Lotus 1-2-3 and Database Software Applied to AIS Cases

W. Ken Harmon
Arizona State University

James P. Borden
Villanova University

John Wiley & Sons, Inc.
New York Chichester Brisbane Toronto Singapore

ACKNOWLEDGEMENTS

My family has always been a great source of inspiration and support. This project relied upon the foundation provided by my parents and sisters. My wife, Kay, gave me love and understanding as the demands on my time became greater. Ashley, my daughter, supplied the joy to keep it all in perspective.

Thank you.

W. Ken Harmon

I would like to thank my family for their support, encouragement and love during this project. They shared in my excitement the three times I announced "I finished the book!" as well as eased the frustration when I was wrong the first two times. They helped to keep the book in its proper perspective, and I look forward to spending more time with them now that "I finished the book!"

James (Quincy) P. Borden

CONTENTS

CHAPTER 2   Using Advanced 1-2-3 Commands and Functions to Enhance Master and Transaction Files

CHAPTER 3 Using 1-2-3 Print and Graph Commands to Create Accounting Reports

CHAPTER 4   Using 1-2-3 Database Commands to Sort and Query Master and Transaction Files

PART II: DATABASE SOFTWARE— APPLIED TO AIS CASES

CHAPTER 6 Designing and Accounting Database Using a Database Management System

CHAPTER 8   Designing Queries to View and Update Multiple Files Using a Database Management System

CHAPTER 9   Designing and Printing Reports Using a Database Management System

CHAPTER 10   Transaction Processing and Controls Using a Database Management System

PREFACE

INTRODUCTION

Our motivation to write this book came from experiences in teaching our own Accounting Information Systems (AIS) courses and from listening to our colleagues' experiences. In summary, the book provides what we feel is an excellent way to teach students Lotus 1-2-3 (Release 2.2) and/or a data base software package (specifically dBase IV or Paradox) without investing too much class time and while keeping the focus on Accounting Information Systems. In this preface, we will describe ways that we think the book can be incorporated into the traditional AIS course, regardless of the students' backgrounds.

OVERVIEW OF THE BOOK

For the past few years, we have taught the AIS course using a somewhat two-pronged approach. We wanted the students to learn the study of Accounting Information Systems, but we also felt the desire to introduce the students to some software package. It was felt that knowledge of a software package would give the students (1) good skills that could be taken to virtually any job, (2) skills that could be applied in other courses, and (3) a mechanism with which they could design their own accounting system, or portion thereof. Traditionally, the software package used for such applications was Lotus 1-2-3. Lotus 1-2-3 still seems to be the package of choice; however, many professors are seeing similar benefits to be gained from knowledge of a data base package.

So, in order to execute our two-pronged approach to AIS, we usually had to devote some class time to the teaching of the software and then assign individual, and team, projects to be worked outside the class environment. This approach has actually met with considerable success, but we have felt one overriding problem exists: no textbook for teaching the course in this fashion. That is, most software books were "reference" books and were therefore not structured for a teaching environment. Or, if the books were structured for teaching, they lacked depth or did not have an AIS perspective. Furthermore, the existing books did not address the problem of having students with different levels of computer expertise. We also felt the need for a book that would allow self-study by the student. This latter consideration was especially important for data base software, because very few students have had much, if any, exposure to a data base package before coming into the AIS course. In order to get these students to a working knowledge of data base simply required too much class time.

All of these concerns and considerations led us to write this book. While the book cannot be for all teaching paradigms, we do think it has many unique features, including:

- The book has a *tutorial approach* that allows students to learn at their own pace and on their own time.
- All levels of expertise are accommodated. A student with no prior knowledge of spreadsheets or data base software can gain a good, working knowledge. Students with prior exposure to such packages can gain insight into more advanced applications.
- All examples and cases in the book have an *AIS focus*. The book reinforces the accounting cycles that are taught in chapters 11 through 15 of Joe Wilkinson's Accounting and Information Systems text (third edition). Because accounting cycles are a universal theme, this book can be used with other AIS textbooks as well.
- The cases provide a good basis for *individual projects* and/or *team projects*.
- The approach requires very little on the part of the professor. In fact, the professor does not need to have much exposure to the software.
- Students can gain a working knowledge of both Lotus 1-2-3 and a data base package, or they can gain an in-depth knowledge of either.

APPROACHES TO TEACHING THE LOTUS 1-2-3 SECTION

Chapter Overview

Part I contains 5 chapters devoted to Lotus 1-2-3. Each chapter is outlined below:

- Chapter 1 teaches the basics of Lotus 1-2-3 to the student who has had little or not exposure to the software package.
- Chapter 2 addresses more advanced topics of Lotus 1-2-3 but should also be review for students who have had some instruction on the package.
- Chapter 3 teaches the student how to produce printed reports and graphs. We have found that even those students who have had considerable exposure to Lotus 1-2-3 are still very weak on the printing and graphing routines.
- Chapter 4 introduces the student to the data base commands in Lotus 1-2-3. This is another topic that students have usually not been exposed to, even if they are very comfortable with the 1-2-3 package. Furthermore, these commands can prove invaluable in accounting applications and are therefore more important in the AIS course.

- Chapter 5 introduces macro programming. If students have experience with 1-2-3, they are probably aware that macros exist. Indeed, many students report that they have seen one or two small macros (usually involving only a few keystrokes). This chapter presents some of the common (and useful) macro commands that will allow the students to design fairly sophisticated accounting applications.

Chapter Organization

Each of the 5 chapters is organized in a very similar fashion. The basics of the Lotus 1-2-3 subject are presented in a tutorial fashion, followed by a series of cases. Each item in the chapter is explained below:

- Text - The material is presented in a tutorial format with examples used throughout. Because of the heavy use of examples and sample screens, we recommend that students read the material while sitting at the computer.
- Case - Each chapter takes the student through the solution of an AIS case, keystroke by keystroke. Except for Chapter 1, data files for all cases can be found on the student diskette.
- Follow-Up Case - The follow-up case is intended to be virtually identical to the case just presented. The follow-up case allows the student to see another application without venturing too far from the material just presented.
- Assignment Case - Each chapter contains two assignment cases from the same accounting cycle as the Case and Follow-Up Case. These assignment cases are intended to stretch the student in an application somewhat different than the ones just presented.
- Review Questions - Each chapter contains a few straightforward review questions. These questions are intended to be used as homework assignments simply to ensure the students have read the material.

Possible Approaches Within the AIS Course

In most AIS classes, one of three situations is encountered:

1. Virtually no students have prior exposure to Lotus 1-2-3,
2. Some students have prior exposure to Lotus 1-2-3, or
3. All students have prior exposure to Lotus 1-2-3.

If virtually no students have exposure to Lotus 1-2-3, we recommend that the students cover at least the first 3 chapters from the section on 1-2-3. After covering these chapters, the professor should decide whether the students should use the remaining time to gain an understanding of the more advanced 1-2-3 topics (namely, data base commands and macro programming) or to be introduced to a data base package.

If some students have Lotus 1-2-3 experience while others do not, then chapters 1 and 2 of Part I can be used to give the latter students some understanding of the 1-2-3 software. Then, all students could be introduced to the more advanced material.

If all of the students have previously been exposed to Lotus 1-2-3, then the entire class could proceed directly to chapters 4 and 5 and then cover all of Part II on data base software. Meanwhile, even though the students have been exposed to 1-2-3 previously, they would have the earlier chapters available as a review.

APPROACHES TO TEACHING THE DATABASE SECTION

Chapter Overview

Part II contains 5 chapters devoted to using either dBASE IV (version 1.1) or Paradox 3.5 database software. Each chapter is outlined below:

• Chapter 6 introduces the student to database software and teaches fundamental skills such as moving through the menus, creating and modifying the structure of a database, entering and editing data, and saving data. Students will begin to build their own transaction processing system.
• Chapter 7 will lead the students through the procedures necessary to design useful input forms. Along the way, they will learn firsthand some of the edit and input controls, such as limit checks, range checks, field checks, etc., discussed in the Wilkinson AIS text as well as most other AIS textbooks.
• Chapter 8 introduces the students to the power of databases through its query language. Students will gain hands-on knowledge of the relational operators select, project, and join. They will also learn about the use of indexes, what a "view" means, and how to update the database.
• Chapter 9 teaches the students how to prepare reports from a database. While from a conceptual viewpoint the outputs, or reports, are designed first, they are by necessity presented last from a detailed design perspective. This is due the fact that you need to have created your database structure first in order to build reports, as well as the fact that several reports are created using "views" that have been created in the previous chapter.
• Chapter 10 allows the students the opportunity to integrate all the work they have done in the previous 4 chapters. Students are given a set of data that they can enter into the database using the input forms created in Chapter 2, update the database using the queries created in Chapter 3, and finally generate useful outputs from the system using the reports created in Chapter 4. This gives the students a good perspective on designing a batch transaction processing system from start to finish.

Chapter Organization

Each of the 5 chapters is organized in a similar manner, which is slightly different than the Lotus 1-2-3 chapters. Each part of the chapter is explained below:

• Case Setting - Each chapter starts off with a brief description of the information requirements of the owner of a toy store in regards to its inventory. The same company setting and inventory cycle is used throughout the book to allow the student to see the diversity of issues involved in designing an accounting information system. From creating a database structure to designing reports, the student will learn to appreciate the power of a DBMS in helping to meet user needs.

• Case Solution - After describing what the owner of the toy store would like, each chapter then goes into a detailed tutorial on using either dBASE IV or Paradox to help satisfy the owner's requests. The tutorial provides step by step guidance in using the software, and supplements the text through generous use of screen shots to enhance the student learning process.

• Follow-Up Cases - Each chapter allows the student to do some additional exercises to both increase their proficiency with the software as well as to enhance their knowledge of transaction processing and the cycle approach to AIS. Follow-up cases include working with the revenue cycle, the expenditure cycle, or the payroll cycle. As with the case setting, the students will build on the chosen cycle as they progress through the chapters.

• Review Questions - Each chapter concludes with a set of basic questions that helps the students review and/or reinforce some of the basic concepts that were learned in the chapter.

Possible Approaches Within the AIS Course

Student exposure to database software varies from school to school, and within the same school, sometimes from instructor to instructor. While most students who are taking AIS will have heard of database software, a significant number may have never had hand-on experience with packages such as dBASE IV and Paradox. One assumption that probably can be made without much argument is that student knowledge of spreadsheet software, such as Lotus 1-2-3, is at least equal to, and most likely exceeds, their knowledge of database software. This part of the book was written based on this assumption, and thus takes a slightly different approach than the first part of the book on Lotus.

For the most part, all students need to work through the tutorial included in each chapter, from Chapter 6 through Chapter 9. The tutorials work on the design of the inventory cycle for a small retail toy store. At the end of each chapter, there are follow-up cases that require the students to have worked through the tutorial. The only exception to this is if the instructor has decided to work through the payroll cycle exercises, which are standalone in nature (i.e., they do not require the student to have completed the inventory cycle exercises, which include the chapter tutorials.)

After the students have worked through the tutorial in each chapter, the instructor has the option as to where to go from here. If the instructor's purpose is to just expose the students to database software, then there is no need to select the revenue, expenditure or payroll cycle follow-up cases. There are additional exercises at eh end of some of the chapters which serve to complete the tutorial related to the inventory cycle. Thus, if a student were to just work through the tutorials and the follow-up exercises related to the inventory cycle, they would have gained a basic knowledge of database software and its capabilities without much of a time commitment. Chapter 10 would not be assigned under this option.

Another option is for the instructor to select either the revenue or expenditure cycle follow-up cases which appear at the end of the chapters. If this is the option chosen, the students will have to work through the tutorial, complete any end of chapter exercises related to the inventory cycle, and then apply their newly acquired skills to either the revenue or expenditure cycles. This option will require more of a time commitment on the student's part, but the benefits should be well worth it. This option allows the students to work through Chapter 10, which introduces students to batch processing and leads them through the steps necessary to properly handle a set of transactions involving the firm's AIS.

Another option is to allow the students to just work through the payroll cycle follow-up cases. This case does not require the students to work through the tutorials, thus it may be useful to assign to students who are fairly comfortable with one of the database software packages.

The choice of options also gives the instructor the ability to switch from semester to semester the required cases. There are also several different options available concerning how the students work on the exercises and present their solutions. The students could work through the cases on their own, and hand in the required case solutions per the instructor's guidelines. Another possibility is to have the students present their solutions to the class. If your school has overhead projection systems connected to a PC, this would be an ideal opportunity for students to get exposed to their use. Another suggestion would be to have students document what they are experiencing as they go through the exercises, including the frustrations (many), the joys (a few), and the perceived strengths and weaknesses of the software. Finally, the cases could be handled either individually or assigned as group projects, each approach having their own merits and drawbacks.

PART I:

LOTUS 1-2-3
Applied to AIS Cases

CHAPTER 1
USING SIMPLE 1-2-3 COMMANDS TO CREATE MASTER AND TRANSACTION FILES

INTRODUCTION

Lotus 1-2-3 has enjoyed tremendous success as an *electronic spreadsheet* software package. One primary reason for this success is that 1-2-3 is quite simple to use. However, at the same time, 1-2-3 is a very powerful software package, capable of supporting large and complicated applications.

Lotus 1-2-3 is particularly useful as an accounting tool. It is simple enough to be used as a calculator yet powerful enough to accommodate a full accounting system. Between these two extremes, 1-2-3 is being used in a myriad of accounting applications, such as preparing payroll, monitoring inventory, maintaining accounts receivable, and preparing reports and supporting schedules of all types. In summary, whatever the business, the accounting system could likely benefit from some 1-2-3 application.

The purpose of this chapter is to explore 1-2-3's basic features, thereby giving you a quick introduction (or review) of the software's abilities. The specific topics we will discuss in this chapter are:

1. Accessing the Lotus 1-2-3 system
2. Moving the cursor
3. Entering and erasing data
4. Expanding and formatting cells
5. Creating formulas
6. Referencing cells
7. Accessing the 1-2-3 menu
8. Saving files

At the end of the chapter, we show how 1-2-3 could be used in an actual accounting system. Then, an additional accounting case is described for you to solve using 1-2-3.

BASIC 1-2-3 COMMANDS

Accessing the 1-2-3 Worksheet

Regardless of the computer system being employed, Lotus 1-2-3 is a simple software package to access and use. If your computer is connected to a local area network (LAN) or has a hard disk, access may be as simple as selecting an option from a menu. If, instead, your computer has only diskettes, the operating manual should be referenced, but access is usually as easy as typing either **LOTUS** or **123** at the DOS prompt. If you enter **LOTUS** at the prompt, then a menu will appear showing the various programs that can be executed. The options are 1-2-3, PrintGraph, Translate, Install, View, and Exit. To access the 1-2-3 spreadsheet, select the 1-2-3 option. For more direct access to the spreadsheet, you can simply type **123** at the DOS prompt.

At this point, you are ready to use 1-2-3. Before describing specific commands, though, it may be helpful to understand how 1-2-3 works. At the heart of the 1-2-3 spreadsheet are the individual *cells*. Each cell is referenced by a *column* and a *row*. For example, the cell at the top left corner is referred to as A1. The cell to the right of that is B1, and so forth. Any cell can have numbers or words entered into it or can contain formulas that use numbers, cell references, or a combination of numbers and cell references.

Moving the Cursor

To enter anything in a cell, you must first place the *cursor* on that cell. The cursor can be moved by any of the following methods:

1. Arrow keys - These keys can be used to move the cursor one cell at a time in the direction indicated on the key.
2. GOTO (F5) key - You can move the cursor directly to any cell (or cell range) by striking the **F5** key and then entering the cell reference for that cell (or the name of the cell range).
3. HOME key - Wherever the cursor is located in the spreadsheet, striking the HOME key will cause the cursor to move directly to cell A1.
4. PAGE UP key - Striking the **PAGE UP** key will cause the cursor to move up one page. For example, if the cursor is positioned at B22, striking **PAGE UP** will move the cursor to B2.
5. PAGE DOWN key - Striking the **PAGE DOWN** key will cause the cursor to move down one page.
6. BIG RIGHT - Holding down the **CTRL** key while striking the right arrow key will cause the cursor to move one screen to the right. For example, if the cursor is positioned at cell C4, striking **CTRL** and the right arrow key would move the cursor to I4. Similarly, if the cursor is at cell A4, striking **CTRL** and the right arrow key would move the cursor to I4. In other words, BIG RIGHT will move

the cursor to the first column to the right of the current screen.

7. BIG LEFT - Holding down the **CTRL** key while striking the left arrow key will move the cursor to the leftmost column of the screen to the left of the current screen. For example, assume the current screen reveals columns P through W. The screen to the left would reveal columns H through O. If, with columns P through W showing, the cursor is in cell V7 and BIG LEFT is invoked, the cursor will move to H7. If the cursor is in P1, BIG LEFT would cause the cursor to move to H1.

8. END key - The **END** key, when used in conjunction with one of the arrow keys, will move the cursor to the next boundary between blank and non-blank cells. For example, assume a continuous column of numbers exists from cell D4 to cell D12, as shown in Figure 1-1. The cursor is in cell D5 in Figure 1-1. Figure 1-2 shows the position of the cursor after striking the **END** key and the down arrow key. The cursor has moved to D12, which is the last cell with contents in the continuous column from D4 to D12. The **END** key is used in exactly the same fashion with any of the arrow keys, and you will find it very useful in numerous applications.

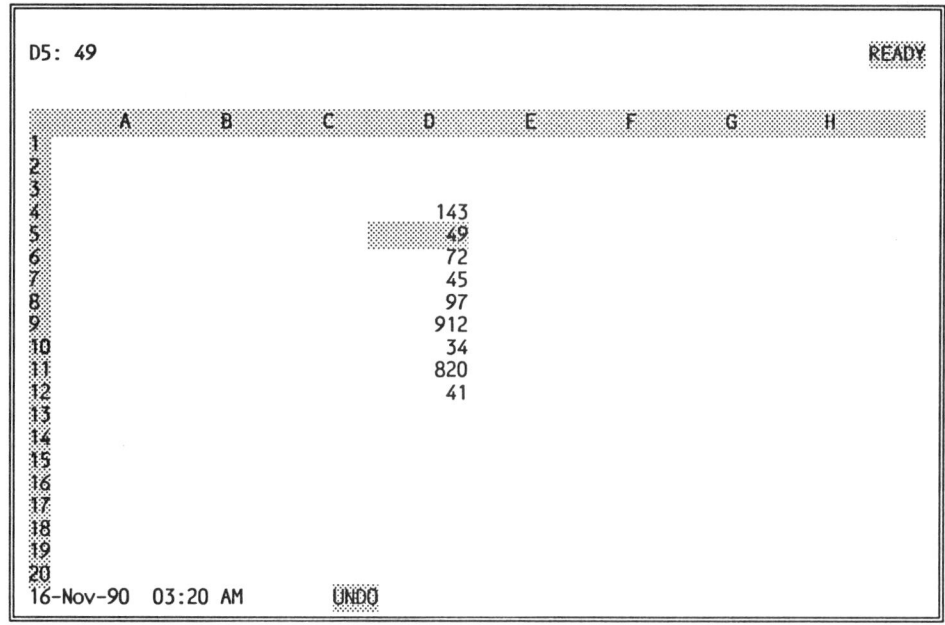

Figure 1-1 Position of Cursor Before Striking END-DOWN

Accessing the 1-2-3 Menu

Lotus 1-2-3 has a myriad of options that can be accessed through a series of *menus* and *submenus*. The main menu is accessed by striking the slash (/) key. When the menu is first accessed, the cursor will be on the first option. That particular option could then be selected by hitting the **ENTER** key. Similarly, any other option could be selected by moving the cursor key to the option and striking the **ENTER** key. A menu option can also be selected by simply striking the first letter of the menu option. For example, the Copy option could be selected by simply striking the letter **C** or Print could be selected by striking **P**. As you become more comfortable with 1-2-3, you will probably avoid using the cursor method for selecting menu items, as the "letter" method is more efficient.

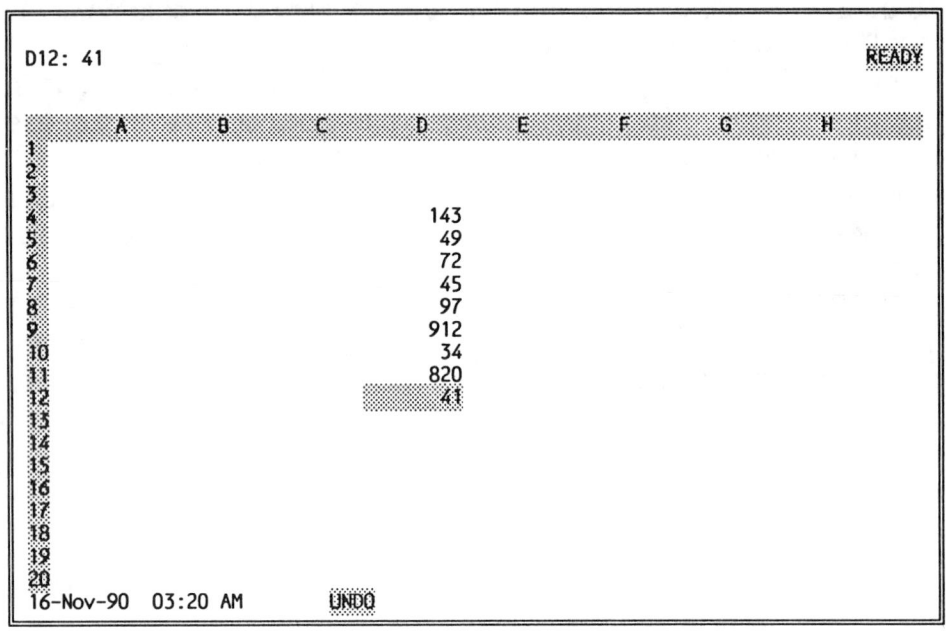

Figure 1-2. Position of Cursor After Striking END-DOWN

When any menu is accessed, the *control panel* (the area at the top of the worksheet) shows both the menu options and the explanation for the highlighted option (that is, the option with the cursor on it). Notice the main menu as shown in Figure 1-3. On the second line of the control panel is the set of menu options. On the third line of the control panel is the explanation for the Worksheet option. In this situation as in numerous others, the explanation is simply the set of menu options that will be displayed when that particular option is selected. The main menu has the following options (shown with their individual explanations):

- Worksheet - Global Insert Delete Column Erase Titles Window Status Page Learn
- Range - Format Label Erase Name Justify Prot Unprot Input Value Trans Search
- Copy - Copy a cell or range of cells
- Move - Move a cell or range of cells
- File - Retrieve Save Combine Xtract Erase List Import Directory Admin
- Print - Print a range on a printer or to a print file
- Graph - Type X A B C D E F Reset View Save Options Name Group Quit
- Data - Fill Table Sort Query Distribution Matrix Regression Parse
- System - Leave 1-2-3 temporarily and use operating system
- Add-In - Attach, Detach, Invoke or Clear 1-2-3 add-in programs
- Quit - End the 1-2-3 session

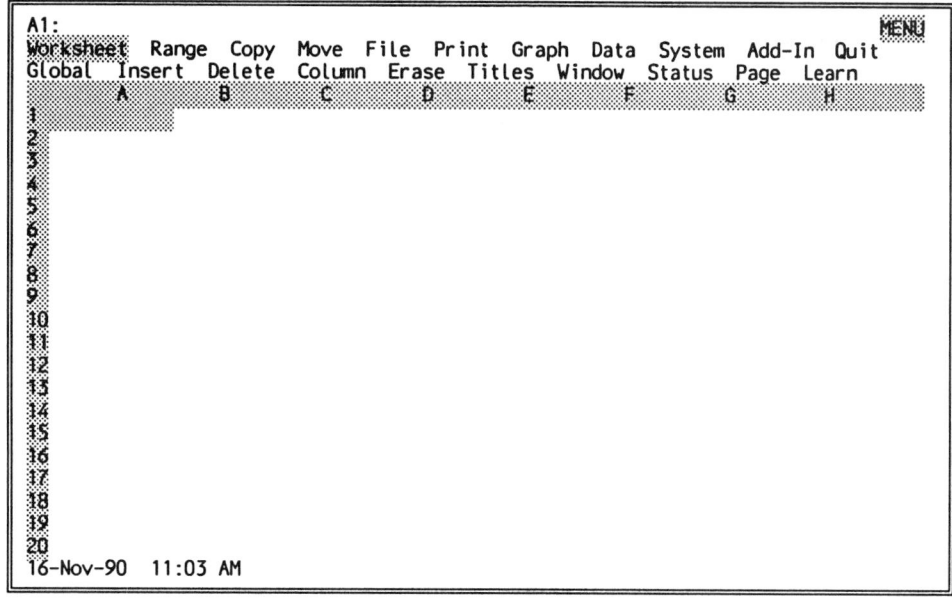

Figure 1-3. The Main Menu

Once you access a menu, you can strike the **ESCAPE** key to back out of that menu and return to the previous menu. Pressing **ESCAPE** at the main menu returns the spreadsheet to the original (READY) mode.

Widening Columns

The columns in Lotus 1-2-3 are originally set to be nine characters wide. This width will of course not be appropriate for every application. Therefore, 1-2-3 allows you to change the width of any column through the menu system.

Assume you wanted to change the D column from the *global* width (nine characters) to a width of 15 characters. First place the cursor on any cell in the D column. Next, access the main menu by striking the slash key. The Worksheet option allows you to alter various characteristics of the worksheet itself, so the Worksheet option should be selected by striking **W** or by moving the cursor to that option and striking the **ENTER** key. The Worksheet menu now appears with numerous options. The Column option of this menu should be selected, because it allows you to alter certain characteristics of a column, including column-width. Selecting the Column option reveals the options of Set-Width, Reset-Width, Hide, Display, and Column-Range. The Set-Width option should be selected. Upon selecting Set-Width, a message appears at the top of the screen, as shown in Figure 1-4. You would simply enter the desired column width of 15 and strike **ENTER**.

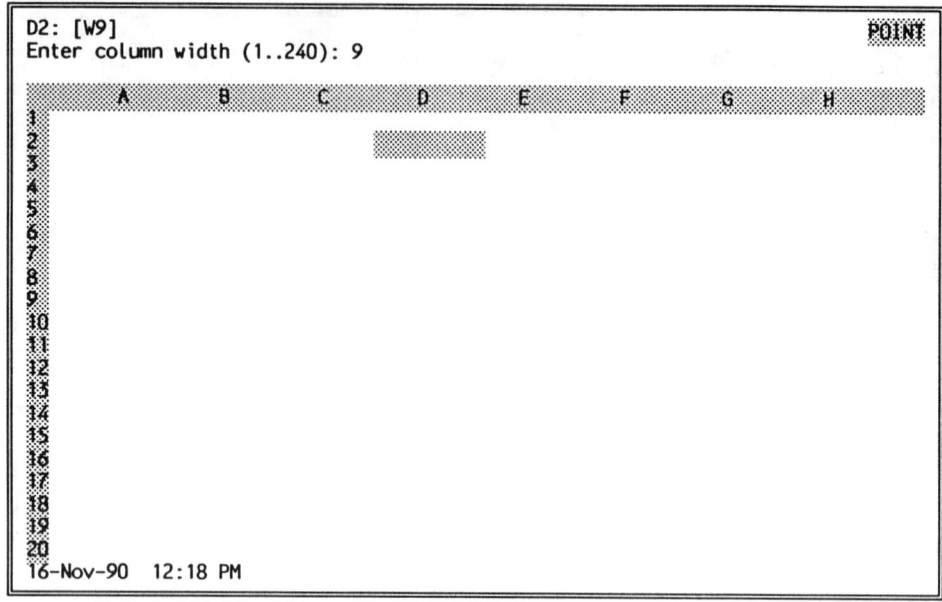

Figure 1-4. Prompt for Set-Width Command

Entering and Editing Data

To enter data into a cell, you simply place the cursor on a cell and start typing. At the time of typing, the cell still appears blank, but the data appear in the upper portion of the screen (the control panel). Striking **ENTER** will cause the data to appear in the cell. Similarly, moving the cursor after typing will cause the data to be entered into the cell.

Before data are entered into a cell, the **BACKSPACE** key can be used for erasing. Once data are entered, though, *editing* and *erasing* are effected by any of the following methods:

1. EDIT (**F2**) key - Striking this key causes the contents of a cell (whichever cell the cursor is on) to be displayed in the control panel. You can then edit the data as needed by using the **BACKSPACE** keys, the arrow keys, the **DELETE** key, and so forth. After editing, striking **ENTER** will place the edited data in the cell.
2. **/Range Erase** - Choosing the Range option from the main menu displays another menu of options. You can select the Erase option to eliminate the contents of a cell or of an entire range of cells.
3. Replacing - At any time, you can replace the contents of a cell by typing new data into the cell. For example, assume a cell contained the number 187 and you wanted to put the number 203 in that cell. Simply place the cursor on the cell, type the number 203, and the cell would then contain the new number. The contents of a cell do not need to be erased or edited to be replaced.

1-2-3 considers each cell entry to be either a *label* or a *value*. A label is simply any entry, usually made up of words, on which arithmetic cannot be performed. Values are defined as either numbers or formulas.   Numbers are just that, any series of digits entered into a cell. Formulas involve some arithmetic manipulation of numbers and/or cell references.

1-2-3 defines a cell entry as a label or a value according to the first character in the cell. Any cell entry with one of the following characters as the first character is considered a value:

0 1 2 3 4 5 6 7 8 9 + - . (@ # $

If the first character is not one of those just listed, the entry is considered a label.

Formatting Cells

Once data have been entered into a cell, the contents of the cell can be *right justified*, *left justified*, or *centered*. Or, when the cell contains a number, the number can be displayed with a dollar sign, a fixed number of decimal places, or any one of a number of other options. These format options allow you to create attractive and therefore more useful reports with 1-2-3 spreadsheets.

Labels can be right-justified, left-justified, or centered. A *label prefix* at the beginning of the entry determines how the contents will be displayed. The following prefixes are the most commonly used:

1. ' - Causes the label to be left-justified
2. ^ - Causes the label to be centered
3. " - Causes the label to be right-justified

When a label is entered into a cell, 1-2-3 assumes the entry should be left-justified and places a label prefix of ' at the beginning. This prefix can be seen on the first line of the control panel when the cursor is on the cell or when entering EDIT mode by using the **F2** key.   If you type a label prefix at the beginning of the label, 1-2-3 will not place any prefix of its own into the cell contents.

Alternatively, a cell containing a label or an entire range of cells containing labels can be formatted by selecting the **/R**ange **L**abel option from the 1-2-3 menu system. Selecting this option will cause a menu to be displayed which allows you to left-justify, right-justify, or center the contents of one cell or a group of cells. Also, **/W**orksheet **G**lobal **L**abel-Prefix can be selected if you want 1-2-3 to default to other than left-justifying.

Values are formatted through the 1-2-3 menus. Selecting **/R**ange **F**ormat from the menus will display a menu with numerous formatting options, as shown in Figure 1-5. Each option is explained below:

- Fixed - The value is displayed with a specified number of decimal places. This option is frequently used to produce financial reports, because it aligns numbers on the decimal point. Negative numbers are displayed with a minus sign.

- Scientific - This option shows the value in exponential format and is primarily used for very large or very small numbers. Negative numbers in this format are displayed with minus signs.
- Currency - A dollar sign is displayed at the far left of the value, and a specified number of decimal places are shown. Commas are added to very large numbers, and negative numbers are represented with parentheses.
- Comma (,) - This option causes commas to be added to very large numbers, making them easier to read and interpret. Negative numbers are shown with parentheses.
- General - This is the default option for 1-2-3. Numbers are displayed without commas, and the only decimal places shown are those actually typed in by the user. A negative number is represented with a minus sign.
- +/- - A graph is displayed using a series of + signs or - signs, depending on the value. For example, the number 5, if formatted as +/-, will actually be displayed as "+++++". The number -3 is displayed as "---". While this format option is useful for very limited applications, the /Graph option in the main menu allows the user to design much more sophisticated, and therefore much more useful, graphs.
- Percent - Numbers are displayed as percentages. Quite simply, this option multiplies the number by 100 and puts a percent sign at the end. For example, .05 would be shown as 5%. Negative numbers have leading minus signs.
- Date - This option allows the user to select one of numerous date formats. Each date format option is shown in a menu when the **Date** option is selected.
- Text - When a formula is placed in a cell, the cell will simply display the result of the formula. However, at times you may want to have the formula itself displayed. The Text format will cause the formula to be displayed rather than the result. For example, a cell would show +9+5 instead of the result, 14. Selecting this option does not change the functioning of the formula, however.
- Hidden - A cell formatted as Hidden will always display a blank. This option is particularly useful in designing reports where certain calculations would only clutter the presentation. The contents of the cell are unaffected when using Hidden.
- Reset - This format option causes the cell to return to the default format. The default format is General, unless you change this setting through /**W**orksheet **G**lobal **F**ormat.

Entering Formulas

Lotus 1-2-3 allows you to enter a formula in any cell. At the simplest level, a formula may only contain numbers. For example, you could enter **5+3+7** in a cell, and 1-2-3 would display the result of 15. But, as you may expect, 1-2-3 also allows much more sophisticated formulas to be constructed.

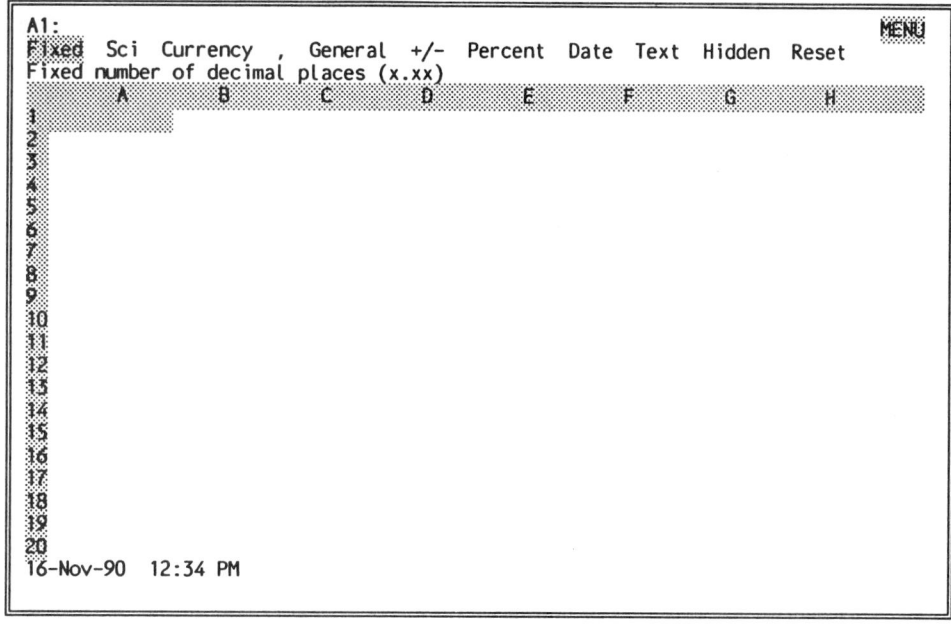

Figure 1-5. Options for /Range Format Command

In order to design sophisticated formulas, you must first be familiar with the *operators* that can be used in numerical formulas. They are presented below, in their *order of calculation*:

1. ^ - Exponentiation
2. *,/ - Multiplication, Division
3. +,- - Addition, Subtraction

The order of calculation is the sequence in which 1-2-3 evaluates a formula. For example, the formula 3^2+1 would yield 10, because the exponentiation of 3^2 would first be calculated to yield 9. Then, 1 would be added to this result to yield 10. At any time, you can override the order of calculation by inserting parentheses into the formula. To use the previous example, if the formula had been entered as 3^(2+1), the value in parentheses would be calculated first, yielding 3. The formula would therefore equal 27, because 1-2-3 would interpret it as 3^3.

While formulas can be constructed with only numbers, most of your applications will require formulas with references to other cells in the worksheet. Assume cell A3 contains the number 53, cell B7 contains the number 42, and you would like to multiply the two numbers, showing the result in cell D10. You would simply move the cursor to D10 and enter the formula +A3*B7. Upon striking the **ENTER** key, the cell would display the result, 2226. This example is demonstrated in Figure 1-6.

While the result of the formula is actually displayed, the formula itself is still in the cell, as shown in the first line of the control panel. In the example just presented, if after entering the formula in D10 you were to change the number in A3 to 2, D10 would immediately display the new result of 84.

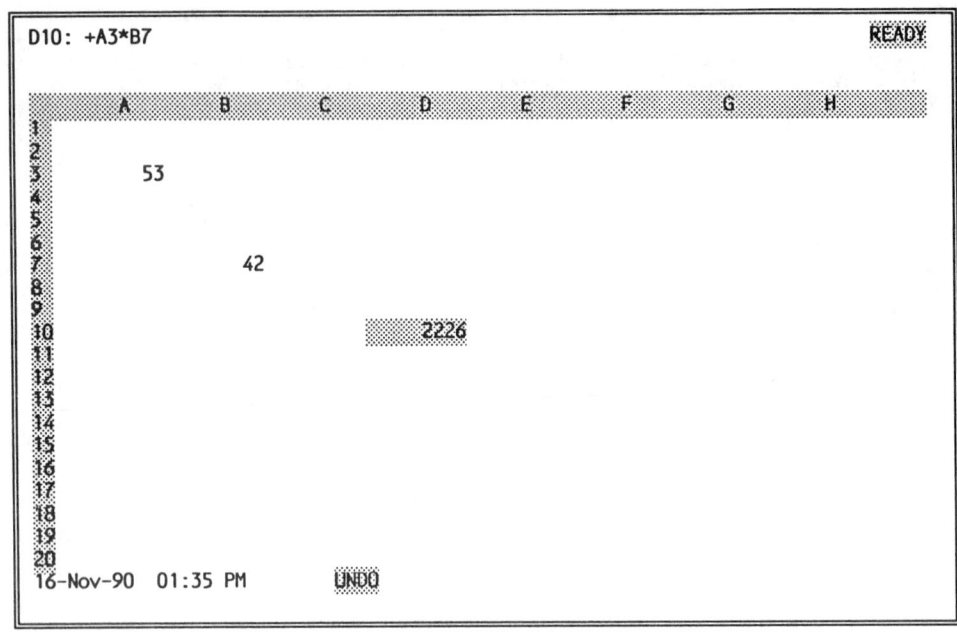

Figure 1-6. Example of Formula Construction

The formula can be reviewed and/or edited at any time by striking the edit key **(F2)**. This will cause the formula to be displayed in the control panel. There are also times when you will not want the formula to change even if the number in a referenced cell were to change. In these cases, you can actually convert from the formula to the number by striking edit **(F2)**, CALC **(F9)**, and then **ENTER**.

You may notice that in this example, the formula was actually started with a plus sign. By starting a formula with a plus sign, you are telling 1-2-3 that you are indeed entering a formula and not a label. If a formula happens to start with a number, then 1-2-3 will automatically format the cell as a value, and you will experience no problem. If, however, the formula starts with a label character, as in A3*B7, then 1-2-3 will format the cell as a label and not perform any calculation. Rather than try to remember which characters result in label versus value formatting, you should probably get in the habit of starting every formula with a + sign (or some other appropriate operator).

As you become more familiar with 1-2-3, you will find yourself *pointing* to cells rather than typing exact cell references. In our previous example, you were typing the formula **+A3*B7** in cell D10. Rather than typing the cell references yourself, you could simply use the cursor to point to the cells. In this example, you would move the cursor to D10 and type a + sign. You would then move the cursor to cell A3. Do not type **ENTER** at this point, or 1-2-3 will assume you are finished entering the formula. Once the cursor is at A3, you would then type the multiplication symbol (*). You will now notice that the cursor has returned to D10. You can now move the cursor to B7, strike **ENTER**, and 1-2-3 will display the result of your formula in D10.

Copying and Referencing Cells

You will frequently find it easier to copy cells rather than retyping information, especially formulas. In the case of formulas, before attempting to make copies, you should first be familiar with the concept of *relative* versus *absolute addressing*.

1-2-3 normally uses what is known as relative addressing. With this form of addressing, 1-2-3 assumes that when you copy a formula containing cell references, the formula should be adjusted for the new location. For example, notice the formula in cell E2 in Figure 1-7.   The formula is +A2+B2+C2+D2. Assume you wanted to have a similar formula in G7, which would add the numbers in cells C7 through F7. Because 1-2-3 uses relative addressing, you only need to enter the /Copy command to copy cell E2 to G7. Because the cell is 2 columns to the right, every column reference (letter) in the formula is adjusted by 2. For example, A becomes C, B becomes D, and so forth. G7 is 5 rows below E2, so when the formula is copied, every row reference is increased by 5. After copying the formula in E2, cell G7 would be +C7+D7+E7+F7, as shown in Figure 1-8.

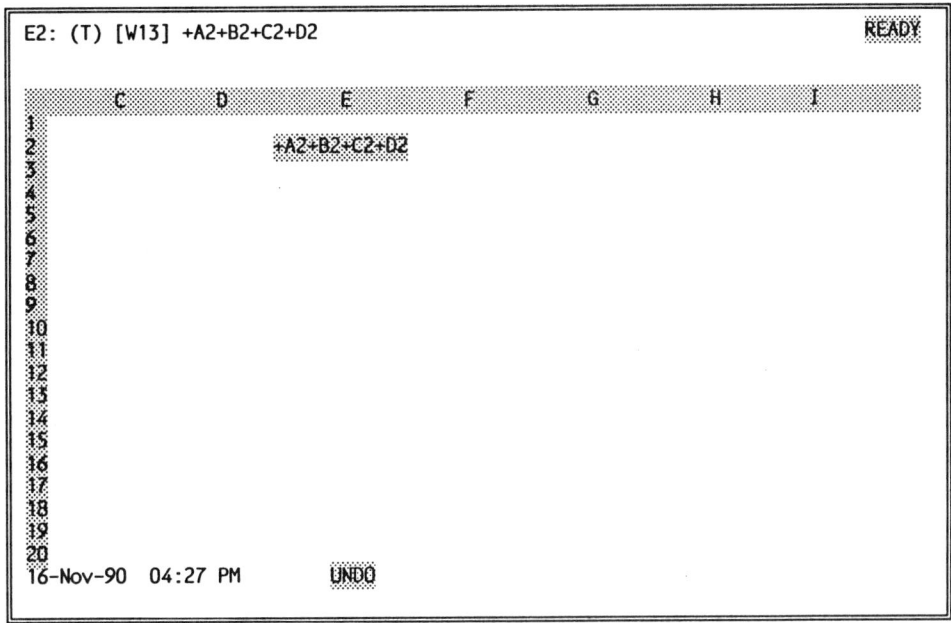

Figure 1-7. Formula to be Copied Using Relative Addressing

There are times when you do not want a formula adjusted. In these situations, you will want to use absolute references in the formula to be copied. Quite simply, to keep 1-2-3 from adjusting a column reference, you place a dollar sign in from of the column reference. Putting a dollar sign in front of a row reference likewise keeps it from being adjusted when copied. The dollar signs can either be typed into the formula directly or the ABS (**F4**) key can be used. To use the ABS key, simply strike the **F4** key immediately after typing any cell reference in a formula, and 1-2-3 will put dollar signs in front of both the column and row reference. Striking **F4** a second time only places a dollar sign in front of the row reference, and striking **F4** a third time places a dollar sign in front of only the column reference.

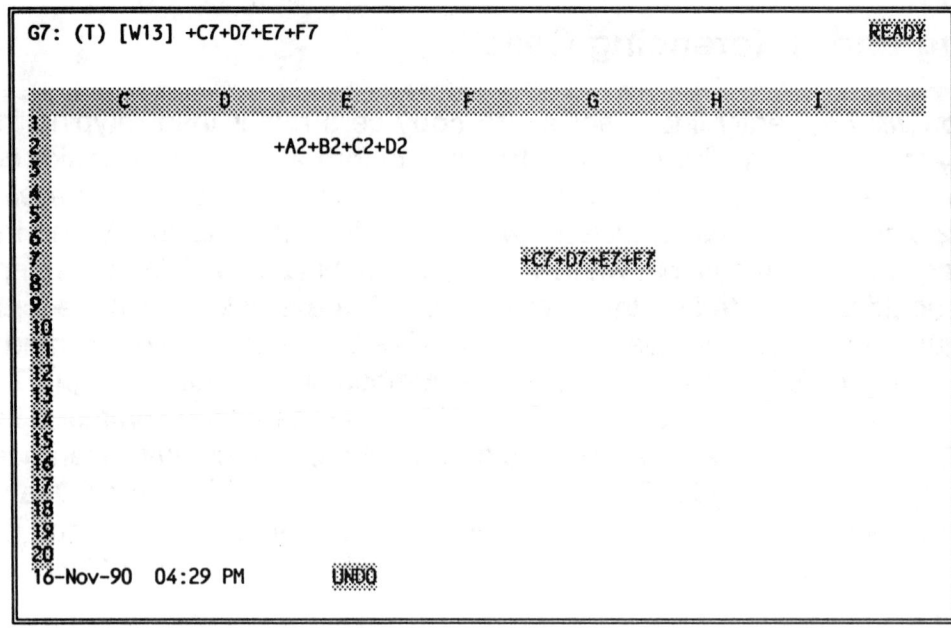

Figure 1-8. Result of Copy Using Relative Addressing

Consider the example shown in Figures 1-9 and 1-10, where the formula in J15 has been copied to M12 without having the cell references adjusted by the /Copy command. Notice that the formula in J15 has dollar signs in front of all column and row references. Also, notice that after the copy, the formula remained intact without having the cell references adjusted.

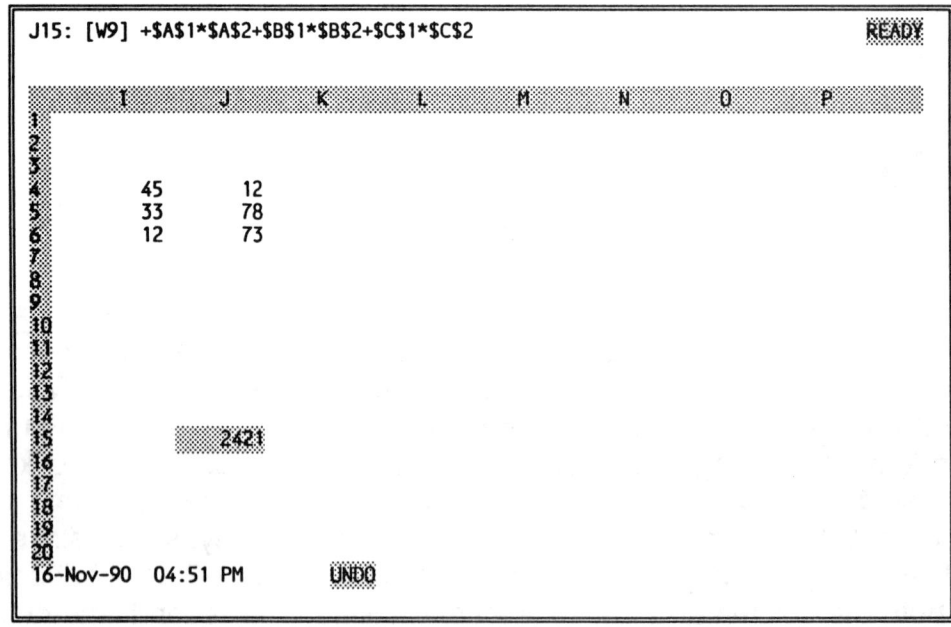

Figure 1-9. Formula to be Copied Using Absolute Addressing

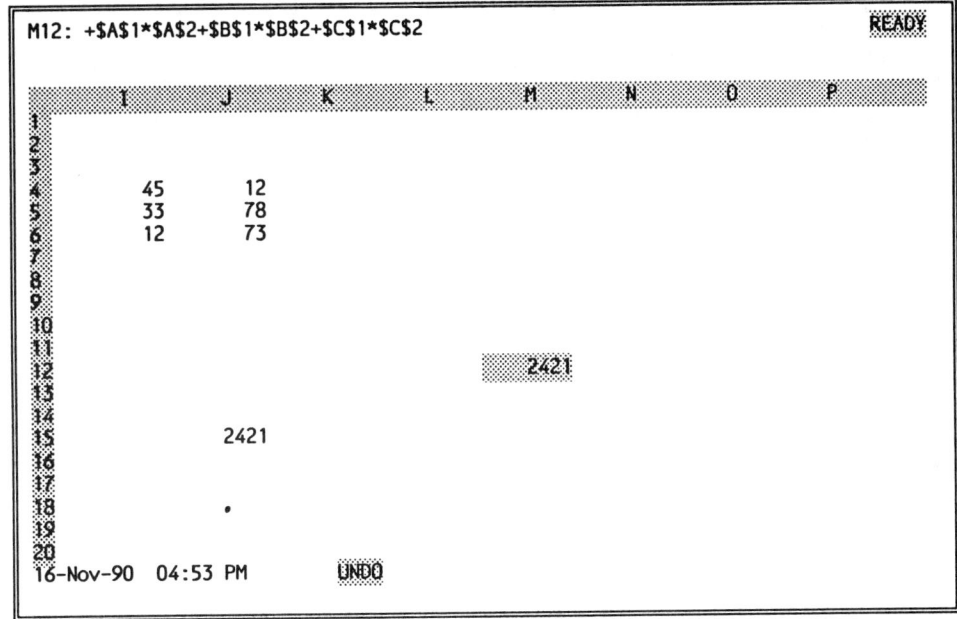

Figure 1-10. Result of Copy Using Absolute Addressing

Saving and retrieving files

Once you have created a spreadsheet, you may want to save it on a diskette. You save the spreadsheet as a *file* by using the /File Save command. For example, assume you had just created a spreadsheet containing travel expenses and wanted to save it as a file. Upon entering /File Save, you would see a message similar to the one shown in Figure 1-11. You are allowed to enter a *file name* of up to 8 characters, with a 3 character *file extension*. In this example, let's say you want to call the file TRAV_EXP. You would simply enter **TRAV_EXP** at the prompt shown in Figure 1-11. While you can put your own extension on the file name, you will probably find it most useful to let 1-2-3 place the default of .WK1 on the file for you. Having the .WK1 extension tells 1-2-3 that this is indeed a Lotus 1-2-3 file.

In the example just shown, the prompt showed the default *directory* of C:\123\. This particular directory is on a hard disk drive and not a diskette drive. In most computers, the diskettes are in drive a: or b:. To save a file on one of these drives, you have three primary options:

1. After entering /File Save, press ESCAPE and type **A:** or **B:** before the file name. This option is illustrated in Figure 1-12.
2. Temporarily change the default drive/directory by entering /File Directory. For example, you might enter /File Directory and then **A:**. Then, any files saved would go to the a: drive.
3. Change the default drive/directory by entering /Worksheet Global Default Directory. To make this default applicable every time you access 1-2-3, be sure to choose Update from the menu that appears upon striking /Worksheet Global Default.

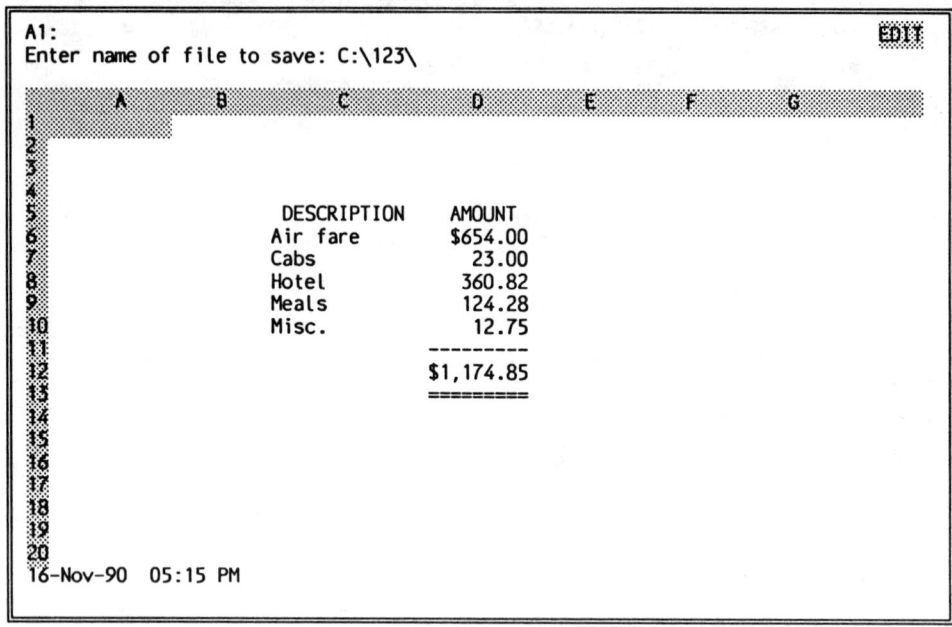

Figure 1-11. Prompt from /File Save Command

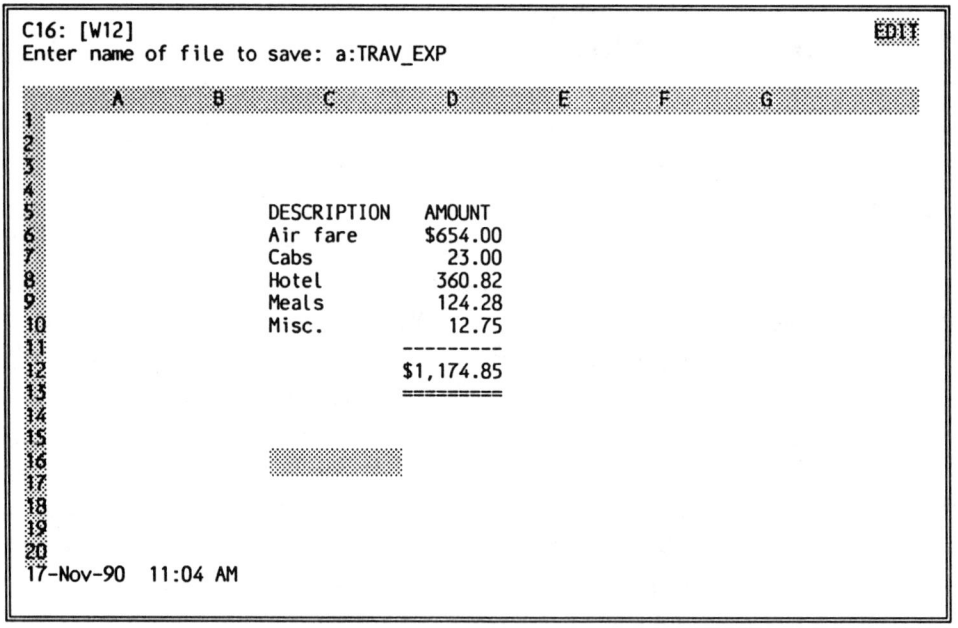

Figure 1-12. Saving File TRAV_EXP on Disk Drive a:

To *retrieve* a previously saved file, you simply enter **/File Retrieve** and then enter the file name. As shown in Figure 1-13, upon entering **/File Retrieve**, 1-2-3 displays the file names of all files with a .WK1 extension on the default directory. To retrieve one of these files, you can either type the file name or move the cursor to the desired file and press **ENTER**.

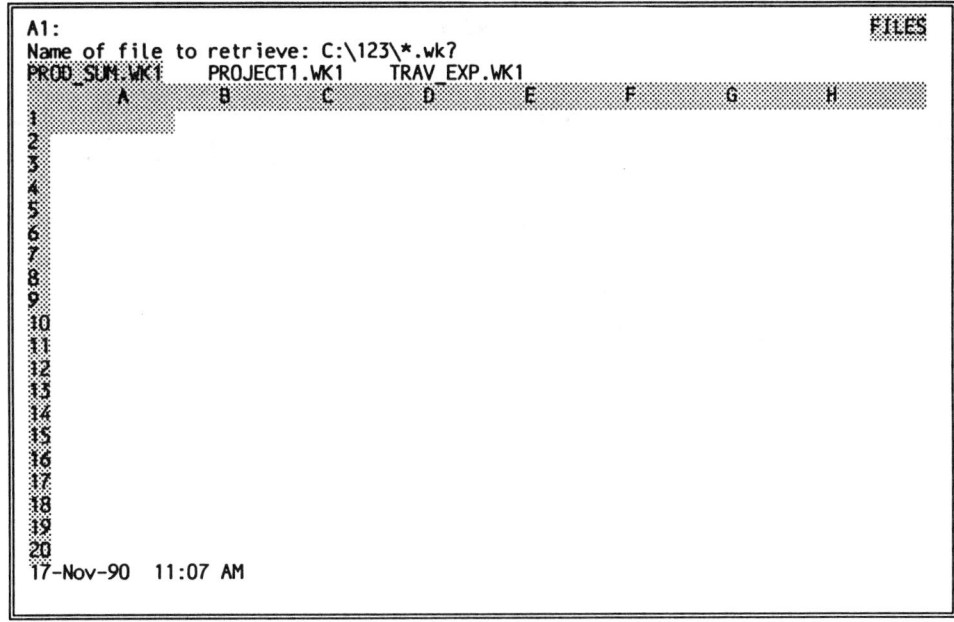

Figure 1-13. Prompt from /File Retrieve Command

As just noted, 1-2-3 displays the files with a .WK1 extension on the default directory. You can also retrieve a file from a directory other than the default directory by (1) specifying the other directory in the file name or (2) changing the default directory as described previously.

CONTROL CONSIDERATIONS

Because you will be working with Accounting data, you must be certain that the *data integrity* is maintained. That is, your 1-2-3 spreadsheets must generate information as you intended, they must be easy to understand and to use, and they should be error-free. To ensure that these data integrity standards are met, you should follow proper control policies and procedures.

Standardizing File Names

In this chapter, we presented the procedures for saving files. In any organization, 1-2-3 users will create numerous files with various names. The problem arises, however, when those individuals leave or when those individuals simply need to retrieve an old file and have forgotten the file's name. To remedy these pitfalls, organizations should adopt *naming conventions* for all computer files, including 1-2-3 files. For example, they could require that dates be included in file names or that certain codes be used. Whatever the naming standards, the organization should adopt some policy and ensure that it is followed.

Using Absolute and Relative Addressing

As you recall, 1-2-3 employs relative addressing when you copy formulas. In other words, 1-2-3 adjusts for the location of the formula when you copy it from one place to another. While this feature is usually quite helpful, it also provides a danger to data integrity. Users oftentimes forget the rules of relative and absolute addressing and therefore forget that the result of a formula is changed whenever that formula is copied elsewhere (unless absolute addressing has been selected). The primary control to overcome potential problems with relative and absolute addressing is to carefully review formula results whenever the spreadsheet is considered finished. Such review may include the use of test data, which is discussed in the following section.

Employing Test Data

1-2-3 users, and especially new users, are frequently unsure of their spreadsheet design. Therefore, all 1-2-3 users should at least test their spreadsheets before they decide to rely on the information those spreadsheets generate. The best way to test a spreadsheet is to use some sample data for which you know the results. While using test data may be considered time-consuming, it presents far less hassle than the potential problems from using incorrect information.

Using Documentation

Before you consider a spreadsheet to be complete, you should take the time to place appropriate *documentation* at some point in the spreadsheet. For example, you should place appropriate headings and dates within every spreadsheet. For those spreadsheets that require a little more elaboration, you should include an explanation section. A simple rule to follow is to imagine what information you think an uninformed user of your spreadsheet would require and then include that information.

Creating Backup Copies

If you have been working with computers for awhile, you know that diskettes present a problem. They can suddenly have errors that render them virtually useless. Furthermore, you can potentially lose some vital information.

Once you have gone to the effort of creating a 1-2-3 spreadsheet, you certainly would not want a disk error to eliminate your hard work. Therefore, you should get in the habit of creating a *backup* copy on your file whenever you save the file. If you have a hard disk, you may find it simple just to save one copy of the file to the hard disk and one copy to diskette.

REVIEW QUESTIONS

1. What is meant by BIG RIGHT and BIG LEFT?

2. How does the END key work?

3. How is an option selected from a 1-2-3 menu?

4. What is the control panel?

5. How can you edit the contents of a cell?

6. What is a "label"?

7. What is a label prefix?

8. Describe the Comma (,) format.

9. Describe the +/- format.

10. Why is Fixed formatting often used for financial reports?

11. When a formula is typed into a cell, the result of the formula is displayed. How can the formula be displayed instead?

12. Why should formulas be started with a plus sign (+)?

13. What "order of calculation" is used for formulas?

14. What is relative addressing?

15. What is absolute addressing, and how is it accomplished?

16. When using /File Save, how can you save the file on some directory other than the default directory?

CASE: SPLASH POOL SUPPLY CO.
Merchandise Inventory Master File
(The Expenditure Cycle)

The Splash Pool Supply Company is a relatively small sole proprietorship that retails chemicals, accessories, and sporting equipment for swimming pools. Barbara Cole started the company in 1985 and still operates it in its original location.

To date, Ms. Cole has maintained the Splash inventory using a manual system. She would like to convert to a computerized system, feeling that computerization would make the calculations less tedious, allow more frequent updating of inventory, improve customer service, and possibly facilitate some expansion of the business. Under the current system, the inventory is updated only monthly using physical observation and latest invoices for the information. A *sample* of a worksheet from the latest inventory appears below:

Product #	Description	On-Hand	Ordered	Cost	Total
22-143	1-inch Chlorine	183	20	$15.00	$2745.00
43-934	Strainer Basket	22	0	$ 5.50	$ 121.00
31-101	pH Increaser	24	7	$ 4.75	$ 114.00
31-102	pH Decreaser	40	11	$ 5.30	$ 212.00
37-227	Med-Gauge Float	7	0	$12.75	$ 89.25
25-114	Basketball Set	6	2	$18.50	$ 111.00

Requirements

Using the data illustrated above, create a Lotus 1-2-3 spreadsheet for the Splash Pool Supply Company inventory. Because Ms. Cole likes the current format, try to emulate that format to the extent possible.

Solution

Assuming you have accessed the Lotus 1-2-3 software by one of the methods described earlier in the chapter, we are now ready to construct the spreadsheet for Splash.

Before entering the titles, we must first decide where to put the spreadsheet. For this application, we have decided to start the titles on row 10, thereby allowing room above for other titles (such as the company name and the date). When the titles are first entered and the columns have not been widened, the spreadsheet appears as illustrated in Figure 1-14. (Note that we have centered each of the titles by placing the character ˆ at the beginning of each.) The next step then is to widen each by entering /Worksheet Column Set-Width and entering the appropriate column width. (Alternatively, you may elect to use the arrow keys after entering /Worksheet Column Set-Width.) We reset the A, B, and F column widths on the illustrated spreadsheet to 11, 17, and 10, respectively. The spreadsheet would then appear as shown in Figure 1-15.

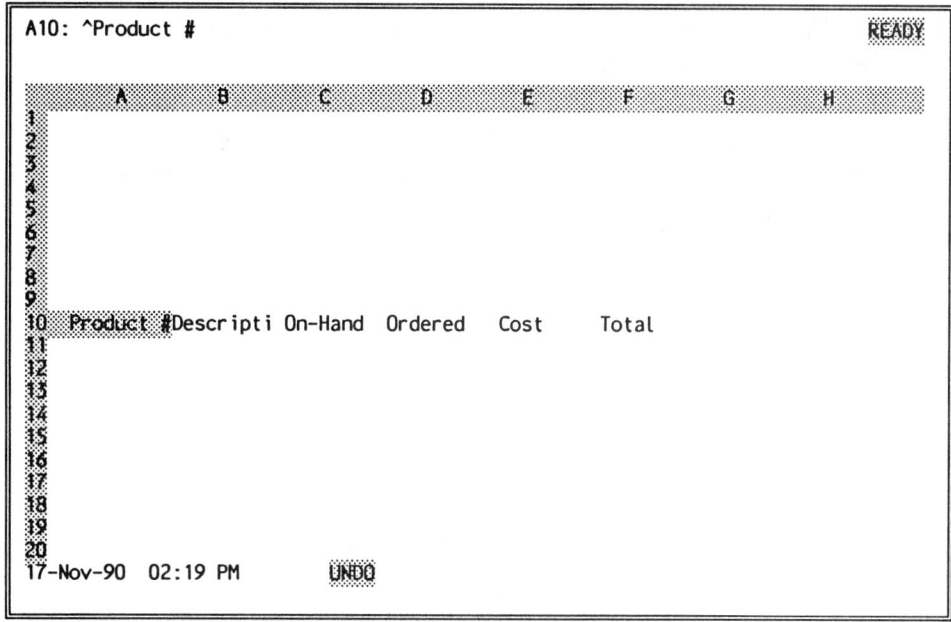

Figure 1-14. Spreadsheet Before Resetting Column Widths

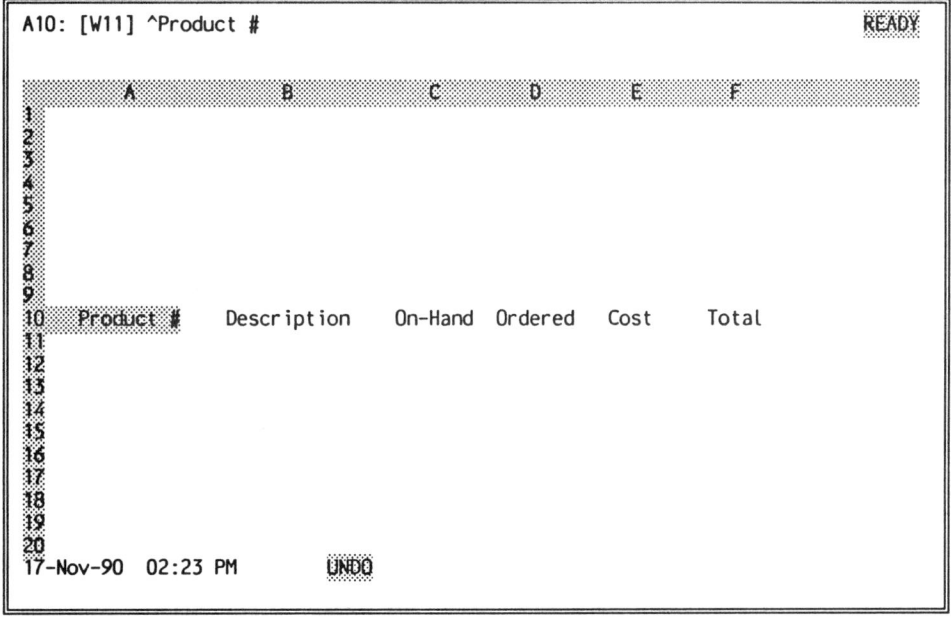

Figure 1-15. Spreadsheet After Resetting Column Widths

Remember that any cell can be formatted as a value or a label. If you simply enter the Item Numbers as they appear, you will find that 1-2-3 assumes the hyphen is actually a minus sign. For example, upon entering the first Item number of 22-143, the cell appears as -121. To make the numbers display correctly, you can:

1. Format the cells as text, by placing the cursor on cell A11, entering /**R**ange **F**ormat **T**ext, and striking the down arrow key a few times. This option causes the numbers to display correctly but still stores them as values.
2. Enter each number as a label by first striking ', ^, or ". This of course causes each Item Number to be correctly stored and displayed as a label. The drawback to this option is that a user would always have to know, and remember to first strike the appropriate label prefix.

The same concerns apply for many of the item Descriptions. That is, some of the Descriptions begin with a number (for example, 1-inch Chlorine). The only option for these items is to enter each as a label by first typing the appropriate label prefix.

The On-Hand amount, Ordered amount, and Cost would be entered directly as numbers. We would of course like to have the numbers in the Cost column displayed with dollar signs. Therefore, the cells in this column should be formatted as currency with 2 decimal places. To do this, simply place the cursor on cell E11, enter /**R**ange **F**ormat **C**urrency, strike **ENTER** to record 2 decimal places, and hit the down arrow key the appropriate number of times. Once you have entered everything but the formulas for the Total column, your screen should appear as in Figure 1-16.

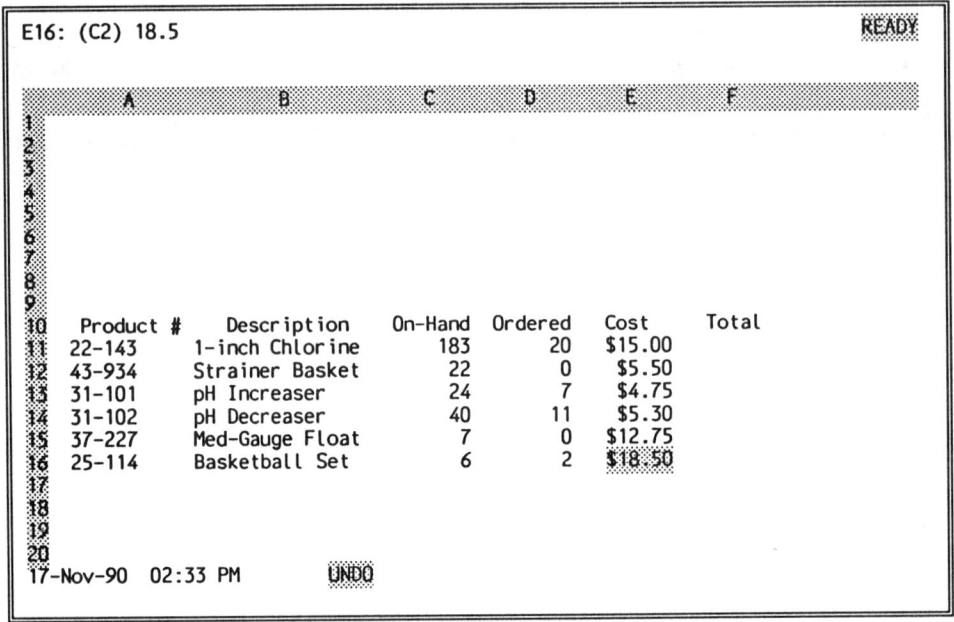

Figure 1-16. Spreadsheet Before Entering Totals

The Total Value cells should all be entered as formulas (On-Hand * Cost). The easiest way to accomplish this is to enter the correct formula in the top cell and copy that formula down the column. To enter the first formula, place the cursor on cell F11 and first enter a plus sign (+). You may now enter the cell reference for the On-Hand amount (cell **C11**). Alternatively, you could simply point to cell C11 by striking the left arrow key 3 times. You next enter the multiplication symbol (*) and then the cell reference for the Cost (cell **E11**). Upon hitting **ENTER**, the cell shows the result of 2745. The formula should appear as shown in the control panel in Figure 1-17.

```
F11: [W10] +C11*E11                                              READY


        A              B            C        D       E        F
1
2
3
4
5
6
7
8
9
10    Product #      Description   On-Hand  Ordered  Cost     Total
11    22-143         1-inch Chlorine   183    20    $15.00       2745
12    43-934         Strainer Basket    22     0     $5.50
13    31-101         pH Increaser       24     7     $4.75
14    31-102         pH Decreaser       40    11     $5.30
15    37-227         Med-Gauge Float     7     0    $12.75
16    25-114         Basketball Set      6     2    $18.50
17
18
19
20
17-Nov-90  02:36 PM           UNDO
```

Figure 1-17. Formula for Calculating Totals

To copy the formula to the remaining cells, enter **/C**opy, strike **ENTER**, and move the cursor down one cell. To anchor the cursor on this cell, strike the period (.). Now simply move the cursor down 4 times. Remember that 1-2-3 defaults to relative addressing; therefore, upon striking **ENTER**, each cell will show the correct result. These cells should now be formatted as currency with 2 decimal places, as described previously. At this point, the Splash Pool Supply Co. Inventory File is completed, as illustrated in Figure 1-18.

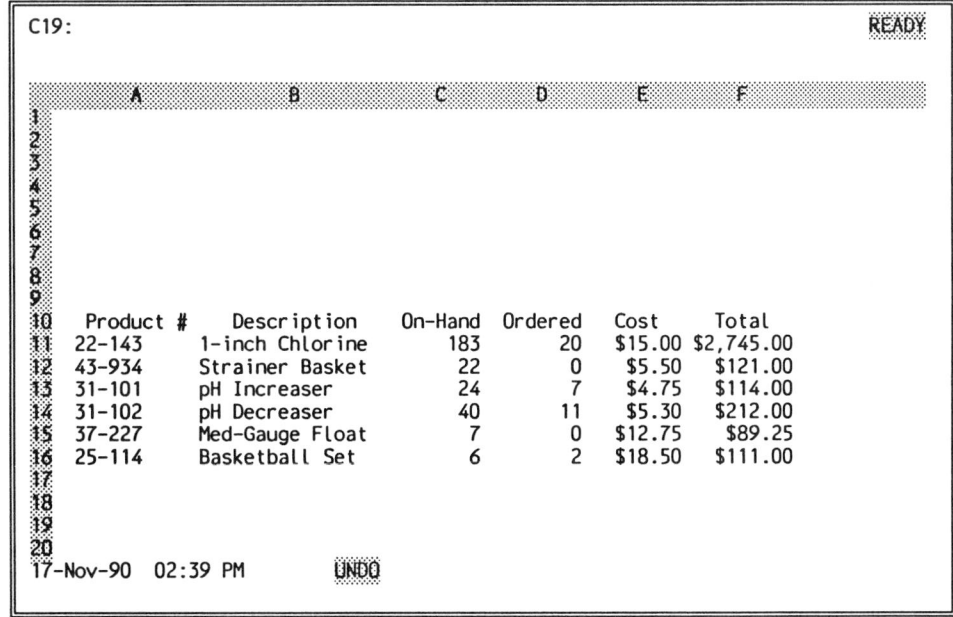

```
C19:                                                            READY


        A              B            C        D       E        F
1
2
3
4
5
6
7
8
9
10    Product #      Description   On-Hand  Ordered  Cost     Total
11    22-143         1-inch Chlorine   183    20    $15.00  $2,745.00
12    43-934         Strainer Basket    22     0     $5.50    $121.00
13    31-101         pH Increaser       24     7     $4.75    $114.00
14    31-102         pH Decreaser       40    11     $5.30    $212.00
15    37-227         Med-Gauge Float     7     0    $12.75     $89.25
16    25-114         Basketball Set      6     2    $18.50    $111.00
17
18
19
20
17-Nov-90  02:39 PM           UNDO
```

Figure 1-18. Completed Spreadsheet

FOLLOW-UP
CASE: Al's Pro Golf Shop
Merchandise Inventory Master File
(The Expenditure Cycle)

The Farragut Country Club offers a full range of athletic and social activities for its members. Within the club is the golf pro shop, run by golf pro Al Kampras. Al carries a basic supply of sportswear and golf equipment. To date, Mr. Kampras has simply maintained the inventory on index cards, which are updated every two   weeks. Equipment is maintained on orange cards and clothing (sportswear) on green cards. Each card contains the following information:

1. Description
2. Inventory Number
3. Supplier
4. Quantity
5. Cost per Unit

Al would like to put the inventory system on Lotus 1-2-3. He feels that having the inventory on computer would allow him to keep more accurate records, possibly expand his offerings, and provide better member services (such as golf lessons and tournaments). To assist in the conversion, Al has summarized the inventory on a worksheet, as shown below:

Type	Description	Inv Number	Supplier	Number	Cost	Total
Equipment	Putter	48231	Zorroc	3	$ 65.00	$ 195.00
Equipment	Metal Woods	12994	Trynor	2	$225.00	$ 450.00
Clothing	Cotton Shirt	99128	Koron	23	$ 12.00	$ 276.00
Equipment	Putter	48901	Fisher	9	$ 78.00	$ 702.00
Clothing	Cap	97831	Acme	46	$ 7.00	$ 322.00
Clothing	Shorts	98112	Koron	17	$ 23.50	$ 399.50
Equipment	Sand Wedge	33943	Sander	3	$ 57.25	$ 171.75
Equipment	Irons	14200	Fling	5	$450.00	$2250.00
Equipment	Irons	21200	McGyver	4	$300.00	$1200.00
Equipment	Golf Balls	00202	Trynor	41	$ 12.00	$ 492.00
Clothing	Poly Shirt	99125	Koron	18	$ 10.75	$ 193.50
Equipment	Driver	12900	Zorroc	2	$150.00	$ 300.00

Requirements

As requested by Mr. Kampras, prepare a Lotus 1-2-3 spreadsheet for his inventory system.

ASSIGNMENT
CASE: T.J. Manufacturing Company
Check Disbursements File
(The Expenditure Cycle)

Tom and Jack Martin own and operate T.J. Manufacturing Co. The company manufactures special heating and air conditioning filters for hospitals, convalescent centers, and some individual homes. These filters are chemically treated and are much more dense than traditional filters, thereby allowing fewer dust, pollen, and other particles to pass through. While the manufacturing process is relatively simple, fitting the filters to the numerous available heating and air conditioning units requires precise measuring and manufacturing. The Martins have become well known for their service and excellent manufacturing standards and are therefore experiencing tremendous growth.

Because of the growth of T.J. Manufacturing, Jack Martin (who handles most of the administrative matters) has decided to replace the manual check register with a computerized check disbursements file, using Lotus 1-2-3.

Requirements

Jack would like your assistance in creating the March, 1992 Check Disbursements File. The information for the file is shown below (because the file references the purchase order numbers, the payee is not listed for each check). In creating the file, you are to consider the following requirements:

1. Center all headings.
2. Format the Amount fields to currency with 2 decimal places.
3. Using a formula, create a Cumulative Total field to the right of the Amount of Payment field. This field should contain a running total for the checks disbursed to date. For example, the first cell would contain $349.10, the second cell would contain $1008.54 ($349.10 + $659.44), the third cell would contain $1151.64 ($1008.54 + $143.10), and so forth.
4. The data are as follows:

Check #	Supplier's Acct. #	Related P.O. #	Date of Payment	Amount of Payment
15001	450002	33802	March 1, 1992	$349.10
15002	350011	33801	March 1, 1992	$659.44
15003	350003	33796	March 1, 1992	$143.10
15004	300021	33814	March 2, 1992	$10.65
15005	450002	33806	March 5, 1992	$239.15
15006	350029	33816	March 5, 1992	$23.93
15007	250034	33804	March 7, 1992	$436.67
15008	250019	33807	March 7, 1992	$754.80
15009	250014	33817	March 8, 1992	$821.99
15010	350011	33809	March 10, 1992	$280.40
15011	450007	33810	March 11, 1992	$368.71
15012	350006	33818	March 16, 1992	$440.59
15013	300012	33812	March 16, 1992	$798.42
15014	350014	33813	March 16, 1992	$994.24
15015	450001	33800	March 16, 1992	$69.82
15016	350022	33815	March 22, 1992	$132.11
15017	250018	33805	March 22, 1992	$487.83
15018	250014	33808	March 22, 1992	$604.80
15019	450024	33811	March 22, 1992	$605.01
15020	300019	33819	March 23, 1992	$596.73
15021	300004	33828	March 24, 1992	$291.54
15022	250009	33821	March 24, 1992	$716.01
15023	300001	33830	March 27, 1992	$640.16

ASSIGNMENT
CASE: Completely Stuffed, Inc.
Open Invoice File
(The Expenditure Cycle)

Completely Stuffed, Inc. purchases teddy bears and other unique stuffed animals from manufacturers in the U.S. and Canada and distributes them to specialty stores in the Northwest region of the U.S. Of the manufacturers, approximately one-third are actually individuals who manufacture the stuffed toys in their homes.

The company has always kepts its invoices in a "To-Be-Paid" drawer of the file cabinet. Because the business is growing and so many manufacturers are relatively small, the number of open invoices is increasing at a rapid rate. The company would therefore like to use Lotus 1-2-3 to monitor its accounts payable. The invoices would continue to be filed as before; however, the review of the invoices would be simplified by using a 1-2-3 file.

Requirements

Using the data shown below, create an Open Invoice File for Completely Stuffed. In creating the file, you should also accommodate the following requests:

1. Center all headings.
2. Format the Discount field as a percentage.
3. Create a Net Due field just to the right of the Discount field. Amounts in this field should be the result of the formula: Net Due = Gross Amount - (Discount * Gross Amount).
4. Format the Gross Amount and Net Due fields as currency with 2 decimal places.
5. The data are as follows:

Invoice Date	Due Date	P.O. Number	Gross Amount	Discount
June 21, 1991	July 11, 1991	9012	$248.02	0.02
June 21, 1991	July 11, 1991	9011	$210.44	0.02
June 22, 1991	July 12, 1991	8979	$219.33	0.015
June 22, 1991	July 22, 1991	9022	$218.55	0
June 22, 1991	July 22, 1991	9014	$453.78	0
June 23, 1991	July 23, 1991	9035	$200.14	0
June 23, 1991	July 13, 1991	9027	$420.47	0.03
June 23, 1991	July 13, 1991	9028	$122.56	0.02
June 24, 1991	July 14, 1991	8999	$105.92	0.025
June 24, 1991	July 24, 1991	8992	$495.02	0
June 24, 1991	July 14, 1991	9001	$493.41	0.02
June 25, 1991	July 25, 1991	9004	$268.29	0
June 26, 1991	July 16, 1991	9019	$56.37	0.015
June 26, 1991	July 16, 1991	9020	$81.15	0.015
June 26, 1991	July 26, 1991	9005	$437.94	0
June 26, 1991	July 26, 1991	9007	$298.88	0
June 27, 1991	July 17, 1991	9031	$153.37	0.02
June 27, 1991	July 17, 1991	8998	$420.70	0.02
June 27, 1991	July 17, 1991	9035	$359.20	0.02
June 27, 1991	July 27, 1991	9009	$95.56	0
June 28, 1991	July 18, 1991	9015	$265.36	0.03
June 28, 1991	July 18, 1991	9017	$283.37	0.025
June 29, 1991	July 19, 1991	9029	$152.97	0.025

CHAPTER 2
USING ADVANCED 1-2-3 COMMANDS AND FUNCTIONS TO ENHANCE MASTER AND TRANSACTION FILES

INTRODUCTION

You should now feel relatively comfortable with Lotus 1-2-3 and how it operates. A strength of the 1-2-3 package is its ease of learning. At the same time, 1-2-3 is a very powerful, sophisticated package that allows you to accomplish virtually any task. As you use 1-2-3 more and more, you will undoubtedly appreciate its versatility. Eventually, you may understand why many people claim that the only limitation to 1-2-3 is your own imagination.

The purpose of this chapter is to introduce some of 1-2-3's more advanced features that allow you to design more useful spreadsheets. The features to be explored here relate specifically to spreadsheet applications; 1-2-3's graphing, database, and programming features are explored in the next three chapters. Upon completing this chapter and its assigned case, you should understand the following topics:

1. Ranges
   - Using ranges
   - Naming ranges

2. Functions
   - Using statistical functions
   - Using special functions
   - Using date and time functions
   - Using financial functions
   - Using logical functions

RANGES

Using Ranges

In using 1-2-3, you will frequently need to access groups of cells at one time. 1-2-3 refers to groups of cells as *ranges*. A range is defined as any cell or group of cells. Therefore, you may think of a range as being only one cell, or a column of cells, or a row of cells, or a block of cells that covers multiple rows and columns.

Ranges can be used in a number of 1-2-3 applications, but some of the applications that more commonly use ranges are:

- Copying
- Moving
- Erasing
- Formatting
- Printing

COPYING

Notice the example shown in Figure 2-1. Assume you wanted to copy the expense account titles from column A to column D (thus allowing you to record another month of expenses). Rather than copy one cell at a time, you will want to treat the group of cells from A4 to A11 as a range. You can then copy the range to column D, starting with D4.

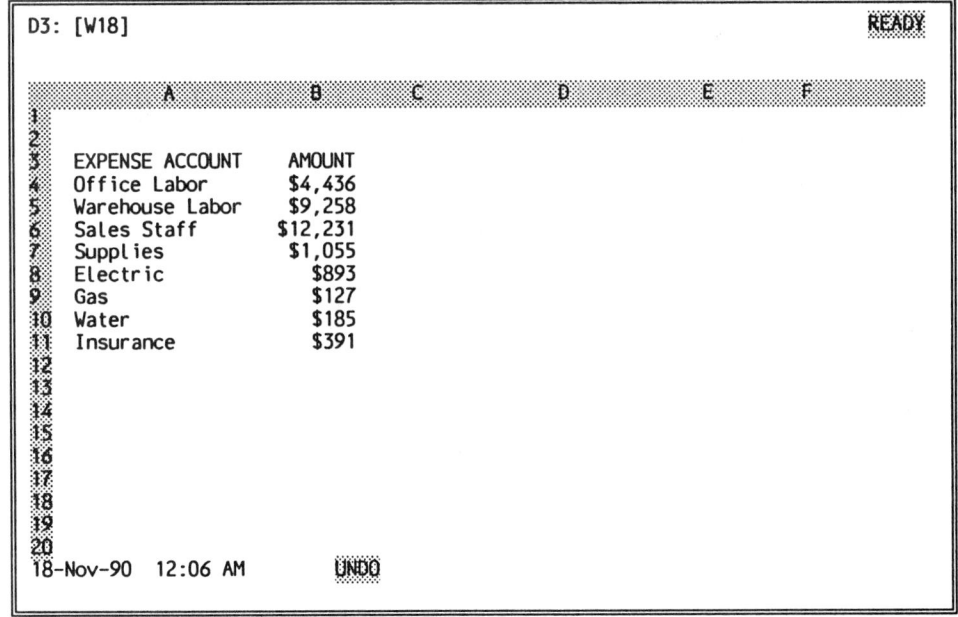

Figure 2-1 Account Titles to be Copied

To accomplish this copy, first place the cursor on cell A4. Then enter the command **/C**opy. In the control panel, the following message appears:

Enter range to copy FROM: A4..A4

The A4..A4 in this prompt is showing the corners of a range (in this case, a one-cell range). At this point, 1-2-3 is defaulting to the current cursor location, A4. Notice what happens as you strike the **DOWN** arrow key. The highlighted area becomes larger, and the control panel indicator will change accordingly. Move the cursor all the way down to A11. The screen should now appear as shown in Figure 2-2.

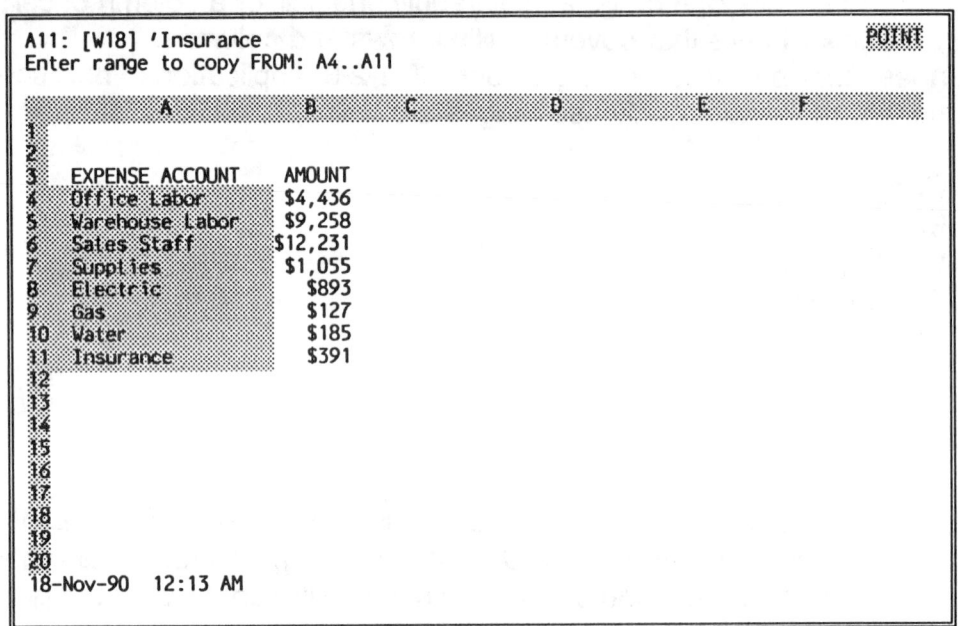

Figure 2-2 Area to be Copied Using /Copy Command

When you originally entered /Copy and A4..A4 appeared, 1-2-3 was telling you that it had *anchored* the cursor. Whenever a cursor is anchored, then any movement of the cursor will cause the highlighted block to become larger by covering more cells. As the highlighted area enlarges, the control panel will show the corners of the highlighted area.

At any time, you can cancel anchoring by pressing the **ESCAPE** key. Alternatively, you can anchor the cursor by pressing the period (.) key.

You have now told 1-2-3 that you want to copy from the range A4..A11. Upon pressing **ENTER**, 1-2-3 will ask for the range (or place) to copy to. In our example, the control panel, upon pressing **ENTER**, looks as shown in Figure 2-3. You will first notice that 1-2-3 has not anchored the cursor for you. This is because you will usually not need to anchor the receiving range in a copy command. In this example, you want the range to be copied over in cells D4 to D11. At the prompt shown in Figure 2-3, you only need to move the cursor to D4 and press **ENTER**. Your screen would then look like Figure 2-4.

MOVING

The Move command also relies on ranges and behaves virtually identically to the Copy command. A primary difference with the Move command is that the information is eliminated from its old location. Also, when you move a formula, the addresses are not automatically changed as with the **/C**opy command.

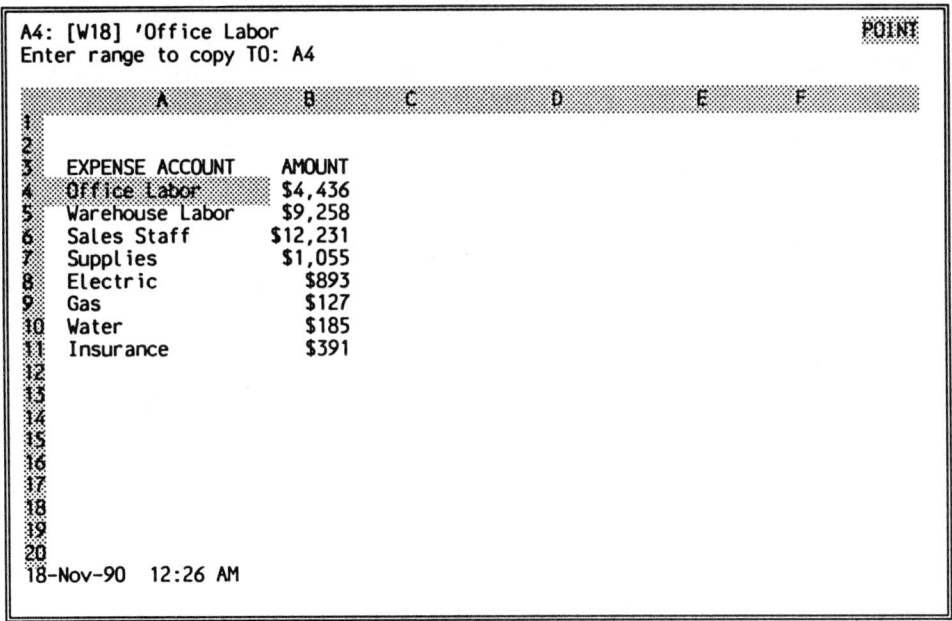

Figure 2-3 Prompt from the /Copy Command

Figure 2-4 Result of Copy Using /Copy Command

ERASING

To eliminate the contents of any cell (or range), the **/R**ange Erase command is used. For example, assume you wanted to erase the contents of cell G15. Upon entering the **/Range Erase** command, the control panel appears as follows:

Enter range to erase: G15..G15

Much like the Copy and Move commands, upon entering **/Range Erase** 1-2-3 assumes you want to anchor the cursor. Upon striking **ENTER**, the contents of the highlighted range will be eliminated.

FORMATTING

In Chapter 1, we introduced formatting. As discussed in that chapter, 1-2-3 will allow you to format any value cell as Fixed, Sci, Currency, Comma, General, +/-, Percent, Date, Text, or Hidden. You will frequently find it easier to format an entire range of cells rather than one cell at a time. Notice the example in Figure 2-5 for travel expenses. You have entered the amounts for each expense and would now like to format them accordingly.

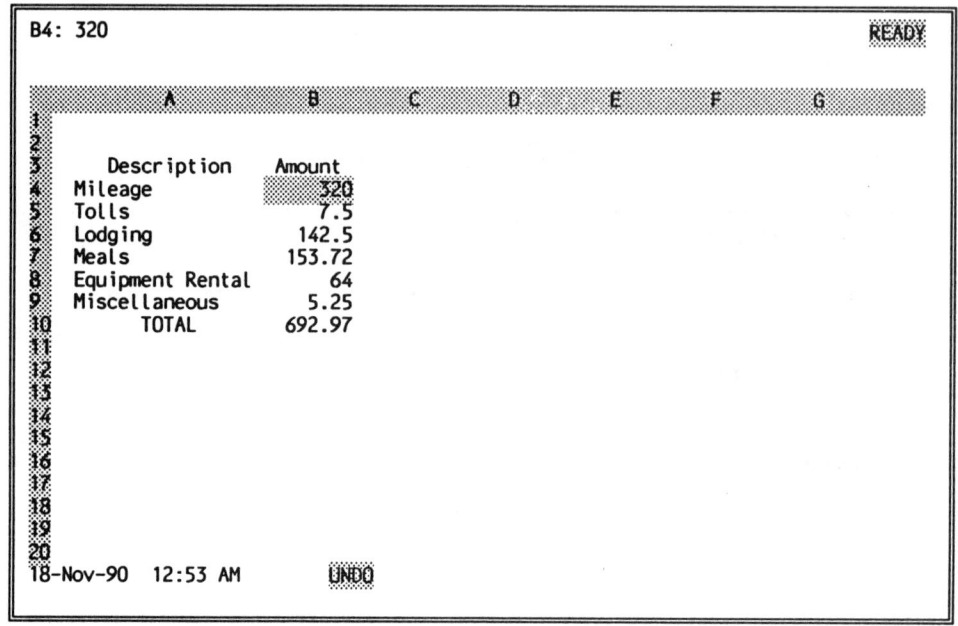

Figure 2-5 Cells to be Formatted

Cell B4 is to be formatted as currency with 2 decimal places. As described in Chapter 1, you should place the cursor on B4, use the **/Range Format Currency** command , and press **ENTER**. Then, when 1-2-3 asks for the range to format, you can simply press **ENTER** again. The spreadsheet would then appear as shown in Figure 2-6.

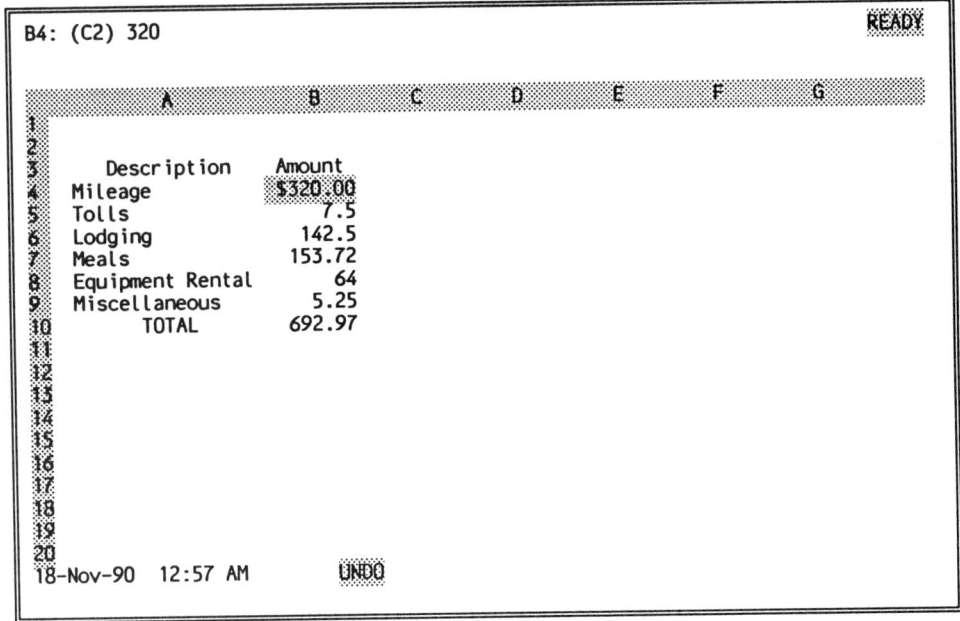

Figure 2-6 Result of Formatting Cell B4 as Currency

Cells B5 through B9 are to be formatted as fixed with 2 decimal places. You would enter the **/R**ange **F**ormat **F**ixed command with 2 decimal places. Then, you would want to anchor the cursor at B5 and move the cursor down four times and strike **ENTER**. Assume, however, that the cursor was positioned on cell B4 when you entered the **/R**ange Format Fixed command. In this case, you would need to first press **ESCAPE** to get out of anchor mode, press the **DOWN** arrow key to move the cursor to B5, press the period (.) key to anchor the cursor at B5, and then move the cursor down four times and strike **ENTER**. After formatting B5 through B9, you would want to format B10 as currency with 2 decimal places in exactly the same way B4 was formatted. The formatted cells would then appear as shown in Figure 2-7.

To this point, we have used only pointing to indicate ranges. That is, we have been anchoring the cursor in one cell and then expanding the highlighted area with the arrow keys. You should note that at any time you can also simply type the cell references. In the previous example, we were formatting B5 through B9 by anchoring on B5 and then striking the down arrow key to B9. In this same situation, you could simply type **B5..B9** at the **Enter range to format:** prompt.

NAMING RANGES

As defined previously, a range is any one cell or group of cells. When referencing cells, in formulas or commands, you will frequently find it more meaningful to use actual names rather than non-descriptive cell references. 1-2-3 has a provision to let you name any range and use it in any place you would ordinarily use the cell references. In fact, you will probably become so accustomed to using range names that you will incorporate them into most of your spreadsheets.

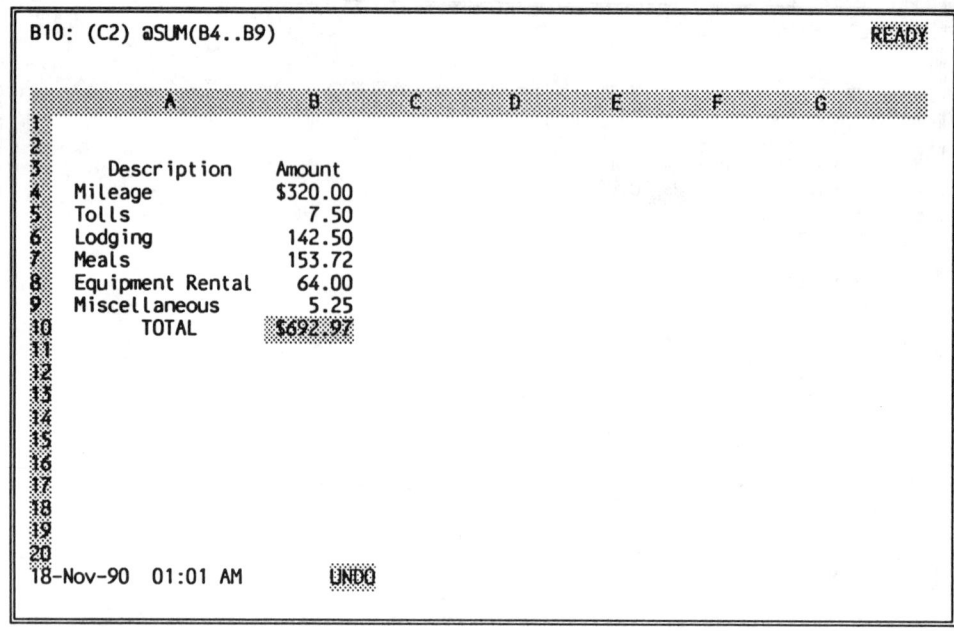

Figure 2-7 Result of Formatting Operation

To give a range of cells a particular name, you simply use the **/R**ange **N**ame **C**reate command. To demonstrate the naming of a range, assume you entered an appropriate report heading for the Qualls Company budget, as shown in Figure 2-8. You know that you will be using this heading over and over; accordingly, you would like to give this group of cells the range name "HEADING". Giving the cells a descriptive name achieves two benefits: (1) you can reference the name and therefore not have to remember the actual cell references for the heading's location and (2) range names are more intuitive and therefore allow you to execute commands more easily.

To give the cells C3 through C5 (the location of the heading) the range name of "HEADING," place the cursor on cell C3 and enter **/R**ange **N**ame **C**reate. 1-2-3 will prompt you with **Enter name:**. Enter the name **HEADING** and press **ENTER**. Upon pressing **ENTER**, the screen now prompts you with **Enter range: C3..C3** (notice that 1-2-3 assumes you will want to anchor the cursor). Press the **DOWN** arrow key two times. Your screen would now appear as in Figure 2-9.

Upon pressing **ENTER**, you have saved the range C3..C5 as the range name HEADING. Even though you have saved these cells as a range name, altering the contents of any of those cells will not affect the range name. For example, even if you erased the contents of cells C3 through C5, the range name HEADING would still be attached to those cells.

USING RANGE NAMES

Using the example just described, we will now show how you can use range names to make some tasks much more simple. Assume that in preparation of generating another budget, you wanted to copy the range HEADING to cell P3. To accomplish this copy, you would only need to enter the **/Copy** command. At the prompt **Enter range to copy FROM:**, you would simply enter the range name HEADING. Then at the prompt **Enter range to copy TO:**, you would type **P3**.

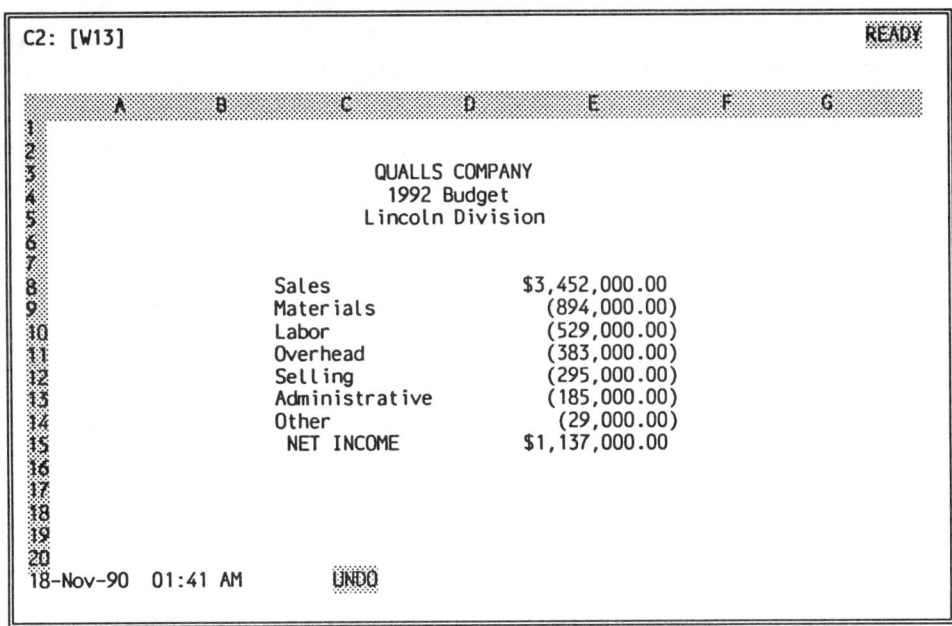

Figure 2-8 Qualls Company Budget

Figure 2-9 Prompts from the /Range Name Create Command

In the examples given thus far, range names have been used to simplify certain 1-2-3 commands. Range names can also be placed on cells containing values, so that the range names themselves can be used in formulas. Figure 2-10 shows part of a spreadsheet that contains departmental budgets for personnel expenses. This company actually has 6 departments; therefore, the spreadsheet extends to cell Y12. We would like to have a summary of departmental expenses at the beginning of the spreadsheet, and this is shown in Figure 2-11. In this example, each department's total personnel budget has been given the range name of the department itself. For example, the total for Accounting's personnel budget is in cell J11. This cell has been given the range name ACCTG. All other departments have been likewise named.

Notice the formula shown in the control panel for cell B4. Rather than trying to remember the cell reference for each department's total, we have simply typed the range names into the formula. The resulting formula is:

$$+ACCTG+INVNTRY+MRKTG+PROD+PERSNL+FINANCE$$

```
I15: [W16]                                                      READY

        H              I              J              K
1
2
3              ACCOUNTING DEPT.
4
5         Supervisor          $62,000
6         Asst. Supervisor     43,000
7         Clerk (Level 1)      26,000
8         Clerk (Level 1)      26,000
9         Clerk (Level 2)      18,000
10                            --------
11                           $175,000
12                           ========
13
14
15
16
17
18
19
20
18-Nov-90  02:03 AM        UNDO
```

Figure 2-10 Accounting Departmental Budget

When you get more comfortable using range names, you may find it difficult to keep up with all the range names you have created. It is therefore helpful to use the **/R**ange **N**ame **T**able command. This command will generate a list of all range names in the spreadsheet and their location. For the example shown in Figure 2-11, assume the **/R**ange **N**ame **T**able command was issued, placing the table in column A, starting at A7. The result would appear as shown in Figure 2-12.

Another convenience of using range names is in moving the cursor. As you may recall from Chapter 1, the F5 key is known as the GOTO key. Pressing this key allows you to move the cursor directly to any cell in the spreadsheet. Remember, too, that range names can be used in any place cell references can be used. You can therefore use range names with the GOTO command to move directly to any named range. In those instances where the range name covers more than one cell, the cursor will move directly to the upper left corner of the range.

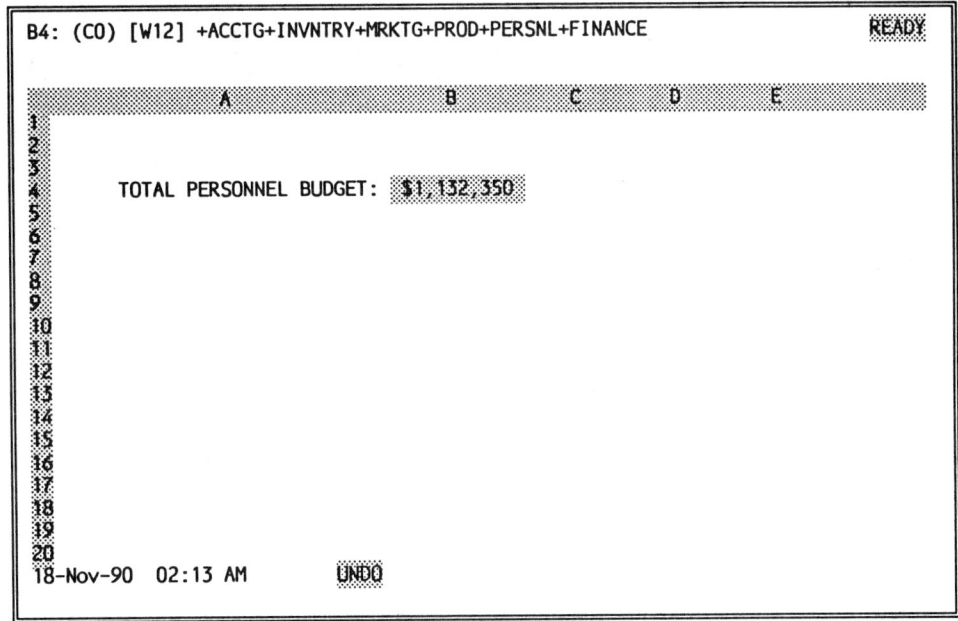

Figure 2-11 Summary of Departmental Budgets

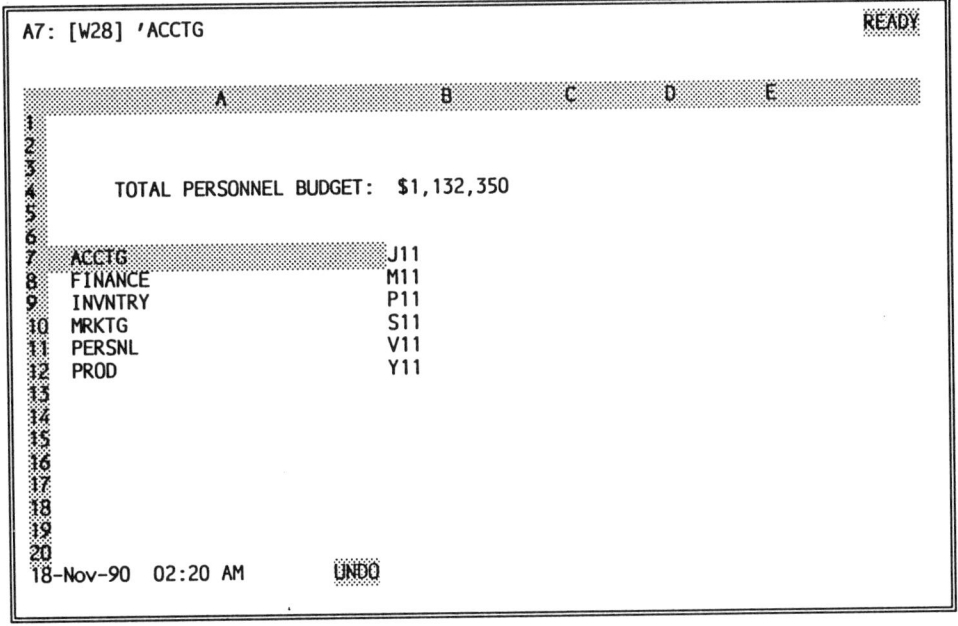

Figure 2-12 Result of /Range Name Table Command

DELETING AND MOVING RANGE NAMES

To delete a range name, you simply use the **/R**ange **N**ame **D**elete command. This command only asks you to specify the range name and not the cell address(es) of the range. This is because 1-2-3 remembers the cells associated with the range name. For example, assume you have a range named HEADING that covers cells D4 through D6. Also assume that you want to delete this range name. You simply issue the command **/Range Name Delete**. At the prompt in the control panel, you then type the name to be deleted, **HEADING**. Upon pressing **ENTER**, the range name would be deleted.

Remember earlier when discussing /Range Erase, we noted that if you erase the contents of a cell, the range name will stay intact. Similarly, if you delete a range name with **/Range Name Delete**, the contents of the cell will be unaffected.

There are times when you will only want to move a range name to another location. In the earlier example where we had a spreadsheet of departmental personnel budgets, the Accounting budget total was in cell J11. Assume that Accounting received approval to have another Level 1 Clerk for the year. This would require inserting a line after cell I8. In this example, you would simply place the cursor on cell I9, issue the **/Move** command, press the **RIGHT** arrow key, press the **DOWN** arrow key 3 times until the highlighted area covers cells I9 to J12. Then upon receiving the **Enter range to move TO:** prompt, you would place the cursor on cell I10 and press **ENTER**. Your screen would now look like Figure 2-13. Notice that if you now enter a /Range Name Table command the cell location for ACCTG has moved to cell J12. Just remember that if you move a cell that has a range name on it, the range name will also be moved.

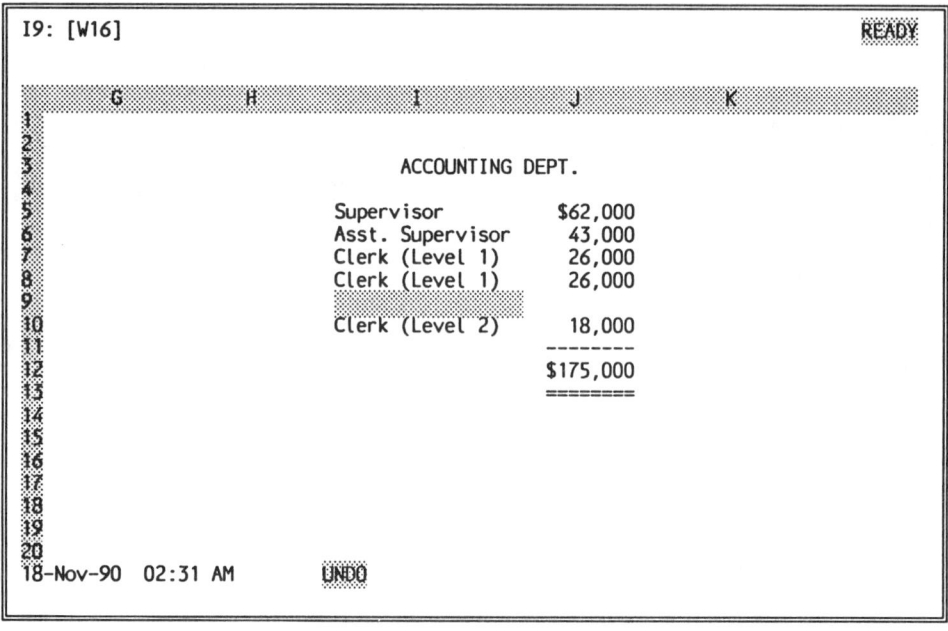

Figure 2-13 Result of /Move Command

FUNCTIONS

1-2-3 has a series of functions built in that can both simplify the execution of frequently used features and assist you in creating much more sophisticated worksheets. Each of these functions begins with the "at" symbol (@); therefore, you may hear people refer to them as *at functions*. 1-2-3 has so many functions that we will only concentrate on those that you will likely find most useful in Accounting applications. The specific functions that we will discuss are:

1. Statistical Functions
   - @SUM
   - @AVG
   - @COUNT
2. Special Functions
   - @VLOOKUP
   - @HLOOKUP
3. Date and Time Functions
   - @DATE
   - @DATEVALUE
   - @TIME
   - @NOW
4. Financial Functions
   - @PV
   - @NPV
   - @FV
   - @IRR
   - @RATE
   - @TERM
   - @CTERM
   - @PMT
   - @SLN
   - @DDB
   - @SYD
5. Logical Functions
   - @IF

Remember that we are only discussing a sample of the functions available in 1-2-3. Once you become comfortable with these, you will be able to incorporate many others into your spreadsheets with little difficulty.

Statistical Functions

In Chapter 1, you learned how to enter basic formulas in cells. You probably realized at that time that to enter more complicated ones would be quite tedious and time consuming. To relieve some of this tedium and to provide more power to some of your formulas, 1-2-3 provides Statistical functions. Quite a few Statistical functions exist, but we have chosen a few that are more frequently used. The Statistical functions we will discuss are:

1. @SUM - Allows you to add a list of numbers very quickly and simply.
2. @AVG - Generates the average of a list of numbers.
3. @COUNT - Examines a list and counts the number of cells in that range that are non-blank.

Notice that we used the word *list* rather than range in defining the functions. In most cases, you will actually put a range in the parentheses. That is, you would put specific cell references or a range name in the parentheses. In the example of @SUM, you would simply type the **@SUM** function into a cell, with a range in parentheses, and the cell would then display the total from adding all the cells in the specified range. The reason we use the list instead of range, though, is that you can also place a group of ranges in the parentheses or you can even place actual numeric values in the parentheses. For example, if you typed the function **@SUM(3,10,9)** into a cell, the cell would display the total 22.

@SUM

The @SUM function works exactly like a formula with plus signs between every cell reference. To illustrate the use of the @SUM function, notice the column of Accounts Receivable numbers in Figure 2-14. Assume you would like to calculate the total Accounts Receivable for the company by adding the column of numbers.

```
C16: [W16]                                                                        READY

          A                      B                       C           D
1
2
3     CUSTOMER              CUSTOMER                 AMOUNT
4      NUMBER                 NAME                RECEIVABLE
5     ----------    ------------------------------    ----------------
6     23-1903       Warren Electronics                  4512.47
7     39-1289       Hickory Distributing               19067.34
8     37-1936       Columbia Corporation                 762.88
9     33-9362       Adams Electronic Corp.            89346.12
10    53-8326       Quinn Steel Co.                    7901.04
11    44-8263       Howard Printers                    9912.65
12    87-4932       Baldwin Consulting Group            832.02
13    91-9372       Baskin Drilling                   63518.33
14    12-2387       Fleet Services Corp.               3521.33
15    87-2342       Poston Realtors                    7823.76
16
17
18
19
20
18-Nov-90   11:05 AM              UNDO
```

Figure 2-14 Column of Numbers to be Totaled Using @SUM

One approach to adding the numbers would be simply to place the cursor in cell C16 and enter a long formula. In entering the formula, you could either enter the cell references or use the cursor to point to each of the appropriate cells. Either way, the process would be overly cumbersome, with the resulting formula appearing as shown in the control panel in Figure 2-15.

The @SUM function would make this process much simpler. The general format for this function is:

@SUM(*list*)

```
C16: (C2) [W16] +C6+C7+C8+C9+C10+C11+C12+C13+C14+C15                    READY

          A                    B                         C              D

1
2
3        CUSTOMER            CUSTOMER                  AMOUNT
4        NUMBER                NAME                 RECEIVABLE
5        ----------  -------------------------------  ----------------
6        23-1903     Warren Electronics                  $4,512.47
7        39-1289     Hickory Distributing               $19,067.34
8        37-1936     Columbia Corporation                  $762.88
9        33-9362     Adams Electronic Corp.             $89,346.12
10       53-8326     Quinn Steel Co.                     $7,901.04
11       44-8263     Howard Printers                     $9,912.65
12       87-4932     Baldwin Consulting Group              $832.02
13       91-9372     Baskin Drilling                    $63,518.33
14       12-2387     Fleet Services Corp.                $3,521.33
15       87-2342     Poston Realtors                     $7,823.76
16                         TOTAL ACCOUNTS RECEIVABLE    $207,197.94
17
18
19
20
18-Nov-90   11:07 AM          UNDO
```

Figure 2-15 Formula for Totalling Amounts

You would use @SUM in this example by placing the cursor on cell C16 and typing the function **@SUM(C6..C15)**. In this situation, you would very likely want to use pointing and the END key to make the process simpler. To use pointing, you would simply type the function **@SUM** (into cell C16 and move the cursor to the top of the range (see Figure 2-16). You would then anchor the cursor at the top of the range by pressing period (.). To move the cursor quickly to the bottom of the range, you would simply press the **END** key and then the **DOWN** arrow key. Notice that the entire column is now highlighted. Upon entering the closing parentheses and then pressing **ENTER**, the function is complete, as shown in Figure 2-17. Alternatively, if you had given the column of numbers a range name, the range name could be typed in the parentheses. For example, assume you had given the column of numbers the range name A_REC, then you could simply type the function **@SUM(A_REC)** into cell C16.

@AVG

The @AVG function works in precisely the same way as the @SUM function. That is, the general formula for this function is:

$$@AVG(list)$$

By typing this function into a cell, the cell will display the average of whatever list (range name, numeric values, etc.) is indicated in the parentheses. In the example used in the previous section, assume the company wants to know the average amount of Accounts Receivable. To calculate the average, you would simply place the cursor on cell C17 and type the function **@AVG(C6..C15)**. Upon pressing **ENTER**, the cell displays the average. See Figure 2-18 for the completed formula.

```
C6: (C2) [W16] 4512.47                                                          POINT
aSUM(C6

         A                     B                        C              D
1
2
3    CUSTOMER              CUSTOMER                  AMOUNT
4    NUMBER                 NAME                  RECEIVABLE
5    ----------    --------------------------------   ----------------
6    23-1903       Warren Electronics                   $4,512.47
7    39-1289       Hickory Distributing                $19,067.34
8    37-1936       Columbia Corporation                   $762.88
9    33-9362       Adams Electronic Corp.              $89,346.12
10   53-8326       Quinn Steel Co.                      $7,901.04
11   44-8263       Howard Printers                      $9,912.65
12   87-4932       Baldwin Consulting Group               $832.02
13   91-9372       Baskin Drilling                     $63,518.33
14   12-2387       Fleet Services Corp.                 $3,521.33
15   87-2342       Poston Realtors                      $7,823.76
16                 TOTAL ACCOUNTS RECEIVABLE
17
18
19
20
18-Nov-90   11:13 AM
```

Figure 2-16 @SUM Formula Before Anchoring

```
C16: (C2) [W16] aSUM(C6..C15)                                                   READY

         A                     B                        C              D
1
2
3    CUSTOMER              CUSTOMER                  AMOUNT
4    NUMBER                 NAME                  RECEIVABLE
5    ----------    --------------------------------   ----------------
6    23-1903       Warren Electronics                   $4,512.47
7    39-1289       Hickory Distributing                $19,067.34
8    37-1936       Columbia Corporation                   $762.88
9    33-9362       Adams Electronic Corp.              $89,346.12
10   53-8326       Quinn Steel Co.                      $7,901.04
11   44-8263       Howard Printers                      $9,912.65
12   87-4932       Baldwin Consulting Group               $832.02
13   91-9372       Baskin Drilling                     $63,518.33
14   12-2387       Fleet Services Corp.                 $3,521.33
15   87-2342       Poston Realtors                      $7,823.76
16                 TOTAL ACCOUNTS RECEIVABLE            $207,197.94
17
18
19
20
18-Nov-90   11:10 AM              UNDO
```

Figure 2-17 @SUM Formula for Totalling Amounts

@COUNT

The @COUNT function displays the total number of non-blank cells in the list. Again, the general format is like that of @SUM and @AVG, and is:

@COUNT(*list*)

You may be wondering what use this particulate function would serve. It is hard to imagine why you would need to know the number of non-blank cells in a list. In practice, the @COUNT function is very beneficial in three primary applications:

1. To know the total number of items in a list. For example, the function could be used to count a long list of customers.
2. To use in conjunction with other statistical functions. For example, you could have calculated your own average of the list in Figure 2-18 by typing the formula **@SUM(C6..C15)/@COUNT(C6..C15)** in cell C17.
3. To assist in designing flexible macros. (Macros are covered in Chapter 5.)

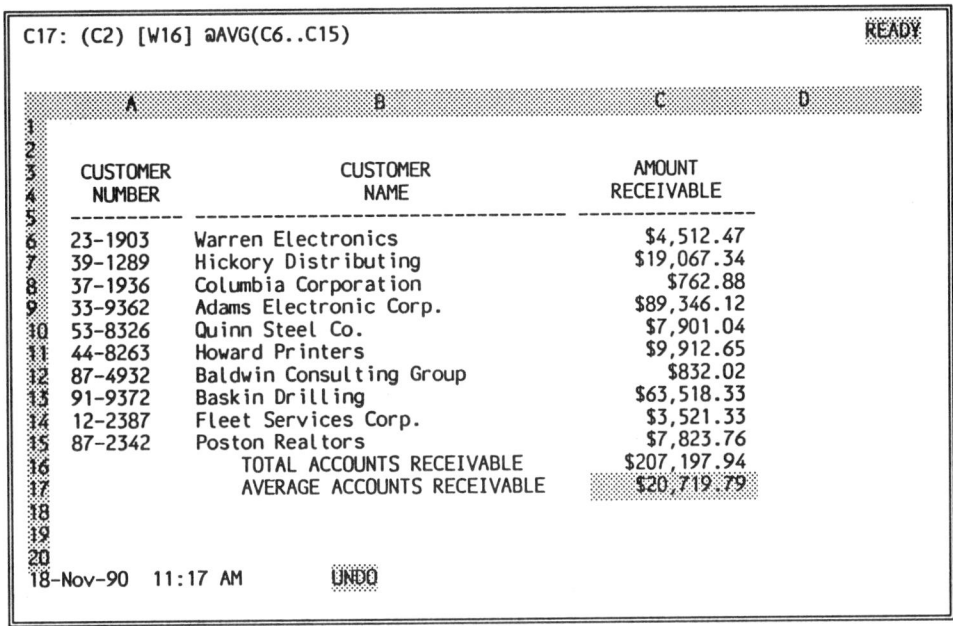

Figure 2-18 @AVG Formula for Averaging Amounts

Special Functions

1-2-3 has a variety of special functions that serve numerous purposes. The two special functions we will focus on are:

1. @VLOOKUP - Allows you to obtain an entry from a vertical table depending on the value specified.
2. @HLOOKUP - Allows you to obtain an entry from a horizontal table depending on the value specified.

@VLOOKUP

To illustrate this function, assume you were constructing a spreadsheet to assist in the preparation of commission checks. The commissions are based on the total amount of sales by employee, with the percentage increasing as the sales amount increases. Figure 2-19 shows each employee's name and the amount of sales attributed to that employee.

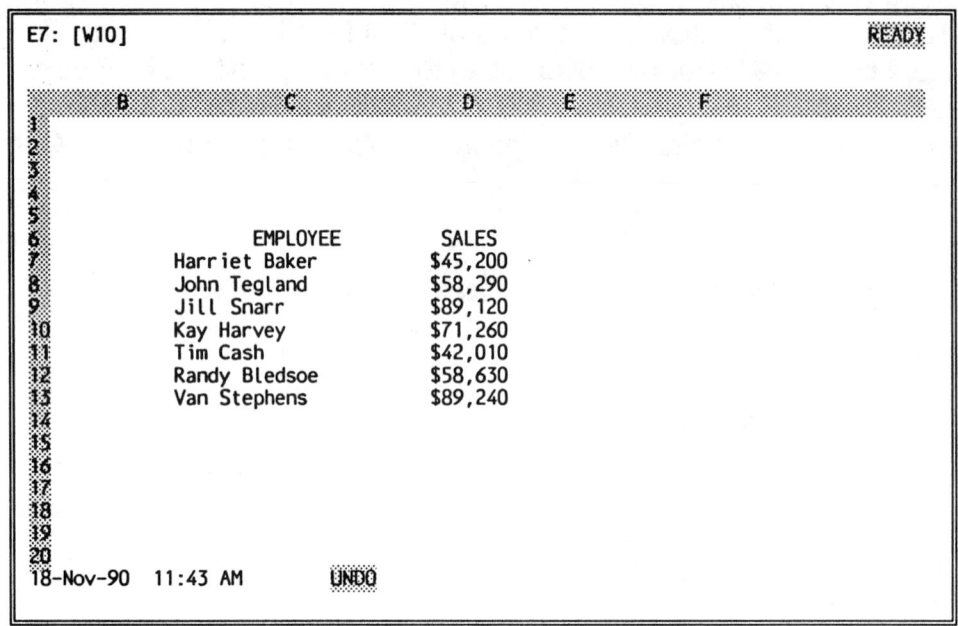

Figure 2-19 Sales Amounts for Calculating Commissions

To use @VLOOKUP, you must first construct a *table of values* to be referenced. The table would simply list the percentage associated with certain critical levels of sales. We have constructed the table, which is shown in Figure 2-20. We have also given the cells J6 through K18 the range name TABLE for future reference.

The @VLOOKUP function has the following general format:

$$@VLOOKUP(x, table\ reference, column)$$

The "x" in this function represents the search key for the table. We are using the sales amount to locate the appropriate location in the table; therefore, the search key is the cell reference of that employee's sales amount.

The "table reference" is simply the cell references or range name for the table to be searched. As mentioned previously, we have already given the table a range name; therefore, the range name of TABLE could be used in this location. Of course, you could also use the actual cell references of J6..K18.

The "column" in the function is actually a column displacement number. For example, the first column in the table would be considered as having a displacement of 0, the next column would have a displacement of 1, and so forth. For our example, we are referencing the second column of the table, so the displacement will be 1.

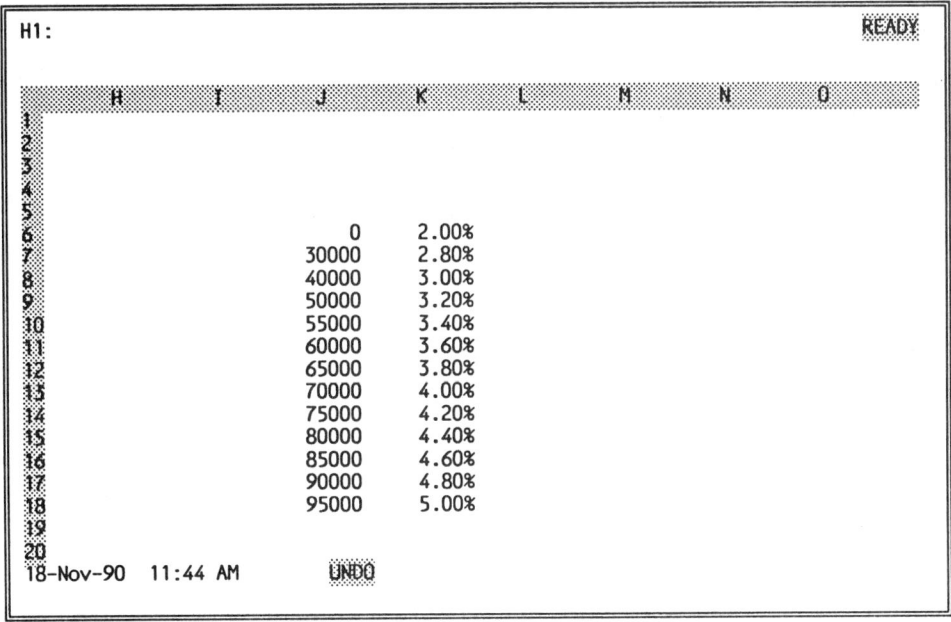

Figure 2-20 Table to be Used in @VLOOKUP Formula

The @VLOOKUP function for the first employee would be entered into cell E7 and would appear as in Figure 2-21. Two things may look peculiar to you and therefore deserve special attention:

1. The range name of TABLE in the @VLOOKUP function has a dollar sign in front of it.
2. The sales amount of $45,200 does not have a corresponding amount in the table. That is, this particular sales amount does not appear in TABLE.

You may remember our earlier discussion of relative versus absolute addressing. With relative addressing, whenever you copy a formula the formula will change depending on where it is moved. Copying or moving formulas containing absolute addresses does not change those addresses. As you may also recall, absolute addressing is denoted by placing a dollar sign in front of the column and/or row reference, depending on what portion of the address you want to remain intact. In this example, we have placed a dollar sign in front of the range name TABLE to give it absolute addressing. This use of the dollar sign with a range name is exactly the same effect as placing dollar signs in front of the column and row references in the range name. In fact, once you enter this formula and press **ENTER**, notice what 1-2-3 does to the table reference; it converts it to the actual cell references in the formula (refer to Figure 2-22). Giving the TABLE reference absolute addressing, we can now simply copy the @VLOOKUP function from cell E7 to cells E8 through E13.

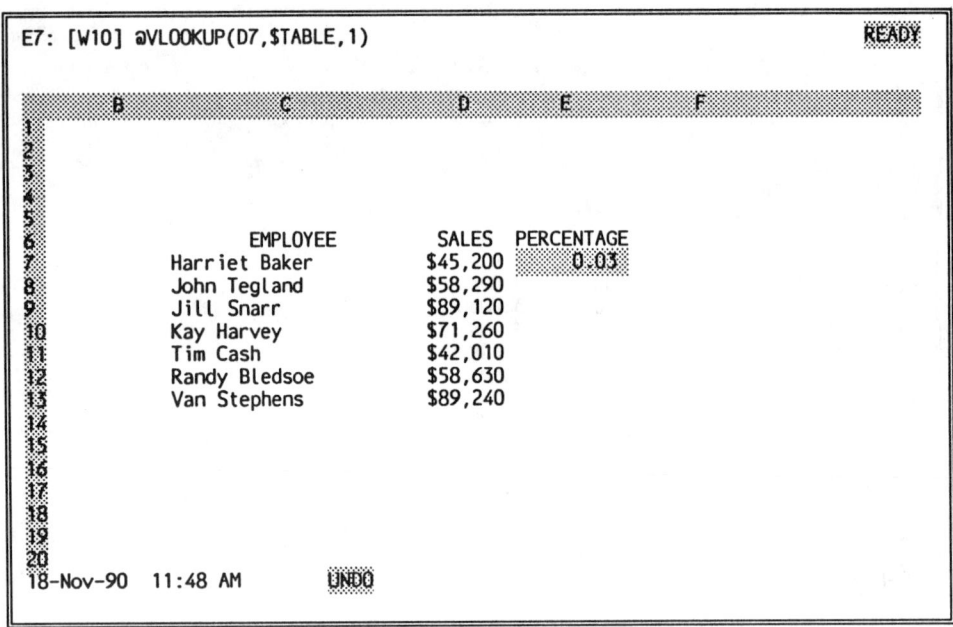

Figure 2-21 @VLOOKUP Formula for First Employee

```
E7: [W10] @VLOOKUP(D7,$TABLE,1)                                              EDIT
@VLOOKUP(D7,$J$6..$K$18,1)
          B              C              D        E          F
 1
 2
 3
 4
 5
 6                    EMPLOYEE         SALES   PERCENTAGE
 7              Harriet Baker       $45,200      0.03
 8              John Tegland        $58,290
 9              Jill Snarr          $89,120
10              Kay Harvey          $71,260
11              Tim Cash            $42,010
12              Randy Bledsoe       $58,630
13              Van Stephens        $89,240
14
15
16
17
18
19
20
18-Nov-90   11:50 AM
```

Figure 2-22 Conversion of Range Name to Cell References

The other peculiarity noted was that not all possible sales amounts were shown in TABLE. It would of course be impossible to predict every sales amount, and constructing a table with all values from 0 on up would be overwhelming. Therefore, 1-2-3 makes the process simpler by matching the search key with the amount that is closest to the search key without exceeding it.

@HLOOKUP

The @HLOOKUP function works in precisely the same way as the @VLOOKUP function, except that the table to be used is constructed horizontally rather than vertically. The general format of the @HLOOKUP function is as follows:

@HLOOKUP(*x,table reference,row*)

Once you understand the @VLOOKUP function, you will have no problem with understanding the @HLOOKUP function (and vice versa). Furthermore, you will find that these functions give you the ability to construct spreadsheets with great flexibility and sophistication.

Date and Time Functions

Date and time functions allow you to perform arithmetic operations on dates and times (such as finding the number of days between two dates). You can also use these functions to display the dates in your spreadsheet. In the case of @NOW, you can improve the documentation in your spreadsheet while giving it a much more professional appearance. As with the previous categories, numerous date and time functions exist, but we will focus on only three of the most important:

1. @DATE - Allows you to perform arithmetic operations on dates by converting a specified date to a *date value*.
2. @NOW - 1-2-3 determines the current date from the computer's clock and then converts that date to the appropriate date value.
3. @YEAR - Retrieves only the year from a date value.

@DATE

This function has the following format:

@DATE(*year,month,day*)

From this function, 1-2-3 assigns a date value, which is a sequential number corresponding to each date from January 1, 1900 (which is assigned the number 1). By assigning this date value to each date, 1-2-3 allows you to perform arithmetic on dates, such as finding the number of days between two dates.

Once 1-2-3 has assigned a date value, the cell can be formatted to present the date in a more understandable fashion. For example, notice the @DATE function in cell D8 in Figure 2-23. (The function itself is shown in the control panel, and the date value for July 2, 1988 is displayed in cell D8.) To have the cell appear as a date, the **/Range Format Date** command should be used. Upon entering this command, the menu depicted in Figure 2-24 would appear. Each format option will display as shown in the option itself. In this example, we selected Option 4 (Long Intn'l), which causes the date to appear as in Figure 2-25. (Remember, even though the cell has been formatted, it still contains the @DATE function.)

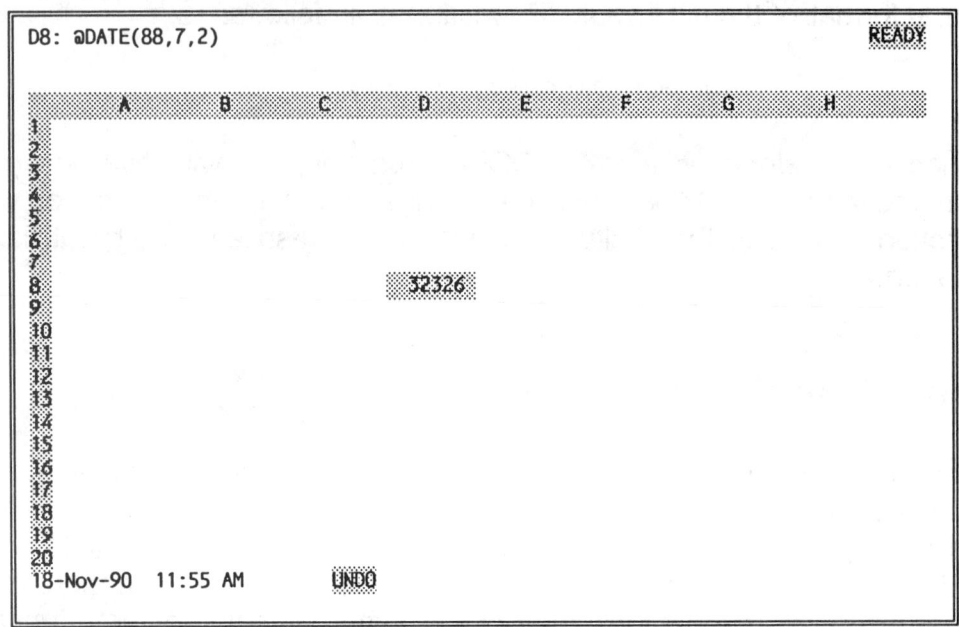

Figure 2-23 Example of a Date Value

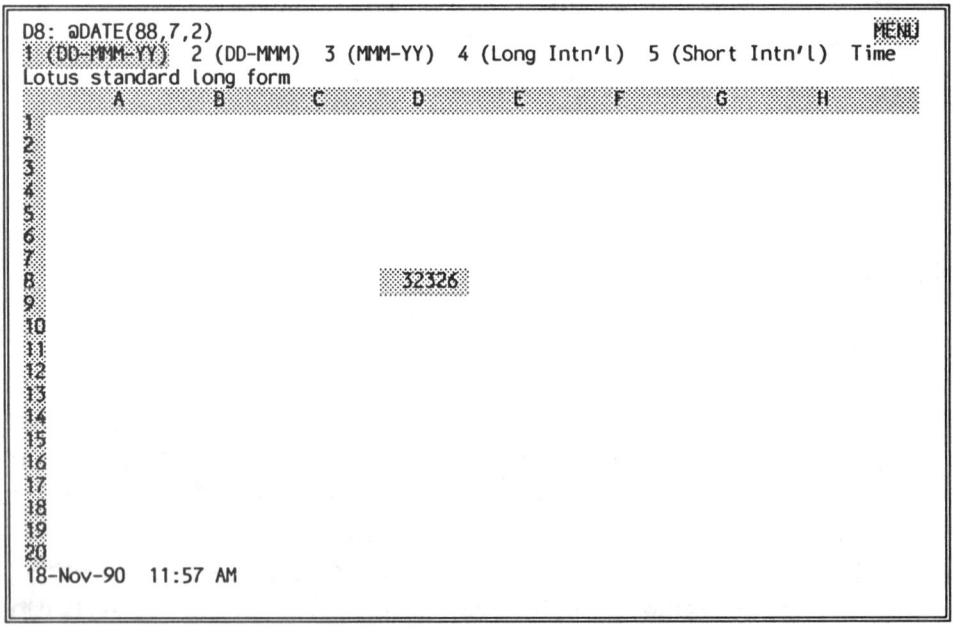

Figure 2-24 Options for /Range Format Date Command

@NOW

Much like the @DATE function, @NOW represents a date as a unique 1-2-3 date value. The difference is that @NOW receives the appropriate date from the computer's clock. To use @NOW, you simply type the function into a cell. The function does not need arguments listed in parentheses, since the function gets its input from the computer itself.

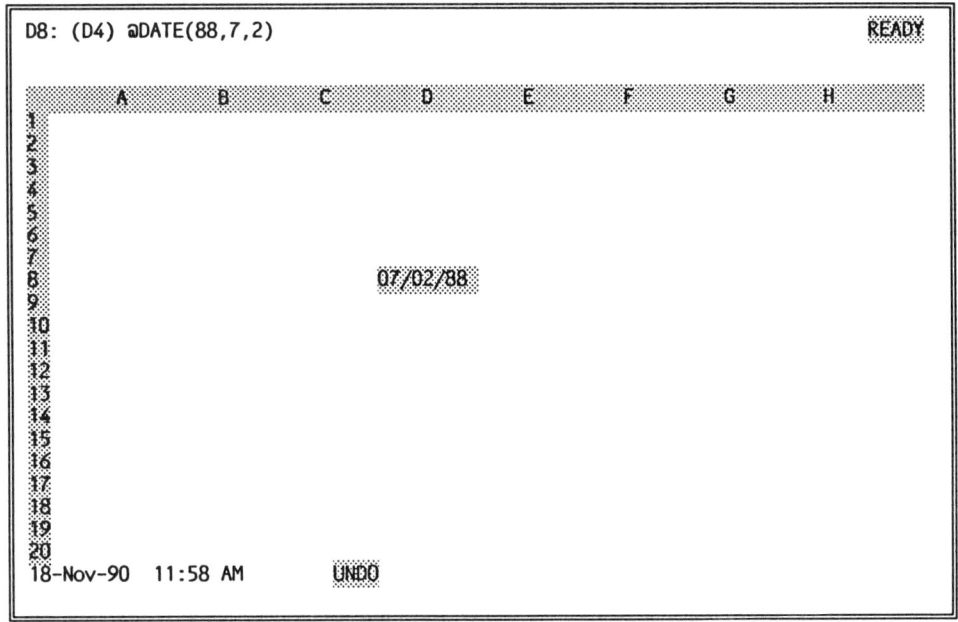

Figure 2-25 Date Value Formatted as Long Intn'l

@YEAR

This function allows you to extract the year from any date value. The format is as follows:

@YEAR(*date value*)

The @YEAR function is most useful when calculating the number of years between two dates. For example, assume you wanted to know the age of a series of assets. In Figure 2-26, we have shown assets and their purchase dates. We would like to calculate the age of each asset, as compared to today's date. The @YEAR function could be used by extracting the year from the formula that computes the number of days between the two dates. (In the example, the "current date" is assumed to be 11/18/90.) The resulting formula would then be as shown in Figure 2-27.

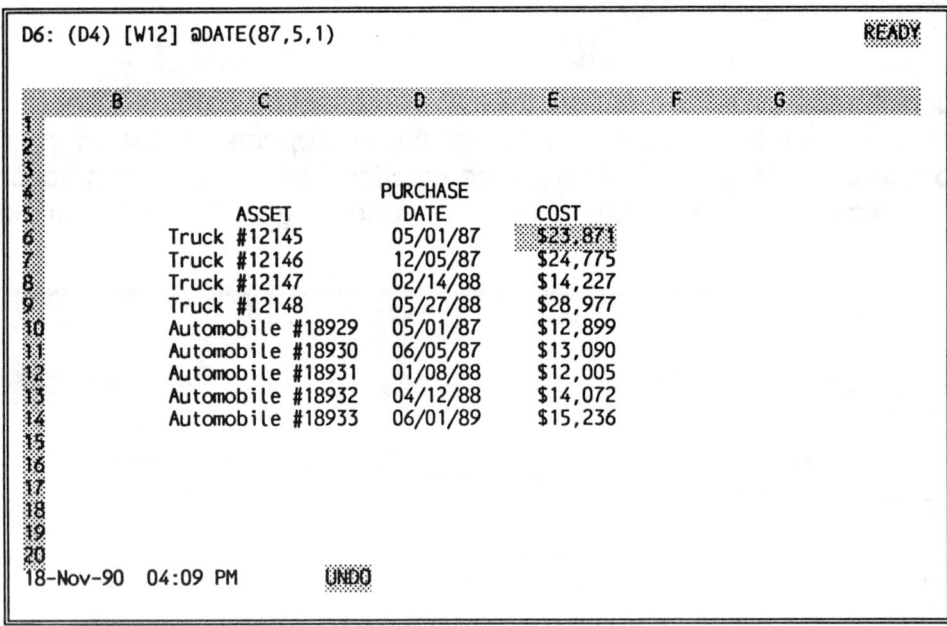

Figure 2-26 Example of Asset Listing

```
F6: aYEAR(aNOW-D6)                                                    READY
          B           C              D            E         F        G
1
2
3
4                                 PURCHASE
5                      ASSET        DATE        COST       AGE
6               Truck #12145       05/01/87    $23,871        3
7               Truck #12146       12/05/87    $24,775        2
8               Truck #12147       02/14/88    $14,227        2
9               Truck #12148       05/27/88    $28,977        2
10              Automobile #18929  05/01/87    $12,899        3
11              Automobile #18930  06/05/87    $13,090        3
12              Automobile #18931  01/08/88    $12,005        2
13              Automobile #18932  04/12/88    $14,072        2
14              Automobile #18933  06/01/89    $15,236        1
15
16
17
18
19
20
18-Nov-90  04:10 PM            UNDO
```

Figure 2-27 @YEAR Function Used to Calculate Asset Age

Financial Functions--Cash Flow

1-2-3 allows you to develop more powerful business applications with the Financial Functions. Because Financial Functions have such potentially wide use in accounting systems, we will discuss all of the Financial Functions available in 1-2-3. These functions can be categorized as Cash Flow Functions and Depreciation Functions.

Cash Flow Functions let you make various calculations related to investing and financing. These functions are summarized and then explained below:

1. @PV - Calculates the present value of a stream of equal future cash flows.
2. @NPV - Calculates the present value of a stream of future cash flows, regardless of whether those amounts are equal.
3. @FV - Calculates the future value of a stream of future cash flows.
4. @IRR - Calculates the internal rate of return from a stream of future cash flows.
5. @RATE - Calculates the interest rate necessary for a present value to achieve a specified future value.
6. @TERM - Calculates the number of times a payment must be made on a loan, given a specified interest rate and future value.
7. @CTERM - Calculates the number of periods required for a specified present value to grow to a specified future value.

@PV

This function calculates the present value of a stream of equal cash flows (an annuity), given an assumed interest rate. The general format of the function is:

@PV(*payments,interest,term*)

The payments represent the amount of money being paid at each interval. The interest is the assumed interest rate for the period, and the term is the number of payments that will be made. Consider the example where an investment will pay $4,000 a year for 12 years (in the case of @PV, the payments are assumed to occur at the end of the year). Furthermore, the assumed interest rate is 10.5% (this may be the rate of return assumed on investments of the cost of funds to the enterprise). In Figure 2-28, the @PV function can be seen in the control panel.

@NPV

The @NPV function is very similar to the @PV function, except that the @PV function assumes the stream of cash flows to be equal, while @NPV can handle uneven amounts. @NPV does, however, assume the cash flows are at equal intervals, just as @PV does. Furthermore, when we think of net present value calculations, we assume the present value of the stream of cash inflows is compared to the cost of the original investment to generate the *net* return on our investment. @NPV does not include the original cost in its formula. To include the original cost in the analysis, you simply subtract the original cost of the investment from the @NPV function.

The general format of the @NPV function is:

@NPV(*interest,range*)

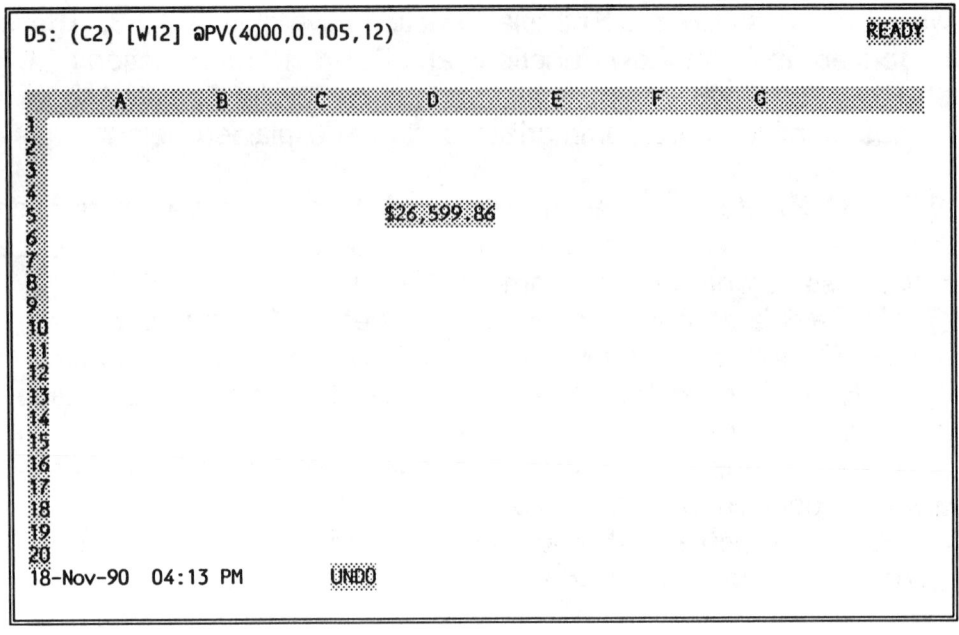

Figure 2-28 Example of the @PV Function

Obviously, the "interest" in this function is the interest rate considered appropriate. The range is actually a reference to a series of cells which contain the actual future cash flow amounts.

Figure 2-29 shows an example of the @NPV function. In this example, the original investment was $45,500. The stream of inflows for the life of the investment (9 years) is shown in cells D6 through D14. The assumed interest rate is 9.6% (.096). Notice that the @NPV formula references cells D6 through D14; the original investment of $45,500 is not considered in the @NPV calculation. Cell D18 shows how the original investment can easily be accommodated by simply subtracting it from the result of the @NPV function.

@FV

The future value of a stream of equal cash flows is calculated with the @FV function. This function is of the following general format:

@FV(*payments,interest,term*)

Just as in the @PV function, the payments argument is the amount of cash flow per period (for example, the amount of interest paid per year), the interest is the assumed interest rate, and the term is the number of payments that will be made.

```
D16: (C2) [W11] aNPV(0.096,D6..D14)                          READY

         A      B           C              D        E        F
 1
 2
 3             Investment:           $45,500
 4
 5             Inflows:
 6                    Year 1         $6,000
 7                    Year 2         $7,500
 8                    Year 3         $7,800
 9                    Year 4         $8,000
10                    Year 5         $8,200
11                    Year 6         $8,400
12                    Year 7         $8,800
13                    Year 8         $9,500
14                    Year 9         $9,800
15
16             NPV of Inflows:       $46,708.60
17
18             NPV of Investment:    $1,208.60
19
20
18-Nov-90  04:21 PM          UNDO
```

Figure 2-29 Example of the @NPV Function

@IRR

The internal rate of return function, @IRR, calculates the return that would be required to cause the future stream of cash inflows to equal the original investment. In other words, the IRR is the interest rate that would cause the net present value to equal zero. @IRR has the following format:

$$@IRR(guess,range)$$

If you were to calculate IRR "by hand," you would find that it is a trial-and-error process. 1-2-3 also uses a trial-and-error process, and you must give it a "reasonable" interest rate as your best first guess. 1-2-3 will then attempt to converge on a solution, adjusting the interest rate each time in an attempt to make the present value equal to zero. At times, 1-2-3 will not find a solution for IRR, and in these situations you should simply try a different "guess" argument. The range in parentheses is the cell references for those cells containing cash flow amounts. Figure 2-30 shows an example of the @IRR function being used to evaluate the purchase of a new inventory system that costs $135,000. The people selling the system have provided the projected cash inflows, which are shown in cells D9 through D16. (Notice that the first number in the range argument must be a negative number, representing the original investment in the asset.)

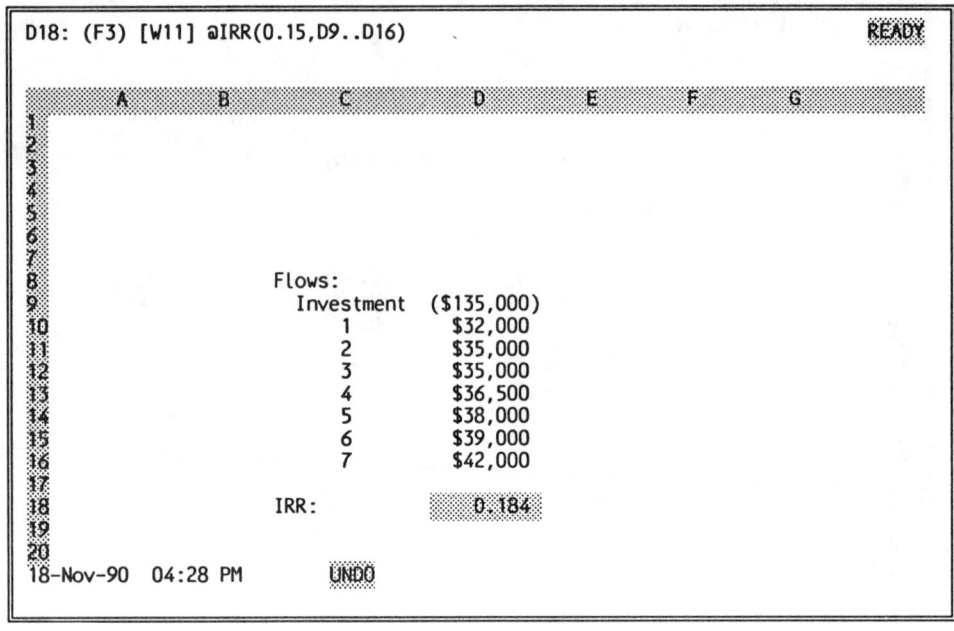

```
D18: (F3) [W11] @IRR(0.15,D9..D16)                              READY

          A         B          C            D          E         F         G
1
2
3
4
5
6
7
8                   Flows:
9                     Investment    ($135,000)
10                        1          $32,000
11                        2          $35,000
12                        3          $35,000
13                        4          $36,500
14                        5          $38,000
15                        6          $39,000
16                        7          $42,000
17
18                  IRR:                0.184
19
20
18-Nov-90   04:28 PM              UNDO
```

Figure 2-30 Example of the @IRR Function

@RATE

@RATE calculates the interest rate required to generate a desired future value from a present value and a specified number of periods (which could be years, months, etc.). The format for this function is:

$$@RATE(\textit{future-value},\textit{present-value},\textit{term})$$

To illustrate the @RATE function, assume the present value of an investment is $30,000 and the desired future value is $45,000 after 6 years. As shown in Figure 2-31, the required interest rate to generate these results is 7%, as shown in cell D16.

@TERM

This function calculates the number of payments needed to attain a specified future value, given an interest rate. The format of the @TERM function is:

$$@TERM(\textit{payments},\textit{interest},\textit{future-value})$$

The payments argument specifies the amount of each payment to be made, the interest of the interest rate that the account will be accumulating, and the future-value is the amount the balance the user wants to attain.

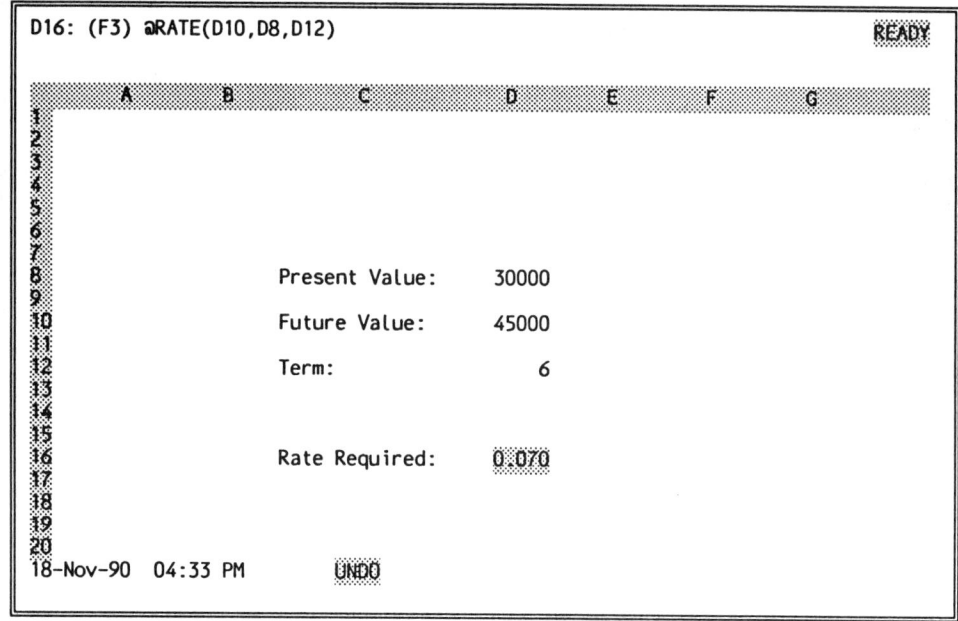

D16: (F3) ᵃRATE(D10,D8,D12)   READY

```
        A       B         C          D        E       F       G
1
2
3
4
5
6
7
8              Present Value:      30000
9
10             Future Value:       45000
11
12             Term:                   6
13
14
15
16             Rate Required:      0.070
17
18
19
20
```
18-Nov-90 04:33 PM   UNDO

Figure 2-31   Example of the @RATE Function

For example, assume you wanted to invest $100 a month into an interest-bearing account that is earning 7% annually. You would like to know how many payments are required before you would accumulate a balance of $10,000. This example is illustrated in Figure 2-32, showing that you would make approximately 79 monthly payments to attain the $10,000 balance. Note that the interest rate in the formula is expressed as .07/12. The interest rate in any financial function should be expressed in the same period of time as the term. In this particular case, we are making monthly contributions, so the interest rate should be expressed in monthly interest rather than annual interest.

@CTERM

@CTERM is very similar to the @TERM function; however, with @CTERM you are determining the number of periods required before a given amount will grow to some desired balance. The format of this function is as follows:

@CTERM(*interest,future-value,present-value*)

Financial Functions--Depreciation

The Depreciation Functions allow you to calculate depreciation using the straight-line method, the double-declining-balance method, or the sum-of-years'-digits method. The depreciation functions are listed and explained below:

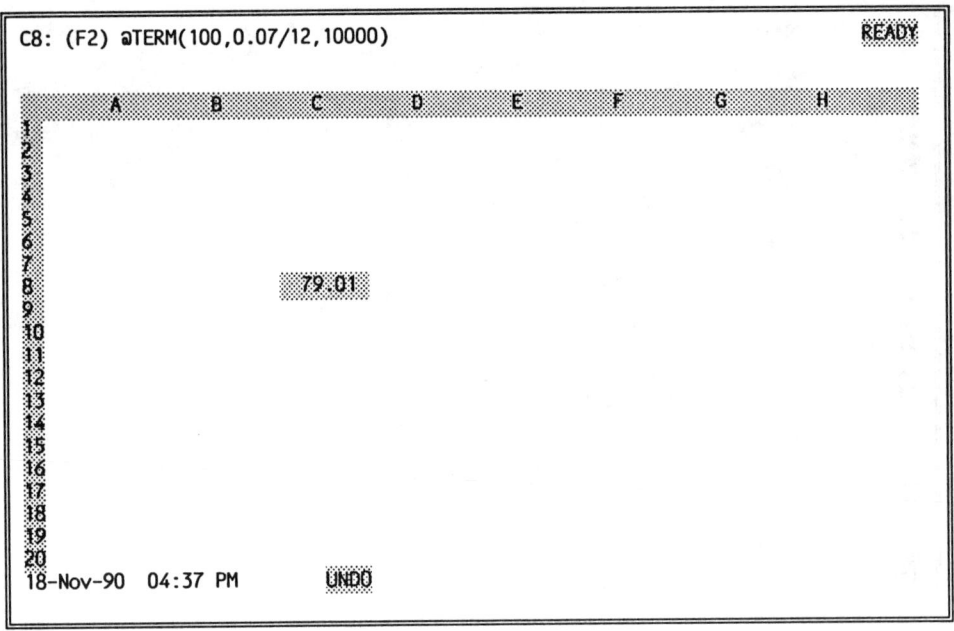

Figure 2-32 Example of the @TERM Function

1. @SLN - Calculates straight-line depreciation of an asset, given the cost, salvage value, and life.
2. @DDB - Calculates double-declining balance depreciation of an asset, given the cost, salvage value, life, and period.
3. @SYD - Calculates sum-of-the-years'-digits depreciation of an asset, given the cost, salvage value, life, and period.

@SLN

@SLN calculates annual depreciation for an asset by using the straight-line method. The format for this function is:

@SLN(*cost,salvage-value,life*)

Once you know the cost of an asset, have made assumptions about its salvage value at the end of its useful life, and the assumed useful life, then the @SLN function will calculate the annual depreciation expense. For example, assume that a company has an asset that cost $25,000, has an assumed useful life of 14 years, and an assumed salvage value of $3,000 at the end of those 14 years. The annual depreciation expense under the straight-line method for this asset would be $1571.43, as shown by the @SLN function in Figure 2-33.

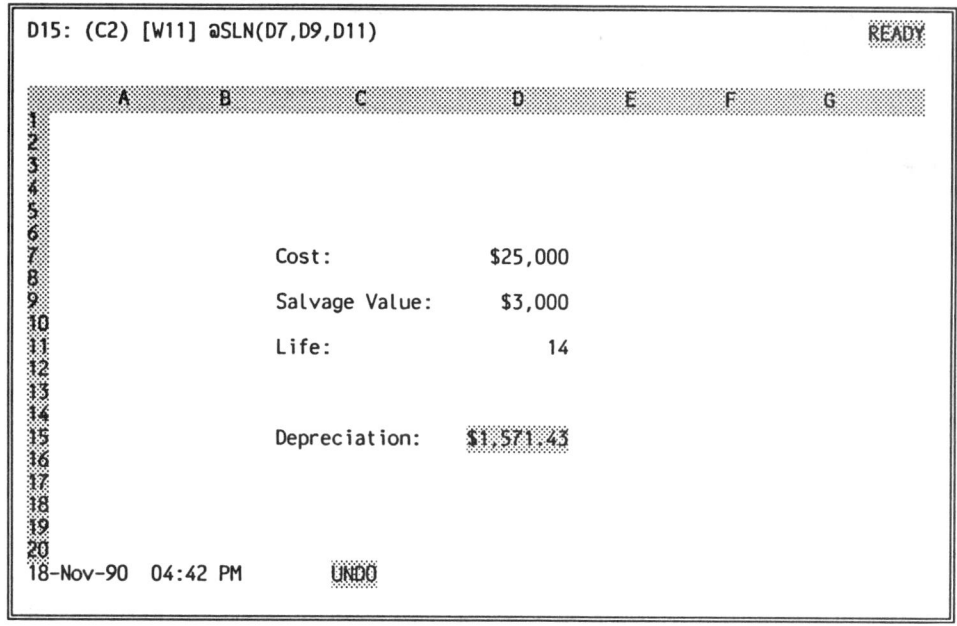

Figure 2-33 Example of the @SLN Function

@DDB

@DDB also generates an annual depreciation amount for an asset, but it uses the double-declining-balance method. The general format for @DDB is as follows:

@DDB(*cost,salvage-value,life,year*)

The arguments for @DDB are identical to those under @SLN, except for the "year" argument.   Under the double-declining-balance method, the depreciation expense decreases from one year to the next.   Therefore, when asking 1-2-3 to calculate the annual depreciation expense, you must indicate the year for which you want the expense. The year argument serves this purpose.

To illustrate @DDB, assume the same information as for the @SLN function, except that we are wanting the depreciation expense for the asset's second year. The function would return the value of $3061.22, which is illustrated in Figure 2-34.

@SYD

@SYD calculates the depreciation expense for a given year using Sum-of-the-Years'-Digits depreciation. Just like @DDB, the general format for @SYD is:

@SYD(*cost,salvage-value,life,year*)

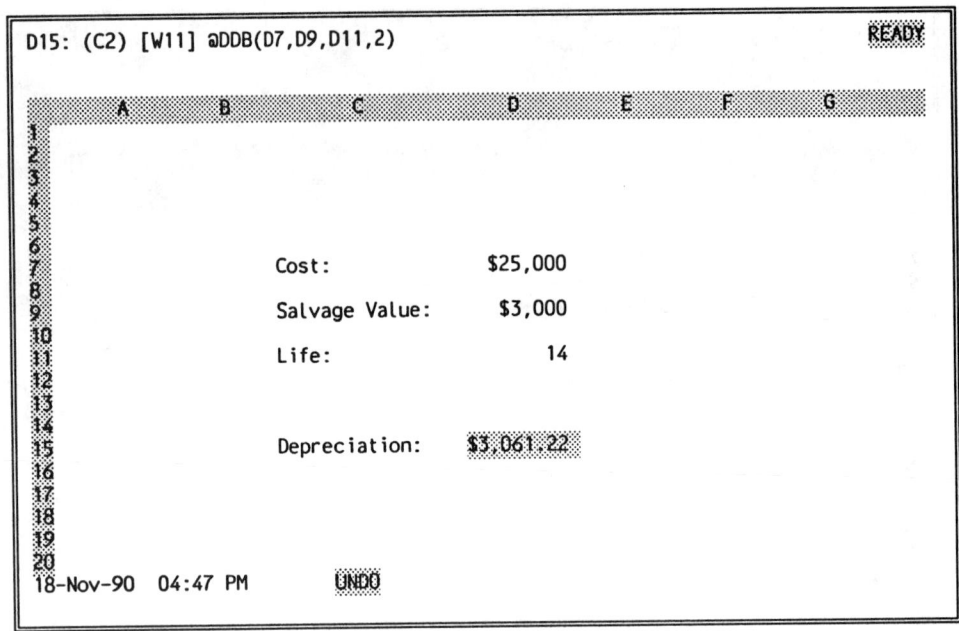

D15: (C2) [W11] @DDB(D7,D9,D11,2)   READY

	A	B	C	D	E	F	G

Cost: $25,000

Salvage Value: $3,000

Life: 14

Depreciation: $3,061.22

18-Nov-90   04:47 PM   UNDO

Figure 2-34 Example of the @DDB Function

Logical Functions

The Logical Functions are quite possibly the most powerful functions available in 1-2-3. These functions allow you to test conditions and then take actions accordingly. By combining these functions with other functions or formulas, your spreadsheet design possibilities are virtually endless.

We will only cover the @IF function. While the other logical functions are undoubtedly useful, the @IF function is the most widely used and powerful Logical Function. Furthermore, once you have mastered the @IF function, the others should be relatively easy to learn. The general format for the @IF function is shown below:

@IF(*condition,true-result,false-result*)

The condition is the item being tested. The true-result is the value that should be placed in the cell if the condition is true, and the false-result is the value that should be placed in the cell if the value is false.

Consider the inventory example shown in Figure 2-35. The BALANCE field shows the amount of uncommitted inventory for that particular item. In other words, BALANCE is calculated as follows:

BALANCE = OLD_BAL + PURCHASES - SHIPMENTS - ORDERS

```
F3: [W13] aIF((+B3+C3-D3-E3)<0,"BACKORDER",B3+C3-D3-E3)          READY

       A          B         C         D         E          F          G
 1
 2     ITEM_NO   OLD_BAL  PURCHASES SHIPMENTS  ORDERS      BALANCE
 3     4432-192      45        23        69         6   BACKORDER
 4     4267-938      88       213       312         7   BACKORDER
 5     5938-823     234        56       231        12             47
 6     2398-196     456        59       512         6   BACKORDER
 7     0864-734     341       200       348        60            133
 8     8975-382     676        34       429        34            247
 9     2340-165      12       231       211        45   BACKORDER
10     3876-187     456       342       651       113             34
11     2039-125      56        83        96        12             31
12     2309-961     345        38       209        84             90
13
14
15
16
17
18
19
20
18-Nov-90  05:01 PM         UNDO
```

Figure 2-35 @IF Function Used to Calculate Inventory Balance

If the current orders exceed the number of items on hand, this formula would cause BALANCE to be negative. We would prefer not to show a negative balance and would instead prefer to have the cell simply show "BACKORDER". To create this effect, we have used the @IF function. The @IF function for cell F3 is shown below:

$$@IF((B3+C3-D3-E3)<0,"BACKORDER",B3+C3-D3-E3)$$

This formula may look overly complicated at first, but it simply tells 1-2-3 that if the BALANCE is below 0, then place the word BACKORDER in the cell; otherwise, calculate the balance and place that result in the cell.

CONTROL CONSIDERATIONS

The risks presented by the commands and functions shown in this chapter are virtually no different from those addressed in Chapter 1. That is, you must be concerned that names are standardized, data are tested, and backup copies are maintained. However, the concept of *test data* is much more important than ever before. As you noticed, many of the formulas for the functions (such as the @IF function) become quite lengthy; it is often difficult to be certain the function is performing as desired. Test data should be used in all cases and especially in those where lengthy, complicated functions are employed.

One unique control feature discussed in this chapter is the use of the **/Range Name Table** command. This command simply generates a list of all range names that you have created and their location. But such a table can easily be used as part of the documentation for the spreadsheet itself.

REVIEW QUESTIONS

1. What is a range?

2. What are two primary differences between /Copy and /Move?

3. What does /Range Name Table do?

4. Differentiate between /Range Erase and /Range Name Delete.

5. Discuss two methods for converting a formula to its result.

6. What does the function @COUNT do?

7. What is the primary difference between @VLOOKUP and @HLOOKUP?

8. Explain the number that @DATE generates.

9. Differentiate between @PV and @NPV.

10. Explain the "guess" argument in the @IRR function.

11. Differentiate between @TERM and @CTERM.

12. Why do @DDB and @SYD each have the "year" argument?

13. Explain how the @IF function works.

14. What does the following command accomplish?

@YEAR(@NOW)

CASE: Carter Brokerage Group
Fixed-assets Master File
(The Facilities Management Cycle)

Richard Carter and Ben Fangmann own and operate the Carter Brokerage Group (which was originally started by Mr. Carter three years ago). They represent certain clothing manufacturers to retail clothing stores. That is, they act as the local sales representatives for clothing manufacturers who do not have sales forces in their area.

While the business was started only three years ago and is still relatively small, the prospects for tremendous growth are very promising. With growth, Carter and Fangmann feel they will need to purchase many more fixed assets. Accordingly, they would like to computerize their current fixed asset accounting system, so that the system could more easily accommodate the expected growth. (The information for the assets they currently own is located in the CARTER.WK1 file on your student disk.)

Requirements

Prepare a 1-2-3 spreadsheet to computerize the annual depreciation for each of the Carter Brokerage fixed assets. Some of the assets are to be accounted for under the Accelerated Cost Recovery System (ACRS). Even though this system is double-declining-balance, we feel it would be easier to handle with a table, which is supplied. The other assets are accounted for on the straight-line basis. Each asset's life must be tested to be certain no depreciation is being recorded after the end of the asset's life. All assets are being depreciated over a 5-year life. For assistance in record-keeping, totals should be placed at the bottom of all columns.

Solution

The information has all been typed into the spreadsheet as shown in Figure 2-36. As you will notice, the columns have been widened to accommodate all of the information, and the cells have been formatted appropriately. Under the PURCHASE DATE column, each entry has been made with the @DATE function, and then the column of cells was formatted with **/R**ange Format Date **4**(Long International). We must now write the formula to calculate each asset's depreciation expense.

The depreciation for the first asset (a desk) is to be calculated using the straight-line method. Because the cost is listed in cell C4, the salvage value in D4, and the useful life in H4, the formula would ordinarily be calculated as:

@SLN(C4,D4,H4)

However, we must first test whether the asset has already been depreciated for its useful life. You could use a number of methods for testing this, but we have chosen to calculate the life since the asset's purchase and compare that to the asset's useful life. To do this, we would simply subtract the year in purchase date from the current year:

@YEAR(@NOW)-@YEAR(B4)

For this example, we are making the simplifying assumption that 100% depreciation is taken for each year when we use the straight-line method (in other words, we are not using the half-year convention). The resulting formula would then be (see also the control panel in Figure 2-37):

```
F4: [W11]                                                             READY
```

	DATE OF			ACCUMULATED	DEPRECIATION
DESCRIPTION	PURCHASE	COST	SALVAGE	DEPRECIATION	EXPENSE
Desk	04/03/89	$650.00	$100	$110.00	
Copier	04/03/89	$1,540.00	$500	$208.00	
File Cabinet	04/19/89	$310.00	$50	$52.00	
Desk	05/16/89	$425.00	$75	$70.00	
Table	01/14/90	$540.00	$75	$0.00	
File Cabinet	04/01/90	$320.00	$50	$0.00	
Credenza	04/01/90	$335.00	$45	$0.00	
Lamp	09/12/89	$175.00	$30	$29.00	
Rug	09/15/90	$800.00	$300	$0.00	
Lamp	09/20/89	$255.00	$50	$41.00	

```
18-Nov-90   10:57 PM        UNDO
```

Figure 2-36 Carter Brokerage Fixed Assets List

```
F4: (C2) [W12] @IF(@YEAR(@NOW)-@YEAR(B4)>=H4,0,@SLN(C4,D4,H4))        READY
```

	DATE OF			ACCUMULATED	DEPRECIATION
DESCRIPTION	PURCHASE	COST	SALVAGE	DEPRECIATION	EXPENSE
Desk	04/03/89	$650.00	$100	$110.00	$110.00
Copier	04/03/89	$1,540.00	$500	$208.00	
File Cabinet	04/19/89	$310.00	$50	$52.00	
Desk	05/16/89	$425.00	$75	$70.00	
Table	01/14/90	$540.00	$75	$0.00	
File Cabinet	04/01/90	$320.00	$50	$0.00	
Credenza	04/01/90	$335.00	$45	$0.00	
Lamp	09/12/89	$175.00	$30	$29.00	
Rug	09/15/90	$800.00	$300	$0.00	
Lamp	09/20/89	$255.00	$50	$41.00	

```
19-Nov-90   03:31 AM        UNDO
```

Figure 2-37 @IF Function Used to Calculate Depreciation Expense

@IF(@YEAR(@NOW)-@YEAR(B4) > =H4,0,@SLN(C4,D4,H4))

As usual, the @IF function appears complicated, but can be summarized as simply testing whether the difference between the current year and the purchase year is greater than or equal to the asset's useful life. If the condition is true, then no depreciation expense would be recorded. If the condition is false, then the straight-line expense would be calculated using @SLN.

The function in cell F4 can then be copied to the remaining cells for the assets using straight-line depreciation.

We must now calculate the ACRS depreciation. As mentioned in the statement of the problem, we have decided to use a table for this depreciation method. The table is as appears in Figure 2-38. To simplify the remaining functions, we have also given the ACRS table a range name of TABLE1. Specifically, the cells M4..O10 have been given the range name TABLE1. You may notice two unique features about the ACRS table, which deserve special mention:

1. The table uses 6 years rather than 5.
2. The table has a 0 for year 7.

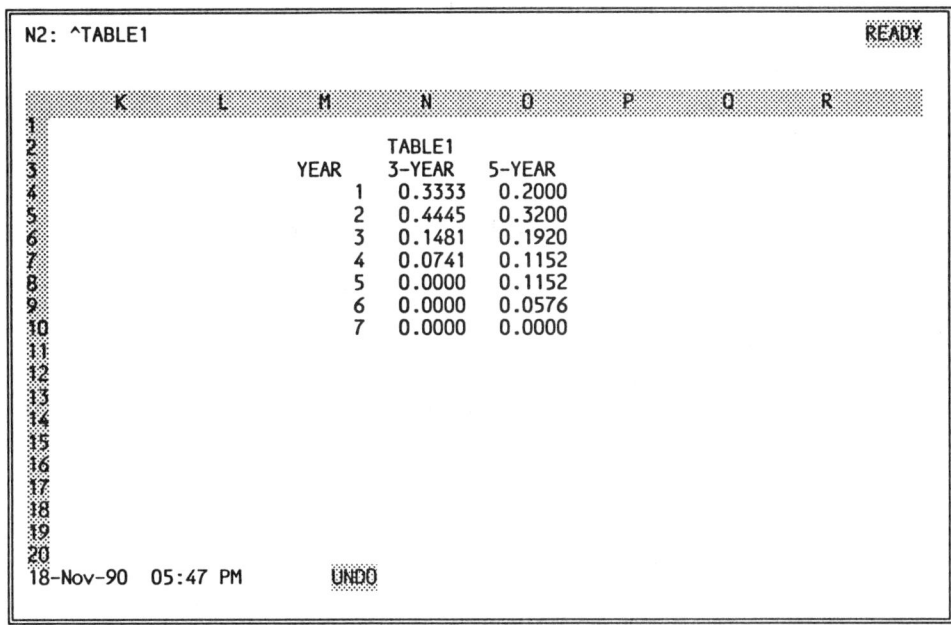

Figure 2-38 Table to be Used for @VLOOKUP Function

This table comes from the *tax method*, which employs the half-year convention, in which an asset is assumed to be placed into service half-way in its first year and placed out of service half-way in its last year. Of course, this still results in five full years of depreciation expense for the asset. This half-year convention also explains the low percentage in the first year (which is one-half the normal double-declining-balance rate for a full first year).

The second unique item for the ACRS table is the 0 in year 7. The 0 is needed so that the @VLOOKUP will return a percentage of 0 when an asset's life is beyond its useful life.

In order to use the ACRS table, the @VLOOKUP function is used. The depreciation expense will change depending on the asset's life. Therefore, we must calculate the asset's life within the @VLOOKUP function. The *first* argument within the function would therefore appear as:

@VLOOKUP(@YEAR(@NOW)-@YEAR(B8)+1,

This portion of the function simply calculates the year of the asset's use. For example, if an asset was purchased in 1991 and we are calculating depreciation expense for 1991, the asset is in its 1st year of use (even though it is not 1 year old). Because we are using the "year of use", we must add 1 to the calculation.

After determining the year of use, the @VLOOKUP function is relatively simple, as follows:

$$@VLOOKUP(@YEAR(@NOW)-@YEAR(B8)+1,\$TABLE1,2)$$

The TABLE1 argument simply tells 1-2-3 that the table to be referenced can be found at that location. We have placed a dollar sign in front of the range name so this function can be copied to other cells without changing the cell references for TABLE1. The argument of 2 conveys the column displacement to be used within the table. In this example, 1-2-3 should return the value in the third column (a displacement of 2 from the first column).

At this point, we have only determined the percentage to be used for ACRS depreciation. That percentage must of course be multiplied by the original cost to determine the current year's depreciation. The final formula, therefore, is:

$$@VLOOKUP(@YEAR(@NOW)-@YEAR(B8)+1,\$TABLE1,2)*C8$$

This formula is shown in the control panel in Figure 2-39 and has been copied to the cells where ACRS is to be used.

```
F8: (C2) [W11] @VLOOKUP(@YEAR(@NOW)-@YEAR(B8)+1,$M$4..$O$9,2)*C8        READY


            A            B          C         D         E          F
1
2                     DATE OF                        ACCUMULATED DEPRECIATION
3       DESCRIPTION   PURCHASE     COST     SALVAGE  DEPRECIATION  EXPENSE
4       Desk          04/03/89   $650.00    $100      $110.00     $110.00
5       Copier        04/03/89 $1,540.00    $500      $208.00     $208.00
6       File Cabinet  04/19/89   $310.00    $50        $52.00      $52.00
7       Desk          05/16/89   $425.00    $75        $70.00      $70.00
8       Table         01/14/90   $540.00    $75         $0.00     $108.00
9       File Cabinet  04/01/90   $320.00    $50         $0.00      $64.00
10      Credenza      04/01/90   $335.00    $45         $0.00      $67.00
11      Lamp          09/12/89   $175.00    $30        $29.00      $29.00
12      Rug           09/15/90   $800.00    $300        $0.00     $100.00
13      Lamp          09/20/89   $255.00    $50        $41.00      $41.00
14
15
16
17
18
19
20
18-Nov-90   11:03 PM          UNDO
```

Figure 2-39 @VLOOKUP Function for Depreciation Expense

The ACCUMULATED DEPRECIATION amounts must also be updated to reflect the current year's Depreciation Expense. While this update may appear as simple as adding a cell from column F to a cell in column E, the process is complicated by the need for updating. That is, the worksheet is to be used every year and must therefore allow for cells in column F to change each year.

Consider the first item in the list, which has Accumulated Depreciation of $110 and Depreciation Expense of $110. You would first want to go to cell E4 and add the Depreciation Expense in cell F4 to it. This addition would most easily be accomplished by putting cell E4 into Edit mode by placing the cursor on the cell and striking **F2**. Notice that upon doing this the cell contents appear in the control panel, as shown in Figure 2-40. You can now press the + key and then enter the cell reference of **F4**. Upon striking **ENTER**, the cell would display the result of $220. However, notice in the first line of the control panel that the cell still contains the formula 110+F4 (see Figure 2-41).

```
E4: (C2) [W12] 110                                    EDIT
110

         A            B          C        D        E           F
 1
 2                  DATE OF                     ACCUMULATED DEPRECIATION
 3    DESCRIPTION   PURCHASE     COST    SALVAGE DEPRECIATION  EXPENSE
 4  Desk           04/03/89   $650.00    $100    $110.00      $110.00
 5  Copier         04/03/89 $1,540.00    $500    $208.00      $208.00
 6  File Cabinet   04/19/89   $310.00     $50     $52.00       $52.00
 7  Desk           05/16/89   $425.00     $75     $70.00       $70.00
 8  Table          01/14/90   $540.00     $75      $0.00      $108.00
 9  File Cabinet   04/01/90   $320.00     $50      $0.00       $64.00
10  Credenza       04/01/90   $335.00     $45      $0.00       $67.00
11  Lamp           09/12/89   $175.00     $30     $29.00       $29.00
12  Rug            09/15/90   $800.00    $300      $0.00      $100.00
13  Lamp           09/20/89   $255.00     $50     $41.00       $41.00
14
15
16
17
18
19
20
18-Nov-90    11:06 PM
```

Figure 2-40 Cell E4 in EDIT Mode

If the formula in cell E4 were allowed to remain as it currently exists, then the Accumulated Depreciation would be wrong once next year's Depreciation Expense was entered into cell F4. Therefore, you should convert the formula to the result of the formula. You accomplish this conversion by using one of two commands:

1. EDIT CALC
2. /Range Value

To illustrate the EDIT CALC command, place the cursor on cell E4 and strike the **EDIT** key **(F2)**. Notice that the formula now appears in the control panel as 110+F4. Press the CALC key **(F9)**, and the formula is replaced with its sum. Now, upon pressing **ENTER**, the formula has been replaced in the cell with the result of the formula. You can now perform future updates and maintain the correct Accumulated Depreciation balance.

Each cell in column E would now have to be edited to place the correct formula in the cell. **EDIT-CALC** would then be pressed for each cell to be converted from the formula to the result of the formula. As you may imagine, there is a much quicker way to perform this entire operation.

```
E4: (C2) [W12] 110+F4                                                 READY


              A              B          C         D         E          F
1
2                        DATE OF                        ACCUMULATED DEPRECIATION
3          DESCRIPTION    PURCHASE      COST     SALVAGE  DEPRECIATION EXPENSE
4     Desk                04/03/89    $650.00     $100     $220.00     $110.00
5     Copier              04/03/89  $1,540.00     $500     $208.00     $208.00
6     File Cabinet        04/19/89    $310.00      $50      $52.00      $52.00
7     Desk                05/16/89    $425.00      $75      $70.00      $70.00
8     Table               01/14/90    $540.00      $75       $0.00     $108.00
9     File Cabinet        04/01/90    $320.00      $50       $0.00      $64.00
10    Credenza            04/01/90    $335.00      $45       $0.00      $67.00
11    Lamp                09/12/89    $175.00      $30      $29.00      $29.00
12    Rug                 09/15/90    $800.00     $300       $0.00     $100.00
13    Lamp                09/20/89    $255.00      $50      $41.00      $41.00
14
15
16
17
18
19
20
18-Nov-90   11:09 PM            UNDO
```

Figure 2-41   Formula in Cell E4

The quicker way to update the Accumulated Depreciation is with the **/R**ange **V**alue command. This command acts precisely as the **/C**opy command, except it copies from a cell (or cells) that contains a formula and then places the result of the formula in the receiving cell. The command can be much more efficient than having to press **EDIT-CALC** after entering each formula.

The first step in this process is to place a formula in each cell in column E. Then, you would press **/R**ange **V**alue, and the following prompt appears in the control panel:

Enter range to copy FROM: E4..E4

Since the cursor is already anchored on cell E4, you simply press **END** and then the **DOWN** arrow key. The entire column should now be highlighted. Upon pressing **ENTER**, the control panel asks where you want to copy the information just entered. In this example, you only want to copy the information back to the same cells, replacing the formulas with numbers. Therefore, you would leave the cursor on cell E4 and press **ENTER**. Each cell in the column should now have only a number in it rather than a formula.

The @SUM function should be used to place a total at the bottom of the COST, ACCUMULATED DEPRECIATION, and DEPRECIATION EXPENSE columns. The most efficient way to accomplish this task would be first to place **@SUM** at the bottom of one of the columns and then simply copy the function (using the **/C**opy command) to the other appropriate cells. The function can be copied because each column in the spreadsheet contains an identical number of cells. After placing @SUM functions in appropriate cells, the spreadsheet would now be complete and should appear as shown in Figure 2-42.

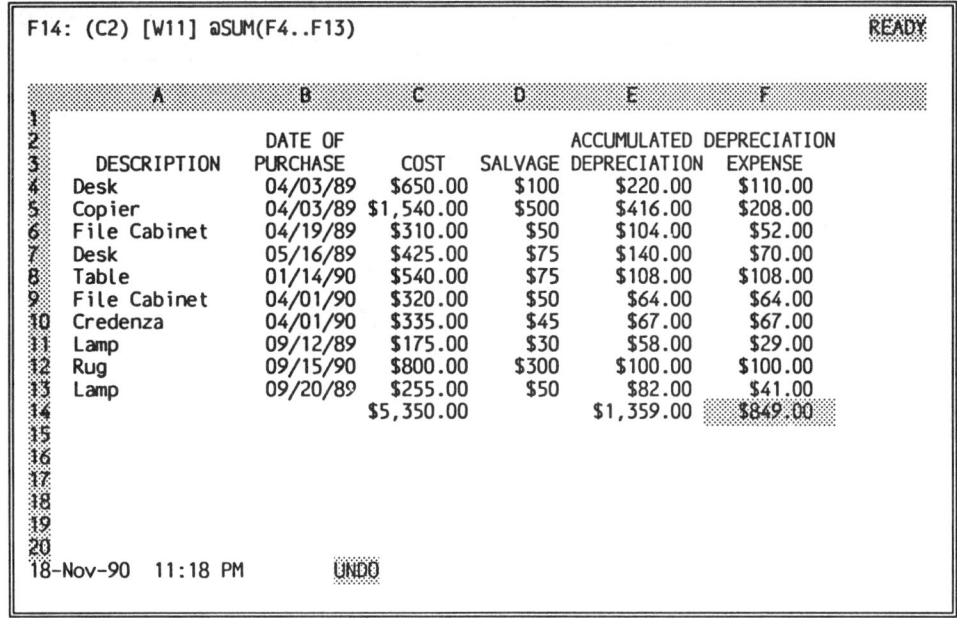

```
F14: (C2) [W11] @SUM(F4..F13)                                    READY

            A              B         C        D        E          F
 1
 2                     DATE OF                        ACCUMULATED DEPRECIATION
 3       DESCRIPTION   PURCHASE     COST    SALVAGE  DEPRECIATION  EXPENSE
 4      Desk          04/03/89    $650.00   $100      $220.00     $110.00
 5      Copier        04/03/89  $1,540.00   $500      $416.00     $208.00
 6      File Cabinet  04/19/89    $310.00    $50      $104.00      $52.00
 7      Desk          05/16/89    $425.00    $75      $140.00      $70.00
 8      Table         01/14/90    $540.00    $75      $108.00     $108.00
 9      File Cabinet  04/01/90    $320.00    $50       $64.00      $64.00
10      Credenza      04/01/90    $335.00    $45       $67.00      $67.00
11      Lamp          09/12/89    $175.00    $30       $58.00      $29.00
12      Rug           09/15/90    $800.00   $300      $100.00     $100.00
13      Lamp          09/20/89    $255.00    $50       $82.00      $41.00
14                              $5,350.00            $1,359.00    $849.00
15
16
17
18
19
20
18-Nov-90   11:18 PM          UNDO
```

Figure 2-42 Completed Fixed Asset Spreadsheet

FOLLOW-UP
CASE: Valley View Video Stores
Fixed-assets Master File
(The Facilities Management Cycle)

Valley View Video Stores is a two-store video-rental business owned and operated by Ron and Caroline Poston. The Postons began with one store in 1988 and last year opened the second store. They have been quite successful in the business to date and have had no major problems with the Fixed Asset Accounting System.

With the opening of a new store, Ron and Caroline feel the Fixed Asset System would be much more efficient if it were on their microcomputer. Specifically, they would like to have the system placed on Lotus 1-2-3. The fixed asset information as of the latest accounting period is in a file entitled VALLEY_V.WK1 (on your student diskette).

Requirements

Place the Fixed Assets System for Valley View Video Stores on Lotus 1-2-3. In addition to calculating the 1991 Depreciation Expense for each asset, you should update the Accumulated Depreciation amount and place a total at the bottom of the Cost, Accumulated Depreciation, and Depreciation Expense columns. In your Depreciation Expense calculations, make sure the Net Book Value does not decline to less than the Salvage Value.

Furthermore, you should assume that the half-year convention (as discussed in the Carter Brokerage Group case) is *not* being using by Valley View Video.

ASSIGNMENT
CASE: Huber Office Supply Co.
Capital Investment Analysis
(The Facilities Management Cycle)

Huber Office Supply sells and delivers all types of office equipment and supplies to the greater Kansas City area. Until recently, all deliveries have been made from one small van that Mr. Huber purchased in 1983, the year the business was started.

Mr. Huber now wants to replace the van. He is considering one of the following options:

1. One large truck to accommodate all deliveries.
2. Two smaller trucks, with deliveries being divided into two regions.
3. Three vans, with deliveries being divided into three regions.

Requirements

Using the cash flow information found in the file HUBER.WK1 (on your student diskette), compare the three delivery alternatives. Mr. Huber wants you to find the alternative with the lowest present value of the total cost, considering the Intital Investment, Annual Cash Expenditures, and Salvage Value in Year 9 (which has already been netted against the Year 9 Expenditures in the case data).

ASSIGNMENT
CASE: Squeaky's Car Wash
Paycheck Transaction File
(The Employee Services Management Cycle)

Mr. Floyd Harris (referred to affectionately as "Squeaky"), owns and operates his own car wash service. The operation is only semi-automated, with the vacuuming, window cleaning, and drying operations being performed manually. Mr. Harris maintains a work force of approximately 15, with most of those being students from the nearby high school.

The employees all work for $5.50 an hour; however, some work as few as 10 hours per week, while others work as much as 25 hours. Furthermore, because Squeaky prides himself in being able to work around the students' exams, athletics, and other activities, the employees' hours may fluctuate widely from one week to another. This fluctuation of hours provides a significant problem in preparing the payroll each week. Therefore, Squeaky would like for you to prepare a Paycheck Transaction File on Lotus 1-2-3.

Requirements

Using the file SQUEAKY.WK1 (on your student diskette), generate the Net Pay amount for each employee. Be sure to address the following requirements:

1. Use an @SUM function to generate the Total Hours.
2. Use an @VLOOKUP function to generate the Withholding Status Percentage. (Note: The table to be used in the @VLOOKUP function is found beginning at cell Z10.)
3. Use an @SUM function to generate a Total for each column, except Withholding Status and Withholding Status Percentage.

CHAPTER 3
USING 1-2-3 PRINT AND GRAPH COMMANDS TO CREATE ACCOUNTING REPORTS

INTRODUCTION

The ultimate objective of any accounting system is to provide information to users. The best means of communicating this information is with a printed report. 1-2-3 allows you to generate reports directly from spreadsheet data. It also can generate various types of graphs to make even more persuasive presentations of information. While 1-2-3 does have limited flexibility on how reports can be generated (even through the Allways add-in option), you will find that the printing and graphing procedures give you the power to produce informative accounting reports.

In this chapter, we explore the range of options 1-2-3 has for generating accounting information. The chapter is divided by the Print and Graph routines. Within each of these areas, the specific topics to be addressed are:

1. Printing
   - Understanding the primary print settings
   - Exploring other print options
2. Graphing
   - Exploring graph types
   - Defining graph ranges
   - Exploring graph options
   - Displaying graphs on the screen
   - Saving graphs
   - Printing graphs

PRINTING

One way to explore the printing function in 1-2-3 is to examine the Print Settings sheet that appears during print operations. This sheet shows print settings you have selected or that are default settings for your version of 1-2-3. A sample Print Settings Sheet is shown in Figure 3-1, and each item is explained below:

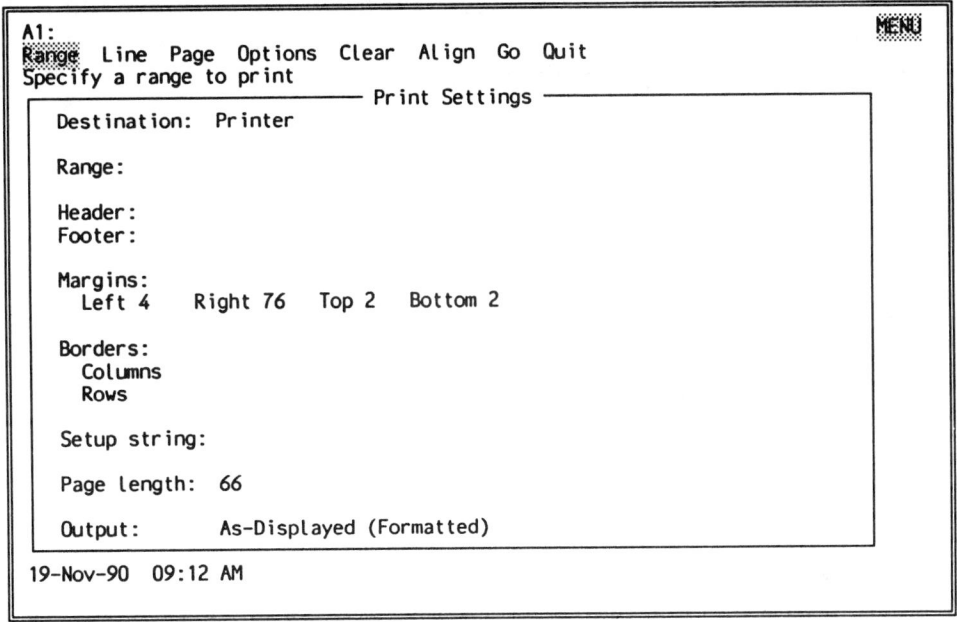

Figure 3-1 Print Settings Sheet

- Destination - The destination of the print operation (the printer or a file).
- Range - The cells that are to be printed.
- Header - A message that is to appear at the top of every page.
- Footer - A message that is to appear at the bottom of every page.
- Margins - The number of character spaces specified for the left and right margin and the number of lines specifies for the top and bottom margin.
- Borders - Titles that will be printed at the top of every page or to the left on every page.
- Setup String - A code sent to the printer to control the printing process.
- Page length - The maximum number of lines on a page.
- Output - The way in which information will be printed.

Destination

When you issue the **/P**rint command, the first menu that appears has a Printer option and a File option. Selecting **P**rinter tells 1-2-3 that you want the output sent to a printer. Selecting **F**ile tells 1-2-3 that the output should be stored on disk as a Text file, which could then be printed (or viewed on the screen) at a later time.

Range

Upon selecting **P**rinter (or after specifying a file name under the File option), a menu appears with the primary print selections. The first option on this menu is Range. Specifying the *Print Range* is as simple as pointing to the appropriate cells or providing a range name.

Headers and Footers

You can improve the appearance of your reports by including *headers* and *footers*. A header is some information you would like to have displayed at the top of every page. A footer is something you would like to have at the bottom of every page. For example, you might want to put the company name, department name, current date, or page number in the header or the footer.

Assume you wanted to have a header displaying the company name in the middle of the page. Then, you would like to have the current date and the page number in the footer, with the current date left justified and the page number right justified. To set up the header, you would press /**P**rint **P**rinter **O**ptions **H**eader. Assuming the company's name was Rational Solutions, Inc., you would type the header as:

|Rational Solutions, Inc.

Notice that the header is preceded in this case with a broken vertical bar. This bar tells 1-2-3 that you want the information following the bar to be centered. Any information before a broken vertical bar is left-justified; any information following a second broken vertical bar is right justified.

In the footer, you wanted the current date and the page number displayed. In headers and footers, you can use two special characters, # and @. The # symbol causes 1-2-3 to place a page number in that position. The @ symbol will place the current date in the place of that symbol (just as with the @DATE function). Just as with any other header or footer text, the broken vertical bars can be used to left-justify, center, or right justify the date and page number. In our example, we wanted to left-justify the date and right justify the page number. To accomplish this, we would type the footer in as:

@||#

Figure 3-2 shows the header and footer for this example as they would be displayed in the Print Settings Status Sheet. Figure 3-3 shows a sample printout with this header and footer.

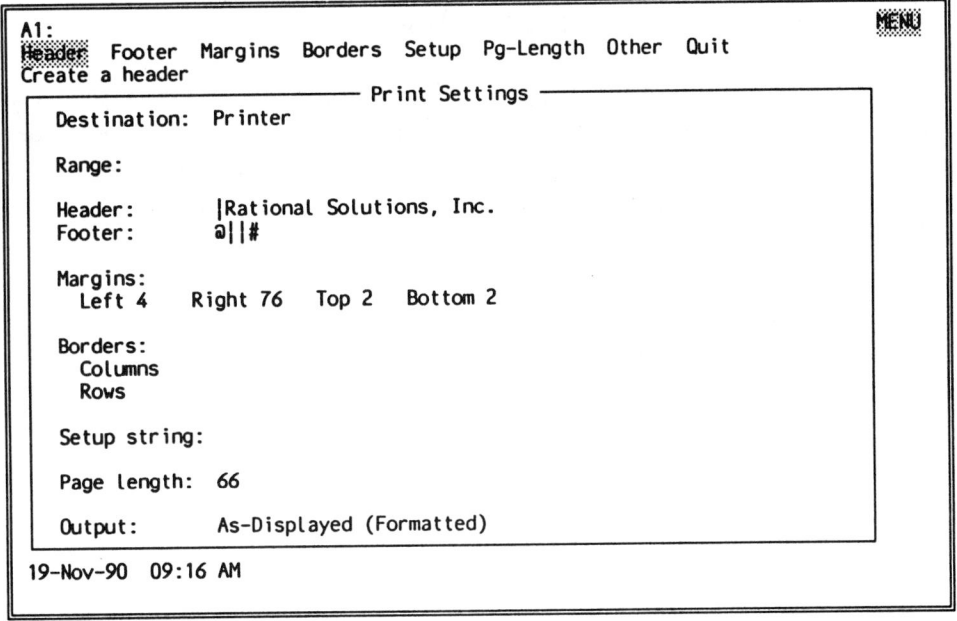

Figure 3-2 Header and
          Footer Settings

Figure 3-3 Sample Header and Footer

Margins

Margins are selected by issuing the **/P**rint **P**rinter **O**ptions **M**argins command. A menu will appear with the following options:

Left Right Top Bottom None

The left and right margins are specified in the number of character spaces that are to be left blank at the left and right side of the paper, respectively. You may specify between 0 and 240 spaces. Because these margins are specified in character spaces, if you change the pitch of your print characters, be aware that the margins will also change and should possibly be adjusted.

The top and bottom margins are specified in the number of lines. You may select any number of lines from 0 to 32. As with the character spacing, anytime the number of lines per inch is changed (usually with a setup string), then the top and bottom margins will be affected.

The **None** selection sets the top, left, and bottom margins to 0 while setting the right margin to 240. This option is used most often for printing data to a file.

Borders

If your report spans more than one page, then you will likely want to have certain titles appear on every page of information. These titles are referred to as *Borders* in 1-2-3. Borders can either be at the top of a page or on the left side of a page.

When setting up your report, you would decide what range of cells (that is, what titles) you wanted to appear on every page of the report. You would then use the **/Print Printer Options Borders** command. A menu would then appear asking you to specify Columns (which would appear to the side of every printed page) and/or Rows (which would appear at the top of every printed page).

Setup String

You may want to print a report using much smaller letters than normal, or you may want to print a report sideways on a page in order to fit more information on one row. These represent just two of the many print options that exist, depending on your printer. Whenever you want to print your text in a unique way, you must first send a message to the printer telling exactly how it is to print. This message is usually in the form of a *setup string*.

A setup string is simply a code telling a printer exactly how to print the upcoming text. Each printer has its own setup strings; therefore, you would need to be familiar with your printer's possible setup strings. For example, in order to print in Landscape Mode, using compressed print and 66 lines per page on a Hewlett Packard LaserJet III requires the following setup string to be sent to the printer:

\027&lo5.45C\027(s0p16.66H

Three options exist for sending setup strings to printers:

1. Enter a setup string using the **/P**rint **P**rinter **O**ptions **S**etup command.
2. Enter a default setup string using the **/W**orksheet **G**lobal **D**efault **P**rinter **S**etup command.
3. Enter the a setup string directly into the text being printed.

Entering a setup string using the **/P**rint **P**rinter **O**ptions **S**etup command or the **/W**orksheet **G**lobal **D**efault **P**rinter **S**etup command is very simple and straightforward. If the default is changed, then it will be applicable for all spreadsheets and is only changed by either altering the default or by using the Options Setup command. Entering setup strings in the text to be printed allows you the flexibility of changing setup strings (and therefore changing print options) during one print job. In order to enter a setup string in the text, you enter double split vertical bars (||) at the beginning of a row, followed by the appropriate setup string. Because 1-2-3 does not print a row starting with double split vertical bars, it is a good idea to place the setup string in a blank row or any other row that you do not want printed. Figure 3-4 shows an example of having two different setups strings embedded in text.

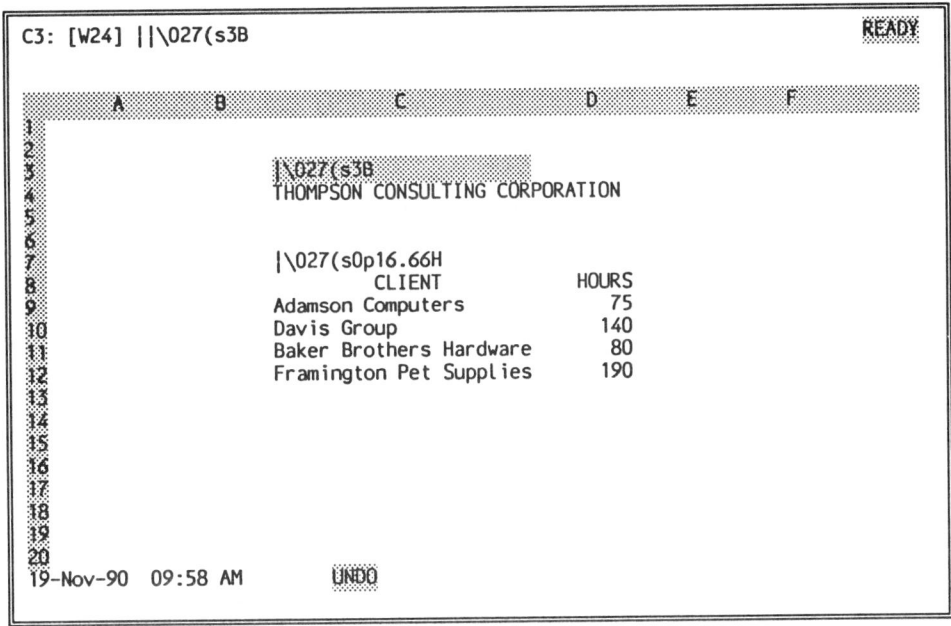

Figure 3-4 Embedded Setup Strings

Page-Length

The standard page length for 1-2-3 is 66 lines. This 66 lines actually includes only 56 lines of text in the body of the report, with 5 lines each at the top and bottom of the page for headers, footers, and margins. This setting can be changed simply by issuing the **/P**rint **P**rinter **O**ptions **P**g-Length command. This command lets you override the default setting, for this session only, by entering the appropriate number of lines that are to constitute a page. The most likely time you will need to change the number of lines per page is when you have changed the number of lines per inch that will be printed.

Output

In most situations, you will want to print the information from a spreadsheet exactly as it appears on the screen and with the headers, footers, page breaks, and so forth that you have specified. Other times, however, you may want to print the cell entries rather than the cell values (in other words, the formulas rather than the results). Also, especially when printing information to a disk file, there may be times you may want to exclude headers, footers, and other formatting. To effect any of these options, you simply select the appropriate item from the menu that appears with the **/P**rint **P**rinter **O**ptions **O**ther command. The menu options that appear are:

As-Displayed Cell-Formulas Formatted Unformatted

Generally speaking, you have two options from this menu. First, you specify whether you want the cells printed as they are displayed on the screen (As-Displayed) or you want the cell entries printed (Cell-Formulas). If you want to have the cell entries printed, then the output is generated with one cell listed per line.

The second option from this menu is the formatting option. Obviously, you can have your information printed Formatted or Unformatted. Selecting **F**ormatted (the default value) prints the headers, footers, page breaks, and margins that you have specified. Selecting **U**nformatted causes the headers, footers, page breaks, and top and bottom margins to be suppressed. The latter option is used primarily when printing data files to disk.

Other Print Menu Selections

We have now described the primary print options that are to be defined for any print job. You should also be familiar with some of the other print menu options that you will encounter. When you press **/P**rint **P**rinter, a menu appears with the following options:

Range Line Page Options Clear Align Go Quit

The Range and Options items have already been discussed, but you should also have some familiarity with the other options.

Three of the options; Line, Page, and Align; control the paper movement. While these three items may appear straightforward, their implementation can be confusing at times. You must first understand that 1-2-3 maintains a count of the number of lines on a page and the number of lines that have been printed. Furthermore, 1-2-3 only knows what commands have been issued through the spreadsheet; that is, if you move the paper with buttons located on the printer, then 1-2-3 will not know that the paper has been moved. For example, if you printed a report that consisted of only a few lines and then advanced the paper in the printer with a button on the printer itself, then 1-2-3 would think that it is still in the middle of a page. If you then printed another report that spanned more than a page, 1-2-3 would insert a page break in the middle of your page.

These problems can be avoided by using the Line, Page, and Align commands on the Print menu. If you select Line, then the paper is advanced by one line, and 1-2-3 increments its internal line counter by one. Similarly, if you select Page, the paper is advanced by one page, and the line counter is reset to zero. If you do decide to advance the paper to the top of a page using one of the buttons on the printer, then selecting Align from the Print menu tells 1-2-3 to consider the current position of the paper to be the top of the page and to reset its line counter accordingly.

Another important item is the Clear option. Selecting this option displays a menu with the following selections:

All Range Borders Format

The All option will clear all print options and reset them to the default values. Selecting Range will only clear the current print range, leaving the other print options as you have specified. Borders clears the setting of certain rows and columns as borders. Selecting Format causes the margins, page length, and setup strings to return to their default values.

The other two options are Go and Quit, which are straightforward. Selecting Go causes the actual printing to take place. The Quit option exits the Print menu and returns you to READY mode.

Other Print Specifications

You will sometimes want to print a report with specific items on separate pages. That is, you may want to insert page breaks at certain places in the report. Also, you may sometimes want to generate output from a spreadsheet without showing all of the cells in the print range. In this section, we describe how to set page breaks within your spreadsheet and how to hide specific columns and cells.

PAGE BREAKS

As was just mentioned, you may want to insert page breaks in strategic points in your spreadsheet, thereby forcing certain cells within the print range to be printed on separate pages. For example, assume you had the budget spreadsheet shown in Figure 3-5. Also assume that you would like to have the departmental figures printed on separate pages. You would use the /Worksheet Page option to cause this separation.

Selecting /Worksheet Page will cause a blank row to be inserted just above the cursor and a page break symbol to be inserted in that row. The page break symbol (::) is entered in the cell as a vertical split bar followed by the page break symbol (|::). When the symbol is placed in the row, however, only the page break symbol appears. Figure 3-6 shows the same spreadsheet with page breaks inserted in the appropriate places.

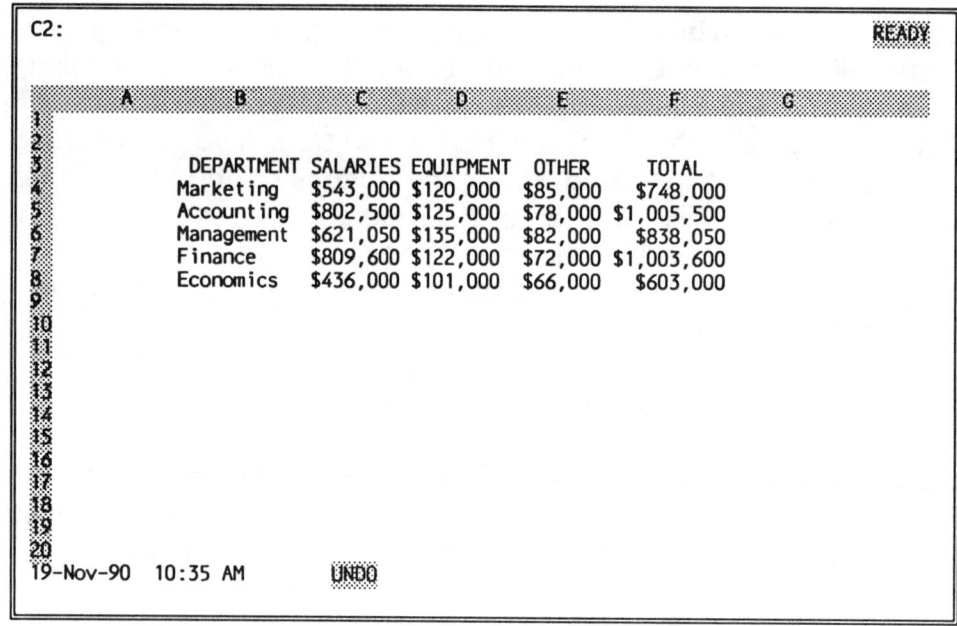

Figure 3-5 Budget Spreadsheet

Figure 3-6 Budget Spreadsheet with Page Breaks

HIDING COLUMNS AND CELLS

Sometimes you may only want to have certain columns of a report displayed. For example, notice the sample inventory spreadsheet displayed in Figure 3-7. Assume you would like to print a report that displays only the beginning balance and the ending balance. You would accomplish this by hiding columns C and D. To hide the columns, you simply press /Worksheet Column Hide and then tell 1-2-3 the columns that are to be hidden. After hiding the columns, your screen would appear as shown in Figure 3-8. Printing the report would now be as simple as printing the columns as displayed.

```
C3: [W11]                                                      READY

         A           B          C          D          E          F
1
2
3
4    ITEM #   BEG-BALANCE PURCHASES      SALES   END-BALANCE
5    33421         2348        238        701       1885
6    34099          231        543        224        550
7    78123          984        567        882        669
8    23498         1095        912       1206        801
9    23409         2271        434       1549       1156
10   98823         1725        611        558       1778
11   12374          674        804        749        729
12   78129          881        231        733        379
13
14
15
16
17
18
19
20
19-Nov-90   10:43 AM              UNDO
```

Figure 3-7 Inventory Spreadsheet

```
E3: [W13]                                                      READY

         A           B          E          F          G          H
1
2
3
4    ITEM #   BEG-BALANCE END-BALANCE
5    33421         2348       1885
6    34099          231        550
7    78123          984        669
8    23498         1095        801
9    23409         2271       1156
10   98823         1725       1778
11   12374          674        729
12   78129          881        379
13
14
15
16
17
18
19
20
19-Nov-90   10:45 AM              UNDO
```

Figure 3-8 Inventory Spreadsheet with Hidden Columns

Just as hiding columns will cause those columns not to be printed, hiding cells also causes those cells not to be printed. Therefore, if you want to suppress the printing of certain cells, simply use **/R**ange **F**ormat **H**idden and then specify the cells that are to be hidden.

GRAPHS

Another powerful tool for communicating accounting information is *graphs*. Graphs can often illustrate trends and relationships in a much more understandable and succinct fashion than can ordinary tables and reports. 1-2-3 has the ability to generate five types of graphs which can then be displayed on the screen or written to a file for later printing. The five types of graphs available in 1-2-3 are (the title of each type matches the "type" submenu):

1. Line - A linear graph used to show trends in data (see Figure 3-9)

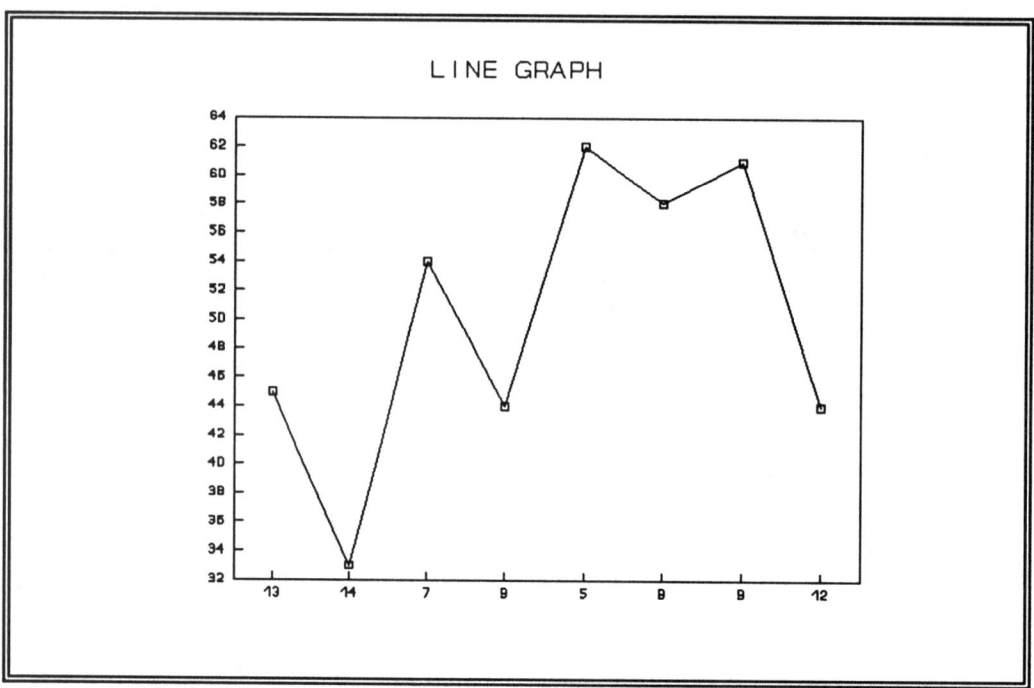

Figure 3-9 Line Graph

2. Bar - A bar graph which is used to show trends and relationships in a more pictoral fashion (see Figure 3-10)

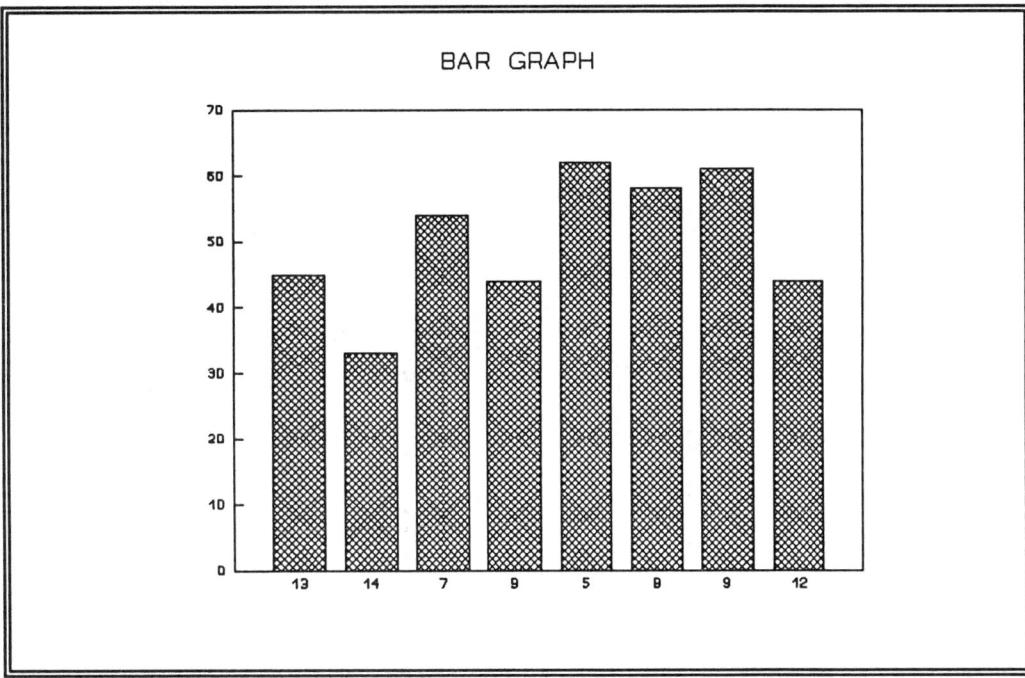

Figure 3-10 Bar Graph

3. XY - Another linear graph type which demonstrates associations between sets of numbers (see Figure 3-11)

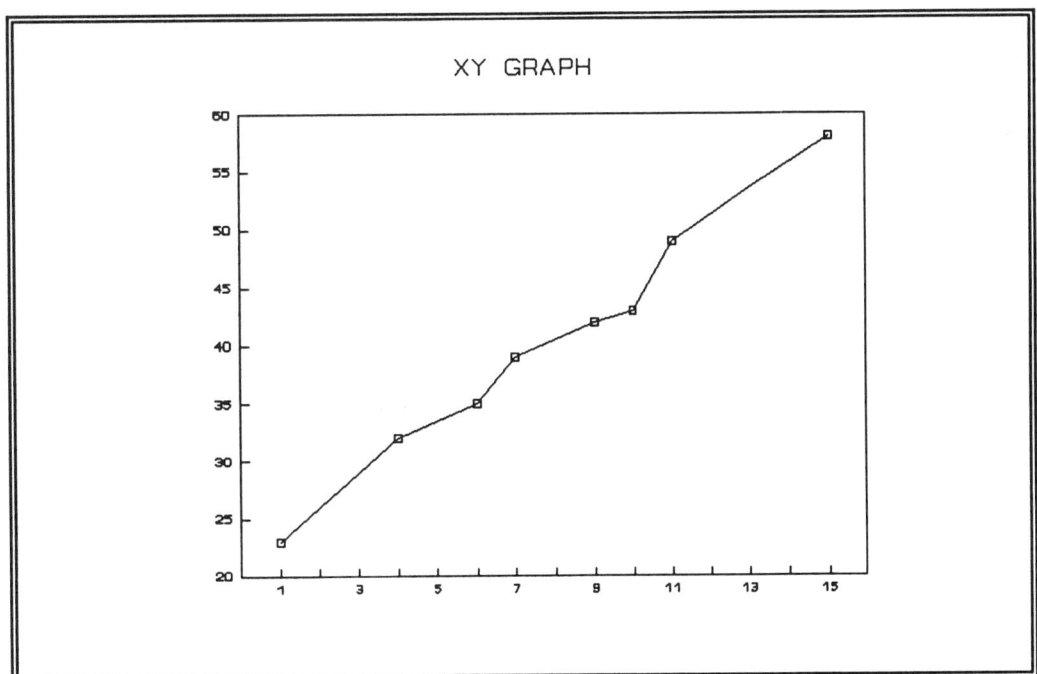

Figure 3-11 XY Graph

4. Stack-Bar - A bar graph that shows component parts of a group by stacking the components on one another (see Figure 3-12)

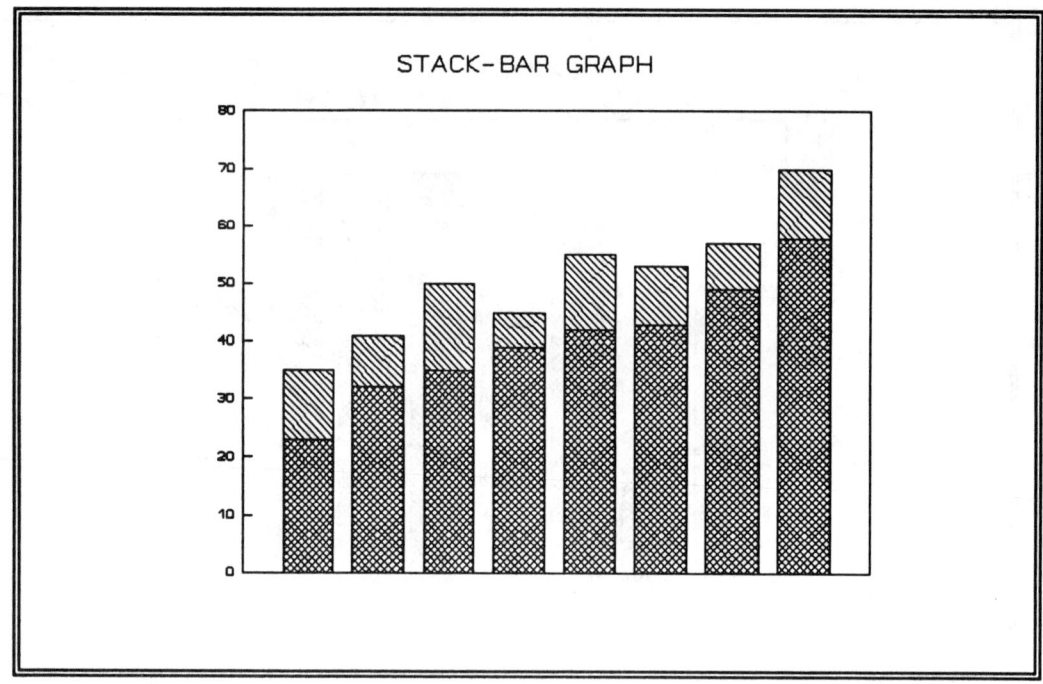

Figure 3-12 Stack-Bar Graph

5. Pie - A pie chart that shows relationships among amounts which themselves are part of some meaningful total (see Figure 3-13)

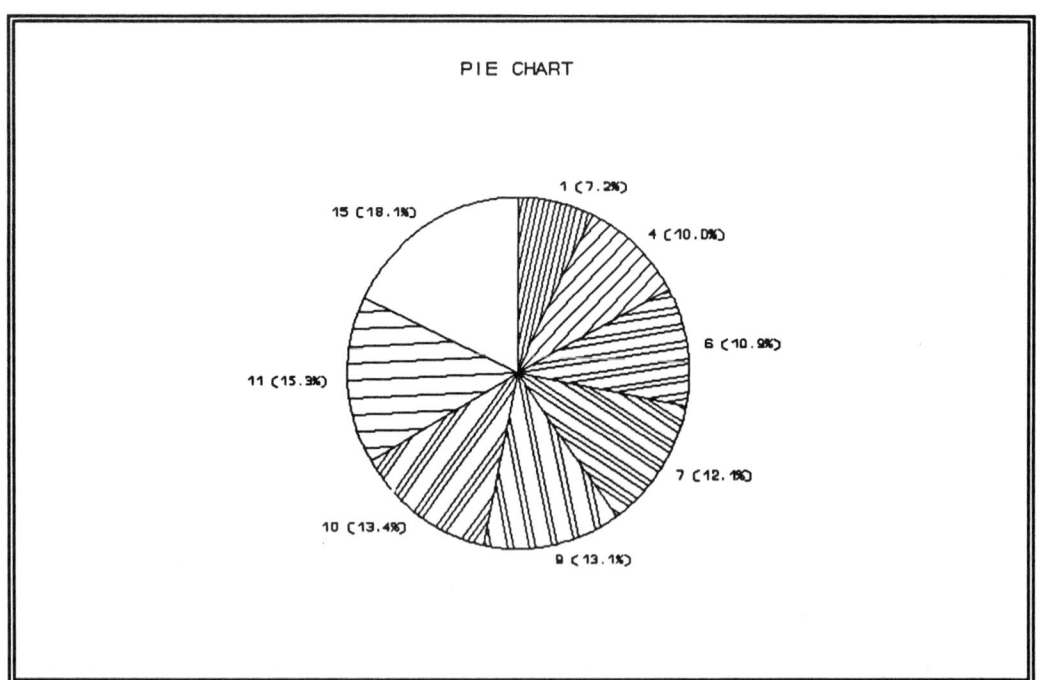

Figure 3-13 Pie Chart

The Graph Settings Sheet

Just as printing was described with the Print Settings sheet, we will use the Graph Settings sheet to describe graph options. Upon pressing /Graph, the Graph Settings sheet is displayed as shown in Figure 3-14. Each setting is defined below.

```
A1:                                                              MENU
Type  X  A  B  C  D  E  F  Reset  View  Save  Options  Name  Group  Quit
Line  Bar  XY  Stack-Bar  Pie
                        ── Graph Settings ──
   Type: Line                Titles: First
                                     Second
   X:                                X axis
   A:                                Y axis
   B:
   C:                                        Y scale:      X scale:
   D:                        Scaling         Automatic     Automatic
   E:                        Lower
   F:                        Upper
                             Format          (G)           (G)
   Grid: None   Color: No    Indicator  Yes                Yes

       Legend:          Format:    Data labels:            Skip: 1
   A                    Both
   B                    Both
   C                    Both
   D                    Both
   E                    Both
   F                    Both

19-Nov-90   11:17 AM
```

Figure 3-14 Graph Settings Sheet

TYPE

As described in the previous section, the five types of graphs available in 1-2-3 are Line, Bar, XY, Stack-Bar, and Pie. Selecting /Graph Type displays each of these options in a submenu.

X AND A-F

The X and A-F settings specify where the appropriate data for the X axis and the Y axis can be found in the 1-2-3 spreadsheet. The X data relates to the X axis and is to be used for the XY graph type only. A-F relate to six possible settings for the y axis. To specify the range(s) for X and A-F, simply select the appropriate letter upon pressing /Graph. Then provide 1-2-3 with the appropriate range where the data can be found.

TITLES

You can specify up to two lines of titles for the graph itself and a one line title for the X axis and the Y axis. To generate titles, simply press /Graph Options Titles. A submenu will appear with the options of:

First Second X-Axis Y-Axis

Selecting any one of the submenu options allows you to type a title for that selection. Alternatively, you can provide a range reference for the location of a title in the spreadsheet.

SCALING

You can adjust the scaling of the numbers presented on the X axis and Y axis of your graph. By selecting **/G**raph **O**ptions **S**cale, a submenu appears with the following options:

Y-Scale X-Scale Skip

The Y-Scale and X-Scale options allow you to specify the scaling for each of those axes. Upon selecting either **Y**-Scale or **X**-Scale, another submenu appears with the following options:

Automatic Manual Lower Upper Format Indicator Quit

If you select **A**utomatic from this menu, 1-2-3 will adjust the graph to the data presented. That is, 1-2-3 will automatically generate a lower limit and an upper limit based on the smallest and largest numbers, respectively, in the data set. If you instead want to set your own upper and lower limits, you must first select the **M**anual option, which tells 1-2-3 that you are going to override its automatic feature. Then you would simply select **U**pper and **L**ower and specify the limits you want displayed.

You can also format the data along the X axis or Y axis by using the **F**ormat option from this menu. This option allows you to use any of the formatting options (General, Currency, etc.). Notice that the scale for the Y axis in Figure 3-15 has been changed to currency.

In order to improve the appearance of your graph, 1-2-3 will scale your numbers. For example, all numbers may be displayed in thousands. Whenever 1-2-3 does adjust the scale of the numbers, it will generate an indicator telling what the scaling is. Notice back in Figure 3-15 that both the X axis and Y axis were scaled in thousands and that the indicator appears next to the title lines. You can remove this indicator from your graph by using the **I**ndicator option from the submenu and then selecting **N**o. Selecting **Y**es will generate the indicator once again.

Recall that the **/G**raph **O**ptions **S**cale menu had the option entitled Skip. You will frequently notice that the labels along the X axis appear crowded. The **S**kip option allows you to display every few labels on the X axis, thereby improving the appearance of the graph. In Figure 3-16, we have selected a skip factor of 2. Notice that only every 2nd X-axis label is displayed.

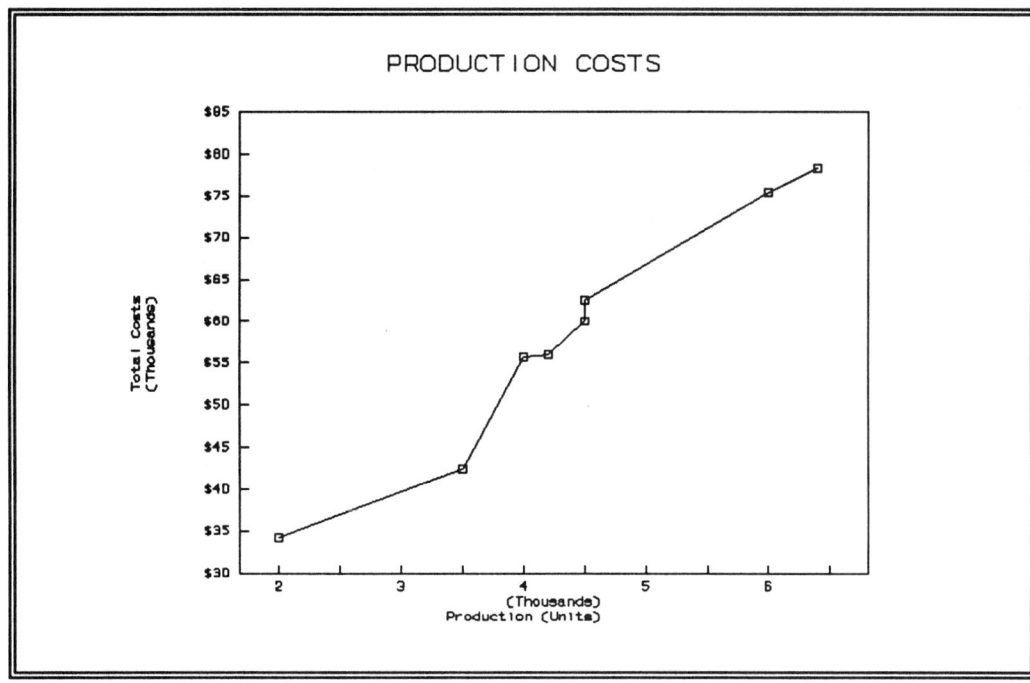

Figure 3-15   Currency Scale for Y Axis

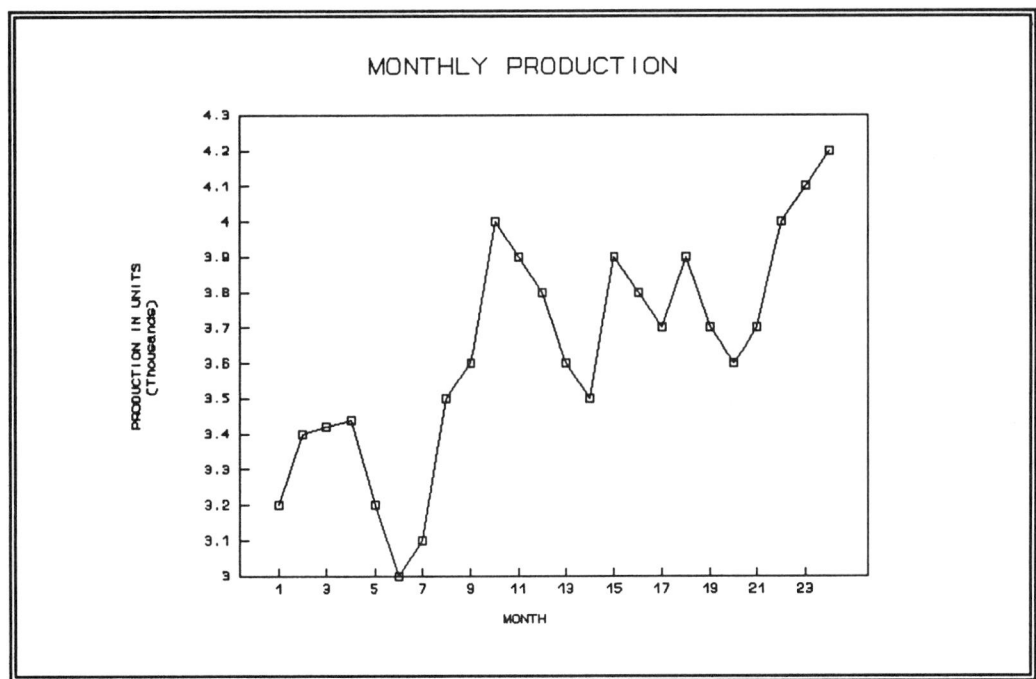

Figure 3-16   Graph with Skip Factor of 2

GRID

The **G**rid option allows you to display horizontal and/or vertical grids on your graph. The graph in Figure 3-17 shows an example of horizontal grids.

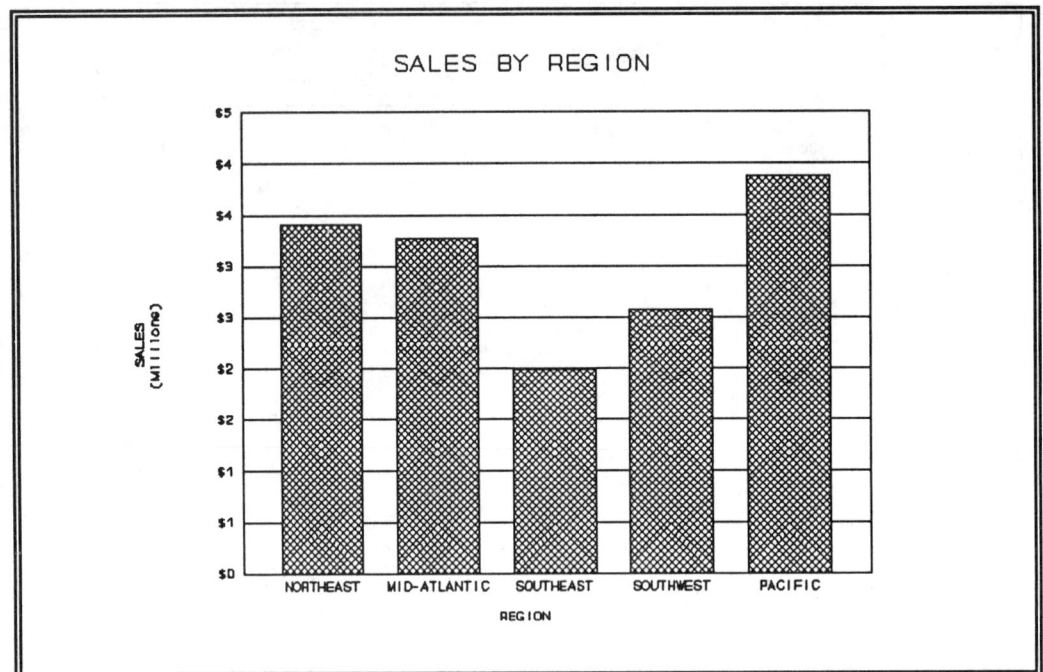

Figure 3-17 Graph with Horizontal Grids

COLOR

You can display your graphs in color, assuming you have a color monitor. You reset the graph to color by pressing **/G**raph **O**ptions **C**olor. The graph is reset to a black and white display by pressing **/G**raph **O**ptions **B&**W.

LEGEND

When you have more than one y-axis setting, 1-2-3 provides different symbols along each of the graphs displayed. Therefore, a legend is often needed to understand what the different graphs are representing. Legends are provided through the **/G**raph **O**ptions **L**egend selection. Upon choosing this selection, a menu appears with the following options:

A B C D E F Range

By selecting any of the A through F options, you can specify the legend to be used for the appropriate y-axis graph. The **R**ange option allows you to define a range in the spreadsheet where the legend titles can be found. The first cell in the range is assumed to correspond to the A setting, the second to the B setting, and so forth. Notice the legends on the Graph Settings sheet in Figure 3-18 and the way those legends appear on the related graph in Figure 3-19.

```
B5: 1985                                                   MENU
Type  X  A  B  C  D  E  F  Reset  View  Save  Options  Name  Group  Quit
Line  Bar  XY  Stack-Bar  Pie
                          ┌─── Graph Settings ───┐
   Type: Line                    Titles: First  SALES/COST HISTORY
                                         Second
   X: B5..B11                    X axis YEAR
   A: C5..C11                    Y axis SALES/COSTS
   B: D5..D11
   C:                                            Y scale:      X scale:
   D:                                   Scaling  Automatic     Automatic
   E:                                   Lower
   F:                                   Upper
                                        Format    (C0)          (G)
   Grid: None        Color: No          Indicator Yes           Yes

      Legend:            Format:    Data labels:              Skip: 1
   A  SALES              Both
   B  TOTAL COSTS        Both
   C                     Both
   D                     Both
   E                     Both
   F                     Both

19-Nov-90  04:11 PM
```

Figure 3-18 Legend Settings in Graph Settings Sheet

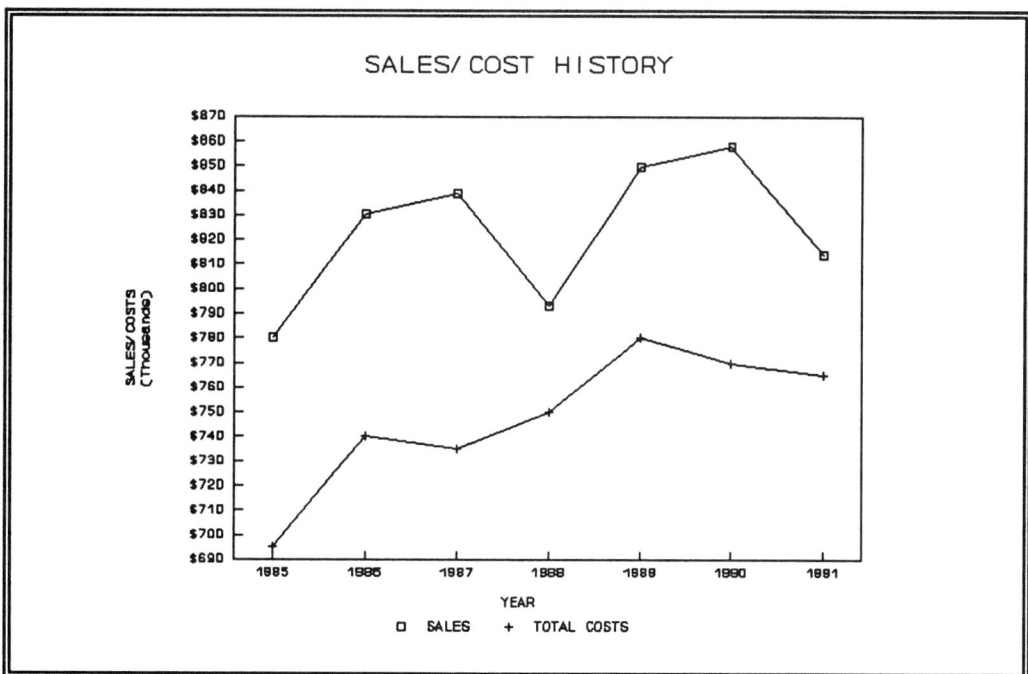

Figure 3-19 Graph with Legends

FORMAT

As noted in the previous section, 1-2-3 provides different symbols for the various y-axis settings. You can alter these graphs by suppressing the display of the symbols and/or suppressing the display of the lines on Line and XY graphs. When you select **/Graph Options Format**, the following menu appears:

Graph A B C D E F Quit

The **G**raph option from this menu allows you to set the display format for all lines on the graph. The A through F options set the format for the respective line. Upon selecting **G**raph or any of the A through F options, a menu appears with the following options:

Lines Symbols Both Neither

Selecting **L**ines causes a line to be drawn between the data points on the graph but does not display a symbol at each data point. **S**ymbols displays a symbol at each data point on the graph but does not draw lines between the data points. The **B**oth option causes both lines and symbols to be displayed. Selecting **N**either causes neither lines nor symbols to be displayed.

DATA LABELS

At times you will want to provide explanations on the graph itself to give further explanation to certain data points. For example, notice the explanation "New Factory" on the graph in Figure 3-20. To provide such labels, you impose the **/G**raph **O**ptions **D**ata-Labels command. This command causes the following menu to appear:

A B C D E F Group Quit

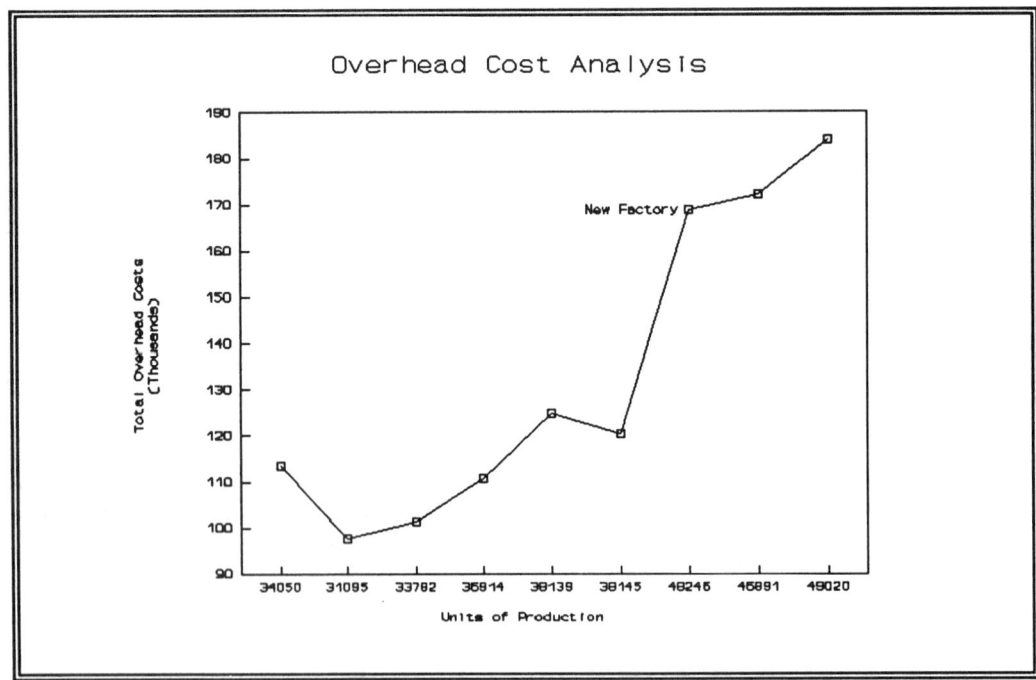

Figure 3-20 Graph with Data Label

You must first understand that a range must be established corresponding to all of the data points in the y-axis range for which you want to provide data labels. Once such ranges have been set up in the spreadsheet, you tell 1-2-3 which of those ranges correspond to each y-axis setting through the above menu.

In the previous example shown in Figure 3-20, the data range was in cells D3 through D11. The data labels were then established in cells E3 through E11, with the title "New Factory" in cell E9.

Naming, Saving, and Printing Graphs

The concept of saving a graph can be somewhat confusing. You must first understand the difference between *naming* a graph and *saving* a graph. A graph is "named" within the current spreadsheet file so that its settings can be recalled within that spreadsheet; however, a graph must be "saved" as a separate file if you want to print the graph.

NAMING GRAPHS

Within a given spreadsheet, a number of graphs could be created. However, once you change any graph settings, the previous graph settings are deleted. To keep yourself from having to recreate the settings every time, you can save those settings by assigning the graph a name. To name a graph, you use the **/G**raph **N**ame command. This command reveals the following menu:

Use Create Delete Reset Table

You can name a graph using the **C**reate option and then retrieve it with the **U**se option. The **D**elete option can be used to eliminate a particular named graph. If you choose **R**eset, though, *all* previously named graphs (in that spreadsheet file) will be eliminated. The **T**able option can be used to create a table of all graph names.

SAVING GRAPHS

If you want to print a graph using the PrintGraph program or any other program, you must first save the graph as a separate file. Remember that the **N**ame option only saves graph settings that can then be retrieved back into the spreadsheet for viewing. Only through the **S**ave option is an actual graph file created. Upon issuing the **/G**raph **S**ave command, 1-2-3 prompts you for a file name. After you input a name, 1-2-3 will place a .PIC extension on the file. This extension tells you (and other software packages) that this file is indeed a graph file.

PRINTING GRAPHS

A PIC file can be printed with PrintGraph, Allways, or any of a number of other software programs. Since you are using 1-2-3, you already have access to PrintGraph. We will therefore focus our discuss on PrintGraph. (While Allways provides more options than PrintGraph, it is not necessarily included in all versions of 1-2-3).

PrintGraph is accessed from the initial Lotus 1-2-3 menu. Upon selecting the **PrintGraph** option, another screen appears, which is shown in Figure 3-21. At the top of the screen displayed in Figure 3-21, notice the menu with the following options:

Image-Select Settings Go Align Page Exit

```
┌─────────────────────────────────────────────────────────────────────┐
│ Copyright 1986, 1989 Lotus Development Corp.  All Rights Reserved. V2.2  MENU │
│                                                                         │
│ Select graphs to print or preview                                       │
│ Image-Select  Settings  Go  Align  Page  Exit                           │
│ ─────────────────────────────────────────────────────────────────────  │
│     GRAPHS    IMAGE SETTINGS                    HARDWARE SETTINGS        │
│    TO PRINT    Size              Range colors    Graphs directory        │
│                  Top      .395   X Black           C:\LOTUS22            │
│                  Left     .750   A Black         Fonts directory         │
│                  Width   6.500   B Black           C:\LOTUS22            │
│                  Height  4.691   C Black         Interface               │
│                  Rotation .000   D Black           Parallel 1            │
│                                  E Black         Printer                 │
│                Font              F Black           HP LaserJet Hi        │
│                 1  BLOCK1                        Paper size              │
│                 2  BLOCK1                          Width      8.500      │
│                                                    Length    11.000      │
│                                                                         │
│                                                 ACTION SETTINGS          │
│                                                 Pause  No   Eject  No    │
│                                                                         │
│                                                                         │
│                                                                         │
└─────────────────────────────────────────────────────────────────────┘
```

Figure 3-21 PrintGraph Screen

Much like the print routine in 1-2-3, you simply tell PrintGraph what you want to print, specify any options you want to set, and then print the graph. To tell the program what you want to print, you choose Image-Select from the menu. Upon choosing Image-Select, you simply follow the directions on the screen to select the graph file (a file with the extension PIC) from the list of graph files presented.

The Settings selection displays another menu with the following options:

Image Hardware Action Save Reset Quit

The Image option allows you to change the appearance of the graph image itself by setting the size, fonts, and colors options. The Hardware option from the menu allows you to change the directory settings, the interface specification, the printer/plotter name, and the paper size. You affect the printer's action between printings by using the Action option.

If you make changes in the graph print settings, you may want to make these the settings for all graphs. You must therefore save the current settings to the PGRAPH.CNF file (the file containing the default settings) by selecting **S**ave from the menu. Selecting **R**eset from the menu (before changing the PGRAPH.CNF file) changes the current settings back to the default settings.

CONTROL CONSIDERATIONS

Accounting reports must be well-designed in order to be used appropriately and to provide adequate documentation. When working with 1-2-3 (as with any software package), it is too easy to generate reports with little attention to headings, etc. In accounting systems, having poorly documented reports is especially risky, because improper decisions can result from misunderstood reports. Furthermore, accounting reports are unique in that they are often used for support of transactions. That support may be considered dubious if the report is not adequately documented.

A frequent problem encountered with graphs is loss of data. This loss frequently results from changing graph settings without giving the previous graph a name. You should get into the habit of naming graph settings frequently. Furthermore, as mentioned in the previous chapters, naming standards should be adopted.

REVIEW QUESTIONS

1. When printing reports in 1-2-3, what are the two possible destinations?

2. How would you create a date within a header or footer?

3. How is information left-justified, centered, or right-justified within headers and footers?

4. What is the largest possible right margin that you can select for printed reports?

5. What are borders, and why would you use them in a printed report?

6. What is the purpose of a setup string?

7. How many lines are on a standard-length page in 1-2-3?

8. Is it possible to print formulas instead of the values from those formulas? If so, how?

9. What happens to your report if you issue the command **/P**rint **P**rinter **O**ptions **O**ther **U**nformatted?

10. What is the purpose of selecting **A**lign before printing a report?

11. How are page breaks inserted into a spreadsheet?

12. The Line and XY graphs often look similar, if not identical. Why would you choose one versus the other?

13. What is the difference between a bar graph and a stack-bar graph?

14. What is the purpose of the Scale option for graphs?

15. What are data labels, <u>and</u> how are they generated for graphs?

16. What is the difference between naming a graph and saving a graph?

CASE: Casey's Restaurants
Budget Analysis
(The General Ledger and Financial Reporting Cycle)

Casey's Restaurants is a regional chain of 8 restaurants operating in the Northwest. The restaurants are all owned by a closely-held corporation, which evolved from the original restaurant owner, Casey Harrison.

The corporation has a centralized budgeting process that involves analyzing the efficiency (and effectiveness) of each store in the prior year before creating the current year's budget. To make the budget process itself more efficient and effective, the owners of Casey's Restaurants have asked for your assistance in performing this analysis.

The company is now attempting to prepare the budget for 1991. Therefore, they will need your assistance in analyzing 1990 data. (The 1990 data for Casey's Restaurants can be found in the file CASEYS.WK1 on your diskette.) As you will see in the 1990 data, the following information has been captured for each store:

1. Square Footage
2. Sales Revenue
3. Costs:
   * Food
   * Personnel--Direct
   * Personnel--Administrative
   * Overhead
4. Net Income

Requirements

The owners would like you to present the following information (using the Lotus

1-2-3 Print and Graph commands):
1. Print the information for each store, with each store's information listed on a separate page,
2. Graph the relationship (using an XY graph) between square footage and Sales Revenue for each store,
3. Graph the stores' costs (using a stack-bar graph), and
4. Using a pie chart, show each store's contribution to total Net Income.

Solution

PRINTING THE REPORTS

Once you have retrieved the data for Casey's Restaurants into a current spreadsheet, you are ready to print the information for each restaurant, as required. Since the owners want each restaurant's information printed on a separate page, you should insert page breaks after each row. You accomplish this by placing the cursor on the second row of data and issuing the /Worksheet Page command. You then perform the same operation at the third row, fourth row, etc. Once you finish inserting page breaks, your spreadsheet should look something like the one in Figure 3-22.

```
B24: [W7]                                                        READY

          B        C         D         E                F          G         H
     6  Store   Square    Total   --------------Costs--------------   Net
     7  Number  Footage  Revenue     Food       Labor    Overhead   Income
     8  ------  -------  --------  ----------  ----------  ----------  --------
     9    1      5000    $600,000  $250,000    $140,000   $165,000   $45,000
    10  ::
    11    2      4500     620,000   230,000     165,000    170,000    55,000
    12  ::
    13    3      5500     790,000   300,000     190,000    220,000    80,000
    14  ::
    15    4      6000     810,000   345,000     220,000    200,000    45,000
    16  ::
    17    5      5000     680,000   270,000     160,000    185,000    65,000
    18  ::
    19    6      4800     700,000   260,000     175,000    195,000    70,000
    20  ::
    21    7      8000     800,000   280,000     215,000    230,000    75,000
    22  ::
    23    8      7000     820,000   295,000     220,000    225,000    80,000
    24          --------  ---------- ---------- ---------- --------
    25  Total          $5,820,000 $2,230,000 $1,485,000 $1,590,000 $515,000
    31-Oct-90  04:19 PM          UNDO
```

Figure 3-22 Casey's Spreadsheet with Page Breaks

The print range must now be specified. The appropriate range for this case is B9..H23. Notice that the titles have not been included in the range, because we will be setting up borders, which will appear on every page. If the titles were included in the print range *and* in the borders, they would appear twice on the first page of output.

You would now need to set up Borders so that the information printed on each page would have appropriate titles. For this case, you would want to have the titles in

cells B2..H8 printed on every page. Therefore, you would simply issue the /**Print Printer**
Options Borders Rows (because you want to specify a row of titles) command and tell
1-2-3 to use B2..H8 for the borders.

 The report would appear more professional with an appropriate header on each
page. Assume you would like to print the header "1990 BUDGET ANALYSIS" in the
center of the top of each page. You define the header by using the /**Print Printer Options
Header** command and then typing the proper header at the prompt. Because you would
like to center the header in this case, the appropriate text to type at the prompt would be:

|1990 BUDGET ANALYSIS

Notice the broken vertical line, which signifies the text should be centered.

 If your Print Settings sheet now looks like the one in Figure 3-23, you are ready to
print. Printing is actually accomplished by simply pressing **G**o at the main Print menu.

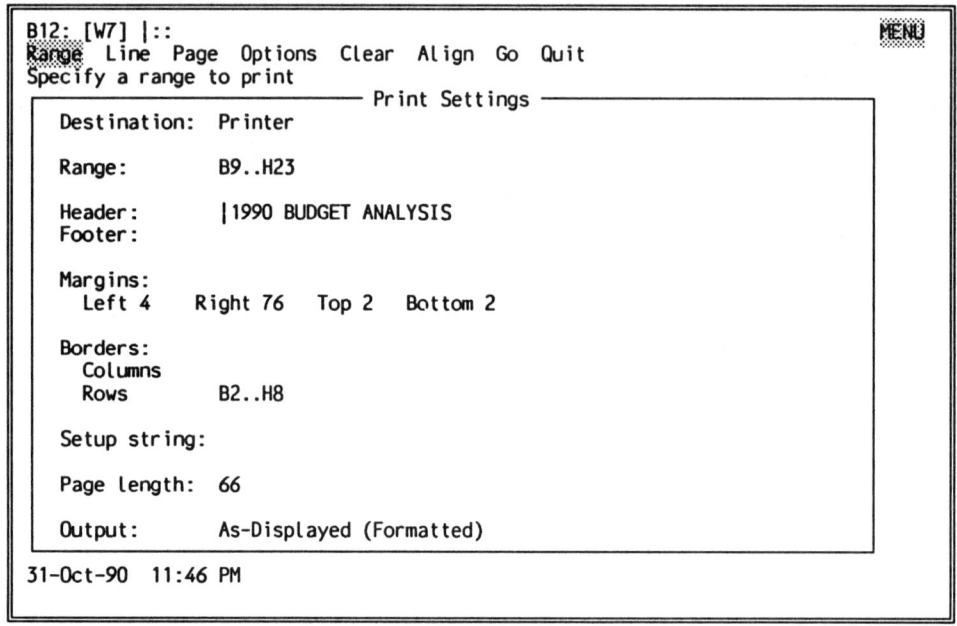

```
B12: [W7] |::                                                    MENU
Range  Line  Page  Options  Clear  Align  Go  Quit
Specify a range to print
                         ┌──────── Print Settings ────────
    Destination:  Printer

    Range:        B9..H23

    Header:       |1990 BUDGET ANALYSIS
    Footer:

    Margins:
      Left 4    Right 76    Top 2    Bottom 2

    Borders:
      Columns
      Rows        B2..H8

    Setup string:

    Page length:  66

    Output:       As-Displayed (Formatted)

31-Oct-90  11:46 PM
```

Figure 3-23 Casey's Print Settings Sheet

PREPARING THE XY GRAPH

 You have been asked to prepare a graph that depicts the relationship between
square footage and Sales Revenue. Remember that the XY graph is the best one to
show relationships between two sets of data. You would therefore select /**Graph Type
XY**.

 The X axis for this graph would be the Square Footage column. Accordingly, you
would simply select **X** at the main Graph menu and specify the column C9..C23. You
would similarly select the range D9..D23 for the A selection, depicting the Sales Revenue
to be used for the Y axis.

 To make the graph appear more professional, you should specify titles. Assume
that for the first line of the graph title you would like to use the text from cell D2. You

would select **/G**raph **O**ptions **T**itles **F**irst and place the expression \D2 at the prompt. For the second title, you would place some appropriate description of the graph's purpose. Specifically, assume you would like to have the following text as the second line of the title:

SALES REVENUE TO SQUARE FOOTAGE

An appropriate title for the X axis would be "Square Footage," which would be input at the prompt following the **/G**raph **O**ptions **T**itles **X**-axis command. The title "Sales Revenue" would similarly be typed in for the Y axis.

When 1-2-3 sets the scaling for you on this type of graph, the lowest value of the Y axis appears along the X axis. You would likely want to improve the appearance of the graph (that is, "tighten it up") by expanding the scale to be used along the Y axis. To change the scale, you issue the **/G**raph **O**ptions **S**cale **Y**-axis **M**anual **L**ower and specify the number 500000 (an arbitrary starting point that is lower than the lowest Y value). You would then specify the Upper limit to be an arbitrary value greater than the Y axis' largest value. We chose the number 900000. While you are changing the upper and lower limits on the Y-axis scale, you can also format the scale to be displayed in currency format. You would simply select the **F**ormat option under the Scale menu and specify currency with 0 decimal places.

While XY graphs do depict the relationship between two sets of numbers, they are often flawed because lines are drawn between successive data points in the range. This often results in a graph with a cluttered, confusing appearance. Such is the case for this graph. To overcome this shortcoming for XY graphs, you can simply suppress the drawing of lines between data points and only show the data points themselves. To accomplish this, you would issue the command **/G**raph **O**ptions **F**ormat **G**raph **S**ymbols.

The symbols would be even more meaningful if they had the associated restaurant number next to each one. You can place the numbers next to the symbols by creating Data Labels, using the **/G**raph **O**ptions **D**ata-labels **A** command. This command asks you to specify a range where the labels associated with each data point can be found. For this case, you would simply respond with the range B9..B23. You then tell 1-2-3 whether you want the Data Labels displayed to the left of the symbols, right of the symbols, and so forth. We have chosen to have the Data Labels displayed to the left of each symbol.

You have now completed the graph. Your Graph Settings sheet should look like the one in Figure 3-24. Also, if you were now to view the graph, you should see something much like Figure 3-25.

Once you are certain you have prepared the graph correctly, you should:

1. Name the graph, using the **/G**raph **N**ame command,
2. Save the graph to diskette, using the **/G**raph **S**ave command (we will discuss how to print the graphs later), and
3. Save the current spreadsheet, using the **/F**ile **S**ave command.

```
D2: [W11] 'CASEY'S RESTAURANTS                                      MENU
Type  X  A  B  C  D  E  F  Reset  View  Save  Options  Name  Group  Quit
Line  Bar  XY  Stack-Bar  Pie
                              ── Graph Settings ──
   Type: XY                Titles: First  \d2
                                   Second SALES REVENUE TO SQUARE FOO...
   X: C9..C16                      X axis Square Footage
   A: D9..D16                      Y axis Sales Revenue
   B:
   C:                                        Y scale:      X scale:
   D:                              Scaling   Manual        Automatic
   E:                              Lower     500000
   F:                              Upper     900000
                                   Format    (CO)          (G)
   Grid: None        Color: No     Indicator Yes           Yes

      Legend:              Format:   Data labels:          Skip: 1
   A                       Symbols   [L] B9..B16
   B                       Symbols
   C                       Symbols
   D                       Symbols
   E                       Symbols
   F                       Symbols

01-Nov-90  12:41 AM
```

Figure 3-24 Graph Settings Sheet

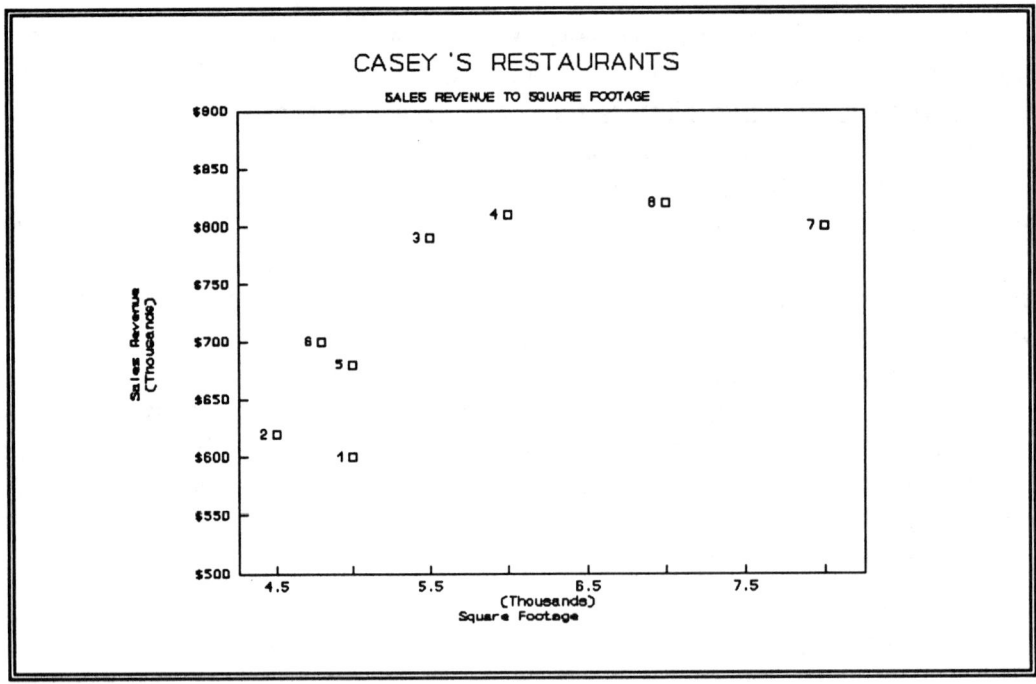

Figure 3-25 Graph of Sales Revenue to Square Footage

PREPARING THE STACK-BAR GRAPH

The stack-bar graph is useful in depicting the components of a total. Casey's Restaurants therefore would like you to prepare a stack-bar graph to show the cost structure for the different restaurants. The first step in preparing the graph would be to issue the **/G**raph Type Stack-Bar command.

A stack-bar graph does not require an X-axis setting; however, you can enhance the appearance of the graph by using an X-axis setting and thereby placing descriptive information along the X axis. For this case, you would use the range B9..B23 for the X axis. The various Y-axis settings would be for the food, labor, and overhead costs. Accordingly, you would use the range E9..E23 for A, F9..F23 for B, and G9..G23 for C.

As with the previous graph, you would want to set appropriate titles. The first line of the main title would be set, as in the previous graph, with the cell reference \D2. The second line of the title to be "COSTS BY STORE." The X axis title would be "Store Hours," and the Y axis title would be "Costs."

This type of graph is often difficult to analyze without some reference lines for comparing the relative heights of the bars. Reference lines can be created with the horizontal grid setting. The appropriate command would be **/G**raph Options **G**rid **H**orizontal.

To make the graph even more understandable, you should include a legend that tells what the different grid patterns are representing. To create a legend, you only need to type **/G**raph Options Legend and then the appropriate letter of the Y-axis range. Upon selecting a letter, you would simply type the appropriate legend. For this graph, you would type **Food** for A, **Labor** for B, and **Overhead** for C.

The only refinement remaining at this point is to format the Y-axis numbers as currency with 0 decimal places. To accomplish this, you would issue the **/G**raph Options Scale **Y**-Scale Format command and then tell 1-2-3 that you want the format to be Currency with 0 decimal places.

Your Graph Settings sheet should now appear as shown in Figure 3-26. If you view the graph, it should look like the one shown in Figure 3-27.

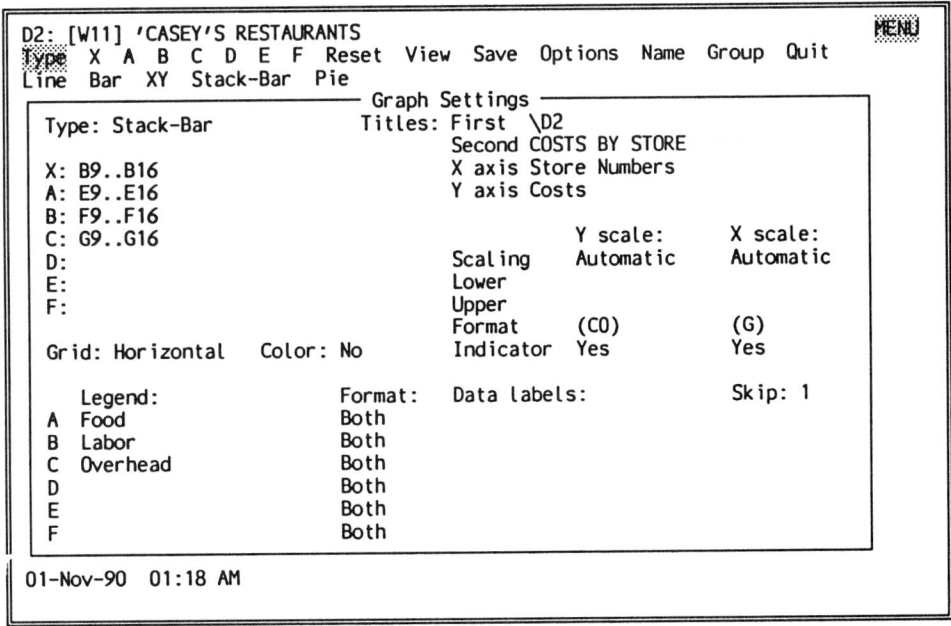

Figure 3-26 Graph Settings Sheet

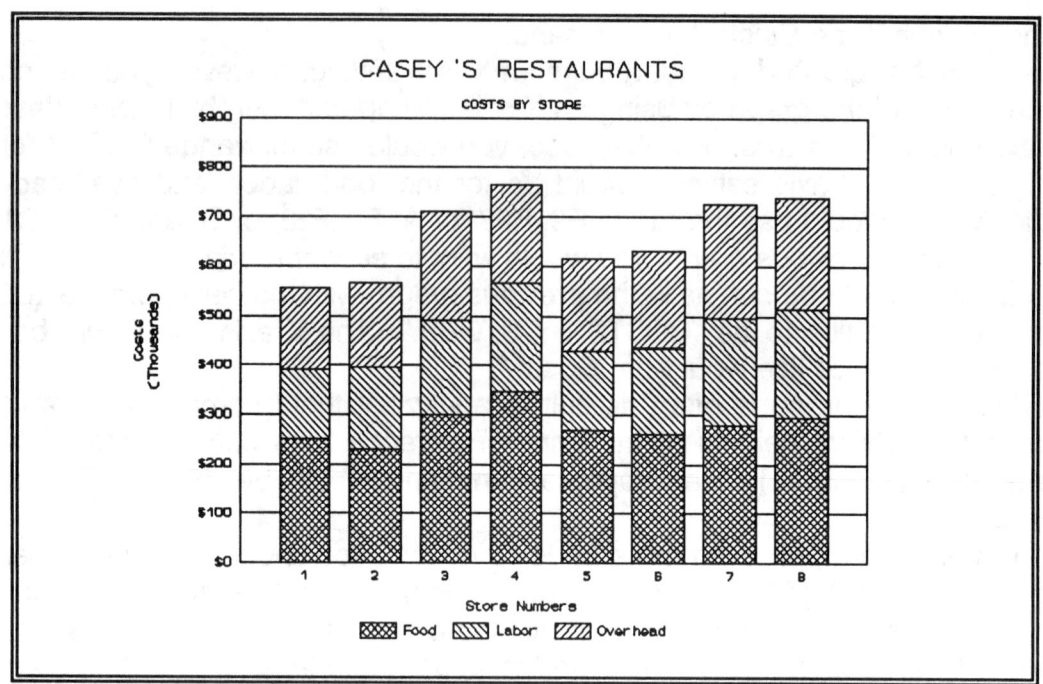

Figure 3-27 Stack-Bar Graph of Costs by Store

Once you are certain you have prepared the graph correctly, you should:

1. Name the graph, using the **/G**raph **N**ame command,
2. Save the graph to diskette, using the **/G**raph **S**ave command, and
3. Save the current spreadsheet, using the **/F**ile **S**ave command.

PREPARING THE PIE CHART

Much like the stack-bar graph, a pie chart is useful in depicting components of a total. In the Casey's Restaurant case, a pie chart is appropriate to show the relative impact of each restaurant's earnings on the total Net Income. The first step in preparing this pie chart is to select the **P**ie option from the **/G**raph **T**ype menu.

The main titles for the chart would be set in exactly the same fashion as for the previous graphs. X-axis and Y-axis titles are not options for a pie chart.

Using store numbers for the X axis provides appropriate descriptions for each "slice" of the pie. The A range would be defined with the net income amounts in cells H9..H23.

At this point, if you were to view the graph, it would appear as shown in Figure 3-28. While this graph is certainly adequate, its appearance could be enhanced through the use of colors or hatching in the different slices of the pie. 1-2-3 allows you to create color or hatching by using a code that is placed in the B range. Hatch codes are numbered 1 through 8. For the Casey's Restaurant case, we have placed hatch codes in cells J9..J16. This column of hatch codes is then used as the B range for the pie chart. Your Graph Settings sheet should now appear as shown in Figure 3-29, and your pie chart should look like the one depicted in Figure 3-30.

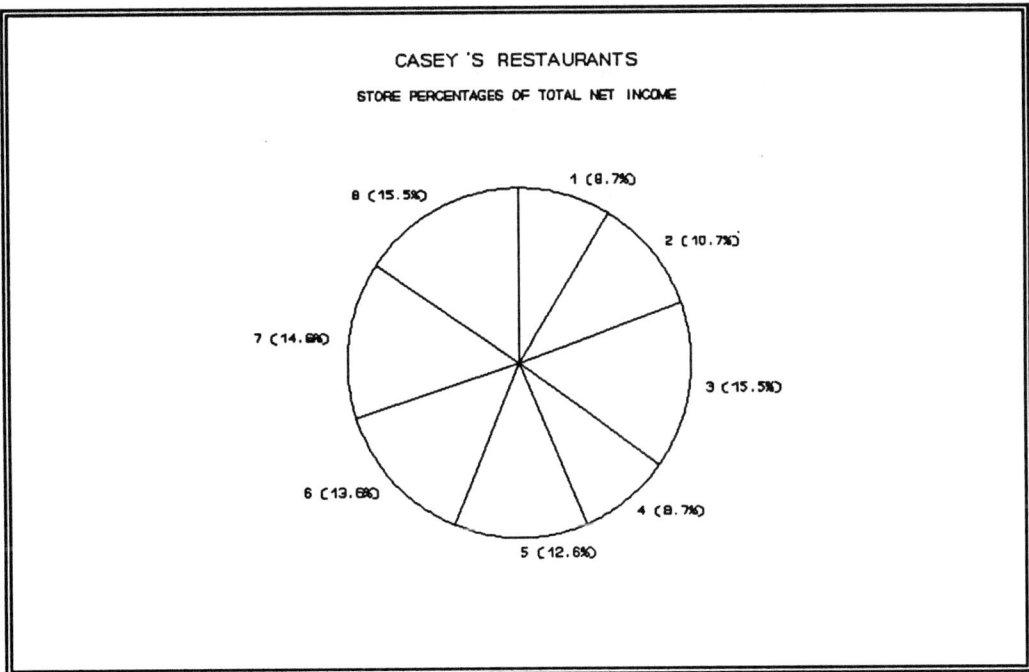

Figure 3-28 Pie Chart without Hatching

```
J17:                                                                    MENU
Type  X  A  B  C  D  E  F  Reset  View  Save  Options  Name  Group  Quit
Line  Bar  XY  Stack-Bar  Pie
                          ┌─────────── Graph Settings ───────────┐
  Type: Pie                  Titles: First  \D2
                                     Second STORE PERCENTAGES OF TOTAL ...
  X: B9..B16                         X axis
  A: H9..H16                         Y axis
  B: J9..J16
  C:                                               Y scale:      X scale:
  D:                                 Scaling       Automatic     Automatic
  E:                                 Lower
  F:                                 Upper
                                     Format        (G)           (G)
  Grid: None       Color: No         Indicator     Yes           Yes

     Legend:             Format:     Data labels:                Skip: 1
  A                      Both
  B                      Both
  C                      Both
  D                      Both
  E                      Both
  F                      Both

01-Nov-90   01:40 AM
```

Figure 3-29 Graph Settings Sheet for Hatch Codes

Once you are certain you have prepared the pie chart correctly, you should:

1. Name the chart, using the **/G**raph **N**ame command,
2. Save the chart to diskette, using the **/G**raph **S**ave command, and
3. Save the current spreadsheet, using the **/F**ile **S**ave command.

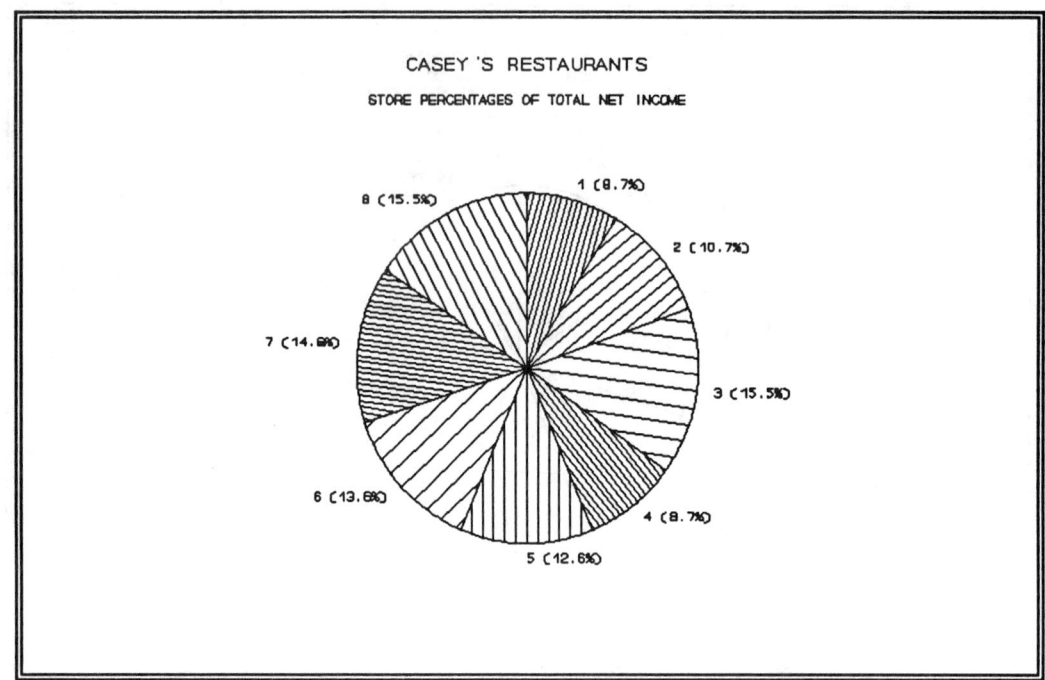

Figure 3-30 Pie Chart with Hatching

PRINTING THE GRAPHS

To print the graphs just created, you should return to the opening menu that is displayed when you first access the Lotus 1-2-3 software (the screen displays the title of "1-2-3 Access System"). Select PrintGraph from this menu.

The printing process is now as easy as selecting the graphs to print and then printing them. In order to tell the PrintGraph system what graph(s) you want to print, you must first be certain the Graphs Directory displayed on the screen is where your graph files (the files with .PIC extensions) can be found. If the correct directory is not displayed, use the Settings Hardware Graphs-Directory commands to change the directory.

You now identify the graphs you want to print by choosing Image-Select. The screen will now display a list of all the graph files found in the Graphs Directory. You simply mark the graph (or graphs) you want to print by highlighting the desired graph(s) and pressing the space bar. Upon striking **ENTER**, you are ready to print, and you only need to select Go from the menu (warning: most printers are very slow in printing graph files).

FOLLOW-UP
CASE: City of Pronto
Budget History and Analysis
(The General Ledger and Financial Reporting Cycle)

Pronto is a city of approximately 20,000 people, with a City Manager form of government. The City Manager wants to start the current year's budget process with an analysis of the Operating Departments' cost information for the previous year. The city employs an indirect-cost allocation plan and therefore categorizes costs as Direct and Indirect. (Pronto's financial information for the previous year is in a Lotus 1-2-3 spreadsheet entitled PRONTO.WK1 on your student diskette).

Requirements

The City Manager would like for you to produce the following reports and graphs:

1. A report showing each department's Direct Costs, Indirect Costs, and Total Costs. Each department's report should be printed on a separate page. Also, a header should be included with "CITY OF PRONTO" centered, and a footer should be included with the current date in the lower left-hand corner.
2. A stack-bar graph showing the Direct Costs in the lower portion of each bar and the Indirect Costs in the top. Titles, legends, data labels, etc. should be used where appropriate to create a professional-quality graph.
3. A pie chart of the 1990 Total Costs by Department. Titles, legends, data labels, etc. should be used where appropriate to create a professional-quality chart.

ASSIGNMENT
CASE: Kelly Corporation
Income Statement Analysis
(The General Ledger and Financial Reporting Cycle)

You have recently been hired by the Kelly Corporation. Your first assignment is to generate a report that analyzes the recent performance of Kelly. You have been given the last 10 years' income statements (found in the KELLY.WK1 file on your student diskette).

Requirements

Using the data from the Lotus 1-2-3 file, generate the following graphical reports:

1. A graph showing the trend in Net Income for the past 10 years.
2. A graph showing the trend in Total Administrative Expenses as a percentage of Sales for the past 10 years.
3. A pie chart illustrating the percentage of Sales comprised of Cost of Sales, Total Selling Expenses, Total Administrative Expenses, and Net Income for the year 1993.

ASSIGNMENT
CASE: Buckley Manufacturing Corporation
Income Statement and Balance Sheet Preparation
(The General Ledger and Financial Reporting Cycle)

You have been given the post-closing Trial Balance of Buckley Manufacturing Corporation and have been asked to generate an Income Statement and Balance Sheet from that information. (The Trial Balance can be found in the BUCKLEY.WK1 file of your student diskette.)

Requirements

Prepare a separate Income Statement and Balance Sheet for Buckley Manufacturing Corporation.

CHAPTER 4
USING 1-2-3 DATABASE COMMANDS TO SORT AND QUERY MASTER AND TRANSACTION FILES

INTRODUCTION

The first 3 chapters presented the Lotus 1-2-3 spreadsheet as a means of inputting data, calculating values, and generating reports. Many times, however, you may have data that you wish to manipulate in other ways. For example, you could have a list of customers you would like to sort by customer name or from which you would like to generate a report of those customers with balances above a certain value. 1-2-3 allows you to perform these types of functions through its database commands. The database commands, which are accessed through the /Data menu, allow you to execute relatively simple database manipulations, such as sorting and extracting. (For more sophisticated database manipulations, you should consider using one of the database management software packages, as presented in the latter portion of this book.)

This chapter examines the database commands 1-2-3 has to offer. Upon completing the chapter, you should be comfortable with each of the following topics:

1. Creating a database
2. Sorting database records
3. Finding database records
4. Extracting database records
5. Deleting database records

CREATING THE DATABASE

A *database* is simply any collection of data. However, in recent years, the term database has been commonly defined as a set of similar records stored on some computer medium. A Lotus 1-2-3 data base certainly fits this latter definition, but it does have some limitations when contrasted with dedicated database software programs (such as dBase IV, RBase, etc.). Some of these database software packages allow you simultaneously to manipulate data records in more than one file, and some permit sophisticated linking of data fields and records throughout the database. The 1-2-3 database (in Release 2.2) does not have these features, but is instead relatively simple in its structure.

A 1-2-3 database is actually just any spreadsheet that contains a series of records which are themselves made up of fields. These records are placed in contiguous rows and across contiguous columns within the spreadsheet. For example, notice the Accounts Receivable data that have been placed in the spreadsheet in Figure 4-1. This set of data could very easily be described as a database.

```
B16: [W30] 'Graves, Michael                                           READY


          A                 B                    C          D         E
 1
 2
 3
 4   CUSTOMER          CUSTOMER
 5    NUMBER              NAME            BALANCE
 6   1-289345 Harris, Bryan                $65.50
 7   2-094731 Wilmont, Kenneth            $391.25
 8   1-234895 Kennedy, Elizabeth           $90.97
 9   1-018462 Adams, Curt                 $128.44
10   2-839482 Basham, Debbie               $23.01
11   3-128394 Thompson, Mary               $72.66
12   1-239847 Roberts, Theresa             $90.97
13   2-019382 Utley, Sarah                $239.10
14   2-911284 Eaton, Frank                 $92.61
15   1-003412 Hutt, Vicky                 $107.88
16   2-091239 Graves, Michael             $184.29
17   3-293041 Bradley, Bob                $277.12
18   3-001651 Wilson, Lynn                $371.50
19
20
19-Nov-90  02:21 AM              UNDO
```

Figure 4-1 Accounts Receivable Database

Notice that each of the records is identical in structure. While not every field must contain data, the structure of the fields within the records is the same across all records. For example, the Customer Number is always in column A, Customer Name is always in column B, and so forth. You should also notice that each of the fields (each column) has a title at the top.

The database illustrated in Figure 4-1 was input to the spreadsheet as any other data would be. That is, the data were entered directly into cells as any other formula, value, or label would be.

A 1-2-3 database can be manipulated by using the /Data command. Upon issuing the /Data command, a menu appears with the following choices:

Fill Table Sort Query Distribution Matrix Regression Parse

This menu shows a number of options that do not directly affect database manipulations and which will therefore not be covered in this chapter. We will only focus on the Sort and Query options. Sorting allows you to sort the records in a data base according to different "keys." The Query option involves locating, extracting, or deleting records according to a stated criterion. The two types of data manipulations, sorting and querying, are discussed in the sections below.

SORTING DATABASE RECORDS

You will often find it necessary to sort some set of data, and 1-2-3 allows you to perform such operations with relative ease. To illustrate a sort, assume you wanted to sort the Accounts Receivable database (presented in Figure 4-1) according to the Balance. Furthermore, assume that if more than one person has the same Balance outstanding, the sort should then default to the customers' last names.

Upon issuing the /Data Sort command, the following menu appears:

Data-Range Primary-Key Secondary-Key Reset Go Quit

The first step in sorting a data base is to tell 1-2-3 the records that are to be sorted. You accomplish this by selecting Data-Range from the Sort menu. At the prompt, you simply input the range of cells where the data base is found. In defining the Data-Range, two notes of caution are warranted:

1. Do not include the titles in the range. If the titles are included, then they too will be sorted among the records in the data base. In our example, the Data-Range would be defined as A6..C18.
2. Be certain *all* fields are included in the Data-Range. For example, if the Data-Range in our example were defined as A6..B18, then only the fields NUMBER and NAME would be sorted. The field BALANCE would remain as is.

You must now tell 1-2-3 how to sort the data. This means that you must define a sort key. The sort key is the field on which you want to sort. In the Accounts Receivable example, we want to sort on the Balance field. To define the Balance field as the sort key, you select the Primary-Key option from the Sort menu. You then simply input any cell reference in the C column (whether or not the cell is in the data base). Upon entering this cell reference, 1-2-3 asks whether you want the data sorted in Ascending or Descending order. This prompt simply requires that you input **A** or **D**.

In some cases, ties will exist in the sort key. For example, more than one person may have the same Accounts Receivable balance. For these cases, you may want to specify a secondary sort key. A secondary sort key causes any records that have the same primary sort key to be sorted by the field defined as the Secondary-Key. The Secondary-Key is defined in exactly the same way as the Primary-Key. Your settings for the Sort option should now appear as shown in the Sort Settings sheet in Figure 4-2.

Selecting Go from the Sort menu causes the sort to take place. Before selecting Go, however, you should save the file. This is necessary in case the sort does not execute as you had hoped. If a problem does occur, you can then retrieve the file as it appeared before the sort. Upon issuing the Go command, the Accounts Receivable database would appear as shown in Figure 4-3.

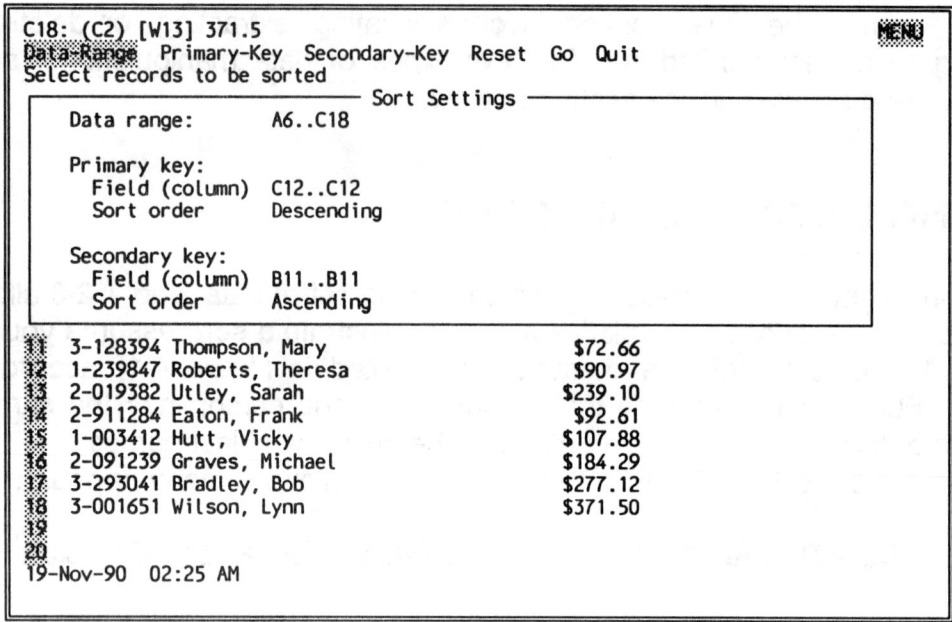

```
C18: (C2) [W13] 371.5                                      MENU
Data-Range  Primary-Key  Secondary-Key  Reset  Go  Quit
Select records to be sorted
┌──────────────────── Sort Settings ────────────────────┐
│   Data range:      A6..C18                             │
│                                                        │
│   Primary key:                                         │
│     Field (column)  C12..C12                           │
│     Sort order      Descending                         │
│                                                        │
│   Secondary key:                                       │
│     Field (column)  B11..B11                           │
│     Sort order      Ascending                          │
└────────────────────────────────────────────────────────┘
11  3-128394 Thompson, Mary                    $72.66
12  1-239847 Roberts, Theresa                  $90.97
13  2-019382 Utley, Sarah                     $239.10
14  2-911284 Eaton, Frank                      $92.61
15  1-003412 Hutt, Vicky                      $107.88
16  2-091239 Graves, Michael                  $184.29
17  3-293041 Bradley, Bob                     $277.12
18  3-001651 Wilson, Lynn                     $371.50
19
20
19-Nov-90  02:25 AM
```

Figure 4-2 Sort Settings

```
C18: (C2) [W13] 23.01                                     READY

        A                B               C        D      E
1
2
3
4   CUSTOMER          CUSTOMER
5    NUMBER             NAME          BALANCE
6   2-094731 Wilmont, Kenneth          $391.25
7   3-001651 Wilson, Lynn              $371.50
8   3-293041 Bradley, Bob              $277.12
9   2-019382 Utley, Sarah              $239.10
10  2-091239 Graves, Michael           $184.29
11  1-018462 Adams, Curt               $128.44
12  1-003412 Hutt, Vicky               $107.88
13  2-911284 Eaton, Frank               $92.61
14  1-234895 Kennedy, Elizabeth         $90.97
15  1-239847 Roberts, Theresa           $90.97
16  3-128394 Thompson, Mary             $72.66
17  1-289345 Harris, Bryan              $65.50
18  2-839482 Basham, Debbie             $23.01
19
20
19-Nov-90  02:27 AM          UNDO
```

Figure 4-3 Sorted Accounts Receivable Database

QUERYING THE DATABASE

The Query option from the **/D**ata menu allows you to locate, extract, and delete certain records from the database. For example, you may want to identify all customers who had a balance greater than $1,000. Alternatively, you could extract a list of records that meet some criterion. The options that are available upon issuing the **/Data Query** command are:

Input Criteria Output Find Extract Unique Delete Reset Quit

Each of these menu options is briefly described below and is then explained in more depth in the sections that follow.

- Input - The range of cells that comprise the data base.
- Criteria - The cell references for those cells containing the query guidelines.
- Output - The cells in which 1-2-3 should place any extracted information.
- Find - Tells 1-2-3 to highlight those records (one at a time) that meet the guidelines specified in the Criteria range.
- Extract - Tells 1-2-3 to copy all or part of those records meeting the guidelines in the Criteria range.
- Unique - Very similar to the Extract command except that only one output record is created if two or more output records would be identical.
- Delete - Tells 1-2-3 to delete those records meeting the guidelines in the Criteria range.
- Reset - Returns the Input range, Criteria range, and Output range to blank entries.
- Quit - Returns you to READY mode.

Defining the Input Range

The Input range simply tells 1-2-3 where the database is that you will be querying. Furthermore, unlike the Data-Range for a sort, the Input range does include the field names (that is, the titles at the top of each column). For example, assume you had a database of Accounts Payable such as the one shown in Figure 4-4, where the first title is in cell E5 and the last record is located in row 17. For this example, the Input range would be defined as E5..G17.

Defining the Criteria Range

The Criteria range is likely the most important feature of any query command. After all, a query is dependent upon having records match those attributes specified in the Criteria range. In the Accounts Payable example from Figure 4-4, assume you wanted to extract information for any record with an Amount Due over $500. To set up the Criteria range, you would first move the cursor to a location on the spreadsheet (you should probably select an out-of-the-way location). We will assume you chose to set up the Criteria range starting in cell Z1. In the first cell of the Criteria range, you specify the field you want 1-2-3 to use in selecting records. In this example, you want 1-2-3 to test amounts in the Amount Due field; therefore, you would place the title **Amount Due** in cell Z1.

```
E5: [W11] ^VOUCHER #                                                    READY

          D          E                    F                    G

  1
  2
  3
  4
  5          VOUCHER #              VENDOR              AMOUNT DUE
  6             145 Baker Brothers                      $3,489.12
  7             146 Adamson Supply                        $782.10
  8             147 Baker Brothers                      $8,823.09
  9             148 Acme Hardware                         $871.23
 10             149 Tryton, Inc.                        $7,165.20
 11             150 Kerston Manufacturing                 $901.27
 12             151 Wallace Construction                  $615.28
 13             152 Acme Hardware                         $948.26
 14             153 Stephens Co.                        $9,012.36
 15             154 Duo Consulting                         $71.12
 16             155 Baker Brothers                        $239.16
 17             156 Christine's Bakery                    $447.80
 18
 19
 20
19-Nov-90  02:38 AM            UNDO
```

Figure 4-4 Accounts Payable Database

A word of caution is warranted at this point. The title that is used for the Criteria range must match exactly the title in the Input range. For example, if you had put two spaces at the beginning of a title in the Input range, the Criteria title must likewise contain two spaces at the beginning. The easiest way to be certain the title is input correctly is to use the /Copy command and simply copy the original title from the Input range to the appropriate cell in the Criteria range.

The next step is to specify the criterion itself. In this example, you want to set up a comparison. This requires that you establish the criterion as a formula, and you should therefore begin the criterion with a plus sign (+). The criterion would therefore be typed in cell Z2 as follows:

$$+G6 > 500$$

You will first notice that we have only specified one cell in the comparison, while the database (Input range) actually contains numerous cells that are to be compared. Simply stated, the rule for establishing Criteria ranges is that you only specify the cell containing the first occurrence of the item of interest. Since we were interested in the Amount Due field, the first occurrence is in cell G6, and that is therefore the cell to be used in the Criteria range. 1-2-3 will simply start at this cell and then proceed downward until hitting the bottom of the Input range.

You may also note that when you first input a criterion that is a formula the cell actually displays as either a 0 or a 1. Notice in Figure 4-5 that cell Z2 is displaying a 1 while the cell actually contains the criterion +G6>500. 1-2-3 is simply making the comparison as stated and returning a value of TRUE or FALSE, where 1 represents TRUE and 0 represents FALSE. In the example in Figure 4-5, Z2 is displaying a 1 because cell

G6 is greater than 500. To make the cell easier to read, you can have it display the criterion itself rather than the TRUE/FALSE value by formatting the cell as **/R**ange **Format Text**. After formatting it as Text, Z2 would appear as shown in Figure 4-6. The Criteria range for this example would simply be cells Z1..Z2.

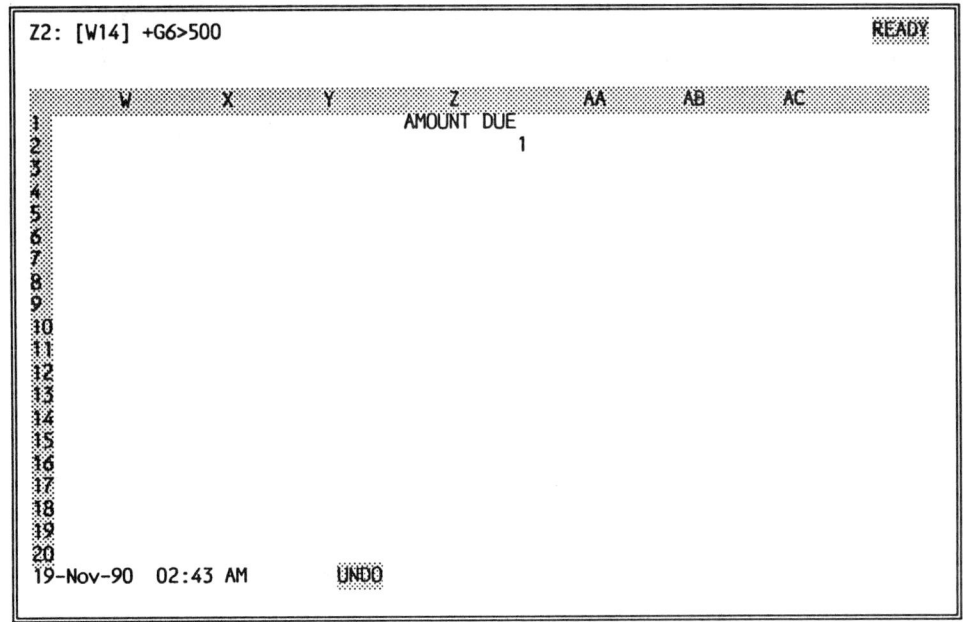

Figure 4-5 Criteria Range Before Formatting as Text

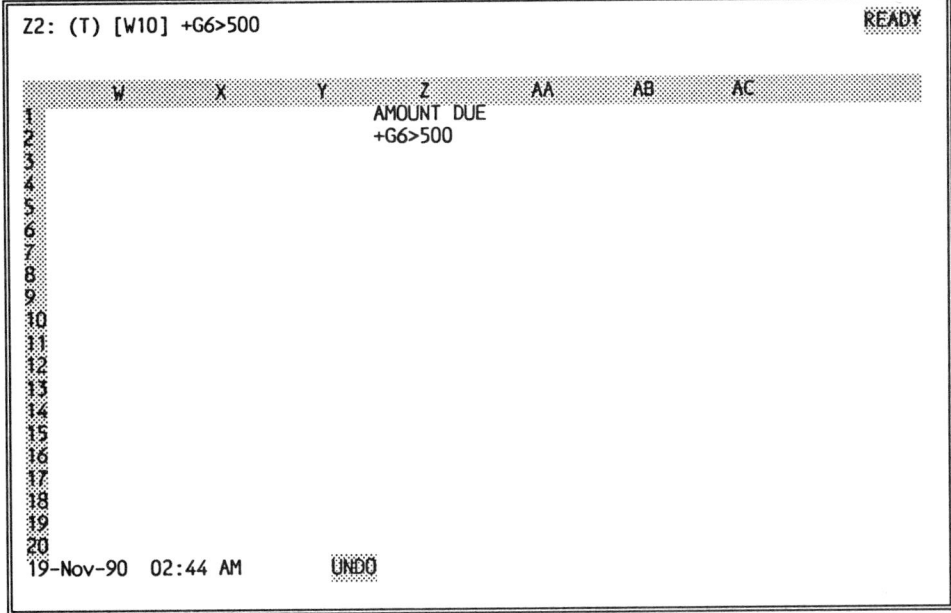

Figure 4-6 Criteria Range After Formatting as Text

The Criteria range used in the previous example is relatively simple, but you will discover that Criteria ranges can become quite complicated. This complication arises from having compound criteria. That is, you can have multiple guidelines for selecting items in a database.

Using the Accounts Payable example from Figure 4-4, assume you want to extract all invoices payable to Baker Brothers that are in excess of $750. Once again, you would first move the cursor to the location where the Criteria range is to be established. We will assume the Criteria range will start in cell M5. Because two fields are required for establishing a match, you would have two field names in the Criteria range. First, copy the title **Payee** to cell M5, and then copy the title **Amount Due** to cell N5. Under the Payee title, you would simply type the name **Baker Brothers**. Notice that a plus sign (+) is not required when you are only matching items from the Input range to the item in the Criteria range. In other words, since no calculation is required, then a formula is not needed. Cell N6 would contain the criterion +G6>750. The Criteria range in this example is shown in Figure 4-7. Notice the Query Settings sheet in Figure 4-8, where the Criteria range is shown now to be cells M5..N6.

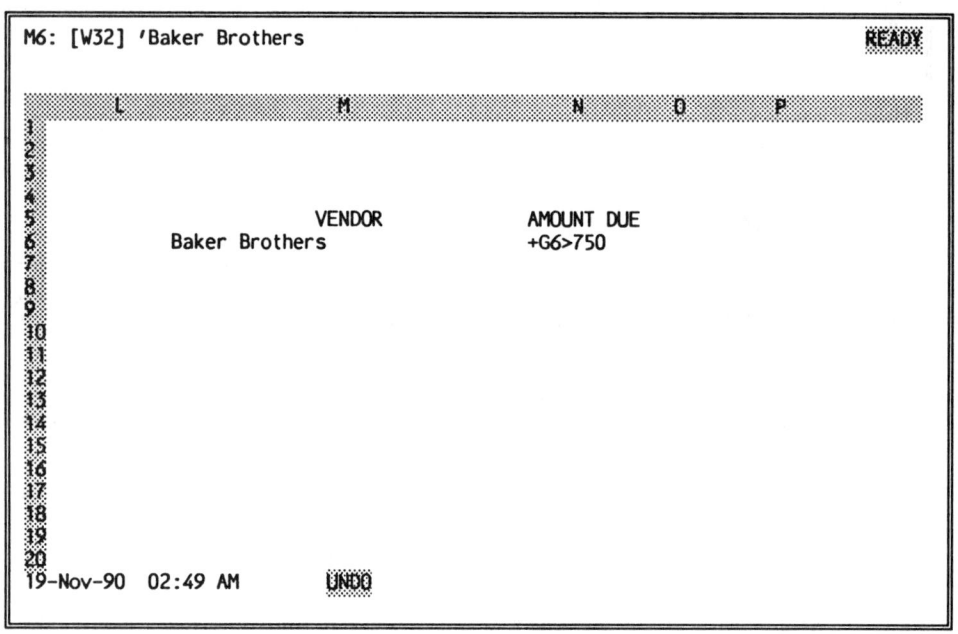

Figure 4-7 Criteria Range with Assumed "AND"

In the example just described, the two criteria were input on the same row of the Criteria range. That is, they were both contained on row 6. Whenever criteria are on the same row of a Criteria range, 1-2-3 assumes that a logical "AND" exists between the cells. For the example depicted in Figure 4-7, 1-2-3 is reading the Criteria range as "Locate a record whose Payee is Baker Corporation *and* whose Amount Due is greater than 75.

If you want 1-2-3 to assume a logical "OR" between criteria, then the criteria should be placed on different rows within the Criteria range. Assume you want to extract any record from Acme Hardware *or* any record whose Amount Due is less than or equal to $1000. For this scenario, the Criteria range would be cells M5..N7 and would appear as shown in Figure 4-9.

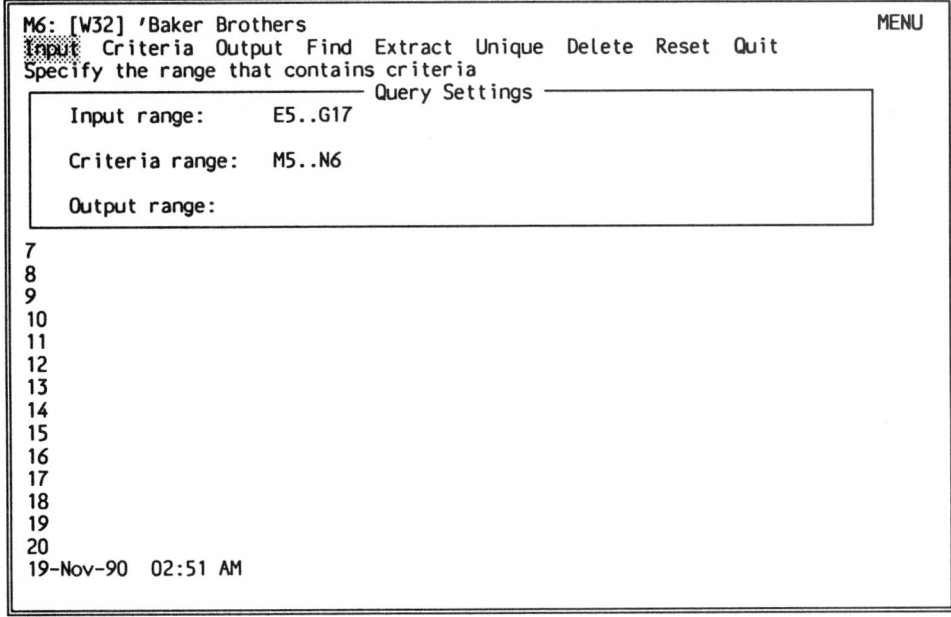

Figure 4-8 Query Settings Sheet

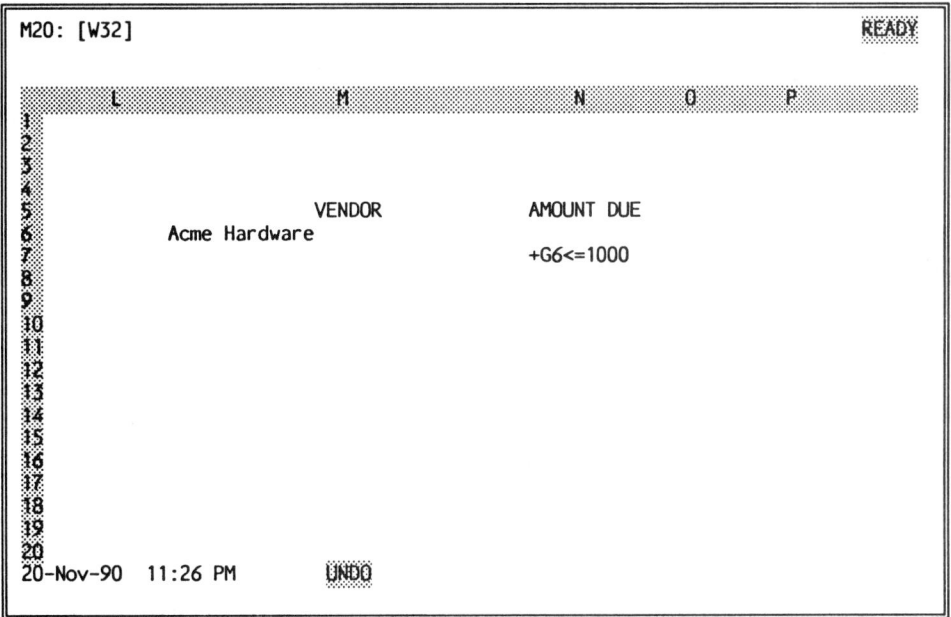

Figure 4-9 Criteria Range with Assumed "OR"

There may be times when you would like to place a logical "AND" or a logical "OR" between criteria within the same field. For example, you might want to find any records where the Amount Due is less than $1000 *and* where the Amount Due is greater than $500. A logical "AND" or "OR" can be placed in a formula by simply enclosing it with the number sign (#). In the situation just described, the Criteria range would be cells M5..M6 and would appear as shown in Figure 4-10.

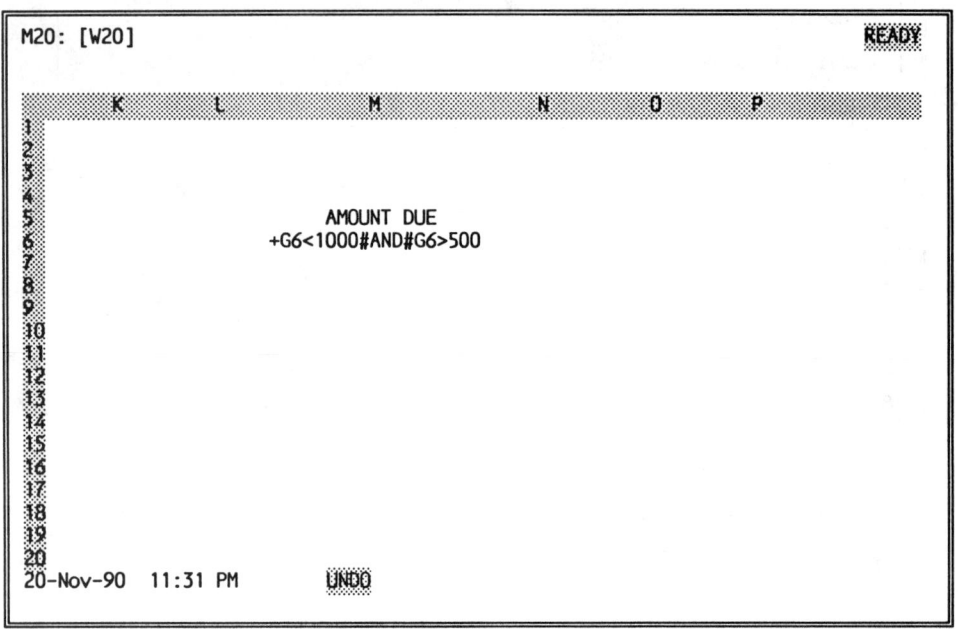

Figure 4-10   Criteria Range with Embedded "AND"

As you can see, the Criteria range is limited only by your imagination. You can combine fields of interest with logical operators to construct very elaborate, sophisticated queries.

Defining the Output Range

When 1-2-3 extracts records from a database (the Extract command is explained later), it must place those records in some specified spreadsheet location. You specify this location by defining the Output range. The Output range is defined as a range of cells containing field names (titles) for those fields you want extracted from the database.

In the Accounts Payable data base, assume you want to extract the Voucher Number and Amount Due for those Vouchers over $2000. The Criteria range would therefore contain the formula +G6>2000. Assuming you want to place the output starting at cell P1, you would need to first copy the field names Voucher # and Amount Due to cells P1 and Q1, respectively. The Output range could therefore be defined as cells P1..Q1. Your Query Settings sheet would then appear as in Figure 4-11.

In this example, two items need to be addressed. First, we were extracting only the Invoice Number and the Amount Due. You do not have to extract entire records, as this example shows. Instead, you place only those fields in the Output range that you want extracted.

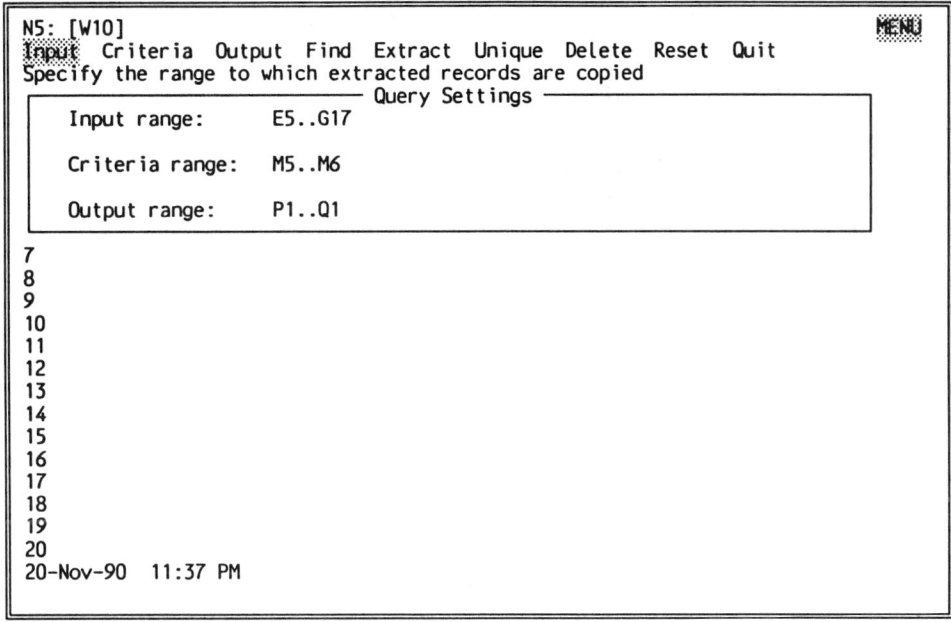

Figure 4-11 Query Settings Sheet

The next item of note is the way the Output range was defined. That is, the range P1..Q1 was defined as the Output range. When the Output range is defined as only the row containing the titles, then any data on rows below that line will be deleted upon executing the Extract command. For example, assume you had some data contained in cells P150..Q160 and then executed the Extract command as specified above. In this situation, the data in cells P150..Q160 would be erased, even though the extracted data does not go beyond row 5.

An alternate way of defining the Output range is to specify a block of cells which includes the cells containing the field names. In our Accounts Payable example, you could have defined the Output range as P1..Q50. The Extract command would have generated the exact same results as before; however, the data in cells P150..Q160 would not have been affected.

You may be wondering why you would ever want to specify only the first row as the Output range if the danger exists of erasing data beneath the Output range. The primary reason for defining the Output range in this way is that you are unsure of the potential number of extracted items. For example, if you specified the Output range as a block of cells with only 10 cells allowed for extracted items and the Extract command were to extract 12 items, then only the first 10 would be extracted. 1-2-3 would give an error message in this situation even though the first 10 items would be extracted correctly.

Invoking the Find Command

If you want only to locate the records in the data base rather than extract or delete them, then you should use the Find option from the /Data Query menu. The Find command highlights each record (one at a time) that matches the criterion. To highlight the next record in sequence, you simply press the **DOWN** arrow key once. Pressing **ENTER** or **ESCAPE** causes 1-2-3 to leave the Find mode and return to the /Data Query menu. To exit the menu, select Quit.

Notice the Inventory database in Figure 4-12. We have placed a Criteria range in cells I4..I5 that appears as follows:

SOLD
+D5>E5

This Criteria range will cause any record where the Units Sold were less than the Units Received to be highlighted. Upon selecting the Find option from the /Data Query menu, Item Number 1423 is highlighted. If you now press the **DOWN** arrow key, Item Number 1120 is highlighted. Pressing the **UP** arrow key at this point would cause 1-2-3 to return to Item Number 1423.

```
B20: [W20]                                                                    READY


          A                B            C         D        E        F         G
1
2
3     ITEM                            PREV    UNITS    UNITS    ENDING
4     NUMBER       DESCRIPTION        BALANCE SOLD     RECEIVED BALANCE
5        2314 MODEL 4412 COMPUTER       45      30       15       30
6        2210 MODEL 4415 COMPUTER       32      40       13        5
7        1423 HR313 LASER PRINTER        4      60       78       22
8        1120 PB220 DM PRINTER          78      23       45      100
9        3281 MODEL 2209 COMPUTER       12      45       23      -10
10       5123 DISK DRIVE (5.25")         9      15        7        1
11       6190 DISK DRIVE (3.5")          0       8       23       15
12
13
14
15
16
17
18
19
20
20-Nov-90   11:52 PM           UNDO
```

Figure 4-12 Inventory Database

While a record is highlighted, you can edit any cell within that record. Returning to the Inventory data base, notice that when Find is selected and Item Number 1423 is highlighted, a small cursor appears in the first cell of the record. This cursor can be moved back and forth among cells within the record by pressing the **LEFT** and **RIGHT** arrow keys. While this cursor is on a particular cell, that cell can be changed by simply typing a new entry or can be edited by using the EDIT (**F2**) key. After the editing is complete, you press **ENTER** to return to Find mode. Pressing **ENTER** again (or **ESCAPE**) will return you to the /Data Query menu.

Invoking the Extract and Unique Commands

The Extract command was covered to a great extent in the discussion of the Output range. One important point to note, however, is that the Extract command really does not <u>extract</u> records from the database. Instead, when the Extract command is invoked, a copy of the appropriate records is made in the Output range. The data remains intact. Furthermore, note that making changes to the records in the Output range has no effect on the records in the data base.

At times, you will want to extract certain database records (or portions thereof) without having any duplication. This is where the Unique command is used. For example, assume that your company had 15 bank accounts in a total of 7 banks (see Figure 4-13). You would like to get a listing of those banks where you have individual accounts in excess of $10,000. For this type of query, you are not interested in duplications. That is, if you had more than one account in excess of $10,000 at a particular bank, you would only want that banks name listed once in the Output range.

```
B3: [W18] '12903-223311-231                                        READY


        A           B                   C                 D           E
1
2                 ACCOUNT #            BANK             BALANCE
3             12903-223311-231   FIFTH INTERSTATE      $12,983.01
4             432-22-1122        MOUNTAIN VIEW BANK    $98,230.87
5             12903-224412-412   FIFTH INTERSTATE      $84,233.58
6             239203912          THIRD FIDELITY           $782.12
7             782-31-2311        MOUNTAIN VIEW BANK    $56,981.23
8             230192739          THIRD FIDELITY         $7,129.45
9             432-22-1123        MOUNTAIN VIEW BANK    $17,910.23
10            432-12-5129        MOUNTAIN VIEW BANK     $8,832.12
11            9031-334422        BUCKEYE NATIONAL       $3,322.93
12            9031-334423        BUCKEYE NATIONAL       $9,012.23
13            12903-224091-119   FIFTH INTERSTATE      $22,334.16
14            8292-298321        BUCKEYE NATIONAL       $8,734.12
15            7831287265         SPRING S & L          $12,503.12
16            901-33-1212-233    MEMPHIS NATIONAL       $9,053.59
17            23912-12-12956     FRANKLIN SAVINGS         $452.09
18
19
20
21-Nov-90   12:02 AM            UNDO
```

Figure 4-13 Database of Bank Accounts

For this example, you would establish an Input range of B2..B17, a Criteria range containing the formula +D3>10000 in cells F2..F3, and an Output range with only the BANK field in cell J2. Upon issuing the **/D**ata **Q**uery Unique command, the Output range would appear as shown in Figure 4-14. Notice that each bank meeting the criterion is displayed only once.

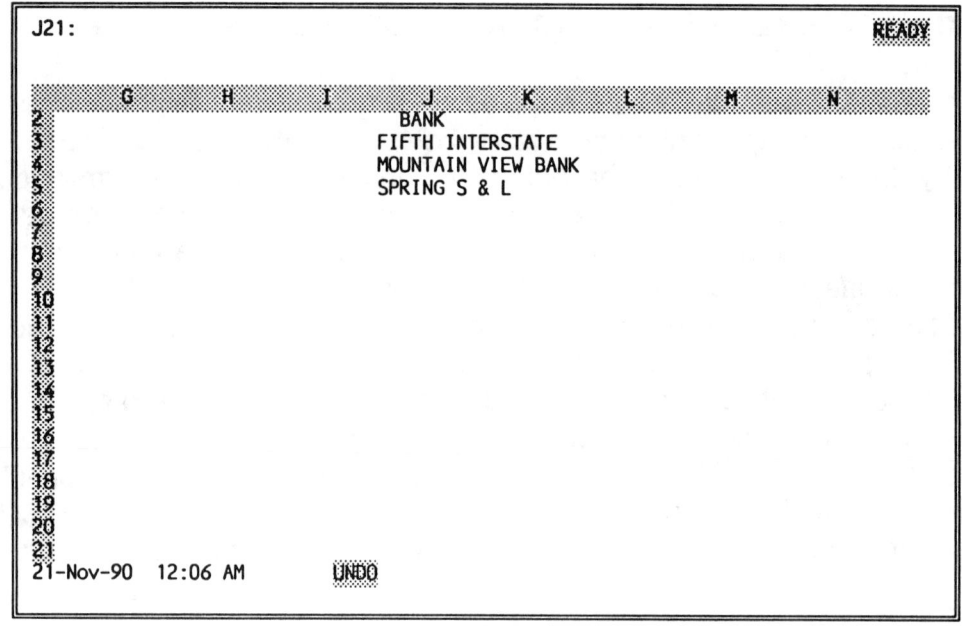

Figure 4-14 Output Range After Extracting

Invoking the Delete Command

The setup of the Delete command is exactly the same as a Find command. You simply specify an Input range and a Criteria range (no Output range needs to be specified, since you are not extracting). When you invoke the Delete command, a submenu appears, as follows:

Cancel Delete

Because the Delete command permanently changes the database, 1-2-3 gives you a chance to cancel the command. If you specify **D**elete at this submenu, the records that match the Criteria range will be deleted from the database. 1-2-3 automatically moves the remaining records up so that no gaps appear in the database.

To illustrate the Delete command, assume you have a Fixed Asset database as shown in Figure 4-15. Notice that some of the assets have a Sales Amount in their record. An entry in this field signifies the asset has been sold. Further assume you want to delete any of these assets that have been sold (that is, the assets with an entry in the Sales Amount field).

The Criteria range is in cells G5..G6 and appears as follows:

AMOUNT
@COUNT(D6..E6)=2

```
B20: [W23]                                                           READY

          A               B              C          D          E
1
2
3
4     ASSET                                    ACCUMULATED   SALES
5     NUMBER       DESCRIPTION        COST      DEPRECIATION AMOUNT
6     82-10992 Desk                   $255         $195        $90
7     84-89213 Filing Cabinet         $196         $136
8     84-23481 Filing Cabinet         $196         $136
9     86-78212 Computer (TRH 8273)  $2,018       $1,518       $400
10    87-12871 Table                 $350         $285
11    87-91283 Building (17 Evans St.) $45,055   $12,050
12    88-19201 Warehouse Shelving   $8,915       $4,200
13    88-26775 Desk                   $644         $303
14    88-39102 Filing Cabinet         $254         $112        $75
15    88-56453 Computer (Negative 342) $4,203     $1,975
16    88-92716 Display Shelving     $1,920         $472
17    89-12813 Desk                   $850         $197
18
19
20
21-Nov-90  12:23 AM          UNDO
```

Figure 4-15 Fixed Asset Database

A few things about this Criteria range may appear confusing and therefore need explaining. First, the only title that is used is "AMOUNT." Because 1-2-3 assumes only one line of titles, we defined the Input range by using only the titles in row 5. That is, even though the titles are in rows 4 and 5, we made 1-2-3 think that the only titles were in row 5 be beginning the Input range in row 5. By using only the titles in the row 5, the title field for the Sales Amount column is assumed by 1-2-3 only to be "AMOUNT."

Secondly, you may not recall the @COUNT function. This function returns a value equaling the number of cells in the specified range that have anything in them (that is, they are non-blank). In this example, if both cells D6 and E6 are non-blank, the @COUNT function would equal 2.

The third item of potential confusion is the use of both D6 and E6 in the @COUNT function. You may wonder why we did not just use E6. A unique characteristic of the @COUNT function is that it does not work properly on just one cell. Therefore, since we knew a value would always appear in the ACCUMULATED DEPRECIATION column, we could specify both the ACCUMULATED DEPRECIATION column and the SALES AMOUNT column and simply ask whether there are 2 non-blank cells.

At this point, if you invoke the **/D**ata **Q**uery Delete command and then select **D**elete once again at the submenu, the three records with amounts in the SALES AMOUNT column would be deleted. Notice that the remaining records are moved up to fill the gap, as shown in Figure 4-16.

```
B23: [W23]                                                                    READY


          A                    B                  C          D             E
  4    ASSET                                               ACCUMULATED   SALES
  5    NUMBER         DESCRIPTION              COST       DEPRECIATION   AMOUNT
  6    84-89213  Filing Cabinet                $196          $136
  7    84-23481  Filing Cabinet                $196          $136
  8    87-12871  Table                         $350          $285
  9    87-91283  Building (17 Evans St.)    $45,055       $12,050
  10   88-19201  Warehouse Shelving          $8,915        $4,200
  11   88-26775  Desk                          $644          $303
  12   88-56453  Computer (Negative 342)     $4,203        $1,975
  13   88-92716  Display Shelving            $1,920          $472
  14   89-12813  Desk                          $850          $197
  15
  16
  17
  18
  19
  20
  21
  22
  23
  21-Nov-90  12:27 AM            UNDO
```

Figure 4-16 Fixed Asset Database After Deleting Records

CONTROL CONSIDERATIONS

The greatest concern in any of the Sort or Query commands is maintaining the integrity of the data base itself. The potential risks are that you could separate some fields from their associated records with the /Data Sort command, execute a Query command with the Criteria range improperly specified, delete the wrong records with /Data Query Delete, or erase desirable data under the Output range when using /Data Query Extract. The following controls will help mitigate these potential risks:

1. Save the file before executing the /Data Sort command to ensure recovery in the event the sort does not execute properly.
2. Be certain the Data-Range in a /Data Sort command covers all data fields (columns) in the data base to eliminate the possibility of sorting only certain fields within records.
3. Save the file before executing the Extract or Delete command to ensure recovery in the event the command does not execute properly.
4. Test Criteria ranges with sample data to be certain their logical structure is as you wanted.
5. Before executing a /Data Query Delete command, test the Criteria range by first executing a /Data Query Extract command.
6. When specifying the Output range as only the first row of the range, test the area under the Output range to be certain it is clear of any data that could be erase upon issuing the /Data Query Extract command.

REVIEW QUESTIONS

1. What is a data base?

2. What is the primary difference between a Data-Range in a Sort and an Input range in a Query?

3. What is a Primary-Key?

4. When is a Secondary-Key necessary?

5. What are two ways the Output range can be defined in a Query? What are the disadvantages of each?

6. How is editing accomplished in a Find command?

7. How do you return from Find mode to the Query menu?

8. When inputting a criterion formula, it will usually appear as a 0 or 1. What determines the number to be displayed?

9. How can you cause a criterion formula to be displayed as the formula itself rather than as a 0 or 1?

10. Why is it recommended that you use /Copy to place the titles in the Criteria range and Output range?

11. How is a logical "AND" represented in the Criteria range?

12. How is a logical "OR" represented in the Criteria range?

13. How can a logical "AND" or "OR" be placed within one cell in a Criteria range?

14. What does the Unique command accomplish?

15. Does the Extract command remove the corresponding records from the data base? If so, how is the data base affected?

16. Can you extract specific fields from a data base rather than entire records? If so, how?

17. Describe the Delete command's built-in safeguard.

18. How many title lines does 1-2-3 allow you to use for Query settings?

19. Which cell is referenced in a Criteria range formula?

20. What should you do before invoking the Delete command to ensure the Criteria range is correct?

CASE: Paradise Food Distributors
Accounts Receivable Data Base
(The Revenue Cycle)

Paradise Food Distributors is a wholesale food distributor that sells canned and frozen foods to institutions such as restaurants, schools, and hospitals. Paradise was started in 1968 by Richard Roberts and Terry Dougherty and is still owned and operated by them. They currently serve 27 customers from one warehouse.

Mr. Roberts and Mr. Dougherty maintain their Accounts Receivable on a Lotus 1-2-3 spreadsheet (see the PARADISE.WK1 file on your student disk). The file contains the Identifier (10-digit telephone number), Name, Type, Current Balance, and Past-Due Balance of each customer.

Requirements

Assume you have recently been hired by Paradise Food Distributors. The owners want you to generate the following reports from the Accounts Receivable data base:

1. A list of all customers with a Current Balance greater than $1,500.
2. A list of all customers with a Current Balance greater than $500 and a Past-Due Balance greater than zero.
3. A list of all Restaurant customers with a Current Balance greater than $1,000 or a Past-Due Balance greater than $500.

After generating these reports, you are to delete any customer with a -999 (this is used as a deletion code) in the Current Balance field. A customer can only be deleted if their Past-Due Balance is equal to zero. After deleting these customers, you are to sort the data base by Customer Name (using Type as the secondary key).

Solution

GENERATING THE FIRST REPORT

The first report requires that you establish a Criteria range for the CURRENT BALANCE field. Assuming you want to establish the Criteria range beginning in cell J1, simply copy the CURRENT BALANCE title from cell D5 to cell J1. The first occurrence within the CURRENT BALANCE field is in cell D6. Therefore the criterion would simply be placed in cell J2 as:

$$+D6>1500$$

Since the first occurrence does not meet the criterion, the cell displays a 0. You will probably want to make the criterion formula easier to read by formatting the cell to Text by striking **/Range Format Text**. To read the entire criterion formula, you will want to widen the column to 17 spaces by using the **/Worksheet Column Set-Width** command. Your Criteria range should then appear as shown in Figure 4-17.

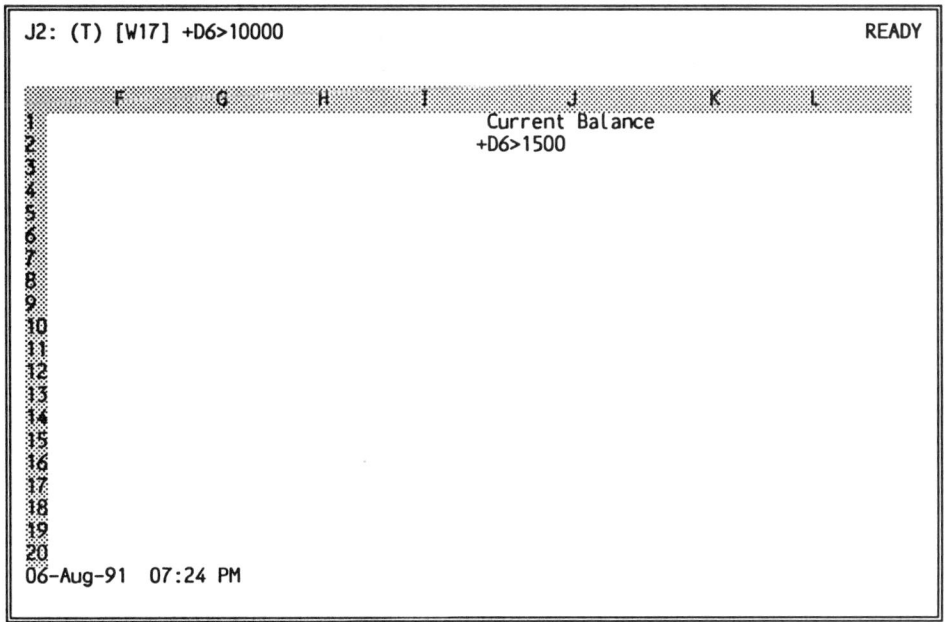

Figure 4-17 Criteria Range

You must now establish the titles for the Output range. Assuming you want the Output range in cells M1..Q1, you simply copy the titles in cells A5..E5 to the cells in the Output range.

You now select **/Data Query** and then select Input from the menu to specify the Input range. In this case, the Input range would be the entire data base. A quick way to define this range is to place the cursor on cell A5 (before entering the **/Data Query** command). Then, after entering the **/Data Query** Input command, you would anchor the cursor, and then press the **END** key, the **DOWN** arrow key, the **END** key again, and the **RIGHT** arrow key. The entire data base should now be highlighted. Pressing **ENTER** defines the highlighted area as the Input range.

The Criteria range option should be selected, and cells J1..J2 should be defined as the Criteria range. The Output range would be selected next. Remember that you can either specify the title row <u>or</u> a block of rows (including the titles) as the Output range. Assuming we know there are no data below the Output range titles, then we will simply specify the cells M1..Q1 as the Output range.

You would now select **Extract** to copy the appropriate records to the Output range.

You then must select **Q**uit from the **/D**ata **Q**uery menu to return to READY mode. Your Output range should appear just as displayed in Figure 4-18. To create a printed report of this information, you would simply follow the procedures from Chapter 3 and print the range M1..Q9.

```
N20: [W26]                                                                  READY


         M                    N                  O              P
1   Identifier             Name               Type       Current Balance
2   6029172901 Guild Nursing Homes         HOSPITAL          $1,900.62
3   6028178991 Pizza Pizzaz                RESTAURANT        $2,090.11
4   6028194927 Mercy Hospital              HOSPITAL          $3,401.72
5   6029017382 Symington Schools           SCHOOL            $3,091.27
6   6023012901 Winner's Wieners            RESTAURANT        $2,991.67
7   6029304918 Sorter School System        SCHOOL            $8,912.37
8   6026356689 Brinkley Restaurant SupplyRESTAURANT          $2,819.26
9   6028123984 Zenith Supply               HOSPITAL          $2,839.10
10
11
12
13
14
15
16
17
18
19
20
21-Nov-90  01:20 AM           UNDO
```

Figure 4-18   Output Range After Extracting

GENERATING THE SECOND REPORT

You are now ready to generate the report of customers who have a Current Balance greater than $500 <u>and</u> a Past-Due Balance greater than zero. This report is very similar to the one just created, and only the Criteria range would need to be changed.

Because you have two criteria involving two fields, you must have an extended Criteria range. Therefore, the first step is to copy the titles for the two fields to the Criteria range. Again assuming you want to start the Criteria range in cell J1, you would copy the title "Current Balance" and the title "Past-Due Balance" to cells J1 and K1, respectively. You are assuming the two criteria have a logical "AND" between them; therefore, they should be placed on the same row. The criterion for the Current Balance would be stated as:

$$+D6 > 500$$

The criterion for the Past-Due Balance would be:

$$+E6 > 0$$

Your Criteria range would now appear as shown in Figure 4-19 (note that we have expanded columns J and K to make the Criteria range easier to read).

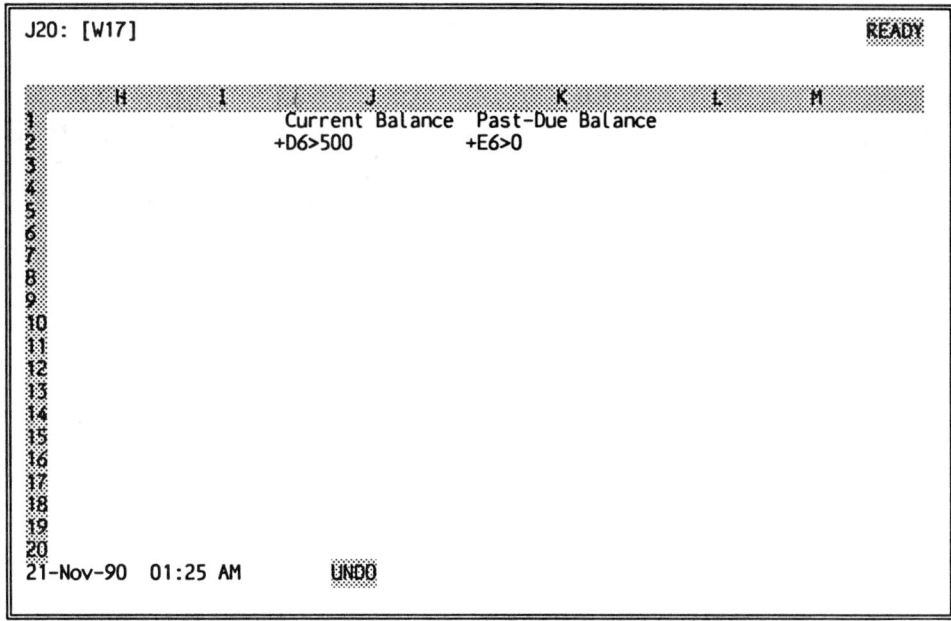

Figure 4-19 Criteria Range

If you now specify the Criteria range to be cells J1..K2, you are ready to perform the Extract. You already specified the Input range and the Output range for the previous report. Therefore, those settings should still remain. Upon selecting **Extract** and then **Q**uit, you can move the cursor to cell M1, and your Output range should have the records shown in Figure 4-20. This range can now be printed to produce the appropriate report.

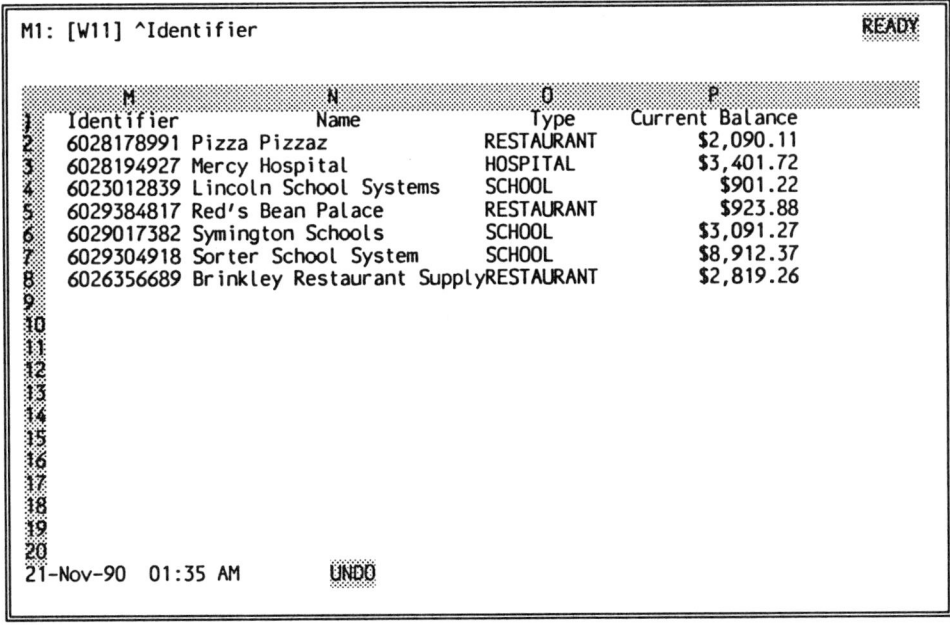

Figure 4-20 Output Range After Extracting

GENERATING THE THIRD REPORT

You are now ready to prepare the report of all Restaurant customers who have a Current Balance greater than $1,000 <u>or</u> a Past-Due Balance greater than $500. Once again, the Input range and the Output range would be identical to those used for the previous reports. The primary concern is the Criteria range.

Note that you must first match the customer Type as a Restaurant. Then you determine if the Restaurant customer has a Current Balance greater than $1,000 or that customer has a Past-Due Balance greater than $500. Because a logical "OR" exists between the two criteria, they must be placed on different rows within the Criteria range. The final Criteria range would therefore appear as shown in Figure 4-21, and the Output range (after Extracting the correct information) would appear as shown in Figure 4-22. This Output range can also be printed to produce a hard-copy report.

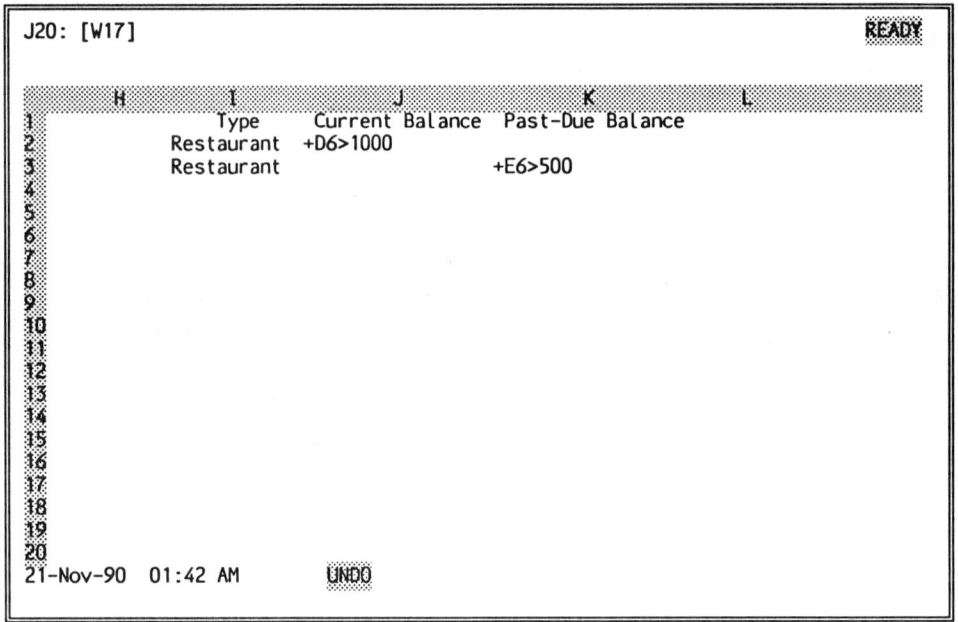

Figure 4-21   Criteria Range

DELETING THE OBSOLETE RECORDS

The next step is to delete those customers who have a deletion code (-999) in their Current Balance field and whose Past-Due Balance is equal to zero. The Input range is defined exactly as before, and no Output range is needed to invoke the Delete command. The Criteria range involves both the Current Balance field and the Past-Due Balance field and would appear as shown in Figure 4-23.

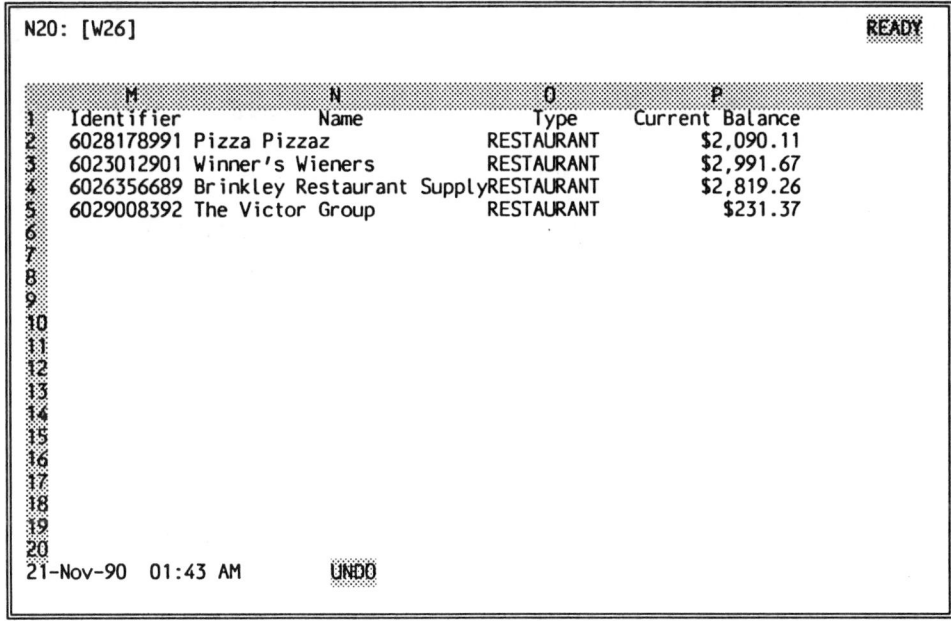

Figure 4-22 Output Range After Extracting

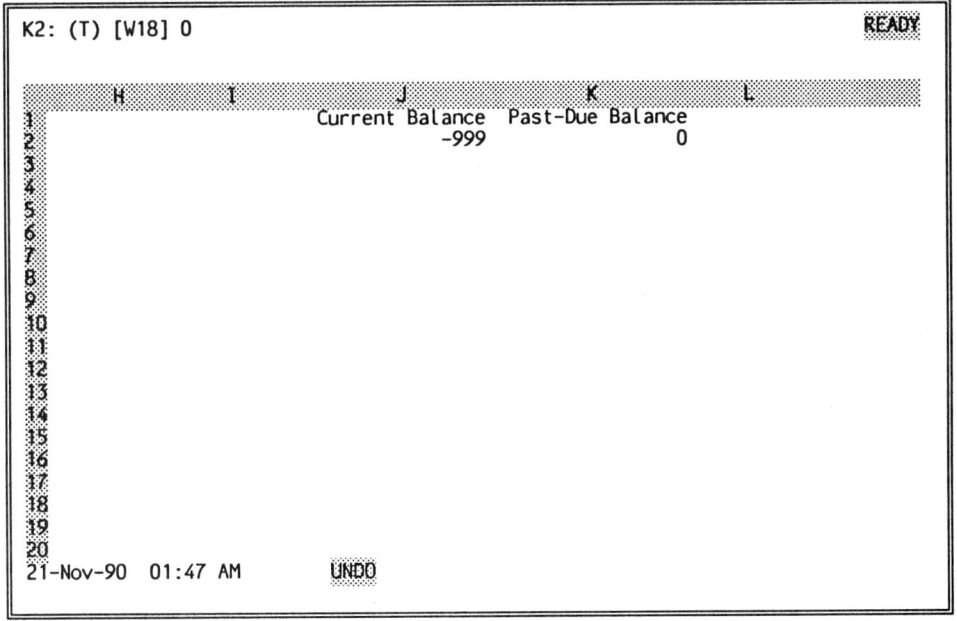

Figure 4-23 Criteria Range

You would then invoke the Delete command by pressing **/D**ata **Q**uery **D**elete and selecting Delete from the submenu that appears at this point. Notice that the matching records are deleted from the database and the remaining records are moved up to close the gaps. The beginning of your database should now appear as shown in Figure 4-24, and the last record should be in row 27.

```
A1: [W11]                                                                    READY

        A                B                    C              D
1                                          Paradise Food Distributors
2                                          Accounts Receivable
3
4
5    Identifier         Name                 Type          Current Balance
6    6025552312 Holmes Hospital Group       HOSPITAL          $789.12
7    6025559160 Chez Cognac                 RESTAURANT        $239.55
8    6029468127 Tara County Schools         SCHOOL            $209.12
9    6029172901 Guild Nursing Homes         HOSPITAL        $1,900.62
10   6028178991 Pizza Pizzaz                RESTAURANT      $2,090.11
11   6028194927 Mercy Hospital              HOSPITAL        $3,401.72
12   6029142948 The Harrison School         SCHOOL             $44.67
13   6028682900 Lovett Hospital             HOSPITAL         ($999.00)
14   6023012839 Lincoln School Systems      SCHOOL            $901.22
15   6024417340 Chez Ferdinand              RESTAURANT         $25.12
16   6029304819 Carey's Home Cooking        RESTAURANT         $92.16
17   6029384817 Red's Bean Palace           RESTAURANT        $923.88
18   6028910001 Barnes, Inc.                HOSPITAL         ($999.00)
19   6029017382 Symington Schools           SCHOOL          $3,091.27
20   6023012901 Winner's Wieners            RESTAURANT      $2,991.67
21-Nov-90  01:52 AM            UNDO
```

Figure 4-24 Database After Deleting

SORTING THE DATABASE

You are now requested to sort the data base by Customer Name and use customer Type as the secondary key. The quickest way to invoke the sort in this case is to first place the cursor on cell A6, which is the first cell of the Data-Range (remember that the titles field is not included in a Data-Range for sorting). You next invoke the commands **/D**ata **S**ort Data-Range. To define the Data-Range, anchor the cursor, and then press the **END** key, the **DOWN** key, the **END** key, and the **RIGHT** arrow key (this is assuming that any previous settings for the Sort commands have been Reset).

The Primary-Key can be defined as any cell in the B column. We have decided to use the cell B8, and since this is an alphabetical range the key should be sorted in Ascending order. The Secondary-Key is defined as any cell in the C column. We chose cell C6 and again prescribed Ascending order. You are now ready to Sort (you may want to save your file at this point just to be safe). Your Sort Settings sheet should look like the one in Figure 4-25.

To sort the data base, select **G**o. The beginning of the database, after sorting, is shown in Figure 4-26.

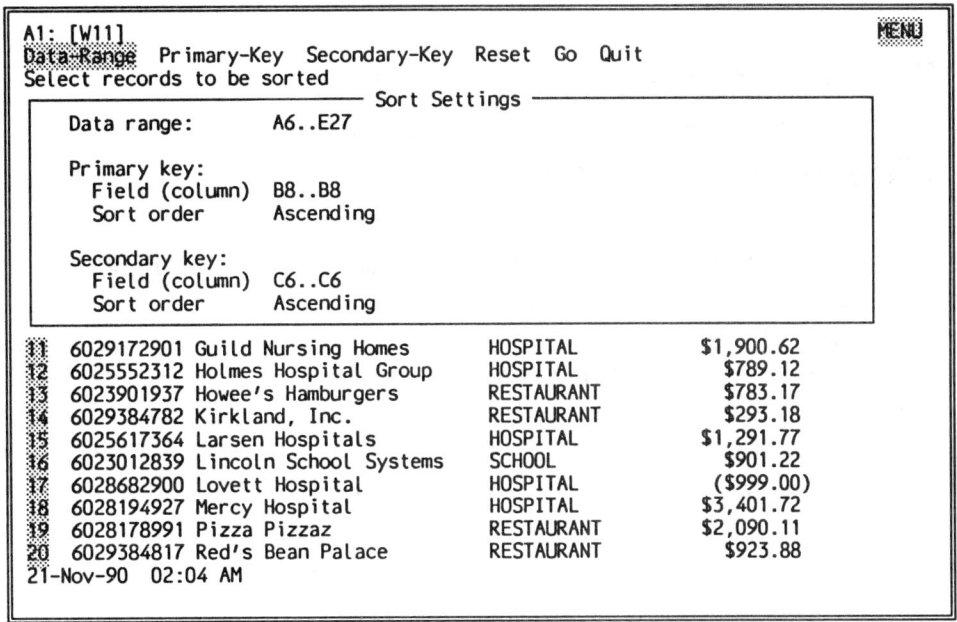

Figure 4-25 Sort Settings Sheet

```
A1: [W11]                                                              READY

          A              B                  C              D
 1                                 Paradise Food Distributors
 2                                 Accounts Receivable
 3
 4
 5    Identifier        Name               Type       Current Balance
 6    6028910001  Barnes, Inc.            HOSPITAL        ($999.00)
 7    6026356689  Brinkley Restaurant SupplyRESTAURANT   $2,819.26
 8    6029304819  Carey's Home Cooking    RESTAURANT       $92.16
 9    6025559160  Chez Cognac             RESTAURANT      $239.55
10    6024417340  Chez Ferdinand          RESTAURANT       $25.12
11    6029172901  Guild Nursing Homes     HOSPITAL      $1,900.62
12    6025552312  Holmes Hospital Group   HOSPITAL        $789.12
13    6023901937  Howee's Hamburgers      RESTAURANT      $783.17
14    6029384782  Kirkland, Inc.          RESTAURANT      $293.18
15    6025617364  Larsen Hospitals        HOSPITAL      $1,291.77
16    6023012839  Lincoln School Systems  SCHOOL          $901.22
17    6028682900  Lovett Hospital         HOSPITAL        ($999.00)
18    6028194927  Mercy Hospital          HOSPITAL      $3,401.72
19    6028178991  Pizza Pizzaz            RESTAURANT    $2,090.11
20    6029384817  Red's Bean Palace       RESTAURANT      $923.88
21-Nov-90  01:59 AM          UNDO
```

Figure 4-26 Database After Sorting

FOLLOW-UP
CASE: Wright's Heating and Cooling
Accounts Receivable Data Base
(The Revenue Cycle)

Patty Wright owns and operates Wright's Heating and Cooling, which was started by her father in 1962. Upon her father's retirement in 1984, Patty took over the business. She installs and repairs air conditioners and furnaces. Most of her customers are businesses in the area, and she maintains between 20 and 30 open accounts at any time.

She maintains her Accounts Receivable on Lotus 1-2-3 (which can be found in the WRIGHTS.WK1 file on your student diskette). The spreadsheet contains each customer's Name, Current Balance, 30-Day Balance, 60-Day Balance, Over 90-Day Balance, and otal Balance.

Requirements

Patty Wright would like your assistance in generating special reports from her Accounts Receivable data. Specifically, she would like the following:

1. Sort the database in descending order of the Total Balances.
2. Generate a report of customers with an Over 60-Day Balance greater than zero.
3. Generate a report of customers with a 60-Day Balance greater than $100 or a 30-Day Balance greater than $500.
4. Delete those customers with a Total Balance of zero.

ASSIGNMENT
CASE: Walker Wholesale
Cash Receipts Transaction File
(The Revenue Cycle)

Walker Wholesale was started by Herbert Walker in 1967. The company distributes cardboard packaging products in the Northeastern U.S. to relatively large companies.

Walker Wholesale maintains a Cash Receipts Transaction File on Lotus 1-2-3. This file, as the name implies, is simply a record of all incoming payments for a period of time (usually one to two weeks). Mr. Walker would like your assistance in performing certain sorting and querying tasks on the Cash Receipts Transaction File.

Requirements

Using the data found in the WALKER.WK1 file of your student diskette, perform the following tasks.

1. Extract all records for Account # 6025557763 (note that the telephone number is used by Walker as the Customer Number).
2. Extract all records for Invoice numbers less than 60000.
3. Sort the file on the Date field, with the most recent payments first (note that the dates have all been input using the @DATE function).
4. Extract all records for payments in excess of $6,000.

ASSIGNMENT
CASE: Crusher Tennis Equipment
Customer Master File
(The Revenue Cycle)

Crusher Tennis Equipment is a tennis equipment distributor located in Nashville, Tennessee. At this time, all of Crusher's customers are located in the state of Tennessee.

Crusher maintains a Customer Master File on Lotus 1-2-3. This file contains each customer's Number, Name, Address, Zip Code, Credit Line, and Balance. Crusher would like for you to use the Lotus 1-2-3 database commands to perform some tasks on this file.

Requirements

Using the data in the CRUSHER.WK1 file of your student diskette, perform the following tasks:

1. Sort the file by Customer Number (in ascending order).
2. Extract the records of all customers from the 95001 zip code *or* from the 90001 zip code.
3. Extract the records of all customers who have a balance greater than their credit line. (Hint: you only need to specify one field in the Criteria Range; however, you can reference more than one field within one cell.)

CHAPTER 5
USING 1-2-3 MACRO PROGRAMMING TO ENHANCE USER PRODUCTIVITY

INTRODUCTION

In the beginning of this section, we described 1-2-3 as a powerful software package that is limited only by your imagination. One feature that truly reflects 1-2-3's power is *macro programming*. Macros (as macro programs are commonly referred) are quite flexible in that they might be only one or two lines long and do nothing but invoke a print command for you. At the same time, however, macros may be a few hundred lines long and used to program entire billing systems, accounts payable systems, and so forth.

In this chapter, we will introduce you to macros primarily at the beginning and intermediate levels. Once you are more comfortable with macros, you will find it easier and easier to make them more sophisticated. Designing advanced macros is nothing more than combining the same commands used for simpler macros into more elaborate logical schemes. We therefore feel that a focus on the basic understanding of macros and macro commands is of primary importance at this stage. This chapter is separated into three topical areas, which are:

1. Designing simple macros for keystroke storage
2. Designing intermediate macros with the macro command language
3. Understanding advanced macros for database manipulation

SIMPLE MACROS FOR KEYSTROKE STORAGE

Let's first get an understanding of what exactly a macro is. A macro is nothing more than a series of keystrokes and/or commands stored in cells of a 1-2-3 spreadsheet. Upon issuing the proper command, 1-2-3 will execute those keystrokes and commands. When more elaborate macro commands are used, macros perform just as any other programming language (such as Basic, Fortran, etc.). That is, by using macro commands, you can have conditional statements, custom-designed menus, subroutines, loops, and virtually any other feature included in a programming language.

Before introducing you to more sophisticated macros, though, we should introduce the simplest form of macro, where you have 1-2-3 invoke keystrokes for you. Let's say that you frequently need to erase the contents of two adjoining cells in a row. You would like for 1-2-3 to take some of the tedium out of having to type the necessary keystrokes over and over again. Therefore, you decide to place the appropriate keystrokes in a macro, which can then be executed at any time.

As you may recall, you erase ranges by pressing **/Range Erase**. Using shorthand notation, this means you simply press the keys **/RE** and then the **ENTER** key. To erase two adjoining cells in a row, you would therefore press **/RE** and then the **RIGHT** arrow key and then the **ENTER** key. You are now ready to store these keystrokes in a cell.

Positioning and Typing Macros

The first decision is where to store the macro. As a rule of thumb, you should always place macros in out-of-the-way locations so they do not interfere with the primary components of the spreadsheet. Assume you decide to store the macro in cell AA1. You move the cursor to AA1 (remember that the F5 key can be used to move the cursor quickly to any cell location). If you attempt to type the sequence **/RE**, 1-2-3 will think that you are ready to actually execute those commands. In other words, if you first type the slash key (/), the main menu will appear. When typing macros in a cell, you should therefore begin the entry with an apostrophe (') or some other appropriate label prefix.

Representing Special Keys

The next problem arises in how to represent the RIGHT arrow key and the ENTER key. While most keys are represented in cells simply by typing the appropriate key (for example, the slash key is placed in a cell by pressing the slash key). However, the arrow movement keys, the ENTER key, and certain other keys require special representation for use in a macro. The arrow keys are represented by typing the word indicating the direction of desired movement within braces ({}). The RIGHT arrow key would therefore be represented in a macro with {RIGHT}. If you wanted the RIGHT arrow key to be pressed five times, you would simply type {RIGHT 5} in the macro. A partial list of special keys and their representation for macros is shown below:

Key	Representation
↑	{UP} or {U}
↓	{DOWN} or {D}
→	{RIGHT} or {R}
←	{LEFT} or {L}
ENTER	
F2	{EDIT}
F5	{GOTO}
F9	{CALC}
Escape	{ESCAPE} or {ESC}
Page Up	{PGUP}
Page Down	{PGDN}
Home	{HOME}

While a number of other special keys exist, this list represents some of the keys more commonly used in macros.

The ENTER key is represented with a tilde (˜). For our example, the proper sequence to type into cell AA1 would therefore be as follows:

'/RE{RIGHT}˜

Upon typing this sequence, your screen should appear as shown in Figure 5-1. Notice the apostrophe (sometimes referred to as a tick mark) at the beginning of the sequence does not appear in the cell itself.

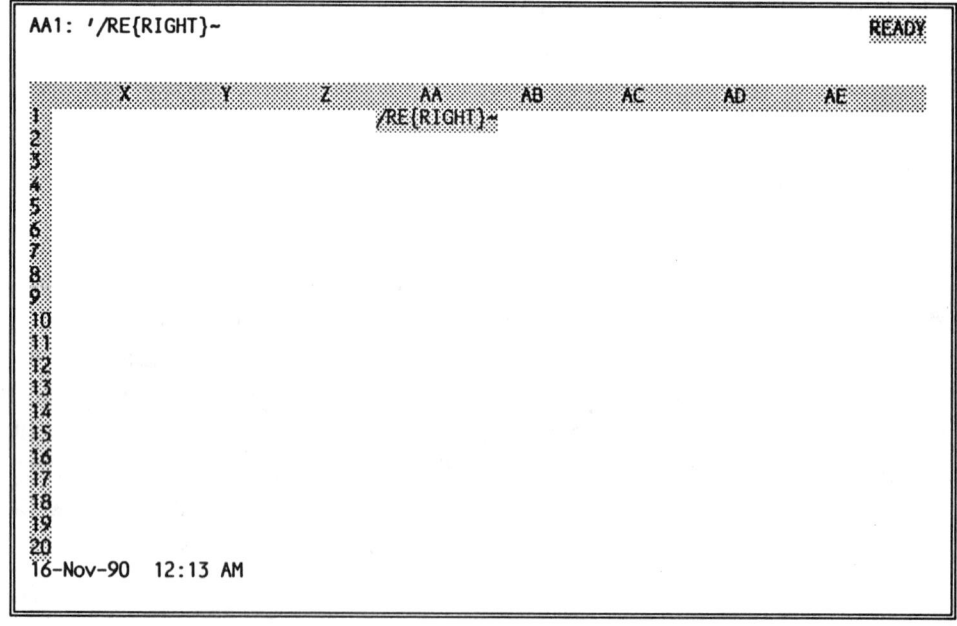

Figure 5-1 Example of Simple Macro

Naming Macros

To be able to execute the keystrokes within a macro, you must first give the macro a name. The rules are very specific for naming macros:

- Macros are named with a backslash (\) and one letter (for example, \K). The only exception to this rule is the AUTOEXEC macro, which is named \0. An AUTOEXEC macro is one that will execute automatically anytime the file containing the macro is retrieved into 1-2-3.
- Only the first cell of the macro is given a macro name. Even though a macro may cover dozens, or even hundreds, of lines, only the first cell of the macro is given a macro name.

Assuming you wanted to name your macro \M, you would simply give the cell AA1 the range name \M. Notice in Figure 5-2 that cell Z1 has the macro name in it. We have placed the macro name in the cell to the left only for documentation. You will find that if you write many macros, it is easy to forget which name you used. Documenting macro names just to the left of the first cell is therefore a good habit to adopt.

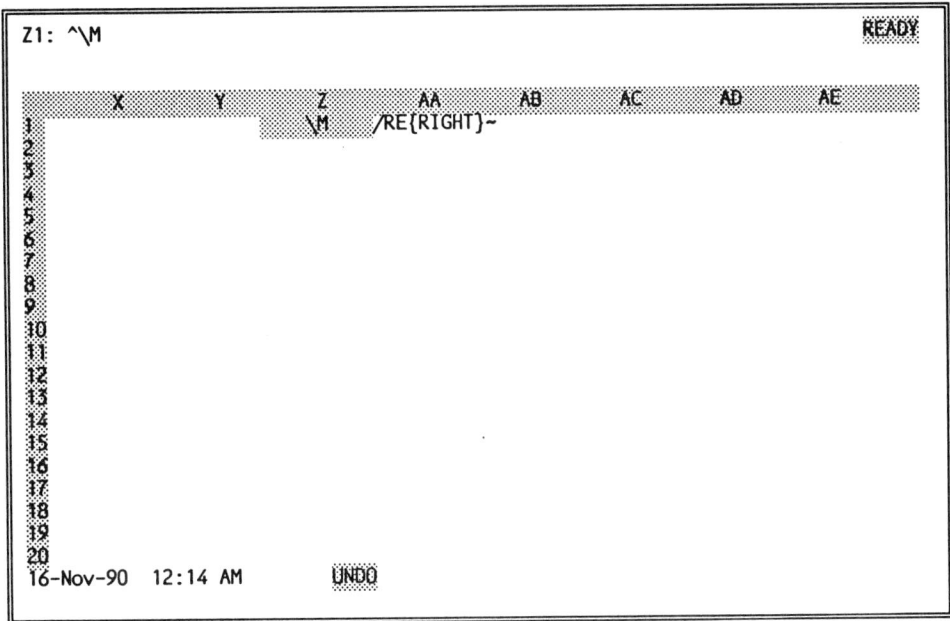

Figure 5-2 Documentation of the Macro Name

Executing Macros

You are now ready to execute the macro. Assume you have some data stored in a worksheet as shown in Figure 5-3. You would like to erase the data in cells B10 and C10. Place the cursor on cell B10 and invoke the macro by holding down the **ALT** key and pressing the letter of the macro's name. In our example, this means you hold down the **ALT** key and then press the letter **M**. Notice that the two cells are erased, and your spreadsheet appears as in Figure 5-4.

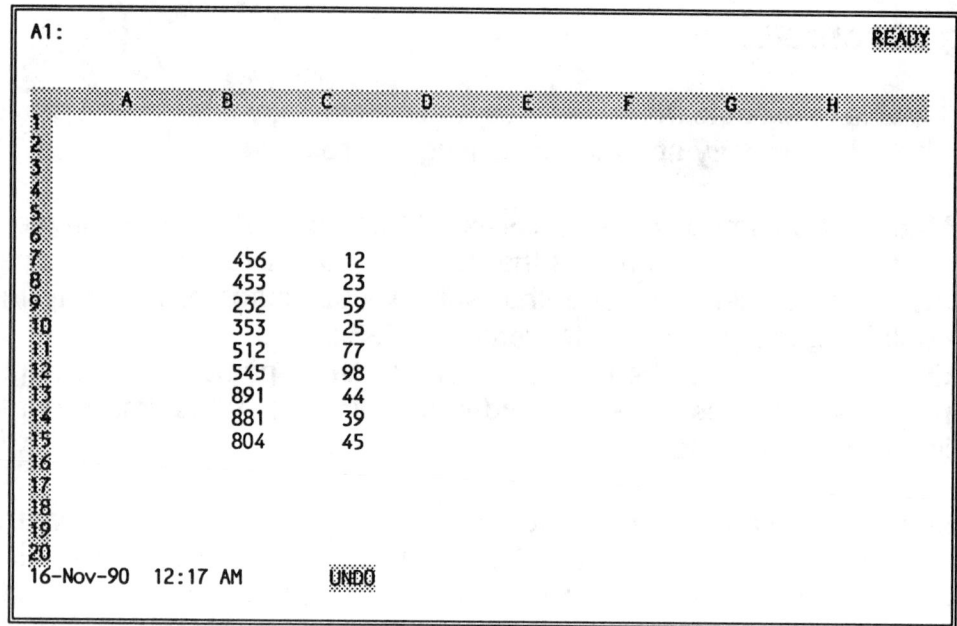

Figure 5-3 Sample Data

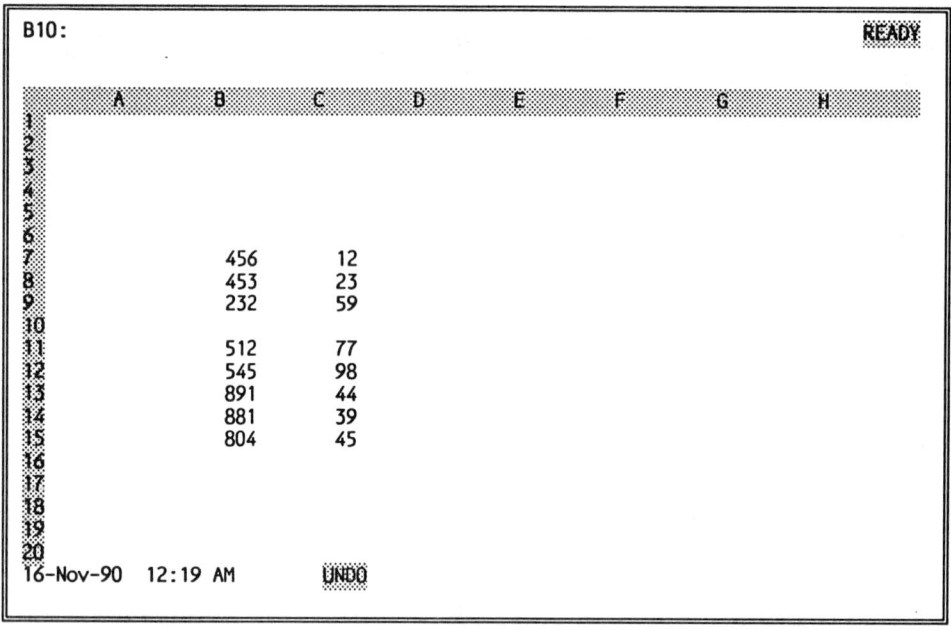

Figure 5-4 Sample Data After Executing Macro

INTERMEDIATE MACROS WITH MACRO COMMANDS

At this point, you should at least understand what a simple macro can do. While relatively lengthy keystroke storage macros could be created, the logical structure remains about the same. To design more sophisticated macros, you will need to incorporate some macro commands.

Testing and Branching

Macro commands are simply programming commands that are recognized by 1-2-3. These commands can be mixed among keystrokes within a macro, and in fact, most macros consist of a mixture of keystrokes and commands. Before presenting an example in which macro commands are used, let's first examine two of the more common macro commands that will be used in the example, {BRANCH} and {IF}.

The {BRANCH} statement simply tells 1-2-3 to continue processing at some other location. Remember that the {BRANCH} command has nothing to do with the cursor movement. It only continues processing of the macro at some specified location.

The {IF} statement tests a condition and then takes action accordingly. If the condition is true, then 1-2-3 will continue processing the remaining commands in the cell in which the {IF} statement is stored. If the statement is false, then 1-2-3 immediately continues processing at the cell immediately below the cell containing the {IF} statement.

A Sample Macro

To illustrate these two commands, assume you had an inventory system as shown in Figure 5-5. You would like to test whether the Ending Balance is less than the Beginning Balance. If it is, you would like to write the word "DECLINE" in the column titled Notes.

```
C2: [W13]                                                           READY

       A              B            C          D          E          F
 1
 2
 3   Inventory   Beginning                            Ending
 4    Number      Balance    Purchases     Sales      Balance    Notes
 5   14-24389        45          23          12          56
 6   14-25091       144           5          17         132
 7   14-25603       207          89          75         221
 8   14-70912        67          12          45          34
 9   14-70994        92           8           3          97
10   15-86508      5509        1208        2017        4700
11   15-88461      6001        1577        1644        5934
12   17-55879        14           2           5          11
13   17-59835        18           5           3          20
14   17-88013        29           1           7          23
15
16
17
18
19
20
13-Nov-90   01:16 AM          UNDO
```

Figure 5-5 Inventory Spreadsheet

There are many ways to approach this problem, but we will focus on only one. We will first present the entire macro and then discuss each line of the macro and its logic. The macro for this problem is shown in Figure 5-6.

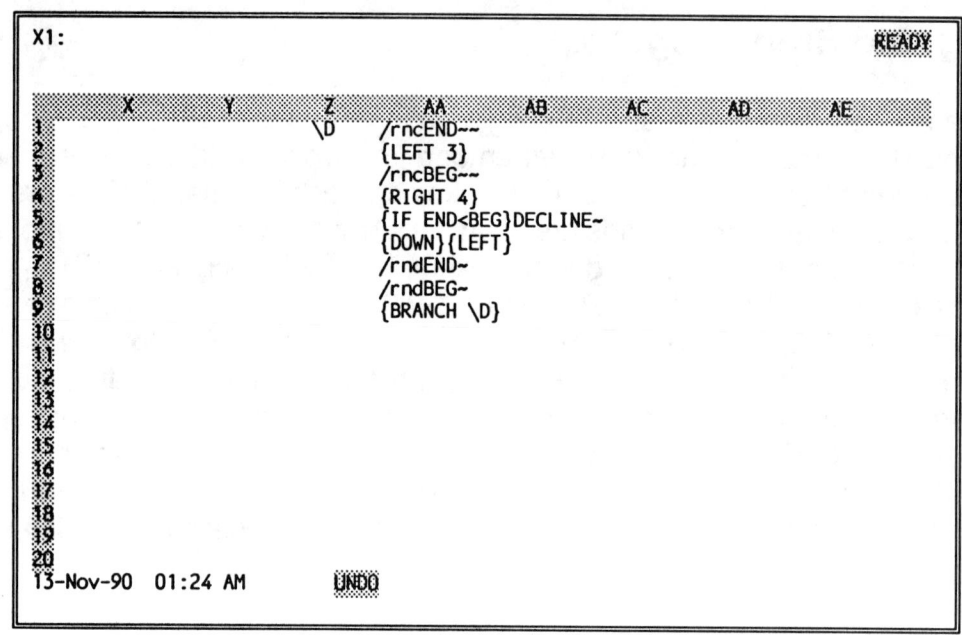

Figure 5-6 Inventory Macro

The first thing you may notice about the macro is that it spans numerous cells down a column. The rule 1-2-3 follows in executing macros is that it will continue processing down from one cell to another until it reaches a blank cell. In this example, we have given the cell AA1 the range name \D. Upon invoking the macro, 1-2-3 will execute all of the cells down the column until it hits a blank cell. (Note that because the last cell contains a {BRANCH} command, 1-2-3 will never encounter a blank cell. The macro does generate an endless loop, the solution for which is discussed later.)

In order for the macro to execute properly, we are assuming the user will first place the cursor on cell E5 and then invoke the macro. The first line of the macro is as follows:

/rncEND˜˜

This line simply contains the series of keystrokes necessary to create a range name of END wherever the cursor is located. If the user starts in cell E5, then that cell will receive the range name of END.

At this point you may be wondering why we are using range names at all. Instead, you may think the exact cell references could be used. Notice, however, that if exact cell references were used, the macro would not work for the cells in row 6, row 7, and so forth. Using temporary range names gives the macro some flexibility.

The next two lines of the program (1) move the cursor to the Beginning Balance column and (2) give that cell the range name BEG. The next line simply moves the cursor to the Notes field in anticipation of inserting the word DECLINE, if appropriate.

Line 5 contains the {IF} statement, which reads as follows:

$$\{IF END < BEG\}DECLINE^\sim$$

This statement tests the condition END<BEG. If the Ending Balance is indeed less than the Beginning Balance, then the remainder of the cell is executed. That is, the word "DECLINE" will be entered into the cell where the cursor is located. If END is not less than BEG, then the remainder of the cell is not executed (DECLINE is not typed into the current cell).

The next few lines of the macro are getting the macro ready to run through the test again for the next row in the data base. To do this, the cursor is first moved to the Ending Balance field of the next row. Then each of the range names END and BEG are deleted, because they will be used again for the next row. Finally, the {BRANCH \D} command tells 1-2-3 to continue processing at the location with the range name \D, which is of course the first cell of the macro.

Stopping Macro Execution

Because, as was stated earlier, this macro is actually an endless loop, you should first know how to stop a macro that has already begun executing. You cease execution by holding down the **CTRL** key and then pressing the **BREAK** key. When you do this, you will hear a beep, and an ERROR message will appear in the upper right corner of the screen. Simply press the **ENTER** key, and you will be out of macro execution and back in READY mode.

After executing the macro described above, your database should appear as shown in Figure 5-7.

```
A1: [W11]                                                        READY

          A           B          C          D          E          F
 1
 2
 3      Inventory   Beginning                        Ending
 4      Number      Balance    Purchases   Sales     Balance    Notes
 5      14-24389        45         23        12          56
 6      14-25091       144          5        17         132 DECLINE
 7      14-25603       207         89        75         221
 8      14-70912        67         12        45          34 DECLINE
 9      14-70994        92          8         3          97
10      15-86508      5509       1208      2017        4700 DECLINE
11      15-88461      6001       1577      1644        5934 DECLINE
12      17-55879        14          2         5          11 DECLINE
13      17-59835        18          5         3          20
14      17-88013        29          1         7          23 DECLINE
15
16
17
18
19
20
13-Nov-90  01:26 AM          UNDO
```

Figure 5-7 Inventory Database After Executing Macro

Other Common Macro Commands

From reviewing the preceding example, you should now see how macro commands can be used to enhance the logic within a 1-2-3 macro. You should also have some understanding of how the {BRANCH} and {IF} commands work. We will now review some of the other common macro commands that you could likely incorporate in your macros. While we are presenting only a subset of all possible commands, you will find that once you master these commands, others are relatively easy to learn. The specific macro commands that we will be discussing in this section are:

1. {GETLABEL} - Allows label input from the user
2. {GETNUMBER} - Allows numeric input from the user
3. {MENUBRANCH} - Causes a custom-designed menu to be executed
4. {?} - Temporarily pauses execution of the macro until the user strikes the ENTER key
5. {BLANK} - Erases a range
6. {FOR} - Executes a range containing macro commands a specified number of times

{GETLABEL}

This command allows you to prompt the user within the control panel and then to receive the user's input to a specific range. The general format of the command is:

{GETLABEL *prompt,range*}

The prompt can be anything that you want to be displayed to the user at that particular point in the program. As a caution, you may want to always enclose the prompt in quotes; otherwise, be certain that you never end the prompt with blank cells.

When the prompt appears, 1-2-3 pauses until the user inputs some data and then strikes ENTER. The range is the place where the user's data will be stored. The range is usually one cell and can either be an exact cell reference or a range name.

To illustrate the {GETLABEL} command, assume you are wanting a user to input a password. When they input the password, it is stored in a location entitled PWORD. The macro should then test the user's password to see if it equals the approved password, which is "SWORDFISH." If the password is correct, then the macro branches to a location entitled NEXT1. Otherwise, the macro branches back to ask for another password to be input.

The macro is shown in Figure 5-8. Notice that the {GETLABEL} command is as follows:

{GETLABEL "Please enter the password: ",PWORD}

Since we want the prompt to be ended with blanks (which improves the appearance of the prompt when the macro is executed), we have enclosed it in blanks.

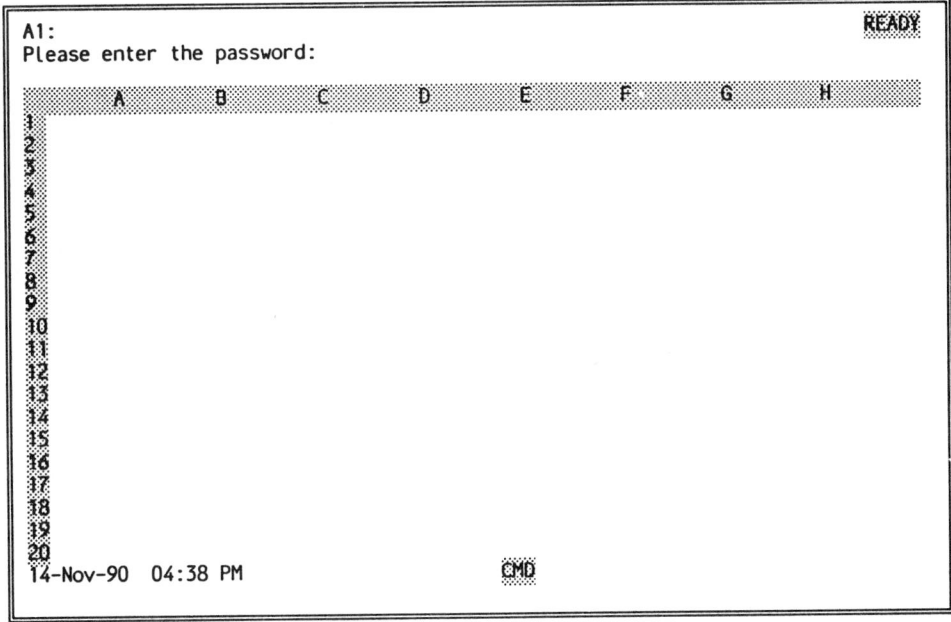

Figure 5-8 Password Macro

When the macro is executed, the prompt will appear in the control panel, as shown in Figure 5-9.

Figure 5-9 Prompt During Macro Execution

{GETNUMBER}

As you may imagine, the {GETNUMBER} command works exactly like the {GETLABEL} command, except the user's input is stored as a number rather than as a label. Therefore, the general format of the {GETNUMBER} command is:

{GETNUMBER *prompt,range*}

{MENUBRANCH}

1-2-3 allows you to custom design your own menus. These menus operate in exactly the same fashion as the menu that appears when you strike the slash (/) key. A primary strength of this feature is that you can design macros that are user-friendly for even those users with very little knowledge of 1-2-3.

The general format of the {MENUBRANCH} command is as follows:

{MENUBRANCH *range*}

The range argument in this command is the top left cell of a range containing the custom designed menu. As usual, the range can be either a range name or a specific cell reference. When 1-2-3 encounters a {MENUBRANCH} command, it branches to the specified location of the menu and causes that menu to appear in the control panel. When the user selects one of the options from the menu, control is passed to the cell two rows below the cell containing that menu option, and the macro proceeds from there.

Because the execution of a menu is somewhat difficult to envision, let's work through an example. Assume you wanted to have a menu at the beginning of a macro that allows a user to specify the program he or she wants to run. Further assume that the available programs are a payroll program, an inventory program, and a cash program. The menu would be typed into a range of cells as shown in Figure 5-10.

Notice that the first row contains the menu options. The next row contains the descriptions you want to appear whenever each menu option is highlighted (even though you cannot see the entire description on the screen, it will appear correctly when the menu is invoked). The third line contains the macro command that you want executed when the user selects that particular menu option. Once that macro command is executed, 1-2-3 continues executing commands down that column, just as in any other macro. To keep this area under the menu from appearing too cluttered, however, you may want to have only one command that branches execution to another location, where the appropriate series of commands can then be displayed in a somewhat neater fashion.

Now notice the spreadsheet in Figure 5-11. The {MENUBRANCH} command contained in cell AA1 is as follows:

{MENUBRANCH MNU1}

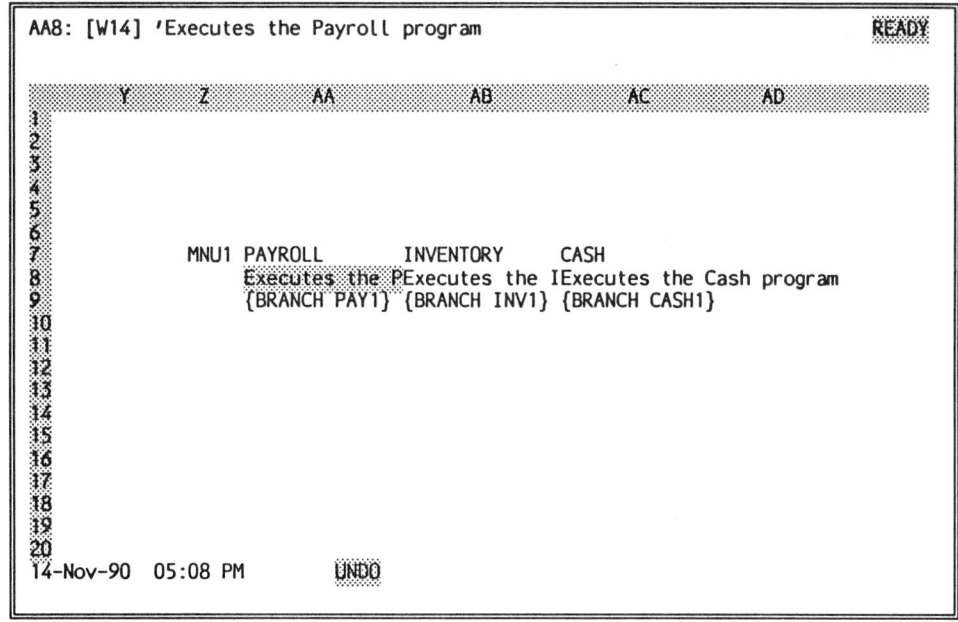

Figure 5-10 Menu Within Macro

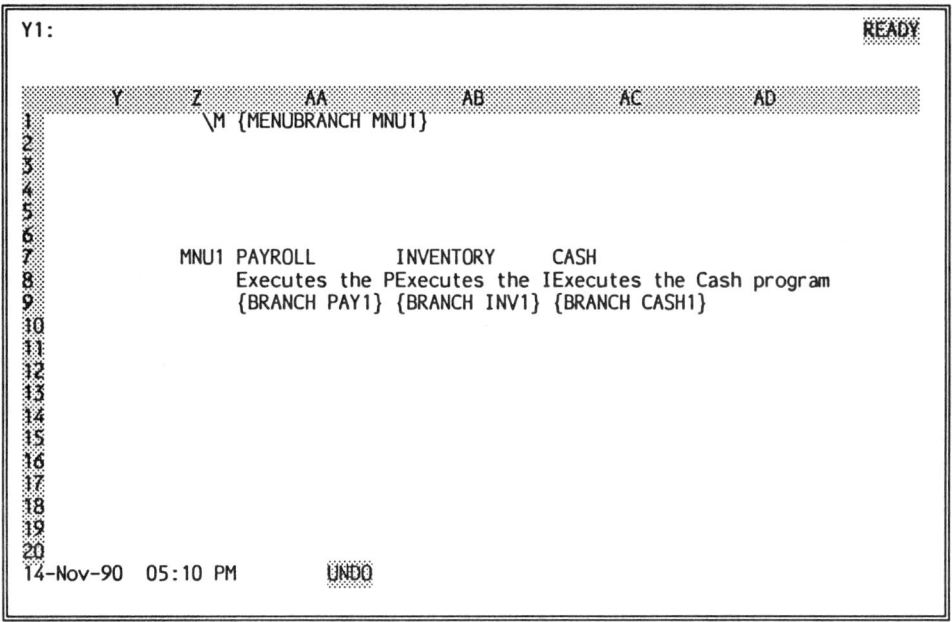

Figure 5-11 {MENUBRANCH} Command

The range name MNU1 has been assigned to the cell AA7. Therefore, when the macro is executed, the {MENUBRANCH} command will be the first line executed, and the menu will appear in the control panel, as shown in Figure 5-12. At this point, if the user selected the PAYROLL option, then the macro would continue processing at the range PAY1.

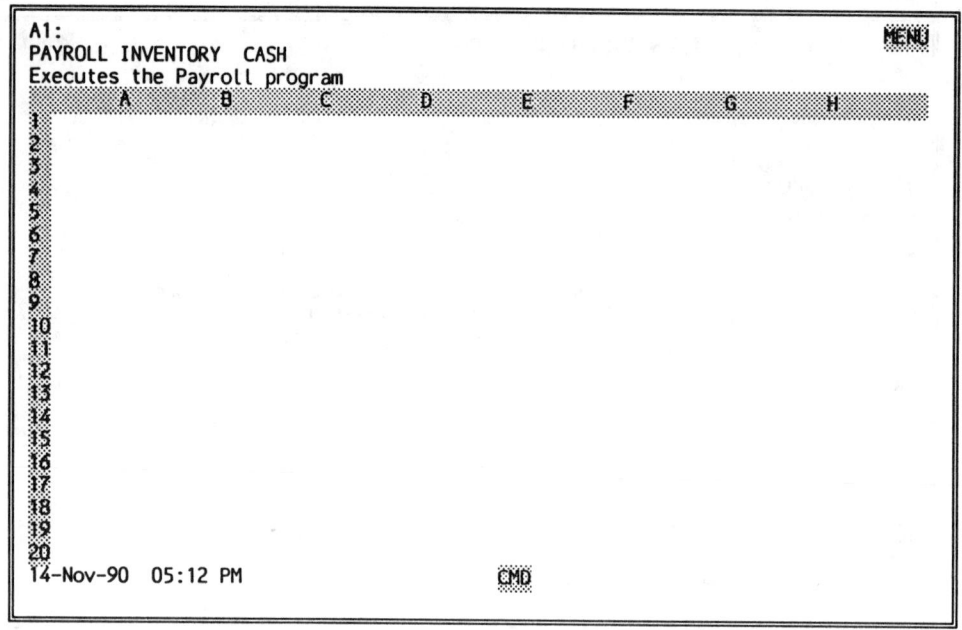

Figure 5-12 Menu Upon Executing Macro

{?}

This command causes 1-2-3 to pause until the user strikes the ENTER key. Whatever the user types will be stored in the cursor location. The {?} command is useful in designing user-friendly screens and for pausing within commands to accept user input.

For example, notice the macro in Figure 5-13. The first command simply causes the cursor to move to cell IP5. When the cursor goes to IP5, the screen appears as shown in Figure 5-14. The {?} then pauses execution of the macro at this point, allowing the user time to read the screen. The screen instructs the user to strike ENTER when he or she is ready to continue. After the user does strike ENTER, the macro proceeds. In this case, a menu would be the next thing to appear.

{BLANK}

This command works exactly like the /Range Erase command discussed previously. That is, the command causes a cell or a series of cells to be erased. The general format of the {BLANK} command is:

{BLANK *range*}

The range argument is simply the range to be erased.

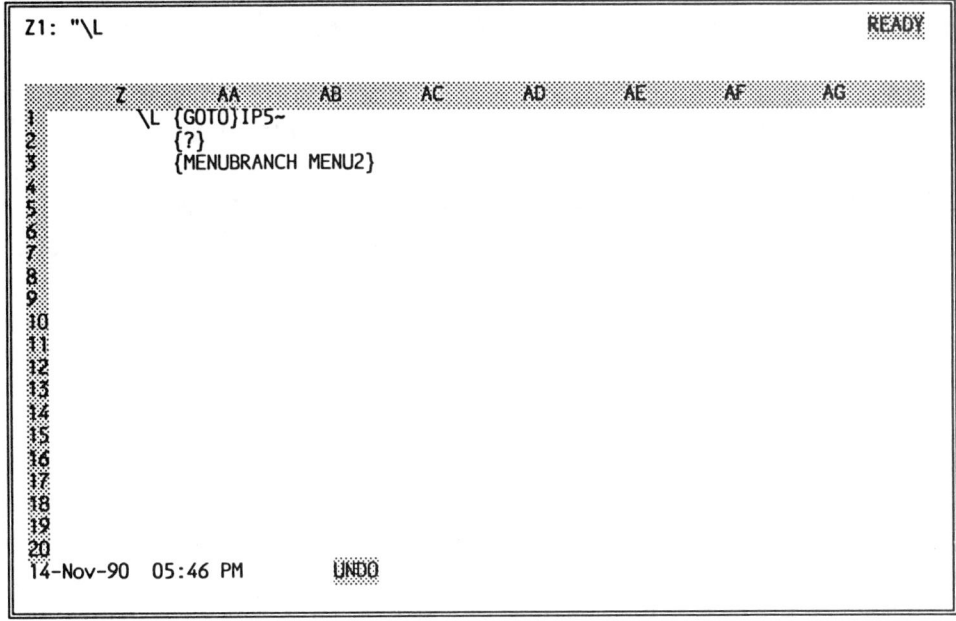

Figure 5-13 {?} Command

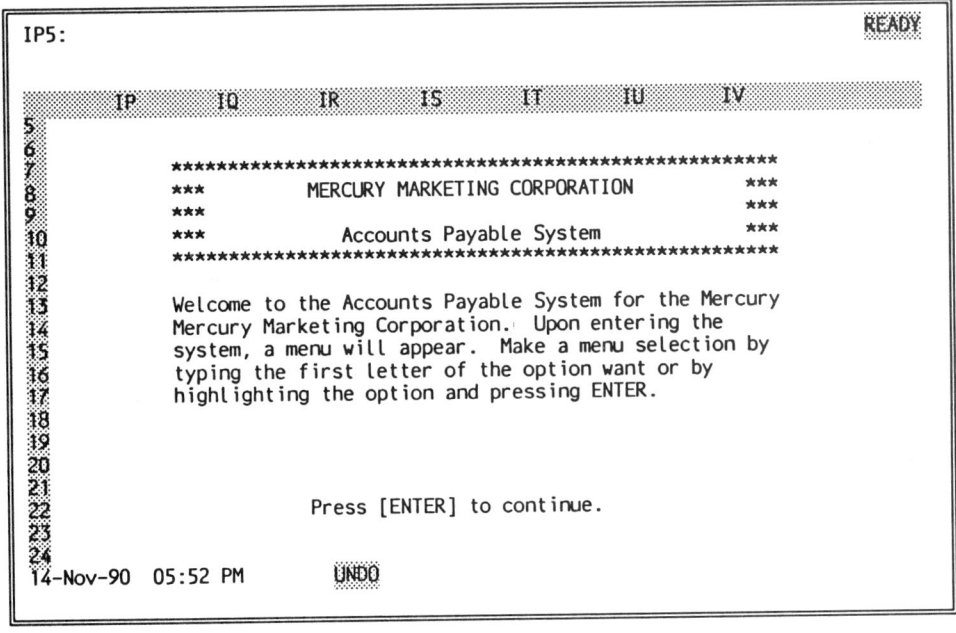

Figure 5-14 Screen Appearing During Macro Execution

{FOR}

The {FOR} command allows you to loop through commands a specified number of times (very much like a "DO LOOP" in some other languages). The general format for the {FOR} command is as follows:

{FOR *counter,beginning,ending,increment,range*}

Before proceeding to an example of the {FOR} command, you should first understand the purpose of each of the arguments. Each one is defined below:

- Counter - The range (specified by range name or cell location) where 1-2-3 should maintain the count of how many times the series of commands has been executed.
- Beginning - 1-2-3 must initialize the counter to some number. You specify this number with the "beginning" argument. For example, if you specify the number 5, then 1-2-3 will initialize the counter to 5.
- Ending - 1-2-3 must also know how many times you want the series of commands executed. This is accomplished through the "ending" argument. After executing the series of commands, 1-2-3 increments the counter and then tests whether the counter is greater than the ending argument. If the counter is greater than the ending number, then the execution if the {FOR} command is ceased, and the line following the {FOR} command is executed.
- Increment - As just mentioned, 1-2-3 increments the counter after each execution of the series of commands. The "increment" argument tells 1-2-3 how much to increment the counter each time.
- Range - This is the range name or cell location of the first cell in the series of commands to be executed.

Assume you have a budget spreadsheet as shown in Figure 5-15. Actually, the screen in Figure 5-15 shows only the first five cities; there are 14 cities across the entire spreadsheet. Notice that the amounts have been put in the cells, but they have not been formatted. You would like to format the first cell in each column to currency with 0 decimal places. Each of the other cells in the column (before the NET figure) you would like to have formatted as comma (,) with 0 decimal places. Then, you would like to have the NET figure formatted as currency with 0 decimal places.

To accomplish this formatting for each column, you could set up the appropriate commands for formatting one column and then simply have those commands executed 14 times. To have them executed 14 times requires a {FOR} command.

The final macro would appear as shown in Figure 5-16. The {FOR} command in the macro appears as follows:

{FOR CNTR,1,14,1,LOOP}

```
A1: [W13]                                                          READY

          A     B    C      D    E    F     G    H    I    J    K    L
 1                          ACE CONSULTING GROUP
 2                          1993 BUDGET PROJECTIONS
 3
 4         ----------  ------- ------- ------- ------- --------
 5                    CHICAGO  PHOENIX  PHILA   L A   SAN FRAN
 6         ----------  ------- ------- ------- ------- --------
 7    BILLINGS         39690   26100   31050   50160   23670
 8    PROF. EXP.       29250   18720   22620   35670   16500
 9    TRAVEL            2550    2140    2490    3210    2310
10    OFFICE STAFF      1620    1150    1530    1890    1200
11    CLERICAL           204     129     174     195     165
12    MARKETING          450     270     279     627     360
13    SUPPLIES           168     120     123     207     102
14    RENT               495     294     297     612     381
15    UTILITIES           69      45      54      72      57
16    MISC.               42      27      33      78      21
17         ----------  ------- ------- ------- ------- --------
18    NET               4842    3205    3450    7599    2574
19         ==========  ======= ======= ======= ======= ========
20
15-Nov-90   12:35 AM         UNDO
```

Figure 5-15 Budget Spreadsheet

```
Y1:                                                               READY

          Y        Z       AA       AB      AC      AD      AE      AF
 1                 \B  {GOTO}C7~
 2                     {FOR CNTR,1,14,1,LOOP}
 3
 4
 5
 6             LOOP  /RFC0~~
 7                   {DOWN}
 8                   /RF,0~{DOWN 8}~
 9                   {DOWN 10}
10                   /RFC0~~
11                   {RIGHT 2}
12                   {UP 11}
13
14
15
16             CNTR
17
18
19
20
15-Nov-90   12:37 AM         UNDO
```

Figure 5-16 {FOR} Command

The CNTR argument is the range name for cell AA16, where 1-2-3 is to maintain its counter. The counter is to start at the number 1, increment by 1 each time, and stop when the counter exceeds 14. The commands that are to be executed during each cycle begin at cell AA6 which has been given the range name LOOP. When the {FOR} command is finished, the macro would then hit the blank cell just below the {FOR} command and would therefore stop. After the macro has been run, your budget data would be formatted correctly, as illustrated in Figure 5-17.

```
A1: [W13]                                                              READY

         A      B     C      D      E     F      G     H     I      J    K   L
1                        ACE CONSULTING GROUP
2                        1993 BUDGET PROJECTIONS
3
4
5  _____       CHICAGO  PHOENIX  PHILA    L A    SAN FRAN
6  -----------       -------  -------  -------  -------  --------
7  BILLINGS          $39,690  $26,100  $31,050  $50,160  $23,670
8  PROF. EXP.         29,250   18,720   22,620   35,670   16,500
9  TRAVEL              2,550    2,140    2,490    3,210    2,310
10 OFFICE STAFF        1,620    1,150    1,530    1,890    1,200
11 CLERICAL              204      129      174      195      165
12 MARKETING             450      270      279      627      360
13 SUPPLIES              168      120      123      207      102
14 RENT                  495      294      297      612      381
15 UTILITIES              69       45       54       72       57
16 MISC.                  42       27       33       78       21
17 -----------       -------  -------  -------  -------  --------
18 NET                $4,842   $3,205   $3,450   $7,599   $2,574
19                 =========================================
20
15-Nov-90  12:39 AM        UNDO
```

Figure 5-17 Budget Spreadsheet After Executing Macro

UNDERSTANDING ADVANCED MACRO DESIGN

While some of the macro commands discussed thus far may seem relatively difficult, you will find that macro sophistication is a function of the macro's logical design rather than of the commands themselves. When designing these advanced macros, you must follow good programming techniques, such as:

1. Keep the user in mind - If your user is someone with little or no knowledge of 1-2-3, you must design the macro to be very user-friendly. Making a macro user-friendly usually requires that you view the macro as a closed system. That is, the macro starts running immediately upon entry to the file (using the \0 macro name); the macro is completely interactive with menus, prompts, and information screens; and the macro exits the file automatically.

2. Design in modules - A sophisticated macro can easily achieve a length of hundreds of lines. You should therefore view the macro as a series of modules with each module being a set of logically related commands. For example, each menu should only be three rows long, with the third row simply a {BRANCH} command for each option.

3. Have a "driver" module - Any lengthy program should have a section that "calls" or initiates the other portions of the program. This main section is sometimes called a driver. With 1-2-3 macros, the driver may very well be a main menu, from which other submenus and commands follow.

Remember that designing advanced macros is not a matter of having complex macro commands (although a thorough understanding of all macro commands facilitates their design). Instead, the advanced macros require that you think through the procedures you want to accomplish and then placing those procedures in a logical sequence. Once the logical structure of the macro is developed, the actual coding of the macro commands is relatively simple.

CONTROL CONSIDERATIONS

Macros present control risks in a number of ways. First, you must be concerned that the macro is designed properly, without errors (or "bugs"). Second, once the macro is designed, you want to be certain that it runs the same way every time. This requires restricting user access to the macro itself. Third, you may want to restrict access to certain users. Alternatively, you may want to restrict access to various portions of the macro (such as certain menu options). Finally, you will want to be certain that the macro can be reviewed and/or updated with relative ease. Each of these four risk areas can be easily address with appropriate controls.

Debugging the Macro

When you first design and input a macro, you will want to test it. Upon testing it, you may find that it contains some errors. The problem, especially with longer macros, is oftentimes simply finding the location of the error. The greatest debugging tool in this situation is to run the macro in STEP mode.

STEP mode allows you to proceed through your macro one command or keystroke at a time. This way, you can easily see the result of each command and keystroke and therefore find the error. To invoke STEP mode, you first hold down the **ALT** key and then press **F2**. You will notice the word STEP appearing in the bottom portion of your screen. Next, you execute the macro in the normal way, by holding down the ALT key and pressing the letter corresponding to the macro name. To proceed through the macro one command or keystroke at a time, you simply press any key on the keyboard. Continue pressing keys until you have discovered the error or reached the end of the macro. If you decide you want to exit STEP mode, simply press **ALT** and **F2** again and press a key.

Restricting Access to the Macro Itself

For various reasons, you may not want the user stopping the macro while it is running. Furthermore, you may not want the user to see the actual commands as they are executing. You can accomplish these objectives by using the following commands:

- {BREAKOFF} - When this command is placed in a macro, the user cannot use CTRL-BREAK to stop the macro. To allow use of CTRL-BREAK once {BREAKOFF} has been used, you can insert the {BREAKON} command.
- {WINDOWSOFF} - This command freezes the portion of the screen below the control panel at its current state even though the macro continues executing. The user therefore does not see what the macro is doing. Another screen cannot be displayed until the {WINDOWSON} command is invoked.
- {PANELOFF} - This command is very similar to the {WINDOWSOFF} command except that it freezes the control panel. Another control panel cannot be displayed until the {PANELON} command is invoked.

Restricting Access to the Macro or Its Components

At times, you may want only certain users to have access to your macro. Alternatively, you may want to restrict access to certain menu options. The best way to provide restricted access is through passwords. As noted in a previous example, you can have the macro prompt the user for a password by using a {GETLABEL} command and then simply testing the user's input against an authorized password. While this method does have its limitations and can be circumvented, it does provide control in certain settings (such as where users are not familiar with 1-2-3).

Documentation

If you design a relatively lengthy macro, you will likely find that it later needs reviewing, updating, or debugging. You will also likely find that you have forgotten the intricacies of the program. You should therefore properly document virtually every line of your macro so that you, or someone else, can easily review the macro without attempting to understand all the keystrokes and commands.

REVIEW QUESTIONS

1. What are the rules for naming macros?

2. Where should a macro be located in the spreadsheet?

3. How is a macro executed?

4. What is an AUTOEXEC macro?

5. Describe three ways that you can stop a macro?

6. How many times will the following {FOR} command process the commands located at LOOP2?

{FOR CNTR2,5,15,2,LOOP2}

7. What is STEP mode, and how is it generally used?

8. How does the {BREAKOFF} command provide control?

9. How does the {IF} statement operate?

10. {GOTO} is often confused with {BRANCH}. Explain their specific functions.

11. Why might you use quotation marks around the prompt in a {GETLABEL} or {GETNUMBER} command?

12. How can the {?} command be used to make a macro more user-friendly?

13. When you design a menu, what is entered on the second row?

14. What does {WINDOWSOFF} accomplish?

15. What does {PANELOFF} accomplish?

CASE: Sierra Clothing Outlet
Accounts Payable Database System
(The Expenditure Cycle)

Sierra Clothing Outlet sells outdoor sport clothing to the public. The majority of the clothing is either factory seconds or closeouts from other stores and can therefore be sold for 30-50% below normal retail prices. The store is owned by Beverly Whitaker and Sarah Davis. Sarah provided the majority of the initial capital; Beverly performs most of the day-to-day managerial duties. Beverly has placed the Accounts Payable database on Lotus 1-2-3 and even uses some of the database features of 1-2-3 to sort and query the database. The database (which is contained in the file titled SIERRA.WK1 on your student diskette) is simply a list of the invoices that have been received along with a reference to the invoices' accompanying Purchase Order number, Receiving Report number, and other pertinent data.

Requirements

Ms. Whitaker is finding the repeated execution of the appropriate database commands to be very cumbersome. She would therefore like for you to design a macro that will perform the following functions:

1. Sort the database by Vendor Name
2. Sort the database by Purchase Order number
3. Extract all Invoice numbers and amounts pertaining to an individual vendor

To make the macro more user-friendly, she would also like for you to make it menu driven.

Solution

As noted in the section pertaining to advanced macro design, you should first imagine the logical structure of the macro. For this case, the logical structure may be described as follows:

Prompt the user with a menu containing the following options:

    a. SORT - Selecting this option causes a submenu to appear with the following options:
       i. VENDOR - Selecting this option causes the data base to be sorted by Vendor Name and then returns the macro to the original menu.
       ii. PO - Selecting this option causes the data base to be sorted by Purchase Order number and then returns the macro to the original menu.
    b. EXTRACT - Selecting this option results in the following:
       i. A prompt appears asking which Vendor's invoices the user would like to see.
       ii. After the user inputs the name, the macro should extract the appropriate Invoice Numbers and Amounts.
       iii. The extracted data is displayed on the screen.
       iv. The macro returns to the original menu.
    c. QUIT - Selecting this option simply causes the macro to stop.

The opening lines of the macro along with the primary menu are shown in Figure 5-18. Notice that the SORT option has a {MENUBRANCH} that invokes the submenu SORTMENU, the EXTRACT option has a {BRANCH} for continuing execution at EXTRCT, and the QUIT option simply has the macro command {QUIT}, which stops execution of the macro.

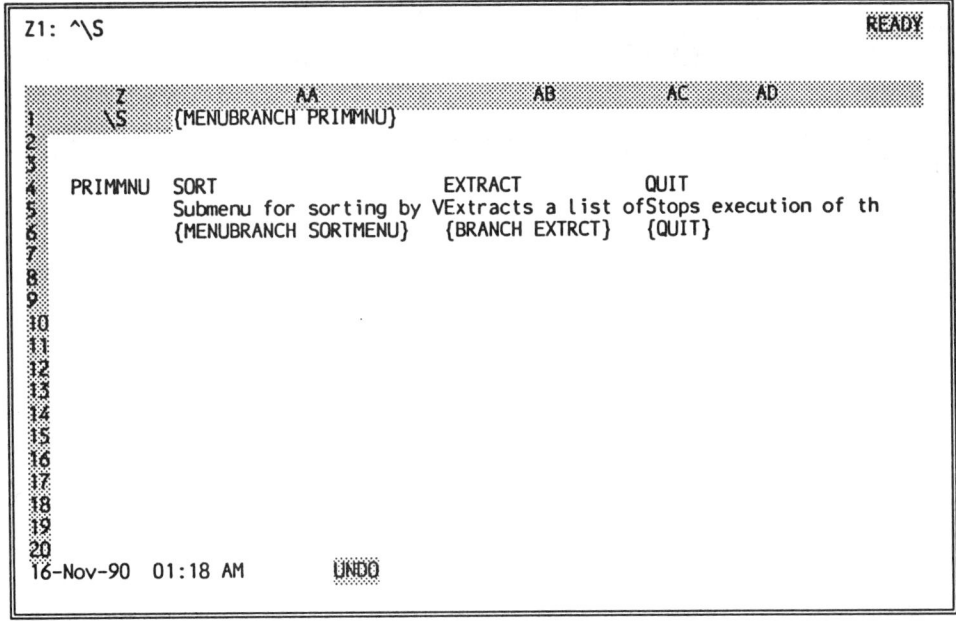

Figure 5-18 Primary Menu for Sierra Macro

Figure 5-19 shows the SORTMENU and its associated routines. Notice that after each of the sort routines, a {MENUBRANCH} returns the macro to the primary menu.

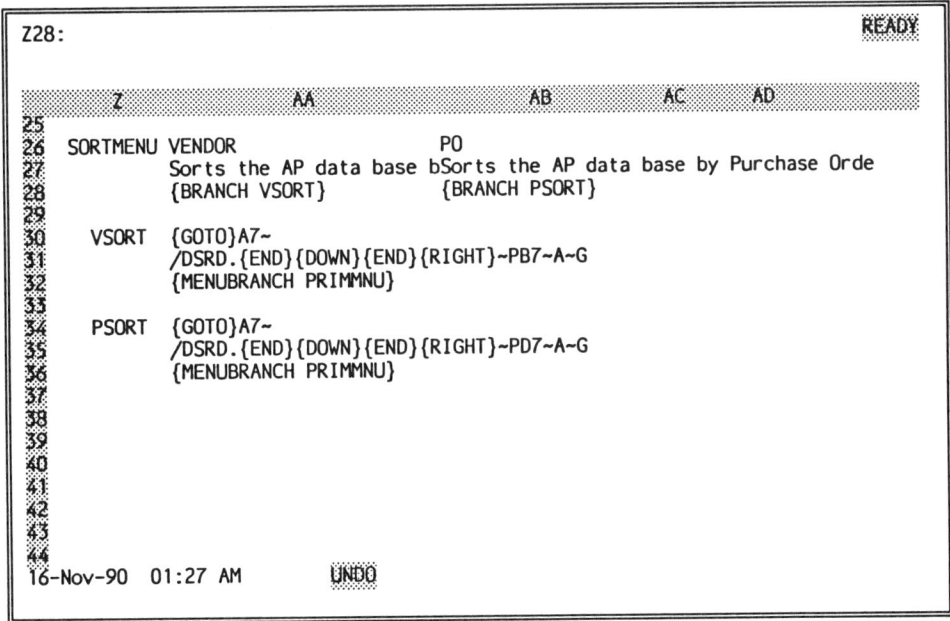

Figure 5-19 Sort Menu for Sierra Macro

The EXTRCT routine is shown in Figure 5-20. Most of the commands in this routine are straightforward; however, the design of the Criteria range may be somewhat confusing. The first line of the macro prompts the user for the Vendor's Name and places it in a cell with the range name VNAME. VNAME is the second cell in the Criteria range (which is entitled CRANGE). That is, CRANGE comprises the cells K1..K2, and cell K2 is named VNAME. Figure 5-21 shows sample output for WOOLY SUPPLIERS.

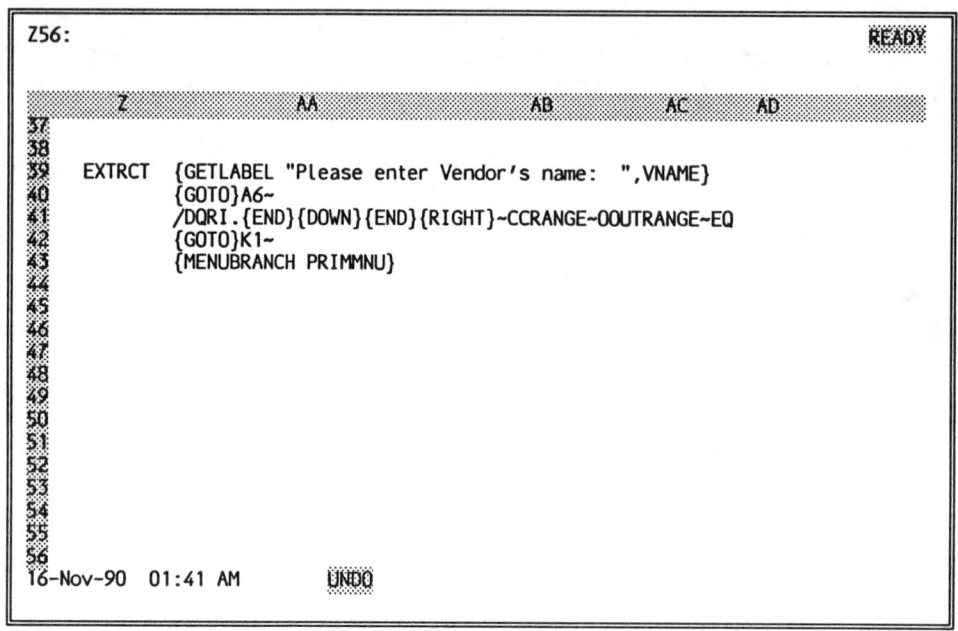

Figure 5-20 Extract Routine for Sierra Macro

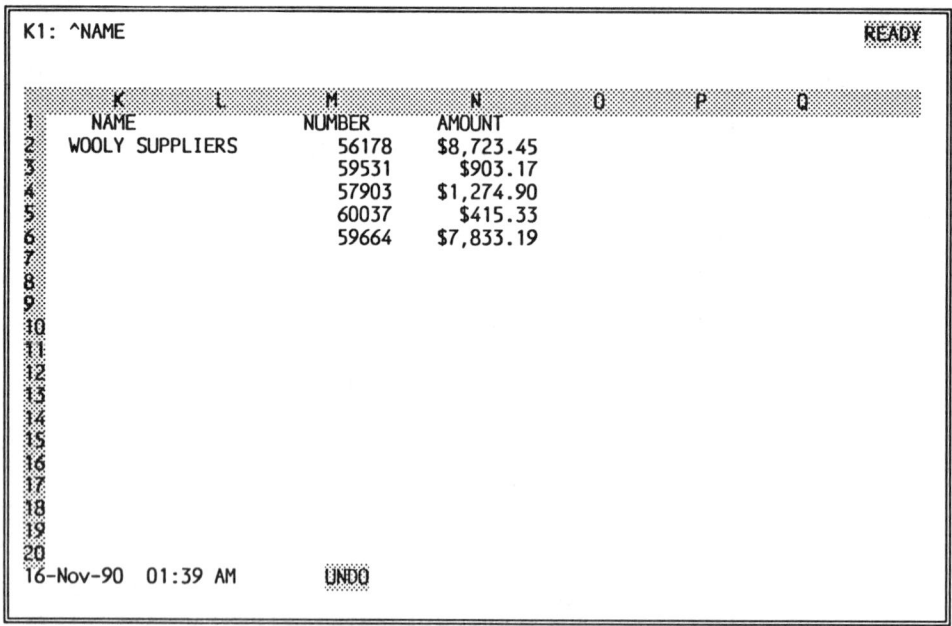

Figure 5-21 Sample Output for Sierra Macro

FOLLOW-UP
CASE: Herrington Furniture Store
Accounts Payable Database System
(The Expenditure Cycle)

Robert Herrington's father began the Herrington Furniture Store in 1957. His father is retired, and Robert now operates the business. The Herringtons have always prided themselves on carrying only quality furniture and have therefore represented only a few furniture manufacturers over the years.

Robert recently put the Accounts Payable data on a Lotus 1-2-3 spreadsheet (contained in the file HERNGTON.WK1 on your student disk). The spreadsheet simply lists each of the outstanding Invoice Numbers, the Vendor's Number (assigned by Herrington), the Amount Due, and other appropriate information. Whenever Mr. Herrington pays an invoice, he simply places a * in the cell just to the left of the Invoice Number.

Requirements

Mr. Herrington would like for you to design a macro that will assist him in the following ways:

1. Sort the database by Vendor Number, with Invoice Amount as a secondary-key.
2. Sort the database by Invoice Amount (in descending order).
3. Extract all invoices over a certain amount. That is, the macro should prompt the user for an amount and then extract any invoices with an amount due greater than that amount specified by the user. (Hint: you may want to consider using a Criteria range formula such as **+D7>$AMT**, where AMT is the range containing the user's input amount. The dollar sign is necessary in the Criteria range formula in order for the Extract to work properly.)

The macro should contain menus, prompts, and any other appropriate user-friendly devices.

ASSIGNMENT
CASE: Walker Wholesale
Cash Receipts System
(The Revenue Cycle)

In Chapter 4, you generated certain reports for Walker Wholesale's Cash Receipts Transaction File. Mr. Walker would now like for you to develop a Cash Receipts

Transaction System that would allow them to easily add to the Cash Receipts Transaction File and to make certain generic queries.

Requirements

Using the WALKER2.WK1 file on you student diskette, write a macro program, as outlined below:

1. The program should open with a menu that has the following options:

   ADD   DELETE   SORT   QUIT

2. If the user selects ADD from the opening menu, the macro should allow a new record to be added to the Cash Receipts Transaction File. For each item, the user should be prompted (using a GETLABEL or a GETNUMBER command). After the user adds a new record, the macro should return to the opening menu.

3. If the user selects DELETE from the opening menu, then the user should be prompted for an Invoice number. The macro should ask the user, **Are you sure (Y or N)?** If the user responds with **N**, the macro should return to the opening menu. If the user responds with **Y**, the macro should then delete the record pertaining to that invoice from the Cash Receipts Transaction File (using the Delete option from the /Data Query menu). After deleting the record, the macro should return to the opening menu.

4. If the user selects SORT, the following submenu should appear:

   INVOICE   DATE   AMOUNT

5. If the user selects INVOICE from the submenu, then the Cash Receipts Transaction File should be sorted by Invoice # (in ascending order). After the file has been sorted, the macro should return to the opening menu.

6. If the user selects DATE from the submenu, then the Cash Receipts Transaction File should be sorted by Date (in descending order). After the file has been sorted, the macro should return to the opening menu.

7. If the user selects AMOUNT from the submenu, then the Cash Receipts Transaction File should be sorted by Amount (in descending order). After the file has been sorted, the macro should return to the opening menu.

8. If the user selects QUIT from the opening menu, then the macro should simply stop running.

ASSIGNMENT
CASE: Crusher Tennis Equipment
Customer Master File Maintenance System
(The Revenue Cycle)

In Chapter 4, you performed some sort and query tasks for Crusher Tennis Equipment. Crusher would like you to write a Lotus 1-2-3 macro that will help them to maintain their Customer Master File.

Requirements

Using the CRUSHER2.WK1 file on your student diskette, write a macro program as outlined below:

1. The macro should open with a menu that has the following options:

    INPUT   CHANGE   QUIT

2. If the user selects INPUT from the opening menu, the macro should allow the user to add a new record to the Customer Master File (using a series of GETLABEL and GETNUMBER commands). After adding the record, the macro should return to the opening menu.
3. If the user selects CHANGE from the opening menu, then a submenu should appear with the following options:

    ADDRESS   ZIP_CODE   CREDIT

4. If the user selects ADDRESS from the submenu, the macro should (1) prompt the user for a customer number, (2) extract the record for that customer, (3) delete the record from the file (leaving the extracted record in the Output region, (4) prompt the user for a new address, and (5) place the extracted record with the changed address back in the file (at the bottom of the file). After this routine, the macro should return to the opening menu.
5. If the user selects ZIP_CODE from the submenu, the macro should (1) prompt the user for a customer number, (2) extract the record for that customer, (3) delete the record from the file (leaving the extracted record in the Output region, (4) prompt the user for a zip code, and (5) place the extracted record with the changed zip code back in the file (at the bottom of the file). After this routine, the macro should return to the opening menu.
6. If the user selects CREDIT from the submenu, the macro should (1) prompt the user for a customer number, (2) extract the record for that customer, (3) delete the record from the file (leaving the extracted record in the Output region, (4) prompt the user for a credit limit, and (5) place the extracted record with the

changed credit limit back in the file (at the bottom of the file). After this routine, the macro should return to the opening menu.

7. If the user selects **Q**UIT from the opening menu, then the macro should simply stop running.

PART II:

DATABASE SOFTWARE
Applied to AIS Cases

CHAPTER 6

DESIGNING AN ACCOUNTING DATABASE USING A DATABASE MANAGEMENT SYSTEM

INTRODUCTION

The purpose of this chapter is to introduce you to the particular database management system (DBMS) package you will be using for the database exercises. We will look at the basic operations of the package and learn the fundamentals of the menu structures. In addition, we will construct a database, learn how to modify the database structure, input data to the database, and discuss how to maintain the individual records that comprise the data files. Finally, the chapter will introduce the case that will be utilized throughout the database chapters.

CASE: Stroudsburg Toy Company

Stroudsburg Toy Company is a large retail store located in Williamsburg, Virginia that carries a full line of toys, games, and books for children of all ages. The store was first opened in 1957 by Tom Jackson and has had steady growth for the past 33 years. Tom would like to start easing off in his day to day management of the business and have his son Bill take on more responsibilities. Bill has just graduated from college with a degree in accounting. For the past 4 years, Bill has worked summers at the store as well as during semester breaks. He has gotten to know the entire business, from stocking shelves and working the register to dealing with suppliers and keeping the books.

Bill is excited about the opportunity to get more involved in the actual management of the store. However, he feels that in many respects the business is still operated as if it were the 1950s. While he is proud of what his father has accomplished, he feels it is necessary to modernize some aspects of the business if it is to continue its success. As one of his top priorities, Bill would like to acquire a microcomputer system that could help improve productivity as well as provide useful information for running the business.

The first area of the business that Bill would like to computerize is inventory. Stroudsburg carries literally hundreds of different products and has always kept track of it by recording on a list each item that is sold. At the end of the day, that amount is subtracted from the previous balance. While this has proved satisfactory, it is time-consuming and subject to errors. Bill feels that his first task should be to set up files for the inventory so that items can be added, deleted, and updated as necessary. He has asked you, a friend from college familiar with computers, to assist him in this task.

Before rushing to the computer, you need to plan what your requirements are. This is done as part of the systems analysis and design phases discussed in your AIS textbook. We will assume that this work has been completed and you are now at the implementation phase. You are not going to put the entire inventory system on the computer at first, but just a small-scale working model of the system known as a *prototype*.

After completing the systems design phase, you determined that three files were necessary to handle the inventory function. You will be referring to these 3 files as:

1. Inventory Master File
2. Inventory Transaction File
3. Inventory History File

We will refer to the collection of these three files as the *Inventory Database*. Your task now is to set up these three files. The following sections will describe how this is to be done, and it is recommended that you follow along with the instructions while at a computer workstation. The instructions are designed to lead you step by step through the creation of the inventory files. Make sure you complete the tutorial since you will be using these files in later chapters.

CASE SOLUTION (dBASE IV)

Introduction

Before starting dBASE IV, make sure you have a newly-formatted floppy diskette. A high density 3.5 inch diskette is highly recommended. It is also recommended that you create a subdirectory on your floppy diskette, perhaps naming the subdirectory DBASE.

Since there are a variety of ways in which dBASE may be accessed, it is not possible to offer one universal method to start the software program. The best advice is to check with your instructor as to how to start dBASE IV. Once you have started dBASE IV and accepted the license agreement by hitting **ENTER**, your screen should look like Figure 6-1. If all that appears on your screen is a dot or a dot followed by the word DEMO, hit the **F2** button or type the word **ASSIST**, and your screen should then look like Figure 6-1.

This screen is known as the *Control Center* in dBASE IV and allows you to perform a wide variety of database tasks without having to learn the dBASE language. Let's explore what the different parts of the screen represent and how you access the various options from the Control Center.

The top left part of the screen is known as the *Menu Bar*. There are two ways to access the menu bar. One method is by hitting the F10 key, and the various options for the Catalog menu would appear. To move within a menu choice, use the up and down arrow keys. To move from one menu option to another, use the left and right arrow keys. To exit from the menu option, you would hit the ESCAPE key. The ESC

```
 Catalog   Tools   Exit                                    12:56:28 pm
                             dBASE IV CONTROL CENTER

                         CATALOG: A:\DBASE\UNTITLED.CAT

        Data        Queries       Forms       Reports      Labels     Applications

     <create>     <create>     <create>     <create>     <create>     <create>




     File:       New file
     Description: Press ENTER on <create> to create a new file


      Help:F1  Use:◄┘  Data:F2  Design:Shift-F2  Quick Report:Shift-F9  Menus:F10
```

Figure 6-1 dBASE IV Control Center

key moves you back one prior menu at a time. Depending on what menu choices you have been making, dBASE may ask you if you want to exit from that operation when you hit the ESC key. If you answer YES, then dBASE will return you to the prior menu. If you answer **NO**, then dBASE will allow you to continue where you left off.

The other method of accessing the menu bar is by holding down the ALT key and then pressing the first letter of your menu choice. For example, to access Catalog, you would hold down the ALT key and hit the letter C (ALT-C). You can then move within and among the menu choices as described above through the use of the arrow keys.

There are multiple levels of menus; the one that appears on your screen when you first start is known as the *Main Menu*. As you select certain menu options, another set of menu options may appear. Again to move back to the prior menu screen, simply hit the ESC key. If you hit the ESC key too many times and the Control Center no longer appears, hit the F2 key or type ASSIST to return to the Control Center.

If you are not currently at the Control Center, return to it now so that you can follow what the other parts of the screen are for. In the top right corner of the screen is the current time. This is updated continuously during your work session.

In the area directly below the words dBASE IV CONTROL CENTER is the name of the current file catalog. We will talk more about catalogs later, but for now think of a catalog as a way to group similar files together. If you are familiar with DOS, it is somewhat analogous to using a subdirectory for file maintenance.

The next part of the screen is referred to as *Panels*. There are six Panels, starting with the Data panel and ending with the Applications panel. The panels indicate various database tasks that may be carried out when you select a certain panel. You can select which panel you want by using the left and right arrow keys. Included in each panel is the name of the files available for that operation. To select a certain file, use the up and down arrow keys to highlight the desired file and then press the ENTER key. If a file is currently active, it is displayed above the horizontal line. When you make your selection, another submenu appears asking you for the specific operation you would like to carry out.

Below the Panel area is information on the current file. This area shows the name of the currently active file, and possibly a description of the file as well. At the bottom of the screen is the *Navigation Line*. This tells you how to move between menus and what some of the function keys can be used for. One important function key is *F1*, which is the help key, and is available at any time. If you get stuck in the middle of an operation, the Navigation Line is a good place to look for help. The Navigation Line changes depending on the current task being performed.

The last part of the screen is referred to as the *Message Line*. During some database operations, messages are displayed concerning the status of the operation, such as whether an error has occurred.

Designing the Inventory Database

To design a database in dBASE IV, you first create the data files that make up the database. The 3 files that you will be creating are:

1. Inventory Master File
2. Inventory Transaction File
3. Inventory History File.

Within each file certain data will be stored that is of interest to Stroudsburg Toy Company. You will want to have the same type of information about each inventory item, such as its name, item number, and quantity on hand. dBASE refers to this type of information as *Fields*. For each Field that you define, you will need to provide some detail for that field, such as its length, the type of data (e.g., numeric, alphabetic), and so on.

After studying the information requirements for Stroudsburg, you have determined that the following fields are needed for the appropriate files.

1. Inventory Master File
   - Item Number
   - Item Class
   - Item Name
   - Unit Cost
   - Unit Price
   - Warehouse Location
   - Reorder Point (Minimum Quantity)
   - Maximum Quantity

2. Inventory Transaction File
   - Item Number
   - Quantity on Hand
   - Quantity Committed
   - Quantity on Order
   - Year to Date Sales (Units)
   - Year to Date Sales (Dollars)
   - Year to Date Cost of Sales
   - Current Month Sales (Units)

3. Inventory History File
   - Item Number
   - Last Year's Unit Sales
   - Sales 1 Month Ago (Units)
   - Sales 2 Months Ago (Units)
   - Sales 3-12 Months Ago (Units)

You are now ready to begin using dBASE IV. The first procedure to learn is how to have dBASE save all the work you will be doing on to your own floppy diskette. This allows you to go from machine to machine as well as hand in your assignment on disk to your instructor. Make sure you are at the Control Center before you proceed. Begin by pressing **ALT-T** to select the Tools menu. When the next menu appears, either move down to DOS utilities using the arrow keys, or press the first letter of the desired menu choice, in this case, **D**. Your screen now shows all the files in the current drive and directory. We want to change the current drive to be your floppy drive. This is done by pressing **ALT-D** (DOS), and then selecting **Set default drive:directory**. You are now asked to type in the name of the drive and directory you want. Depending on whether your floppy diskette is in drive a: or b:, type in the appropriate letter (including the colon), followed by the name of the directory. Assuming that you created a subdirectory called DBASE and that your diskette is in the A drive, you would type in **A:\DBASE** . This will automatically save all your work for the current session to the floppy diskette.

Important: Make sure this is the first thing you do each time you begin your dBASE session! Otherwise, it may be difficult for you to copy your work onto your floppy from either the hard drive or the network, depending on your operating environment. To get back to the Control Center, press **ALT-E** and then hit **ENTER**. You can now begin the exercises.

From the Control Center, your first task is to set up a catalog for keeping all the files you will create in these exercises together. To create a catalog, hit **ALT-C**. Again, holding down the **ALT** key and hitting the first letter of the menu choice selects that option.

Your screen should look like Figure 6-2. Select **Use a different catalog**. A box will appear in the right side of your screen listing any catalogs you have created. To choose one of those catalogs, simply use the up and down arrow keys to highlight the desired catalog and then press **ENTER**. If you have not created any catalogs, you will see two items: <create> and UNTITLED.CAT. The second item is the dBASE default catalog. The .CAT extension indicates that this is a catalog file. As you will see throughout these cases, dBASE uses specific extensions to differentiate the variety of file types that can be created.

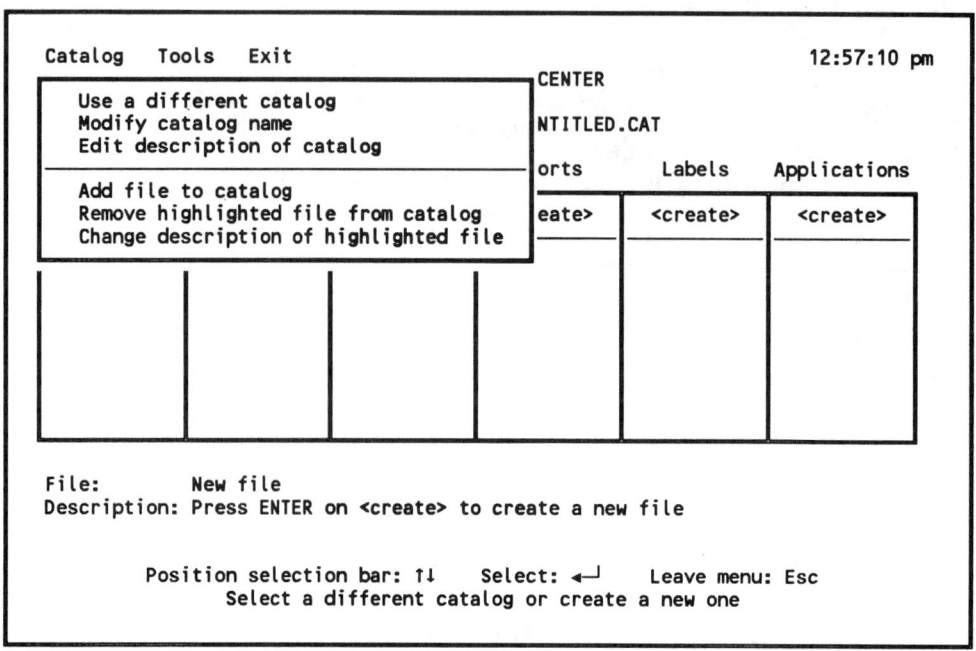

Figure 6-2 The Catalog Menu

Since we want to create a new catalog, select **<create>**, and type in the name of the catalog. It is useful to choose a name that indicates what type of files are kept in the catalog. For this case (as well as all others you may work on), let's type in the name of the catalog as **AIS_FILE**. The purpose of the underscore is to replace a blank space, which is not allowed in naming catalogs, files, or field names. It is designed to make it easier to read a file name. You do not have to add the .CAT extension; dBASE does this automatically. When you are finished typing the name, hit **ENTER**. This will save the catalog name and return you to the Control Center.

The first file we will create is the inventory master file. From the Control Center, use the arrow keys to select the **<create>** option from the Data Panel. After hitting **ENTER**, a blank file structure definition form appears such as the one shown in Figure 6-3.

The menu options at the top of the screen will not be used as part of this exercise. The next part of the screen is where you define the specifications for each field. The following section will describe how to set up the inventory master file. The bottom of the screen indicates what information is required from you and what special key functions are available. Directly above this is the status bar that will change to reflect the current activity.

The cursor should currently be in the column labeled Field Name. A field name can contain up to 10 characters, the first of which must be a letter. No blank spaces are allowed. At this point type in the first field name, which will be **ITEM_NO**, and then hit the **ENTER** key. The cursor then moves to the next column, Field Type. A field type may be character, numeric, floating value, date, logical, and memo. We will only be using character, numeric and date fields.

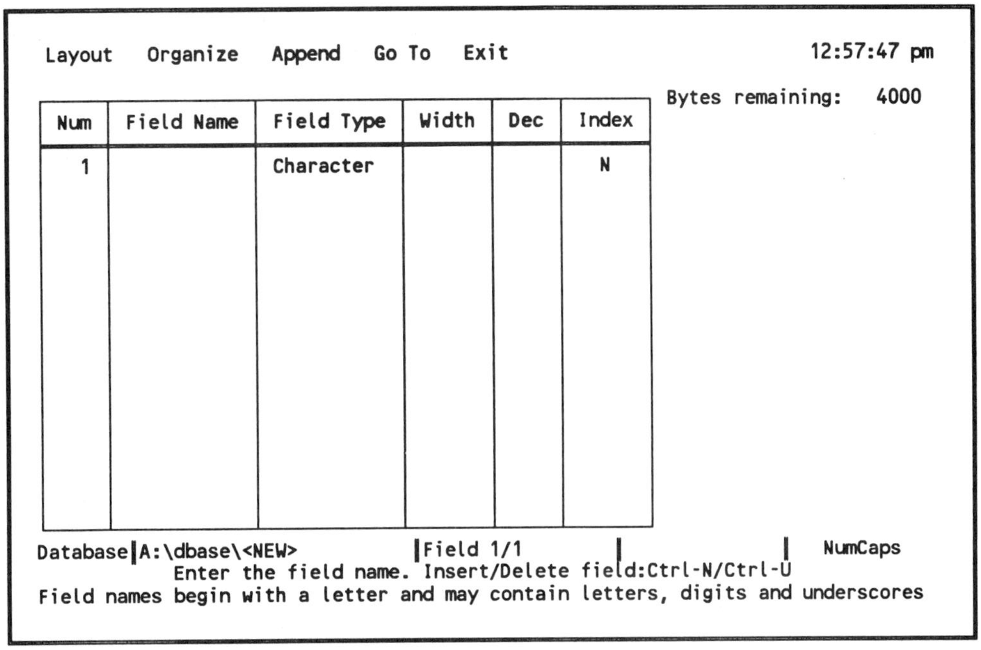

```
 Layout    Organize    Append    Go To    Exit                    12:57:47 pm

                                                          Bytes remaining:    4000
  ┌─────┬────────────┬────────────┬───────┬─────┬────────┐
  │ Num │ Field Name │ Field Type │ Width │ Dec │ Index  │
  ├─────┼────────────┼────────────┼───────┼─────┼────────┤
  │  1  │            │ Character  │       │     │   N    │
  │     │            │            │       │     │        │
  │     │            │            │       │     │        │
  │     │            │            │       │     │        │
  │     │            │            │       │     │        │
  │     │            │            │       │     │        │
  │     │            │            │       │     │        │
  │     │            │            │       │     │        │
  │     │            │            │       │     │        │
  │     │            │            │       │     │        │
  └─────┴────────────┴────────────┴───────┴─────┴────────┘
 Database│A:\dbase\<NEW>              │Field 1/1     │          │    NumCaps
            Enter the field name. Insert/Delete field:Ctrl-N/Ctrl-U
  Field names begin with a letter and may contain letters, digits and underscores
```

Figure 6-3 Blank Database Design Screen

A numeric type field would be selected if you intend to do some calculations on the values that make up that data item. If you intend to use the field for date information, you would select the date field. All other fields, for our purposes, will be character fields. To select the various types of fields, you press the space bar to cycle through the choices. When you find the one you want, hit the **ENTER** key. Thus, for ITEM_NO, select character, which is the default.

The cursor has now moved to the next column, WIDTH. The width of a field determines the maximum number of characters allowed for that field. For a numeric field, you are also prompted for the number of decimal places. If you have defined a field as a date field, the width is set automatically at eight characters. For the ITEM_NO field, enter **4** as the field width. The last field is for *indexing*, which you will ignore for now by selecting the default of N (just press **ENTER**). We will discuss the concept of indexing in Chapter 8.

The cursor should now be in the second row under the Field Name column. Your screen should look like Figure 6-4. At this point you are ready to enter the remaining information for this file structure. Figure 6-5 displays the necessary information for completing the Inventory Master File definition. When you are finished, your screen should match Figure 6-5. The cursor should be on a blank line at this point.

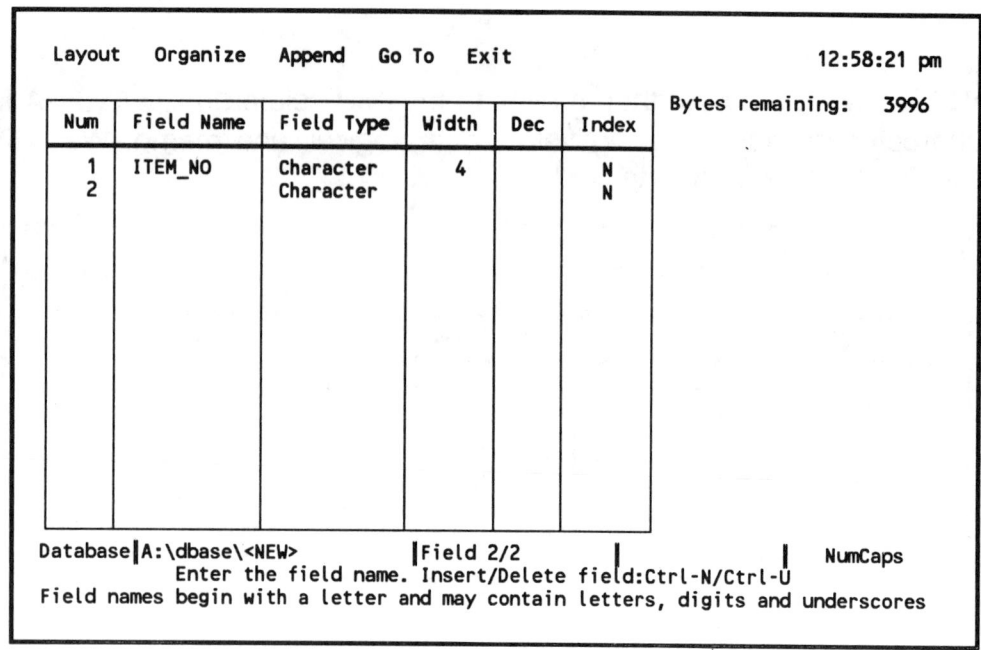

Figure 6-4 Database Design Screen after Adding the ITEM_NO Field

Editing the File Structure

If any mistakes have been made in creating the file structure, there are several editing options available for use. To insert a new field, move the cursor to the field above which you would like to add the new field, then press **CTRL-N**. A new blank field appears, and you may now enter the field attributes. To remove an existing field, first highlight the field by using the arrow keys and then press **CTRL-U**. To edit an existing field, use the up and down arrow keys to move to the selected field, and then use the **ENTER** key to move from column to column. To then change existing information, merely type in the new information in the desired column.

Saving the File Structure

After you have gotten the screen to look like Figure 6-5, you are ready to save the file structure. To do so, you may either press **ENTER** or **CTRL-END**. After doing this, you are prompted for a file name. The name can consist of up to eight characters. Name this first file **INV_MAST**. After typing the name, press **ENTER**, and another prompt appears: Input data records now? (Y/N) Press **Y** to indicate you are ready to input the raw data into the INV_MAST file. The screen displayed now is the default data-entry screen for the file you have just created. See Figure 6-6.

```
 Layout   Organize   Append   Go To   Exit                    12:59:30 pm
                                                        Bytes remaining:   3943
 ┌─────┬─────────────┬─────────────┬───────┬─────┬───────┐
 │ Num │ Field Name  │ Field Type  │ Width │ Dec │ Index │
 ├─────┼─────────────┼─────────────┼───────┼─────┼───────┤
 │  1  │ ITEM_NO     │ Character   │   4   │     │   N   │
 │  2  │ ITEM_CLASS  │ Character   │   4   │     │   N   │
 │  3  │ ITEM_NAME   │ Character   │  25   │     │   N   │
 │  4  │ UNIT_COST   │ Numeric     │   6   │  2  │   N   │
 │  5  │ UNIT_PRICE  │ Numeric     │   6   │  2  │   N   │
 │  6  │ WAREH_LOC   │ Character   │   6   │     │   N   │
 │  7  │ REORD_PNT   │ Numeric     │   3   │  0  │   N   │
 │  8  │ MAX_PNT     │ Numeric     │   3   │  0  │   N   │
 │  9  │             │ Character   │       │     │   N   │
 └─────┴─────────────┴─────────────┴───────┴─────┴───────┘
 Database|A:\dbase\<NEW>            |Field 9/9         |          |  NumCaps
              Enter the field name. Insert/Delete field:Ctrl-N/Ctrl-U
 Field names begin with a letter and may contain letters, digits and underscores
```

Figure 6-5 Completed Database Design Screen

Inputting Data

To input data, use the arrow keys to move to the desired field and enter the appropriate information. If the data exceeds the length of the field, you will hear a beeping noise when you reach the end of the field and you are moved to the next field. If the data does not exceed the length of the field, press the ENTER key when finished, and the cursor moves to the next field. As soon as the data for the last data field is entered, a blank data entry form appears for the next record. The status bar at the bottom of the screen indicates the name of the file you are working on, the current record number, and the total number of records in the file (1/1).

The data for the first record appears below. Enter this data into your file. (**USE ALL CAPITAL LETTERS.**)

```
ITEM_NO     B467
ITEM_CLASS  BOOK
ITEM_NAME   MAKE WAY FOR DUCKLINGS
UNIT_COST   2.50
UNIT_PRICE  4.50
WAREH_LOC   A2S4L5
REORD_PNT   80
MAX_PNT     200
```

After entering the data for the MAX_PNT, you should once again have a blank data-entry form on your screen. The status bar should indicate that the current record is 2 out of a total of 2 records. The remaining data for the INV_MAST file is shown in Table 6-1 below. When you are adding this data to the file, be sure to use all capital letters.

Item_ no	Item_ class	Item_ name	Unit_ cost	Unit_ price	Wareh_ loc	Reord_ pnt	Max_ pnt
B467	BOOK	MAKE WAY FOR DUCKLINGS	2.50	4.50	A2S4L5	80	200
G324	GAME	MONOPOLY	4.25	9.60	A4S3L2	60	300
T219	TOY	TURTLE VAN	12.60	22.50	A3S2L4	30	160
T418	TOY	ECTO MOBILE	11.40	21.90	A3S3L6	30	160
G121	GAME	CANDYLAND	2.60	4.80	A4S3L1	40	250
B119	BOOK	CASEY AT THE BAT	2.10	4.30	A2S3L2	70	180
B187	BOOK	MIKE MULLIGAN	2.70	5.00	A2S3L5	80	220
G043	GAME	KERPLUNK	6.80	14.90	A4S2L4	90	260
B029	BOOK	GOODNIGHT MOON	3.60	7.00	A2S1L2	40	180
T108	TOY	LEGO BLOCKS	12.70	18.40	A3S1L4	20	110

Table 6-1 Data to Input to the Inv_mast Data File

```
 Records   Organize   Go To   Exit
ITEM_NO
ITEM_CLASS
ITEM_NAME
UNIT_COST         .
UNIT_PRICE        .
WAREH_LOC
REORD_PNT
MAX_PNT







Edit    |A:\dbase\INV_MAST      |Rec None      |File |      |  NumCaps
```

Figure 6-6 The Default Data Entry Screen For the INV_MAST data file

When you have entered the last data item for the last record, you should have a blank data entry form on the screen. You are now ready to save the data that you have entered. To do this, press **ALT-E** and select **EXIT**. This will save all the records, except the blank one you were currently working on. At this point you are returned to the Control Center.

The name of the file you just created should appear in the Data Panel above the horizontal line. This indicates that this is an open file.

Viewing the Data

There are two ways to display the data you have just entered. One way is to highlight the file you wish to look at (using the arrow keys), press **ENTER**, and when the next box appears, select the **Display data** option. The data should now appear on the screen. If necessary, press **PgUp** to go to the top of the file. The other method to display a data file is to press **F2**. There are also two different format that dBASE has available for displaying data. The first format, known as *EDIT*, displays the data in a form that looks just like the default data-entry screen. To see the next record, you would push the Page Down key. Page Up would display the previous record. The second format, known as *BROWSE*, displays the data in a table format. Each record is a line and each field is a column. If there are columns that do not appear on the screen, you can use the Tab key or Enter key to move to the next column(s). If there are more than 17 records in a file, you would need to use either the down arrow key or the Page Down key to see the additional records. You can switch back and forth between the two formats by pressing the F2 key while the data is being displayed.

Editing the Data

To edit existing data records, you should be in one of the display formats (EDIT or BROWSE) discussed above. Move the cursor to the desired record using the arrow keys or the Page Up/Page Down keys. When you are at the record you wish to edit, just move to the desired field (using the Tab or Enter key) and you can begin editing. By pushing the INS key you can toggle back and forth between insert mode and override mode. The letters INS will appear in the status bar at the bottom of your screen when you are in the insert mode. Insert mode will allow you to enter data without affecting the existing data. The existing data will just shift to the right as you enter the data. The override mode allows you to edit a data item by replacing the old data with the new data by essentially writing on top of, or erasing, the old data.

To add records to the file, move to the end of the file using the down arrow key or Page Down key. When you get to the end of the file, you will be asked: Add new records?(Y/N) By answering yes, space is created for you to enter data for the new record(s).

You may also add records to a file while you are at the Control Center. To do this, highlight the appropriate file in the Data Panel. Press ENTER and then choose the Modify structure/order option in the menu box. The next screen that appears will show the structure of the file. The option to add records to a file is contained within the Append menu. To use this option, first press ALT-A, or move to that choice using the arrow keys. Next, you would select Enter records from keyboard and the default data entry screen will appear. When you are finished, press ALT-E and select EXIT. The new records will be saved to the file.

To delete a record from a file is a two-step process. First, highlight the record you wish to delete and press CTRL-U (the command to mark a record for deletion). After doing this you will notice the status bar (at the bottom of the screen) has the word Del now showing. However, the record is still not removed from the file. If you wish to undelete a record, highlight the record and press CTRL-U once again. The word Del should no longer appear at the bottom of the screen. The second step needed to delete a record requires you to exit from the display or view mode. This can be done by selecting ALT-E, and choosing Exit. This will bring you back to the Control Center.

At this point you should highlight the desired file in the Data Panel and press ENTER. When the next menu box appears, select the Modify structure/order option. The structure of the file is then displayed, as well as a menu at the top of the screen. The other way to get directly to the Modify structure/order menu is by pressing Shift-F2 from the Control Center. Regardless of the approach used, the menu choice you want is already displayed; all you need to do is move the cursor down to the choice Erase Marked records, and press ENTER. This operation is known as the *PACK* operation in dBASE. After the operation is completed you can exit from the current menu by pressing ALT-E, selecting Save changes and exit, and then pressing ENTER.

The above sections should provide you with the basic skills to create and maintain a database. Routine maintenance activities include adding, deleting, and editing a file. Be sure you are familiar with these operations, since the same general pattern of commands will be used in other database management activities.

Changing the structure of an existing file

As noted above, you can display the structure of a file by highlighting the appropriate file in the data panel, pressing ENTER, and selecting the Modify structure/order option. Alternatively, pressing Shift-F2 will also display the structure of a file. The Organize menu automatically appears when you bring up this screen. To clear the Organize menu from your screen press ESC. The screen should now show only the structure of the file you just created. To change any item, use the up and down arrow keys to move from field to field and the ENTER or TAB key to move within a field. Instructions on how to make specific changes have already been discussed above in the *Editing the File Structure* section. Refer to that section for additional information. When you have finished getting the structure in the desired format, you can save the file structure by pressing ALT-E for the exit menu and selecting Save changes and exit. If you have made any changes, you will be asked if you want to save those changes. Press Y to save the changes. After doing this, you are returned to the Control Center.

Exiting dBASE

To exit from dBASE, first make sure you are at the Command Control Center. Next, make sure there are no open files (above the line in the one of the panels). If there are any open files, highlight the file and then press **ENTER**. Next, select **Close file** and you should be returned to the Control Center, with the file now below the line. To start the exiting process, press **ALT-E**, and select **Quit to DOS**. This procedure will return you to where you were before you started dBASE. Do not remove your diskette until you have returned to this point and the light is off on the floppy drive! You do not have to worry about saving your files before you exit, since you have already done so as part of the tutorial. The transparent saving of files is one of the control features in dBASE; the next section talks about some other controls that are relevant at this point.

Controls

dBASE offers many control features, we will talk about these as they become relevant to each chapter's topics. At this stage of development, there are some important control points that you should be aware of. The first concern a database manager would have is controlling access to the database and its files. dBASE IV has a feature known as *Protect* that allows a data base administrator (DBA) to establish various levels of controls over the data files and their contents. For example, Protect can establish a system of passwords that would allow a particular user to look at a particular file, but not allow that user to make any changes to the file. Protect can also allow the DBA to use passwords that would allow a user to view and change only certain fields within a file. You will not be working with the Protect command, but it is useful to know that such a control device does exist within dBASE.

Another control device that you should get in the habit of using is *backing up* your files. At the beginning of this tutorial, remember that you made your floppy disk drive the default drive for the work session. For a variety of reasons, such as diskette damage or lost diskettes, you should copy each session's work on to another floppy diskette. At this point, the only file you have created is a data file, to which dBASE automatically adds the extension **.DBF** to the file name. If you do not know how to copy files from one floppy to another, ask your lab consultant or instructor.

Conclusion

The exercises at the end of the chapter provide you with the necessary file structures and data to create the Inventory Transaction File and the Inventory History File for Stroudsburg's inventory database. It is important that you complete those exercises since future exercises and tutorials will reference those files. Once you have finished those exercises you will have a "complete" inventory database for Stroudsburg Toy Company. You should also be aware that included on the diskette that accompanied this manual are several other files that you will be using in later sections of this book. There are also review questions at the end of this chapter that allow you to evaluate your knowledge of the skills learned in this chapter.

FOLLOW-UP EXERCISES

Inventory Cycle

Before you start these exercises, make sure that you are using the proper floppy drive and subdirectory (if you have created one) and that the AIS_FILE catalog is selected. If you are not sure how to do this, refer to the appropriate sections in this chapter. When you are finished, remember to exit properly from the Control Center.
This exercise is designed to give you more practice with creating data files in dBASE. It is mandatory that you complete this exercise, since future parts of this manual depend on these files having been created. Figure 6-7 indicates the structure of the Inventory Transaction file. When you are finished creating the file, save the file using the name INV_TRAN. Table 6-2 shows the data that you are to add to the file as part of the data entry process. (Again, be sure to use all capital letters when entering the data).

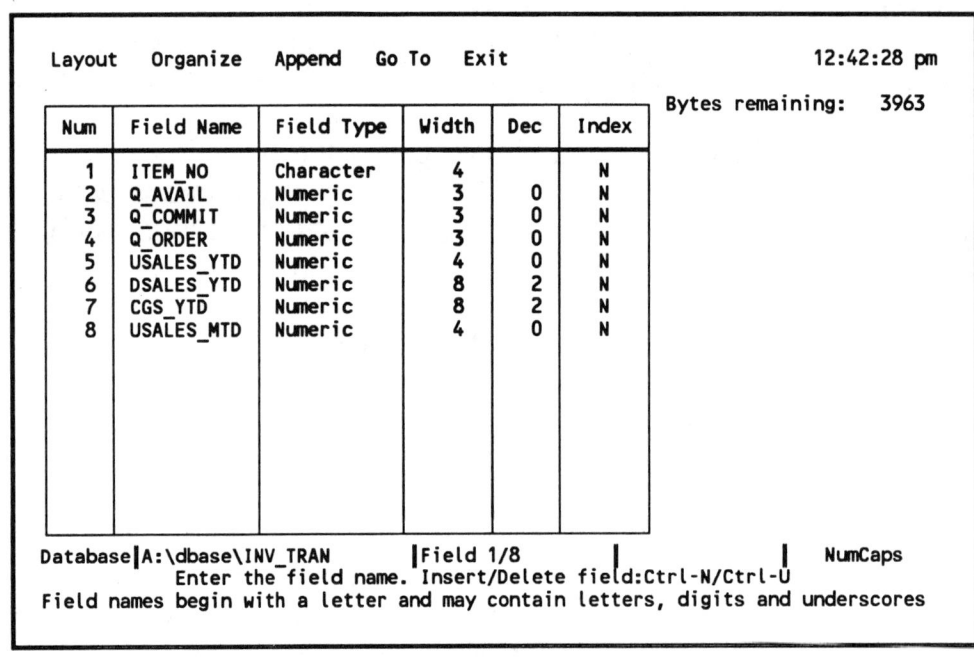

Figure 6-7 Completed Database Design Screen for the INV_TRAN data file

Figure 6-8 displays the file structure for the Inventory History file. Save this file with the name INV_HIST. Table 6-3 supplies the data needed for the History file. (Once more, be sure to use capital letters).

ITEM_ NO	Q_ AVAIL	Q_ COMMIT	Q_ ORDER	USALES_ YTD	DSALES_ YTD	CGS_ YTD	USALES_ MTD
B467	145	20	0	55	247.50	137.50	0
G324	75	0	0	5	48.00	21.25	0
T219	150	30	0	0	0.00	0.00	0
T418	45	25	80	60	1314.00	684.00	0
G121	65	175	190	5	24.00	13.00	0
B119	130	0	0	40	172.00	84.00	0
B187	130	0	0	30	150.00	81.00	0
G043	155	55	0	145	2160.50	986.00	0
B029	150	40	0	0	0.00	0.00	0
T108	20	65	90	85	1564.00	1079.50	0

Table 6-2 Data to Input to the Inv_tran Data File

```
  Layout   Organize   Append   Go To   Exit                    12:42:46 pm

                                               Bytes remaining:   3944
  ┌─────┬─────────────┬─────────────┬───────┬─────┬───────┐
  │ Num │ Field Name  │ Field Type  │ Width │ Dec │ Index │
  ├─────┼─────────────┼─────────────┼───────┼─────┼───────┤
  │  1  │ ITEM_NO     │ Character   │   4   │     │   N   │
  │  2  │ USALES_LAS  │ Numeric     │   4   │  0  │   N   │
  │  3  │ USALES_1MO  │ Numeric     │   4   │  0  │   N   │
  │  4  │ USALES_2MO  │ Numeric     │   4   │  0  │   N   │
  │  5  │ USALES_3MO  │ Numeric     │   4   │  0  │   N   │
  │  6  │ USALES_4MO  │ Numeric     │   4   │  0  │   N   │
  │  7  │ USALES_5MO  │ Numeric     │   4   │  0  │   N   │
  │  8  │ USALES_6MO  │ Numeric     │   4   │  0  │   N   │
  │  9  │ USALES_7MO  │ Numeric     │   4   │  0  │   N   │
  │ 10  │ USALES_8MO  │ Numeric     │   4   │  0  │   N   │
  │ 11  │ USALES_9MO  │ Numeric     │   4   │  0  │   N   │
  │ 12  │ USALES_10M  │ Numeric     │   4   │  0  │   N   │
  │ 13  │ USALES_11M  │ Numeric     │   4   │  0  │   N   │
  │ 14  │ USALES_12M  │ Numeric     │   4   │  0  │   N   │
  └─────┴─────────────┴─────────────┴───────┴─────┴───────┘

  Database│A:\dbase\INV_HIST        │Field 1/14     │         │  NumCaps
          Enter the field name. Insert/Delete field:Ctrl-N/Ctrl-U
  Field names begin with a letter and may contain letters, digits and underscores
```

Figure 6-8 Completed Database Design Screen for the INV_HIST data file

ITEM_ NO	USALES LAST	USALES _1MO	USALES _2MO	USALES _3MO	USALES _4MO	USALES _5MO	USALES _6MO	USALES _7MO	USALES _8MO	USALES _9MO	USALES _10M	SALES _11M	USALES _12M
B467	500	55	0	0	0	0	0	0	0	0	0	0	0
G324	580	5	0	0	0	0	0	0	0	0	0	0	0
T219	280	0	0	0	0	0	0	0	0	0	0	0	0
T418	400	60	0	0	0	0	0	0	0	0	0	0	0
G121	230	5	0	0	0	0	0	0	0	0	0	0	0
B119	170	40	0	0	0	0	0	0	0	0	0	0	0
B187	370	30	0	0	0	0	0	0	0	0	0	0	0
G043	150	145	0	0	0	0	0	0	0	0	0	0	0
B029	450	0	0	0	0	0	0	0	0	0	0	0	0
T108	530	85	0	0	0	0	0	0	0	0	0	0	0

Table 6-3 Data to Input to the Inv_hist Data File

Revenue Cycle

You should first complete the follow-up exercise for the Inventory Cycle described above. When that is complete, there is only one other short exercise that needs to be completed as part of the Revenue Cycle. The disk that accompanied this text already includes all the data files needed for the Revenue Cycle (except the ones you created as part of the tutorial and the Inventory Cycle follow-up exercises). You need to copy these data files from that disk to the disk that has your three inventory data files. The names of the files to copy are as follows:

AR_MAST.DBF
CASH_REC.DBF
CUSTOMER.DBF
SALES_IN.DBF
SALES_OR.DBF

If you have created a subdirectory on your floppy disk, be sure to copy these files to the appropriate subdirectory. When you are finished copying these data files to your diskette, the next step is to add these files to your AIS_FILE catalog. To do this, you first need to be in the dBASE program and have the necessary floppy disk drive and subdirectory as the active drive and subdirectory. See the tutorial for instructions on how to do this. When you are back at the Control Center, select the AIS_FILE catalog to use. After doing this, you should see the three inventory files you created earlier displayed under the Data Panel. While your cursor is in the Data Panel, press **ALT-C** and select **Add file to catalog**. The names of all the data files on the floppy diskette will appear in a window on the right side of your screen. To select a file, move your cursor to the appropriate file name (in this case the first one listed should be the AR_MAST.DBF file) and press **ENTER**. You are then asked for a description of the file. You may either leave this blank or type in a short explanation of what the file contains. When you are finished with the description, press **ENTER**, and the file name should appear under the Data Panel. You need to complete this routine for all five of the revenue-related data files that are on your diskette. When you are finished, remember to exit properly from dBASE.

Expenditure Cycle

You should first complete the follow-up exercise for the Inventory Cycle described above. When that is complete, there is only one other short exercise that needs to be completed as part of the Expenditure Cycle. The disk that accompanied this text already includes all the data files needed for the Expenditure Cycle (except the ones you created as part of the tutorial and the Inventory Cycle follow-up exercises). You need to copy these data files from that disk to the disk that has your three inventory data files. The names of the files to copy are as follows:

AP_MAST.DBF
CASH_PAY.DBF
VENDOR.DBF
VOUCHER.DBF
PURCH_OR.DBF

When you are finished copying these data files to your diskette, the next step is to add these files to your AIS_FILE catalog. To do this, you first need to be in the dBASE program and have your floppy disk drive as the active drive. See the tutorial for instructions on how to do this. When you are back at the Control Center, select the AIS_file catalog to use. After doing this, you should see the three inventory files you created earlier displayed under the Data Panel. While your cursor is in the Data Panel, press **ALT-C** and select **Add file to catalog**. The names of all the data files on the floppy diskette will appear in a window on the right side of your screen. To select a file, move your cursor to the appropriate file name (in this case the first one listed should be the AP_MAST.DBF file) and press **ENTER**. You are then asked for a description of the file. You may either leave this blank or type in a short explanation of what the file contains. When you are finished with the description, press **ENTER**, and the file name should appear under the Data Panel. You need to complete this routine for all five of the expenditure-related data files that are on your diskette. When you are finished, remember to exit properly from dBASE.

Payroll Cycle

Create the following data files using dBASE IV:

PAYCHECK.DBF
PAY_CLAS.DBF
PAY_MAST.DBF
PERSONEL.DBF
TIME_CAR.DBF

Figures 6-9 through 6-13 display the suggested layout for these files. You will input the data to these files in Chapter 7. If you wish you may create a catalog called PAYROLL in order to keep all of these files, as well as later ones, together in one quasi-directory.

```
 Layout   Organize   Append   Go To   Exit                        12:47:27 pm

                                                        Bytes remaining:   3979
 ┌─────┬───────────────┬──────────────┬───────┬───────┬─────────┐
 │ Num │  Field Name   │  Field Type  │ Width │  Dec  │  Index  │
 ├─────┼───────────────┼──────────────┼───────┼───────┼─────────┤
 │  1  │ PAYCHK_NO     │ Character    │   4   │       │    N    │
 │  2  │ SSN           │ Character    │   9   │       │    N    │
 │  3  │ DATE          │ Date         │   8   │       │    N    │
 │     │               │              │       │       │         │
 │     │               │              │       │       │         │
 │     │               │              │       │       │         │
 │     │               │              │       │       │         │
 │     │               │              │       │       │         │
 │     │               │              │       │       │         │
 │     │               │              │       │       │         │
 └─────┴───────────────┴──────────────┴───────┴───────┴─────────┘
 Database│A:\dbase\PAYCHECK          │Field 1/3     │        │         NumCapsIns
                Enter the field name.  Insert/Delete field:Ctrl-N/Ctrl-U
 Field names begin with a letter and may contain letters, digits and underscores
```

Figure 6-9 Completed Database Design Screen for the PAYCHECK data file

```
 Layout   Organize   Append   Go To   Exit                        12:47:57 pm

                                                        Bytes remaining:   3972
 ┌─────┬───────────────┬──────────────┬───────┬───────┬─────────┐
 │ Num │  Field Name   │  Field Type  │ Width │  Dec  │  Index  │
 ├─────┼───────────────┼──────────────┼───────┼───────┼─────────┤
 │  1  │ PAY_CLASS     │ Character    │   1   │       │    N    │
 │  2  │ CLAS_DESC     │ Character    │  10   │       │    N    │
 │  3  │ PAY_RATE      │ Numeric      │  10   │   2   │    N    │
 │  4  │ BASIS         │ Character    │   7   │       │    N    │
 │     │               │              │       │       │         │
 │     │               │              │       │       │         │
 │     │               │              │       │       │         │
 │     │               │              │       │       │         │
 │     │               │              │       │       │         │
 │     │               │              │       │       │         │
 └─────┴───────────────┴──────────────┴───────┴───────┴─────────┘
 Database│A:\dbase\PAY_CLAS          │Field 1/4     │        │         NumCapsIns
                Enter the field name.  Insert/Delete field:Ctrl-N/Ctrl-U
 Field names begin with a letter and may contain letters, digits and underscores
```

Figure 6-10 Completed Database Design Screen for the PAY_CLAS data file

```
  Layout   Organize   Append   Go To   Exit                      12:48:18 pm

                                                     Bytes remaining:   3957
  ┌──────┬────────────┬────────────┬───────┬─────┬────────┐
  │ Num  │ Field Name │ Field Type │ Width │ Dec │ Index  │
  ├──────┼────────────┼────────────┼───────┼─────┼────────┤
  │  1   │ SSN        │ Character  │   9   │     │   N    │
  │  2   │ EXEMPTIONS │ Numeric    │   2   │  0  │   N    │
  │  3   │ MARITAL_ST │ Character  │   1   │     │   N    │
  │  4   │ PAY_CLASS  │ Character  │   1   │     │   N    │
  │  5   │ DEDUCTIONS │ Numeric    │  10   │  2  │   N    │
  │  6   │ YTD_GRPAY  │ Numeric    │  10   │  2  │   N    │
  │  7   │ YTD_DEDUCT │ Numeric    │  10   │  2  │   N    │
  │  8   │ PDATE      │ Date       │   8   │     │   N    │
  │      │            │            │       │     │        │
  │      │            │            │       │     │        │
  │      │            │            │       │     │        │
  │      │            │            │       │     │        │
  │      │            │            │       │     │        │
  └──────┴────────────┴────────────┴───────┴─────┴────────┘
  Database│A:\dbase\PAY_MAST       │Field 1/7      │        │        │ NumCapsIns
             Enter the field name. Insert/Delete field:Ctrl-N/Ctrl-U
  Field names begin with a letter and may contain letters, digits and underscores
```

Figure 6-11 Completed Database Design Screen for the PAY_MAST data file

```
  Layout   Organize   Append   Go To   Exit                      12:48:37 pm

                                                     Bytes remaining:   3917
  ┌──────┬────────────┬────────────┬───────┬─────┬────────┐
  │ Num  │ Field Name │ Field Type │ Width │ Dec │ Index  │
  ├──────┼────────────┼────────────┼───────┼─────┼────────┤
  │  1   │ SSN        │ Character  │   9   │     │   N    │
  │  2   │ LAST_NAME  │ Character  │  15   │     │   N    │
  │  3   │ FRST_NAME  │ Character  │  10   │     │   N    │
  │  4   │ ADDRESS    │ Character  │  20   │     │   N    │
  │  5   │ CITY       │ Character  │  15   │     │   N    │
  │  6   │ STATE      │ Character  │   2   │     │   N    │
  │  7   │ ZIP        │ Character  │   5   │     │   N    │
  │  8   │ HOME_PHONE │ Character  │   7   │     │   N    │
  │      │            │            │       │     │        │
  │      │            │            │       │     │        │
  │      │            │            │       │     │        │
  │      │            │            │       │     │        │
  │      │            │            │       │     │        │
  └──────┴────────────┴────────────┴───────┴─────┴────────┘
  Database│A:\dbase\PERSONEL       │Field 1/8      │        │        │ NumCapsIns
             Enter the field name. Insert/Delete field:Ctrl-N/Ctrl-U
  Field names begin with a letter and may contain letters, digits and underscores
```

Figure 6-12 Completed Database Design Screen for the PERSONEL data file

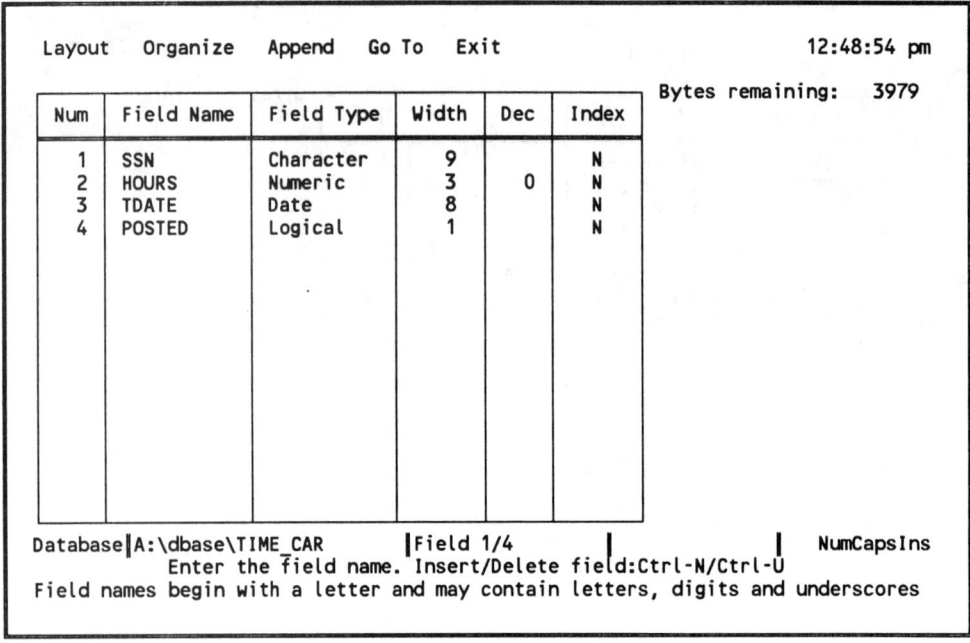

Figure 6-13 Completed Database Design Screen for the TIME_CAR data file

REVIEW QUESTIONS

1. How do you switch to a different drive and a subdirectory using dBASE?
2. What is meant by a catalog?
3. How do you create a catalog?
4. How do you select a different catalog from the one that is currently shown?
5. How do you create a data file?
6. How do you make a file the current or active file?
7. What is meant by file structure?
8. How do you save a file structure?
9. How do you change the structure of an existing data file?
10. How do you add data to a file if you are currently at the Control Center?
11. How do you save a file after you have added or changed data in the file?
12. What is the difference between Edit mode and Browse mode?
13. How do you switch back and forth between Browse and Edit mode?
14. How can you make changes to an existing record in a data file?
15. What steps must you go through in order to delete a specific record from a data file?
16. What are some controls dBASE IV has for limiting access to data?
17. What filename extension does dBASE IV give to data files?
18. How do you add files to a catalog?

CASE SOLUTION: PARADOX 3.5

Introduction

Before starting PARADOX, make sure you have a newly-formatted floppy diskette. A high density 3.5 inch diskette is highly recommended. It is also recommended that you create a subdirectory on your floppy diskette, perhaps naming the subdirectory PARADOX.

Since there are a variety of ways in which PARADOX may be accessed, it is not possible to offer one universal method to start the software program. The best advice is to check with your instructor as to how to start PARADOX. Once you have started PARADOX, your screen should look like Figure 6-14.

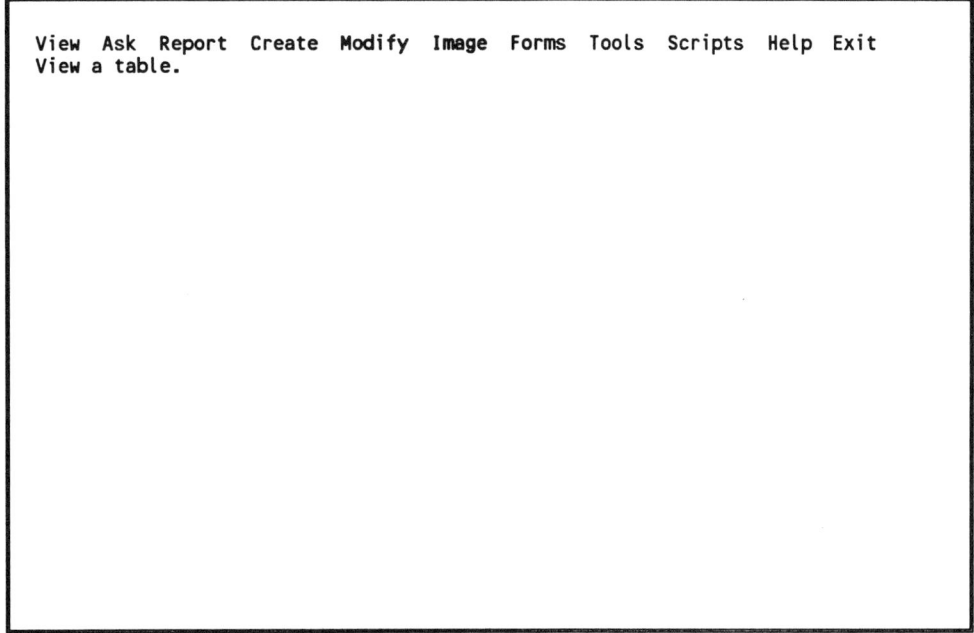

```
View  Ask  Report  Create  Modify  Image  Forms  Tools  Scripts  Help  Exit
View a table.
```

Figure 6-14 PARADOX Main Menu

This screen is known as the *main menu*, and allows you to perform a wide variety of database tasks. There are two ways to select a menu choice. With the first method, you can use the right and left arrow keys to move from one menu option to another and then press ENTER when the desired choice is highlighted. Note that as you move from one menu option to another, the message displayed on the line below the main menu changes. This line gives a brief description of the purpose of that particular menu choice.

The second method requires you to press the first letter of the desired menu choice, whether or not that choice is highlighted. Once you have made a selection, the main menu is replaced by another menu specific to that operation. Since there are multiple levels of menus, it is often useful to move back to a previous menu. This can be accomplished through the use of the Esc key, which brings you back one menu level at a time. To return to the main menu at once from any other menu in PARADOX, press F10.

Designing the Inventory Database

To design a database in PARADOX, you first create the data files that make up the database. PARADOX refers to these files as *Tables*. The 3 tables that you will be creating are:

1. Inventory Master Table
2. Inventory Transaction Table
3. Inventory History Table.

Within each table certain data will be stored that is of interest to Stroudsburg Toy Company. You will want to have the same type of information about each inventory item, such as its name, item number, and quantity on hand. PARADOX refers to this type of information as *Fields*. For each Field that you define, you will need to provide some detail for that field, such as its length, the type of data (e.g., numeric, alphabetic), and so on.

After studying the information requirements for Stroudsburg, you have determined that the following fields are needed for the appropriate tables.

1. Inventory Master File
   - Item Number
   - Item Class
   - Item Name
   - Unit Cost
   - Unit Price
   - Warehouse Location
   - Reorder Point (Minimum Quantity)
   - Maximum Quantity

2. Inventory Transaction File
   - Item Number
   - Quantity on Hand
   - Quantity Committed
   - Quantity on Order
   - Year to Date Sales (Units)
   - Year to Date Sales (Dollars)
   - Year to Date Cost of Sales
   - Current Month Sales (Units)

3. Inventory History File
   • Item Number
   • Last Year's Unit Sales
   • Sales 1 Month Ago (Units)
   • Sales 2 Months Ago (Units)
   • Sales 3-12 Months Ago (Units)

You are now ready to start using PARADOX. The first procedure to learn is how to have PARADOX save all the work you will be doing on to your own floppy diskette. This allows you to go from machine to machine as well as hand in your assignment on disk to your instructor. To do this, select **Tools** from the main menu, then **More** from the next menu, and then **Directory**. You are now asked to type in the name of the drive and directory you want. Depending on whether your floppy diskette is in drive a: or b:, type in the appropriate letter (including the colon), followed by the name of the directory. Assuming that you created a subdirectory called PARADOX and that your diskette is in the A drive, you would type in **A:\PARADOX** and press **ENTER**. You are then given a choice to either Cancel or OK (proceed); select **OK**. You are now returned to the main menu screen, and the bottom right corner of the screen should say Working directory is now A:\PARADOX\. If it does not, repeat the procedures above to make your floppy disk the active directory.

Important: Make sure this is the first thing you do each time you begin your PARADOX session! This will automatically save all your work for the current session to the floppy diskette. If this is not done, it may be difficult to get your tables copied from the hard drive or a network, depending on your operating environment.

We can now start to create our first data table, the Inventory Master table. From the main menu, select **Create** and PARADOX will prompt you for a table name. We will use the name **Inv_mast**; the purpose of the underscore is to make the table names easier to read, since PARADOX does not allow blank spaces when naming tables or any other type of file. After typing in the name, your screen should look like Figure 6-15.

The cursor should currently be on the first blank line of the table, under the column labeled Field Name. A field name can be up to 25 characters in length and there are certain restrictions on what type of characters may be used in naming a field. No blank spaces are allowed. At this point type in the first field name, which will be **ITEM_NO**, and then hit the **ENTER** key. The cursor then moves to the next column, Field Type.

The field types available in PARADOX are alphanumeric, numeric, currency, and date. A numeric type field would be selected if you intend to do some calculations on the values that make up that data item. A currency field will automatically add two decimal places to any number, unless the user inputs the decimal place on their own. If you intend to use the field for date information, you would select the date type. All other fields, for our purposes, will be alphanumeric.

The ITEM_NO field will be classified as an alphanumeric type. If a field is alphanumeric, you also need to specify its length. The length of a field determines the maximum number of characters allowed for that field. For the Item_no field, the length will be four characters. Thus, type **A4** in the Field Type column.

After typing in the Field Type and pressing Enter, your screen should look like Figure 6-16. At this point you are ready to enter the remaining information for the table

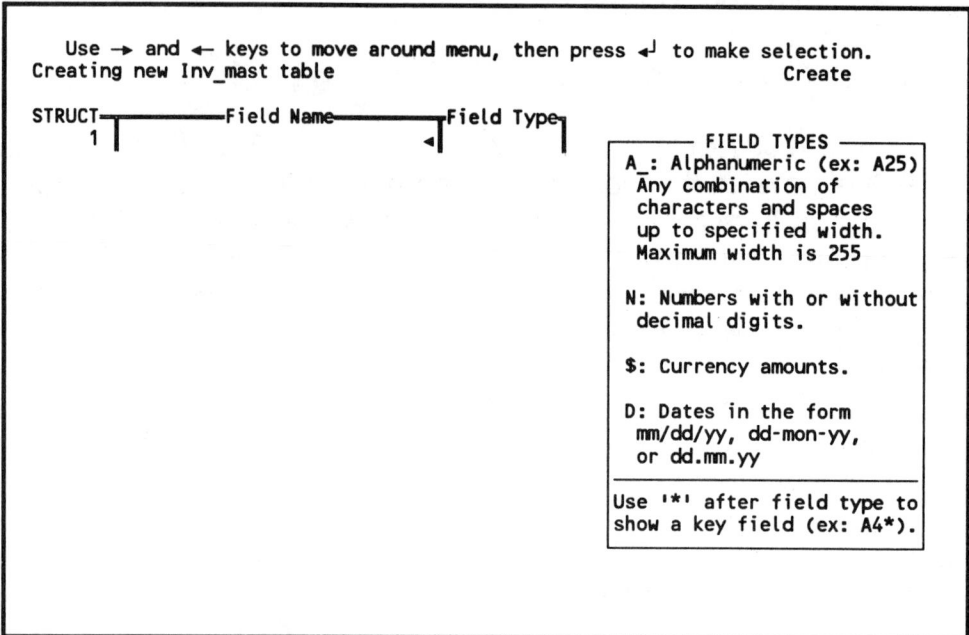

Figure 6-15 Blank Table Structure Screen for the Inv_mast Data Table

structure. Figure 6-17 displays the necessary information for completing the Inventory Master Table definition. When you are finished, your screen should match Figure 6-17. The cursor should be on a blank line at this point.

Editing the table structure

If you have made any mistakes while creating the table structure, there are several editing options available. To insert a new field or move an existing field in the existing structure, first place your cursor at the position where you want to have the new field. Then press INS and a blank field is opened for you to input information for the new field. To delete an existing field, press DEL while your cursor is on that field. To change a spelling error or field type error, you can use the Backspace key to delete a character at a time. You may then type in the correct information.

Saving the table structure

After you have gotten the screen to look like Figure 6-17, you are ready to save the table structure. To do so, press **F10** to bring up the menu related to creating a table. Select **Do-it!**, and PARADOX will save the current table structure. After doing this, you are returned to the main menu. You may also save the table structure by just pressing **F2**, which is the Do-it! function key in PARADOX. This method saves you some keystroke commands.

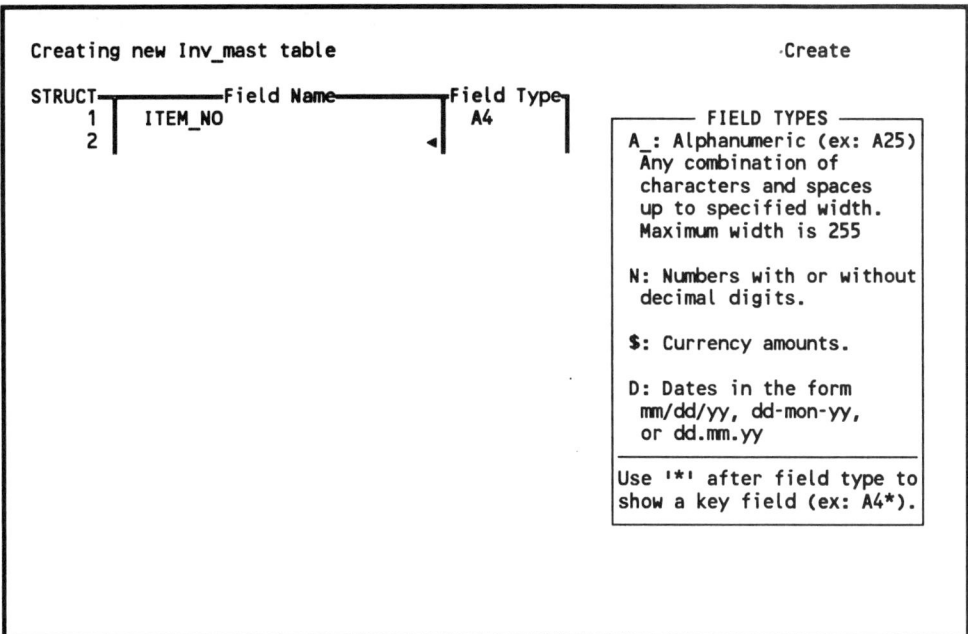

Figure 6-16 Table Structure for the Inv_mast Data Table after Adding the ITEM_NO Field

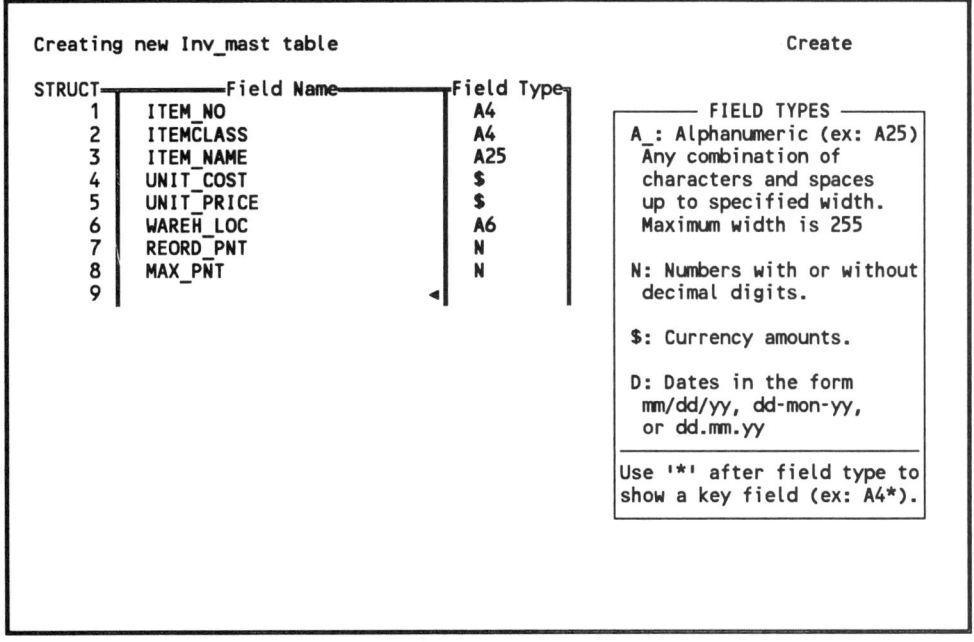

Figure 6-17 Completed Table Structure for the Inv_mast Data Table

Inputting data

To enter data into your INV_MAST table, from the main menu select **Modify** followed by **DataEntry**. Press **ENTER** to display the table names available and select INV_MAST. At this point your screen should look like Figure 6-18, which is the default data-entry screen in PARADOX. After entering data in one field, you would press the **ENTER** key to move to the next field. The data for the first record appears below. Enter this data into your table. (**USE ALL CAPITAL LETTERS.**)

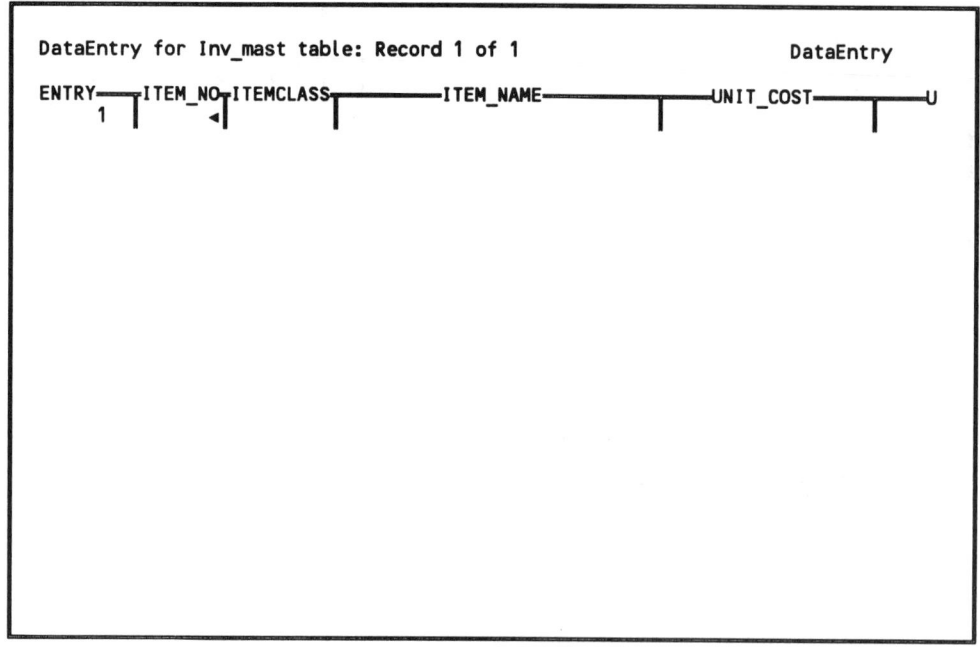

Figure 6-18 Default Data Entry Screen for the Inv_mast Data Table

ITEM_NO   B467
ITEM_CLASS BOOK
ITEM_NAME MAKE WAY FOR DUCKLINGS
UNIT_COST 2.50
UNIT_PRICE 4.50
WAREH_LOC A2S4L5
REORD_PNT 80
MAX_PNT   200

After entering the data for the first record, you are placed on the second line of the table, and the top of your screen should indicate that this is Record 2 of 2. The remaining data that you need to input to the Inv_mast table is shown in Table 6-4. After entering the last record, your screen should look like Figure 6-19. If you make any errors while entering the data, you can move to the record where the error has

Item_ no	Item_ class	Item_ name	Unit_ cost	Unit_ price	Wareh_ loc	Reord_ pnt	Max_ pnt
B467	BOOK	MAKE WAY FOR DUCKLINGS	2.50	4.50	A2S4L5	80	200
G324	GAME	MONOPOLY	4.25	9.60	A4S3L2	60	300
T219	TOY	TURTLE VAN	12.60	22.50	A3S2L4	30	160
T418	TOY	ECTO MOBILE	11.40	21.90	A3S3L6	30	160
G121	GAME	CANDYLAND	2.60	4.80	A4S3L1	40	250
B119	BOOK	CASEY AT THE BAT	2.10	4.30	A2S3L2	70	180
B187	BOOK	MIKE MULLIGAN	2.70	5.00	A2S3L5	80	220
G043	GAME	KERPLUNK	6.80	14.90	A4S2L4	90	260
B029	BOOK	GOODNIGHT MOON	3.60	7.00	A2S1L2	40	180
T108	TOY	LEGO BLOCKS	12.70	18.40	A3S1L4	20	110

Table 6-4 Data to Input to the Inv_mast Data Table

been made and do one of two things. To delete the entire record, press Del; to erase data in only a specific field, use the Backspace key to delete the data and then input the data once more. If you want to insert a record in the middle of an existing table, place the cursor on the line where you want the new record to appear and press Ins. This will create a blank line which you may use to input the correct data.

```
DataEntry for Inv_mast table: Record 11 of 11                    DataEntry

ENTRY───┬─ITEM_NO┬ITEMCLASS┬───────ITEM_NAME───────┬─UNIT_COST───┬───U
      1 │ B467   │ BOOK    │ MAKE WAY FOR DUCKLINGS │        2.50 │ ***
      2 │ G324   │ GAME    │ MONOPOLY               │        4.25 │ ***
      3 │ T219   │ TOY     │ TURTLE VAN             │       12.60 │ ***
      4 │ T418   │ TOY     │ ECTO MOBILE            │       11.40 │ ***
      5 │ G121   │ GAME    │ CANDYLAND              │        2.60 │ ***
      6 │ B119   │ BOOK    │ CASEY AT THE BAT       │        2.10 │ ***
      7 │ B187   │ BOOK    │ MIKE MULLIGAN          │        2.70 │ ***
      8 │ G043   │ GAME    │ KERPLUNK               │        6.80 │ ***
      9 │ B029   │ BOOK    │ GOODNIGHT MOON         │        3.60 │ ***
     10 │ T108   │ TOY     │ LEGO BLOCKS            │       12.70 │ ***
     11 │        ◄
```

Figure 6-19 Completed Data Entry Screen for the Inv_mast Data Table

At this point you are ready to formally add the records to the file and end the data entry process. To do this, press **F10** and select **DO-IT!** or just press **F2** (instead of F10). PARADOX will then add the records to the Inv_mast table; when it is finished, it will display a *View* of the table. View mode allows the user to look at the data contained in the table, but does not allow the user to change any of the data. To clear the table from the screen, press **F8**.

Viewing the data

There are two formats available to display the data you have just entered. To see these different formats select the **View** option from the main menu, press **ENTER** and selecting the Inv_mast table. PARADOX will then display, in table form, the first 22 records of a table. To see the next set of records you may use either PgDn or the down arrow keys. This is known as the *Table View*. The other display format available displays the data for only one record at a time. PARADOX allows you to toggle back and forth between the two display modes by pressing the **F7** key. This other method is referred to as *Record View*. When you initially press the F7 key, your screen should look like Figure 6-20. To go back to the Table display, press F7 again. Remember, the View mode does not allow you to change any of the data directly. To learn how to make changes to your records, see the next section. You should now clear your screen by pressing **F8**.

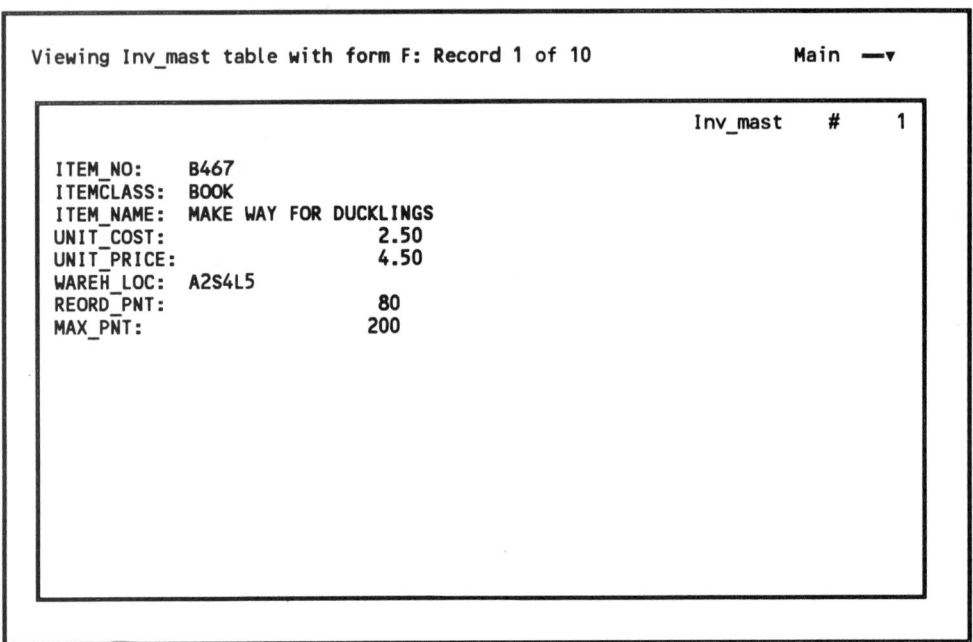

Figure 6-20 Viewing the Inv_mast Data Table using Record View

Editing the data

PARADOX allows you to make changes to the data in existing tables through its editing capabilities. There are two ways to enter the *Edit* mode of PARADOX; the first method is through the Modify command, the other is through the Edit command available while viewing a table. We will look at the use of the Modify command first.

From the main menu, select **Modify** and then **Edit**. You are asked for the name of the table you want to edit; press **ENTER** to see a listing of all the tables. At this point the only table listed should be the INV_MAST table. Select the Inv_mast table by pressing **ENTER** while it is highlighted, and your screen should look like Figure 6-21. At this point you can use the same editing keys we had discussed earlier: to delete an entire record, press DEL; to insert a new record, press INS when the cursor is in the position you want for the new record; to edit a particular field, use the Backspace key to delete the old data, and type in the correct data. You can also add records at the end of the table by moving to the first blank line and entering new data. When you are finished correcting the records, you may either: 1) press **F10** and select **DO-IT!** or 2) press **F2** (the DO-IT! key). Note that the table still appears on your screen, but the top left corner of the screen now says Viewing, not Editing. You can no longer make changes to the table at this point. To clear the table from the screen, press **F8**.

The second way to edit data in a table is to switch to the Edit mode from the View mode by pressing the F9 key. To try this, select **View** from the main menu, press **Enter** to see a list of tables, and select INV_MAST. Your screen should look like Figure 6-22. Note that the top left of the screen says Viewing. Next, press **F9** and you will note that the top left of your screen now says Editing. At this point if you need to edit any records, you may follow the procedures discussed above on how to make changes to the records. To save the changes, press **F10** and select **DO-IT!** (or press **F2**). You are now returned to the View mode. To clear the screen, press **F8**. You should now have a blank screen, except for the main menu at the top.

```
Editing Inv_mast table: Record 1 of 10                        Edit

INV_MAST┬ITEM_NO┬ITEMCLASS┬────────ITEM_NAME────────┬─UNIT_COST─┬────U
       1 │ B467  │  BOOK    │ MAKE WAY FOR DUCKLINGS   │      2.50 │ ***
       2 │ G324  │  GAME    │ MONOPOLY                 │      4.25 │ ***
       3 │ T219  │  TOY     │ TURTLE VAN               │     12.60 │ ***
       4 │ T418  │  TOY     │ ECTO MOBILE              │     11.40 │ ***
       5 │ G121  │  GAME    │ CANDYLAND                │      2.60 │ ***
       6 │ B119  │  BOOK    │ CASEY AT THE BAT         │      2.10 │ ***
       7 │ B187  │  BOOK    │ MIKE MULLIGAN            │      2.70 │ ***
       8 │ G043  │  GAME    │ KERPLUNK                 │      6.80 │ ***
       9 │ B029  │  BOOK    │ GOODNIGHT MOON           │      3.60 │ ***
      10 │ T108  │  TOY     │ LEGO BLOCKS              │     12.70 │ ***
```

Figure 6-21 Editing the Inv_mast Data Table

The previous sections have provided you with the basics of how to create and maintain a database. The last lesson to be learned in this chapter is how to modify the structure of an existing table. This is discussed in the next section.

```
Viewing Inv_mast table: Record 1 of 10                          Main

INV_MAST┬ITEM_NO┬ITEMCLASS┬────────ITEM_NAME────────┬────UNIT_COST────┬────U
       1│ B467  │ BOOK    │ MAKE WAY FOR DUCKLINGS   │         2.50    │ ***
       2│ G324  │ GAME    │ MONOPOLY                 │         4.25    │ ***
       3│ T219  │ TOY     │ TURTLE VAN               │        12.60    │ ***
       4│ T418  │ TOY     │ ECTO MOBILE              │        11.40    │ ***
       5│ G121  │ GAME    │ CANDYLAND                │         2.60    │ ***
       6│ B119  │ BOOK    │ CASEY AT THE BAT         │         2.10    │ ***
       7│ B187  │ BOOK    │ MIKE MULLIGAN            │         2.70    │ ***
       8│ G043  │ GAME    │ KERPLUNK                 │         6.80    │ ***
       9│ B029  │ BOOK    │ GOODNIGHT MOON           │         3.60    │ ***
      10│ T108  │ TOY     │ LEGO BLOCKS              │        12.70    │ ***
```

Figure 6-22 Viewing the Inv_mast Data Table using Table View

Changing the structure of an existing table

To modify the structure of an existing table, you would select Modify from the main menu and then select Restructure. You are asked which table you want to restructure; press ENTER and select INV_MAST. Your screen should look like Figure 6-23.

At this point you could use the DEL keys to delete a field, the INS key to insert a new field in the middle of the table or move an existing field into that position, and the Backspace key to change specific field information. See the previous section on *Editing the table structure* for the specific procedures needed to carry out these changes. When you are finished, press F2 (DO-IT!) to save the new structure. After saving the new structure, the table is displayed in View mode, with the changed structure in use. Remember that F8 will clear the screen and display the main menu.

Exiting PARADOX

To exit from PARADOX, select Exit from the main menu and then answer Yes a the next menu. This procedure will return you to where you were before you started PARADOX. Do not remove your floppy diskette until you have returned to this point and the light is off on the floppy drive. You do not have to worry about saving your files before you exit, since you have already done so as part of the tutorial. This transparent saving of files is one of the control features in PARADOX; the next section talks about some other controls that are relevant at this point.

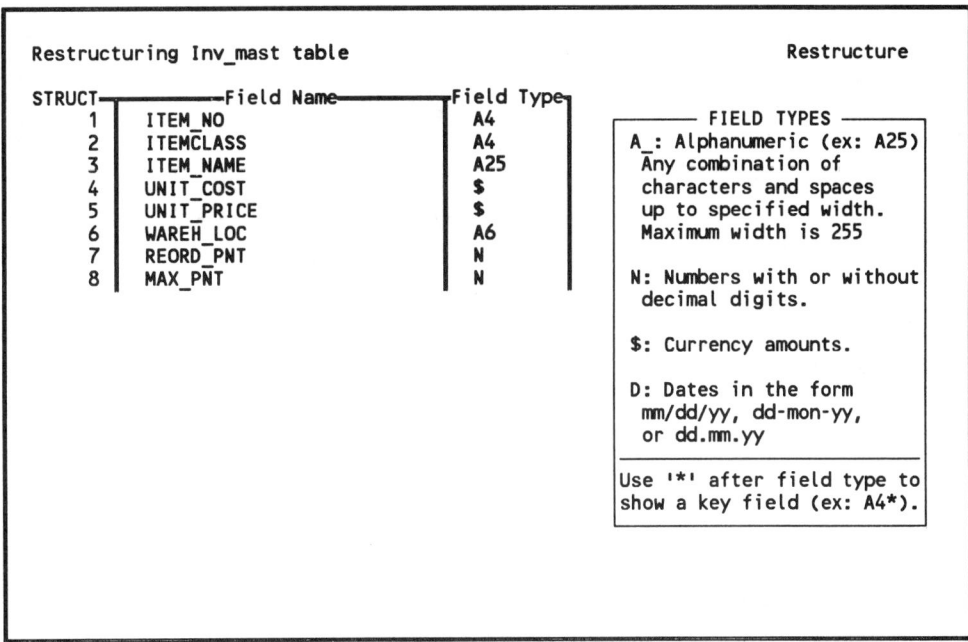

Figure 6-23 Restructuring the Inv_mast Data Table

Controls

PARADOX offers many control features, we will talk about these as they become relevant to each chapter's topics. At this stage of development, the major control that could be implemented is a basic file protection scheme that controls access to various tables and files as well as setting up a hierarchy of table and file privileges.

Under the Tools options there is a feature known as *Protect* (to get to this choice you would need to select Tools followed by More). PARADOX offers two broad levels of controls, *Owner* and *Auxiliary*. The Owner password gives you full power to work with any part of PARADOX; the Auxiliary password offers users limited access to various features and parts of PARADOX.

For example, if someone is assigned an auxiliary password, that person could view a certain table, but not make any changes to the table. The user could also be allowed to make changes to a particular field in a table and not allowed to view or make changes to other fields in the same table. These types of controls are extremely important in a database environment where several people will be using a centralized repository of data, and access to that data must be controlled.

A firm's database administrator (DBA) would likely be the person who has Owner privileges; that person's password should be kept in a secure place so that no one can use it. You will not use any password protection in your exercises, since there is a danger that if the password is lost, you may not be able to read your tables anymore. It is important, however, to realize that such controls do exist, and would be used in a corporate setting.

Another control device that you should get in the habit of using is *backing up* your files. At the beginning of this tutorial, remember that you made your floppy disk drive the default drive for the work session. For a variety of reasons, such as diskette damage or lost diskettes, you should copy each session's work on to another floppy diskette. At this point, the only file you have created is a data table, to which PARADOX automatically adds the extension .DB to the filename. If you do not know how to copy files from one floppy to another, ask your lab consultant or instructor.

Conclusion

The exercises at the end of the chapter provide you with the necessary table structures and data to create the Inventory Transaction Table and the Inventory History Table for Stroudsburg's inventory database. It is important that you complete those exercises since future exercises and tutorials will reference those tables. Once you have finished those exercises you will have a "complete" inventory database for Stroudsburg Toy Company. You should also be aware that included on your diskette that accompanied this manual are several other files that you will be using in later sections of this book. There are also review questions at the end of this chapter that allow you to evaluate your knowledge of the skills learned in this chapter.

FOLLOW-UP EXERCISES

Inventory Cycle

Before you start these exercises, make sure that you are using the proper floppy drive and subdirectory (if you have created one). If you are not sure how to do this, refer to the appropriate sections of this manual. When you are finished, remember to exit properly from PARADOX.

This exercise is designed to give you more practice with creating data tables in PARADOX. It is mandatory that you complete this exercise, since future parts of this manual depend on these tables having been created. Figure 6-24 indicates the structure of the Inventory Transaction table. You should name this table INV_TRAN. Table 6-5 shows the data that you are to add to the table as part of the data entry process. (Again, be sure to use all capital letters when entering the data).

Figure 6-25 displays the table structure for the Inventory History table and Table 6-6 supplies the data needed for the History table. You should name this table INV_HIST.

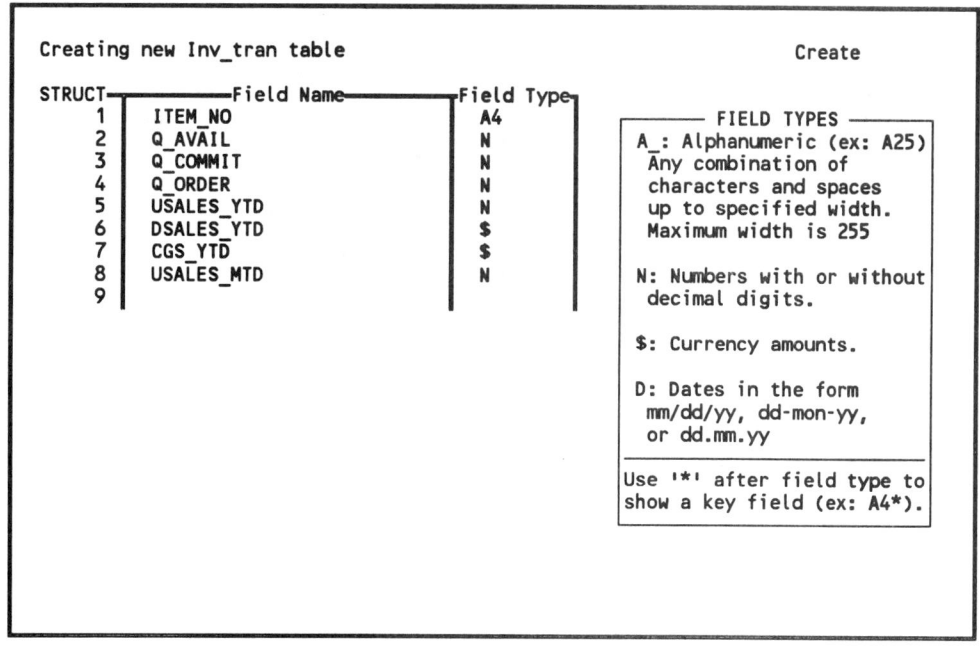

Figure 6-24 Completed Table Structure for the Inv_tran Data Table

ITEM_NO	Q_AVAIL	Q_COMMIT	Q_ORDER	USALES_YTD	DSALES_YTD	CGS_YTD	USALES_MTD
B467	145	20	0	55	247.50	137.50	0
G324	75	0	0	5	48.00	21.25	0
T219	150	30	0	0	0.00	0.00	0
T418	45	25	80	60	1314.00	684.00	0
G121	65	175	190	5	24.00	13.00	0
B119	130	0	0	40	172.00	84.00	0
B187	130	0	0	30	150.00	81.00	0
G043	155	55	0	145	2160.50	986.00	0
B029	150	40	0	0	0.00	0.00	0
T108	20	65	90	85	1564.00	1079.50	0

Table 6-5 Data to Input to the Inv_tran Data Table

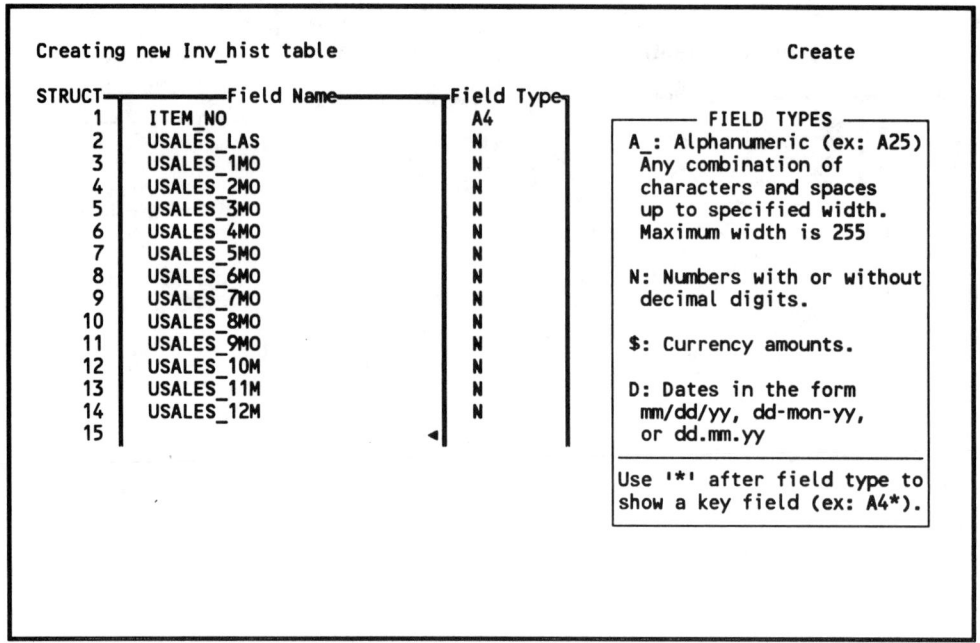

Figure 6-25 Completed Table Structure for the Inv_hist Data Table

ITEM_NO	USALES LAST	USALES _1MO	USALES _2MO	USALES _3MO	USALES _4MO	USALES _5MO	USALES _6MO	USALES _7MO	USALES _8MO	USALES _9MO	USALES _10M	SALES _11M	USALES _12M
B467	500	55	0	0	0	0	0	0	0	0	0	0	0
G324	580	5	0	0	0	0	0	0	0	0	0	0	0
T219	280	0	0	0	0	0	0	0	0	0	0	0	0
T418	400	60	0	0	0	0	0	0	0	0	0	0	0
G121	230	5	0	0	0	0	0	0	0	0	0	0	0
B119	170	40	0	0	0	0	0	0	0	0	0	0	0
B187	370	30	0	0	0	0	0	0	0	0	0	0	0
G043	150	145	0	0	0	0	0	0	0	0	0	0	0
B029	450	0	0	0	0	0	0	0	0	0	0	0	0
T108	530	85	0	0	0	0	0	0	0	0	0	0	0

Table 6-6 Data to Input to the Inv_hist Data Table

Revenue Cycle

You should first complete the follow-up exercise for the Inventory Cycle described above. When that is complete, there is only one other short exercise that needs to be completed as part of the Revenue Cycle. The disk that accompanied this text already includes all the data tables needed for the Revenue Cycle (except the ones you created as part of the tutorial and the Inventory Cycle follow-up exercises). You need to copy these data tables from that disk to the disk that has your three inventory data tables. You will also need to copy some index files, which have an extension of .PX . We will talk about indexing in Chapter 8. The names of the files to copy are as follows:

AR_MAST.DB	AR_MAST.PX
CASH_REC.DB	CASH_REC.PX
CUSTOMER.DB	CUSTOMER.PX
SALES_IN.DB	SALES_IN.PX
SALES_OR.DB	SALES_OR.PX

If you have created a subdirectory on your floppy disk, be sure to copy these files to the appropriate subdirectory. When you are finished copying these data tables to your diskette, start PARADOX and go through the procedures described earlier to switch to your default drive and subdirectory (e.g., A:\PARADOX). Select **View** from the main menu and then press **ENTER.** You should now see 8 tables listed, the three inventory tables you created and the five revenue tables you copied. If not, repeat the steps above to copy those files to your diskette.

Expenditure Cycle

You should first complete the follow-up exercise for the Inventory Cycle described above. When that is complete, there is only one other short exercise that needs to be completed as part of the Expenditure Cycle. The disk that accompanied this text already includes all the data tables needed for the Expenditure Cycle (except the ones you created as part of the tutorial and the Inventory Cycle follow-up exercises). You need to copy these data tables from that disk to the disk that has your three inventory data tables. You will also need to copy some index files, which have an extension of .PX . We will talk about indexing in Chapter 8. The names of the files to copy are as follows:

AP_MAST.DB	AP_MAST.PX
CASH_PAY.DB	CASH_PAY.PX
VENDOR.DB	VENDOR.PX
VOUCHER.DB	VOUCHER.PX
PURCH_OR.DB	PURCH_OR.PX

If you have created a subdirectory on your floppy disk, be sure to copy these files to the appropriate subdirectory.

When you are finished copying these data tables to your diskette, start PARADOX and go through the procedures described earlier to switch to your default drive and subdirectory (e.g., A:\PARADOX). Select **View** from the main menu and then press **ENTER**. You should now see 8 tables listed, the three inventory tables you created and the five expenditure tables you copied. If not, repeat the steps above to copy those files to your diskette.

Payroll Cycle

Create the following data files using PARADOX:

PAYCHECK.DB
PAY_CLAS.DB
PAY_MAST.DB
PERSONEL.DB
TIME_CAR.DB

Figures 6-26 through 6-30 display the suggested layout for these files. You will input the data to these files in Chapter 7.

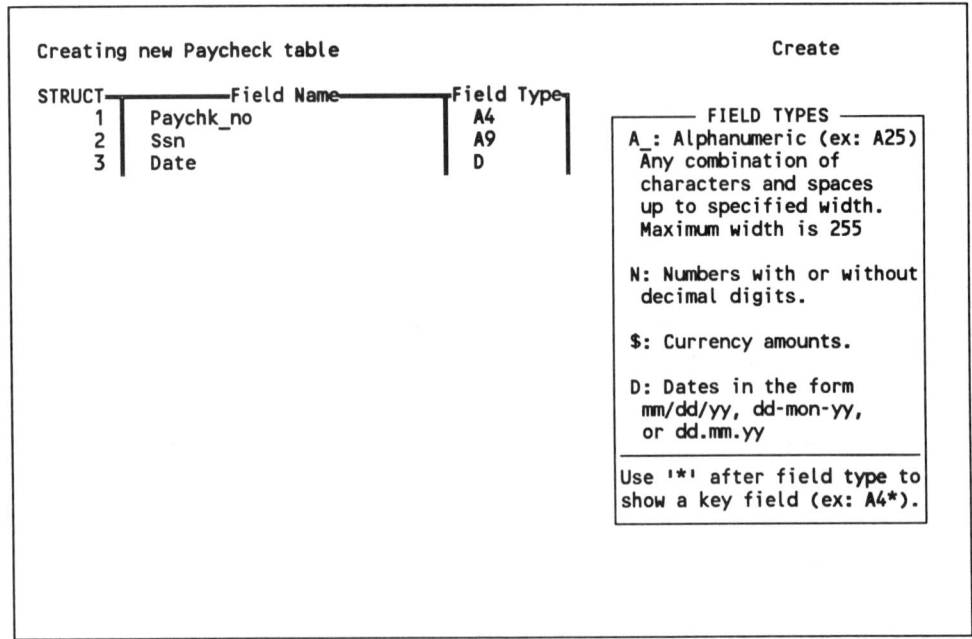

Figure 6-26 Completed Table Structure for the PAYCHECK Data Table

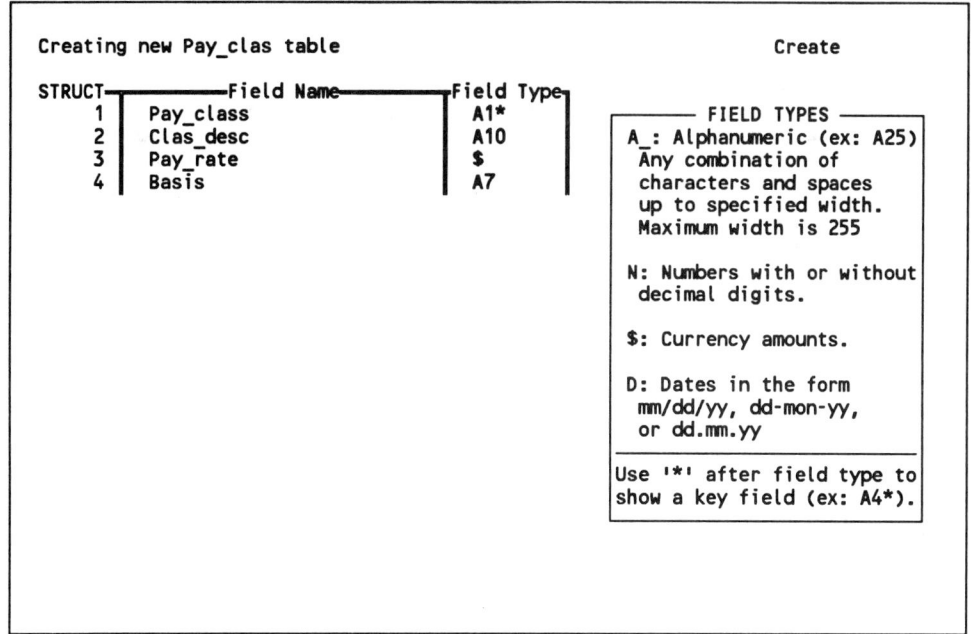

Figure 6-27 Completed Table Structure for the PAY_CLAS Data Table

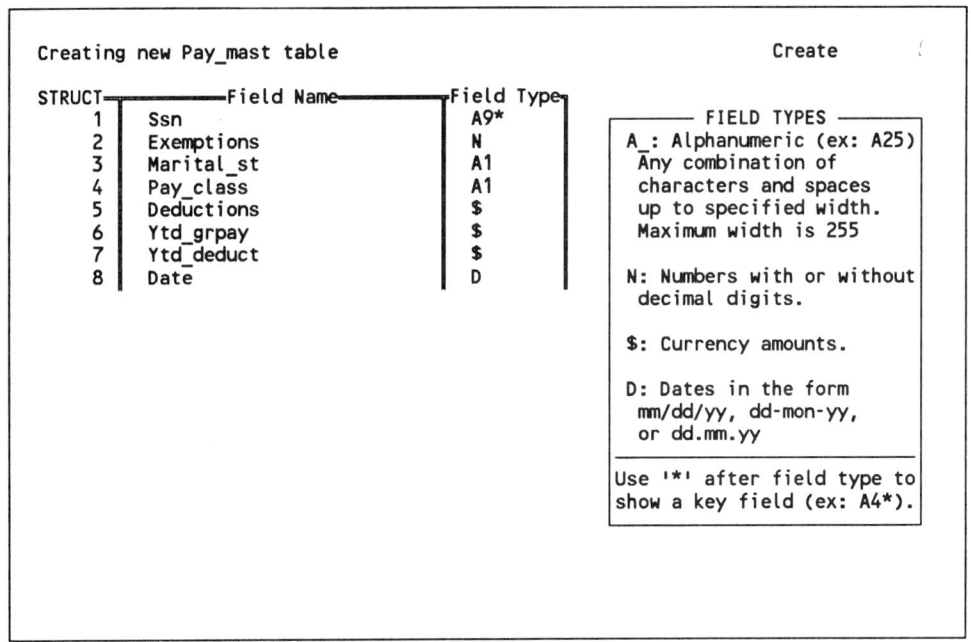

Figure 6-28 Completed Table Structure for the PAY_MAST Data Table

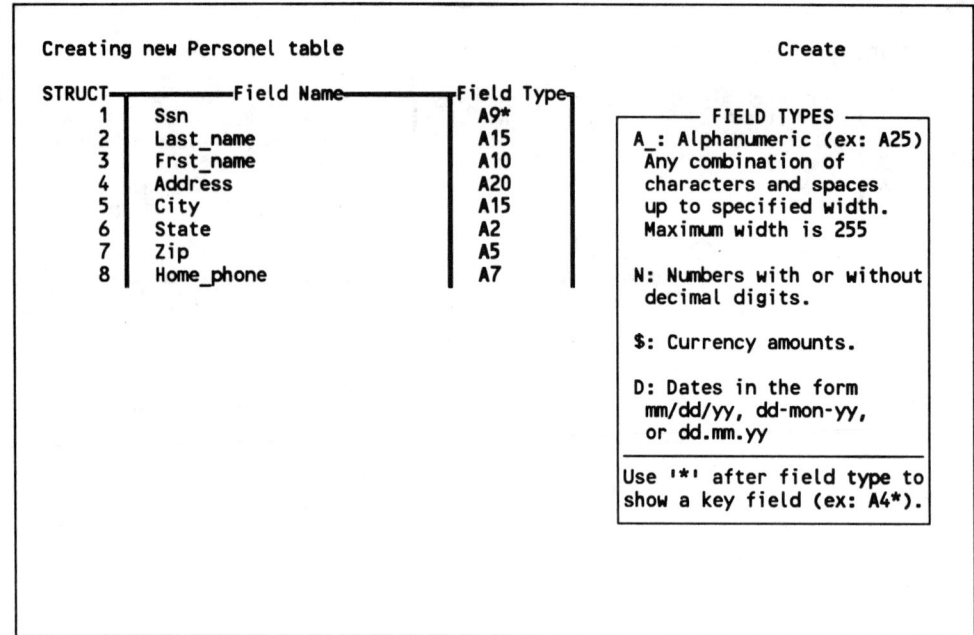

Figure 6-29 Completed Table Structure for the PERSONEL Data Table

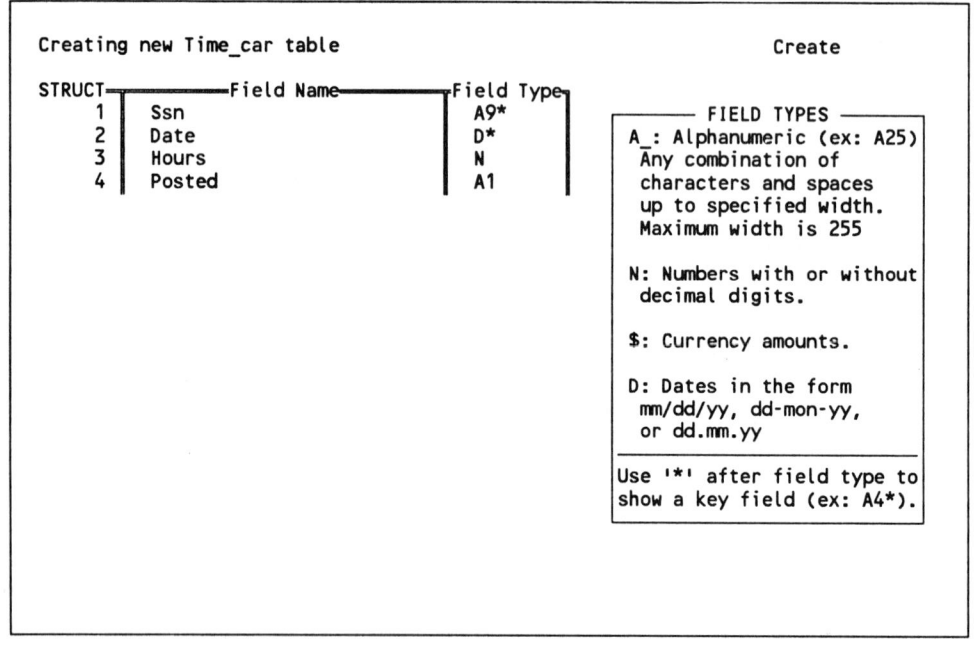

Figure 6-30 Completed Table Structure for the TIME_CAR Data Table

REVIEW QUESTIONS

1. How do you switch to a different drive and a subdirectory using PARADOX?
2. How do you create a data file?
3. What is meant by a file structure?
4. How do you save a file structure?
5. How do you change the structure of an existing data file?
6. How do you add data to a file using PARADOX?
7. How do you save a file after you have added or changed data in the file?
8. What is the difference between Table View and Record View?
9. How do you switch back and forth between Table view and Record View?
10. What is meant by the Edit mode?
11. How can you make changes to an existing record in a data file?
12. How can you delete an existing record in a data file?
13. What are some controls PARADOX has for limiting access to data?
14. What filename extension does PARADOX give to data files?
15. How do you exit from PARADOX?

CHAPTER 7

DESIGNING INPUT SCREENS AND
CONTROLLING DATA ENTRY
USING A DATABASE MANAGEMENT SYSTEM

INTRODUCTION

The purpose of this chapter is to teach you how to create forms that may be used for inputting data into the database. Assuring the accuracy and completeness of data entry can be enhanced through the use of several of the control features available with your DBMS software. We will look at these issues through the use of Stroudsburg Toy Company's inventory database, which you created in Chapter 6.

CASE: Stroudsburg Toy Company

Bill Jackson is pleased with the progress that has been made in developing the inventory database. He has input all the data that shows the current status of Stroudsburg through August 31, 1991. However, he realizes that the database will be constantly changing, due to new items being added to the inventory files, old items being deleted from the inventory files, the selling of goods to customers throughout the year, and the buying of goods from vendors throughout the year.

While it was not difficult to add, delete, or edit data using the default data entry screen used in Chapter 6, it was not a very intuitive or helpful screen for a relative novice to use. Thus, Bill would like your help in designing data entry (input) screens that could help data entry people with their duties more efficiently and effectively.

CASE SOLUTION: dBASE IV

dBASE IV allows the user to develop what are known as *FORMS*. The first task you would normally work on before you sit in front of the computer is to design, on a piece of paper, what you want your data entry screen to look like. Let's assume that we want to create a data entry form that allows us to add new inventory items to the inventory master file. After looking at the structure of the Inventory Master file, you decide that a form such as Figure 7-1 will be useful for this purpose. This chapter will teach you how to design a screen such as Figure 7-1 using dBASE IV.

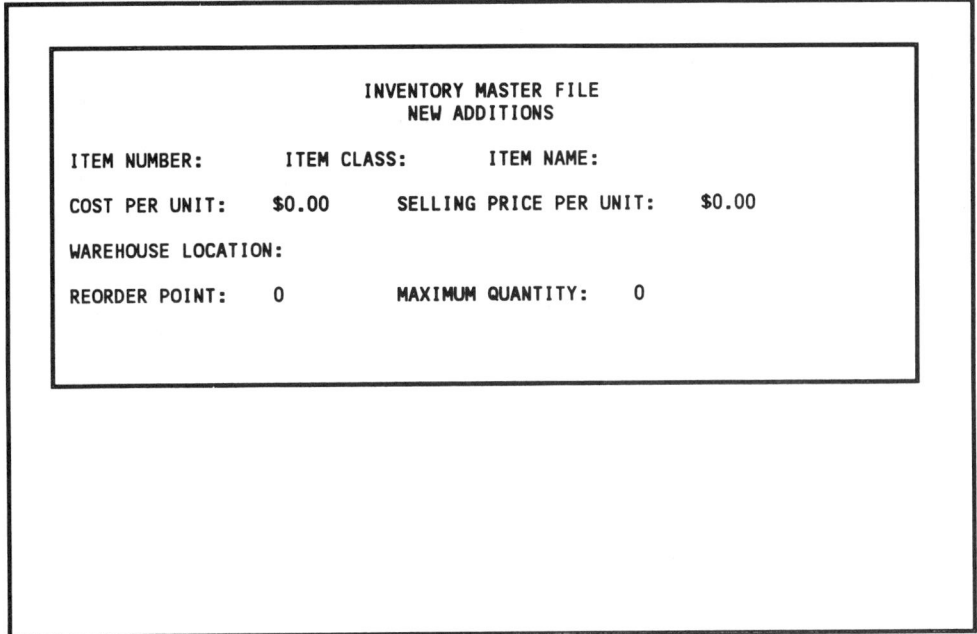

```
                          INVENTORY MASTER FILE
                             NEW ADDITIONS

     ITEM NUMBER:        ITEM CLASS:        ITEM NAME:

     COST PER UNIT:    $0.00      SELLING PRICE PER UNIT:    $0.00

     WAREHOUSE LOCATION:

     REORDER POINT:    0        MAXIMUM QUANTITY:    0
```

Figure 7-1 Sample Data Entry Form for the Inv_mast Data File

Designing a Data Entry Form

Once you have laid out what you want the screen to look like, you can begin working on the computer. After starting dBASE, switch to your default drive and subdirectory (see Chapter 6 for details), and make sure that you are in the AIS_FILE catalog. The name of your current catalog is displayed near the top of the screen. If you are not in the proper catalog, press **ALT_C**, and select **use a different catalog**. The names of any catalogs on the current drive and directory are then displayed; choose the AIS_FILE catalog. Once you are in the right catalog, you should see the three files you created in Chapter 6 displayed in the Data Panel (plus some other data files if you are doing some of the additional follow-up exercises).

Your first step is to select the data file for which you will be creating a data entry form. Since we will be working with the data from the Inventory Master file, you need to select that file and make it the active file. To do this, use the arrow keys to highlight the INV_MAST file and press **ENTER**. When the next window appears, move the cursor to Use file and press **ENTER**. You should now be back at the Control Center, and the INV_MAST file should be above the dotted line in the data panel, indicating that the file is currently in use.

The next step is to enter the Forms Design Module by moving the cursor over to the Forms Panel and pressing **ENTER** while the <create> option is highlighted. After doing this, your screen should look like Figure 7-2. *Note: if you need to exit from this tutorial before you have completed it, go to the section* Saving a Form. *When you are ready to work on the form again, read the section* Modifying a Form.

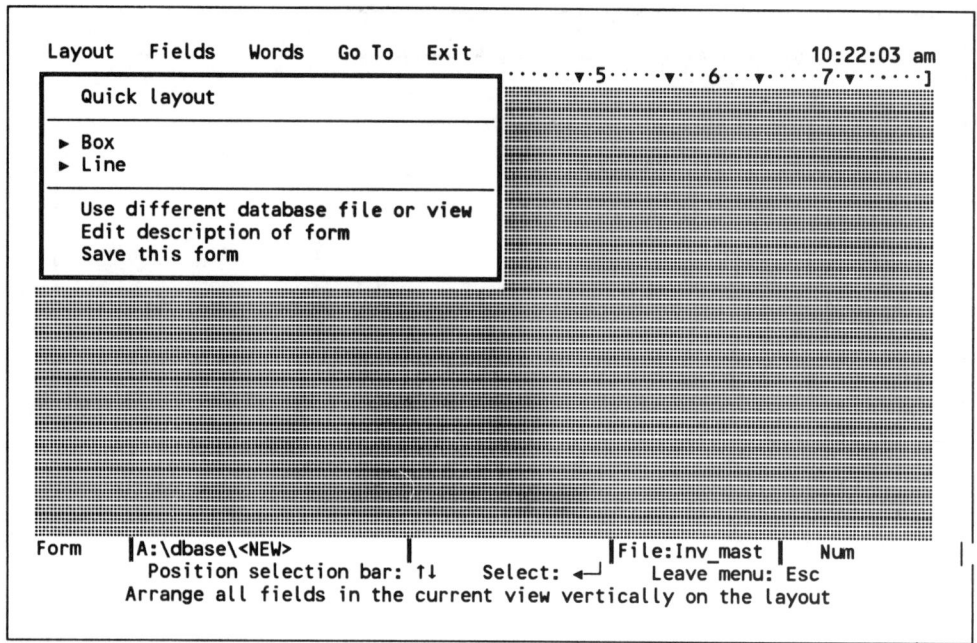

*Figure 7-2 Layout Menu for Designing Data Entry Form for Inv_mast
Data File*

The first part of the form you can design is the heading. The heading should clearly indicate the purpose of the form. Putting useful headings on forms is a good control device. We will use Figure 7-1 as a guide.

You will begin by giving yourself a blank workspace, so that we can design the form from scratch. To do this, press **ESC**, and the pull-down menu under the Layout option should disappear. Next, move your cursor down a few lines and type the words **INVENTORY MASTER FILE**. After that is finished, you want to center these words on your screen. In order to accomplish this, first make sure that your cursor is on one of the letters/characters in the text which you wish to center. Next, select the Words option by pressing **ALT-W**, and move the cursor down to the Position option. Press **ENTER**, and select **Center**. The text will automatically be placed in the center of your screen. Use the down arrow key to move to the next line, and repeat the same steps for adding the next line of text, **New Additions**. After this has been centered, press **ENTER** two or three times to create some blank lines on your screen.

You are now ready to add the fields and their corresponding labels to the form. Move your cursor to a place that would correspond with where the Item Number: label appears in Figure 7-1, and type in those words. Again, labels are a useful control feature and should give the user a clear indication of what data needs to be entered at different locations on the screen. When you are finished typing in this label, move your cursor to the right one or two spaces, using the right arrow key. You will now add the corresponding field to go along with this label, which in this case is the ITEM_NO field.

There are different ways to accomplish the adding of a field to a form. First, if you look at the bottom of your screen, it indicates that the F5 function key is used to add a field. Since this is what you want to do, you could press F5 and a listing of all the fields for the current database would be shown, allowing you to choose the appropriate one. Another way to add a field to a form is through the menu choices at the top of your screen. Note that one of the menu choices is Fields. To select this option, you would press ALT-F. A pull-down menu appears, and you would select Add a field. You would now be at the same point as if you had pushed F5 to add a field.

Let's use the second method described above. Press **ALT-F** and select **Add a field**. Your screen should look like Figure 7-3. Since you want to add the ITEM_NO field, highlight that field and press **ENTER**. A window then appears that allows you to customize how the field will look and what sort of data may be entered into that field. The first item we would like to modify is the template. Currently, the template is {XXXX}, which means the field is four characters in width, and will accept any type of character.

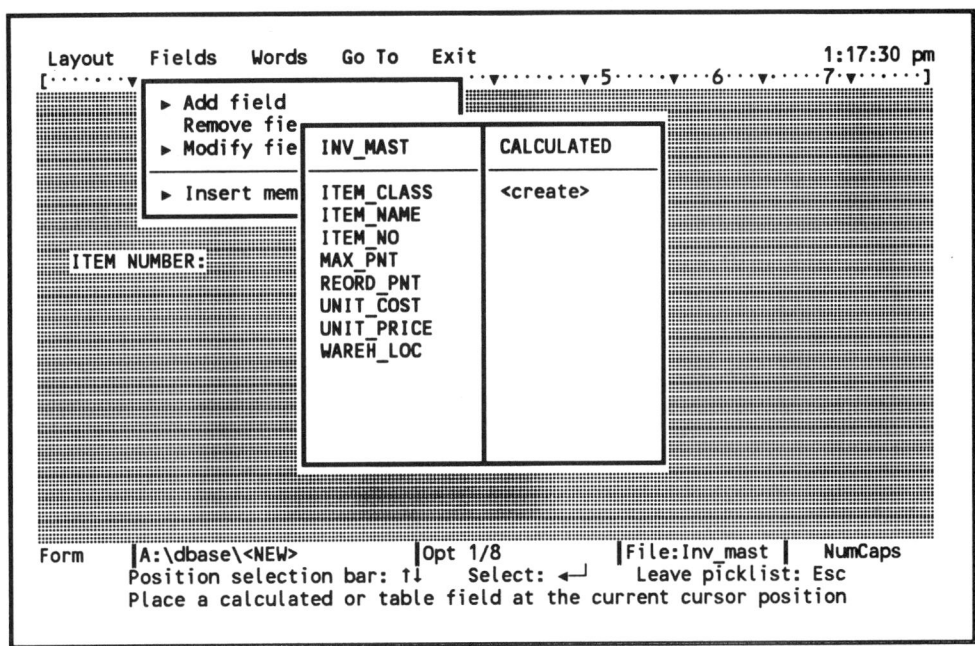

Figure 7-3 Selecting a Field to Add to the Forms Design Screen

Stroudsburg Toy Company has set up their coding system for their inventory file so that the first letter of the code indicates whether the inventory item is a book (B), game (G), or toy (T). After the initial character, there are three numbers. This coding scheme allows for a sufficiently large number of inventory items within each classification.

To control the data entry process for the item number, you can specify that the first character must be a letter, followed by three numbers. This is accomplished by pressing **ENTER** while on the Template option. A box appears that contains a variety of ways to control what sort of data is allowed for that field. Since we want just alphabetic characters in the first position, type **A** in the first position. This will then only allow the letters A-Z to be in the first position. For the last three positions, we just want numeric data, so enter **9** three times, which will limit that part of the item number to only accepting numeric characters. When you are finished, press **ENTER** to save your template. Note that we have not changed this from a character type field. We have merely controlled for the type of characters that may be entered in the various positions.

The next concern Stroudsburg has is making sure that data is entered in a standard fashion. For example, one person may enter the first letter of the item number using uppercase letters and another person may do so using lowercase letters. Since the computer would interpret this as two different characters, item number B467 would be considered a different item when compared to item number b467. What is needed is a built-in data entry control that will accept either upper or lower case entries and have them converted into all upper case. This way, the data is standardized. To do this in dBASE, move down to the Picture functions option and press **ENTER**. When the next window appears, move down to the Upper case conversion option. The default setting is most likely OFF. To switch the option to ON so that all letters entered from the keyboard are converted to capital letters, you may either press the **ENTER** key or the **SPACE BAR** key. Pressing either one of these keys toggles you back and forth between OFF and ON. Once you have turned this option ON, you need to save that option. This is done by pressing **Ctrl-End**. Note that this method of saving the changes is displayed on the screen to remind you of the exact keystroke combination required. Once you have saved this option, you are returned back to the previous window.

The last control we will put in is to have a message displayed to the user that the first letter of the item number must be a B, G, or T. The ability to put a message on the screen allows the system to be more user friendly as well as reduce errors. To install this control, move your cursor down to the Edit options and press **ENTER**. A new window will appear with several options available. The option we are interested in is message. Move your cursor to this menu choice, press **ENTER**, and you can begin typing your message. Let's type the message: **The first letter must be a B, G, or T followed by three numbers.** When you are finished, press **ENTER**. Press **Ctrl-End** to save this option.

These controls are probably adequate for our purposes. Later in this chapter we will talk about some other useful controls that could be implemented through the dBASE programming language. You are now ready to place the ITEM_NO field on the forms screen. To do this press **Ctrl-End**. Your screen should now look like Figure 7-4. We will now go through each of the remaining fields, and discuss what control(s) would be appropriate for each field.

Move your cursor to the position where the Item Class label appears (see Figure 7-1) and type in those words. As noted earlier, Stroudsburg classifies all its inventory as either a BOOK, GAME, or TOY. dBASE has the capability to limit a user's choice for the item class to just one of these three choices. To see how this can be setup, move your cursor one or two spaces to the right of the Item Class: label, press **ALT-F** and select Add a field. Move the cursor to ITEM_CLASS and press **ENTER**. The control we want to install is found under the Picture options, so move your cursor down to that line and press **ENTER**. The option we need is labeled Multiple choice. Place your cursor on that option, and press **ENTER**. You are then prompted to enter the possible choices for this field. Type in the following: **BOOK, GAME, TOY** (make sure you place the commas between the words) and then press **ENTER**. When you are finished typing in the choices, press **Ctrl-End** once to save the multiple choice option, and then press **Ctrl-End** once more to place this field on your screen.

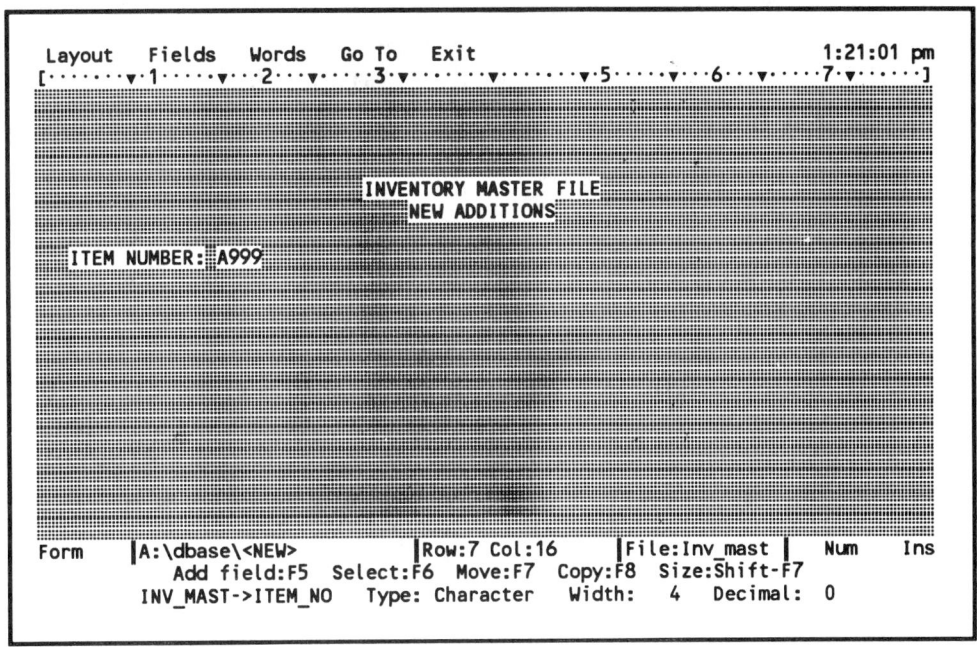

Figure 7-4 Forms Design Screen after Adding the ITEM_NO field to the Screen

The next field to add (again use Figure 7-1 as a guide) is the item name field. First type in the label for the field: **Item Name:** then move your cursor next to the label. Press **ALT-F** select **add a field**, and then choose ITEM_NAME. There is only one control we will place on this field, and that is to make all the letters uppercase. As you may recall, this command is included with the Picture option. Follow the instructions from earlier on using this option, and then when you have saved the option by pressing **Ctrl-End**, press **Ctrl-End** once more to put the item name field on the screen.

The next field we will work on is the unit cost, where we will install two controls not yet discussed. The first step is to move your cursor down a couple of lines, using the down arrow key. Type in the label **Cost per Unit:**. With the cursor next to the label, press **ALT-F**, select **add a field** and select the UNIT_COST field to add. Move the cursor down to the picture options and press **ENTER**. The option that you will select from here is Financial format. To do this move your cursor down until you highlight that option and then press **ENTER** to switch it **On**; press **Ctrl-End** to save this option. The next control to install is included with the *edit* options, so move down to that option and press **ENTER**. The control we are going to use is known as a *Limit Test*. This control will make sure that the cost that is input is greater than a certain amount. In this case, we want the unit cost to be greater than zero. We could almost consider this a *Sign Test* as well, since we are preventing anyone from entering a negative number for the unit cost.

Move the cursor down to the smallest allowed value option and press **ENTER**. At this point you are asked to enter a valid dBASE expression. The expression required here can be satisfied by simply typing in the number **0**. After doing this, press **Ctrl-End** to save that option. Press **Ctrl-End** once more to place the field on the screen.

For the unit price field, first add the label and then follow the directions above on how to make this a financial format field. When you are finished with that, select the edit option next. This will be the last new control that we need to discuss in detail. What we would like to do is compare the unit price with the unit cost to control for the price to be greater than the cost. While in some rare cases this is not always true, we will assume that Stroudsburg's unit cost has never exceeded its unit price for any item. This type of control is known as a *Relationship Check*.

After selecting the edit option, move the cursor down to Accept value when and press **ENTER**. At this point you are asked to enter a valid dBASE expression. The expression required is as follows: **UNIT_PRICE > UNIT_COST**. You must be careful to type in these field names exactly as they have been defined in your file structure. After typing this expression, press **ENTER**, and you are returned to the edit option screen. The last detail needed at this point is for dBASE to display an error message if someone tries to enter a price lower than the cost. To do this, move the cursor down to the Unaccepted message, press **ENTER**, and type in: **The price must be higher than the cost.** When you are finished typing the message, press **ENTER**, and then Ctrl-End to save your editing controls. Remember to press **Ctrl-End** once more to place the field on the screen.

For the remaining fields, there are no new controls that need to be explained in detail. The next field to work on is the warehouse location. After typing the label and selecting the WAREH_LOC field, there are two options we will put with this field. First, the template should control for the type of characters that are entered into this field. The warehouse location for any item is noted by its Aisle, its Shelf, and its Location on the shelf. A sample warehouse location would be A1S2L3, indicating aisle one, shelf two, and location three. Thus for the template, we would want it to be **a9a9a9**. The second control is under the edit option. We want to display a message to help the user know what kind of format is used to indicate a unique warehouse location. This can be accomplished by selecting the message choice under the edit option and then typing in a brief message, such as: **Example: A1S2L3 = Aisle one, Shelf two, and Location three**. When you are finished, be sure to press **Ctrl-End** to save these options. Press **Ctrl-End** once more to place this field on the screen.

The next field is the reorder point. First, add the label and select the REORD_PNT field. Next, under the edit options put **0** for the smallest allowed value, and press **Ctrl-End** twice to save the options and place the field on the screen.

The last field to add to the form is the maximum quantity. The controls we will place on this field are similar to the ones used with the unit price field. First, type the label and select the MAX_PNT field using **ALT-F** and the add a field option. Next, we want to control for the maximum quantity allowable to be greater than the reorder point. Follow the steps described above with the unit price field and use the dBASE expression: **MAX_PNT > REORD_PNT**. Be sure to use the exact field names. When you are finished with that task, type the message: **Maximum quantity must be**

greater than reorder point for the Unaccepted message option. Remember to press **Ctrl-End** twice to save this option and place the field on the screen.

Editing/Enhancing the Form Design

When you have placed the maximum quantity field on the screen, you are now finished with the basic construction of the form. To make sure that you have placed the right fields next to the right labels, move your cursor around to the various fields. At the bottom of your screen dBASE tells you what field is represented at that position. If you have made a mistake, there are a couple of ways to correct it. One way is to place your cursor on the incorrect field, press ALT-F and select Remove a field. By pressing ENTER, the currently highlighted field is removed from the screen. You may then go back and add the correct field in the desired location.

Another method of rearranging the fields is by placing the cursor on one of the fields and pressing F6. You will note at the bottom of the screen that F6 is for selecting a field. That field has now been "captured", or highlighted, by the screen. To move the field to another location, press F7 and you can use the arrow keys to move the field to a different location. Do not place a field on top of an existing field. If there is already a field in the position where you wish to place the currently selected field, first move the currently selected field to a nearby blank location and press ENTER to complete the move. You can then go back to the field that is in the wrong place and either remove that field or move it to its proper location. After doing so, you may go back to capture the original field and use F6 and F7 to place it next to the appropriate label. When you are finished, press ENTER.

To correct a label, the easiest way is to use the DEL key or **Backspace** key to erase the label completely, and then retype the correct label.

To put a blank line on the screen, make sure that the INS key has been activated. You can tell if it is active by looking at the bottom right part of your screen. If the Ins key has been activated, you should see the word Ins. If it is not there, press the INS key, and you will see that word in the lower right corner of the screen. To insert a blank line, all you need to do is press ENTER while the INS key is activated.

The last procedure we will learn is how to enhance the appearance of the form by adding a double line border around the form. To do this, select **ALT-L** for Layout, and choose the **Box** option. Another window appears from which you can select the type of border you want. Choose **Double**, and you will note at the bottom of the screen some further instructions. You should use your arrow keys to move the cursor to the upper left corner of where you want the box to begin. When you get the cursor to the desired position, press **ENTER**, and this will lock the top left corner point of the box. At this point, you can expand the box by using the arrow keys to move the cursor down and over, basically stretching the dimensions of the box. When you reach the bottom right corner of the box, press **ENTER** and the box will be completed.

Saving a form

Your screen should now look like Figure 7-5. To save the screen, press **ALT-L** and select **Save this form**. You will be prompted for a name; type the name **INV_MAST** and press **ENTER** when you are finished. dBASE will now create three files related to the form, one with a .SCR extension, one with a .FMO extension, and the third with a .FMT extension. This may take a little time, so be patient. To exit from the form screen and return to the Control Center, press **ALT-E** and select **Save changes and exit**. You should now be back at the Control Center.

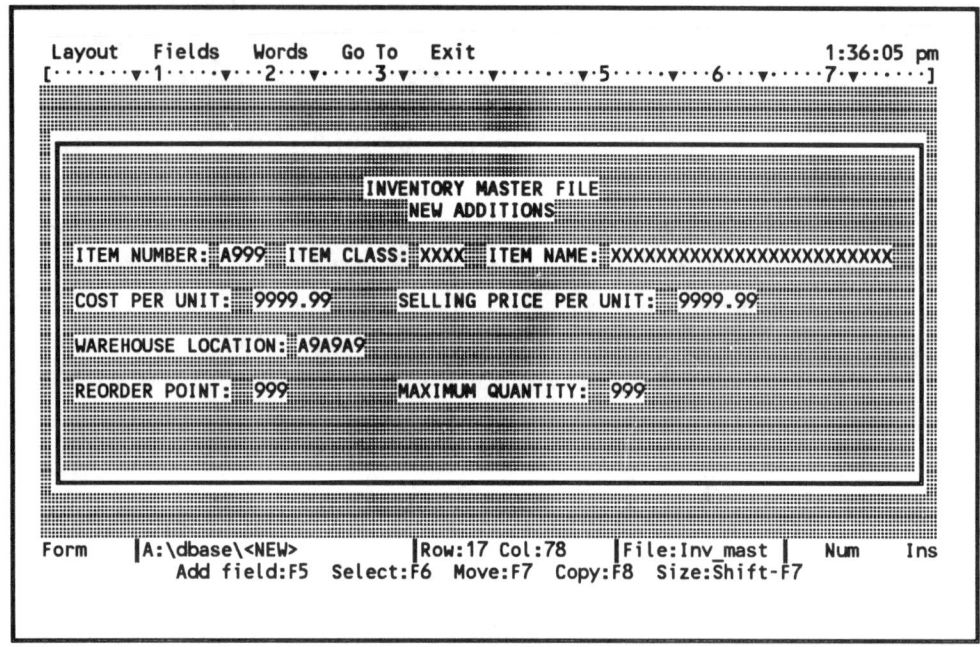

Figure 7-5 Completed Forms Design Screen for Inv_mast Data File

The screen you have created has the .SCR extension; the program code generated to produce the form has the .FMT extension, and the compiled code has the .FMO extension. The file that should be in your Forms panel is the one with the .SCR extension. To check this, just highlight INV_MAST in the Forms panel (not the Data panel) and the bottom of the screen will display the filename INV_MAST.SCR.

Using a form

To see what your form looks like and how to use it, make sure your cursor is in the Forms panel and move it to the INV_MAST file. You should see the name of the file displayed on your screen below the Panels, with the .SCR extension. Press **ENTER**, choose **Display data** and your screen should look like Figure 7-6, which is displaying the first record in the INV_MAST data file. To move through your file, press **PgDn**. To add records to the file, press **ALT-R**, and choose **Add new records**. You are then given a blank form. At this point, you may add new records to your data file.

To practice with using the form, add the following records shown in Table 7-1 for two new items that Stroudsburg has just added to their inventory. While you are entering the data, note the messages at the bottom of the screen. For the ITEM_CLASS field, you need to press the spacebar to cycle through the various choices. When the correct choice is found, press **ENTER**. Try putting in a price lower than the cost to see how the system responds. When you are finished, press **ALT-E**, select **Exit**, and you are returned to the Control Center.

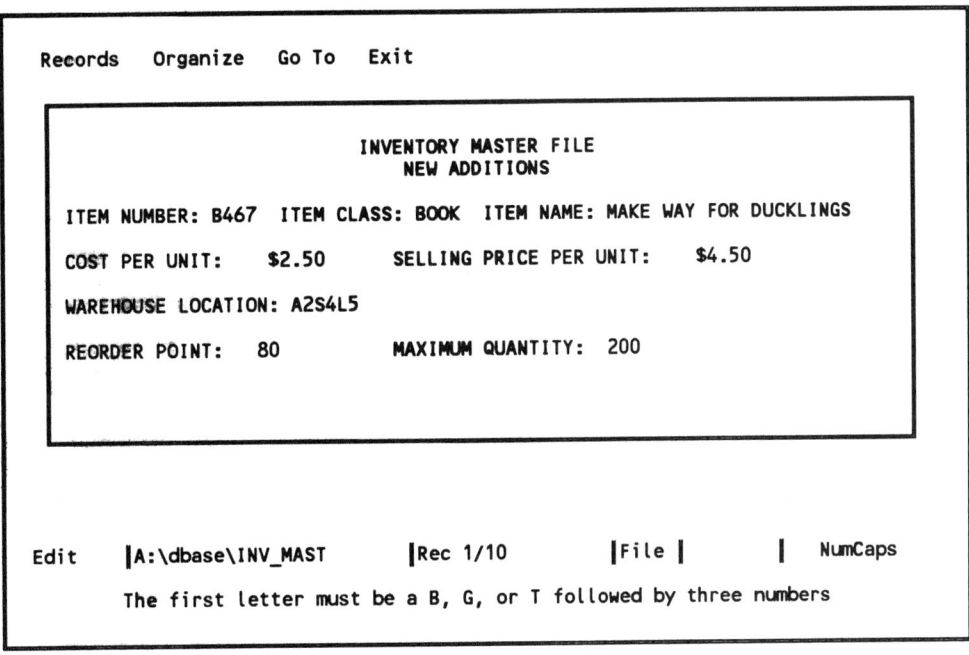

Figure 7-6 Displaying the First Record in the Inv_mast Data File Using Custom Form

Item_ no	Item_ class	Item_ name	Unit_ cost	Unit_ price	Store_ loc	Reord_ pnt	Max_ pnt
G286	GAME	RISK	5.25	11.60	A4S3L7	50	290
T220	TOY	PIZZA THROWER	11.60	21.50	A3S2L5	30	160

Table 7-1 New Data to Add to Inventory Master Data File Using Custom Form

Modifying a form

The last issue to be discussed concerning the design of input forms is how to modify a previously designed screen layout. You may need to do this if you had to exit from the tutorial before you were completely finished, or just to make some changes to your finished form. To do this, select INV_MAST from the Forms panel by highlighting the file and pressing ENTER and then choosing Modify layout. Your screen should now be displaying the form you had created earlier. You may also get to this point by highlighting the file in the Form panel and pressing SHIFT-F2. As a reminder, ALT-F brings up the options for adding, deleting, or modifying a field. If you need to delete or change a label, use the Backspace or Del key to remove the incorrect label. To get rid of the box border, position your cursor anywhere on the box and press Del. You can then add a new box through the Layout menu. When you are finished modifying the screen, press ALT-L and select Save this form. Press ENTER to accept the old file name. When you are ready to return to the Control Center, press ALT-E and select Save changes and exit. You should now be back at the Control Center.

Database integrity

The DBA, as well as everyone in the firm, should be concerned with making sure the database is accurate, consistent, and up-to-date. This is known as *database integrity*. At this point, your database is not consistent, since the inventory master data files contain two item numbers (G286 and T220) that are not in the other two inventory data files. You need to open up the other two inventory data files (INV_HIST and INV_TRAN) and add just the two new item numbers to the files. To do this, highlight the appropriate data file in the Data panel and press **F2**. This will display the data currently in the file. Press **ALT-R**, select **Add new records**, and add the two new inventory item numbers to these files. Place 0's in the remaining fields. When you are finished, remember to press **ALT-E**, and to select **Exit** to save your changes.

Conclusion

This completes the tutorial on using the Forms module of dBASE. Ensuring the accuracy and reliability of the data that enters a firm's database is critical to the firm's success. With the proper use of editing controls, a DBMS can prevent a good number of errors from corrupting a database. These controls were discussed throughout the section on *Designing a data entry form*.

FOLLOW-UP EXERCISES

Inventory Cycle

There are no additional forms that need to be created specific to the inventory cycle. As a reminder, however, be sure that you have added the two new inventory items discussed in this chapter to all three of your inventory data files. See the chapter sections on *Using a form* and *Database integrity* for more detail if necessary.

Revenue Cycle

There are various data entry operations that are performed as part of the revenue cycle. In order to institute some control over this process, Stroudsburg has asked you to design data entry screens as part of the revenue cycle. Name the forms you are about to create the same as their corresponding data file. The names of the data files you will be using are shown below:

- SALES_OR.DBF
- SALES_IN.DBF
- CASH_REC.DBF

Figures 7-7 through 7-9 give you an idea as to how such data entry screens could appear. Feel free to design them as you want, but they should contain the same information as shown on the screen. The most important point that needs to be made is that you should not put any fields on the screen that do not appear on the Figures below. Also, remember to put some controls over the data entry process, using the techniques discussed in the tutorial. In the last chapter we will use these screens to record some revenue transactions for Stroudsburg Toy Company.

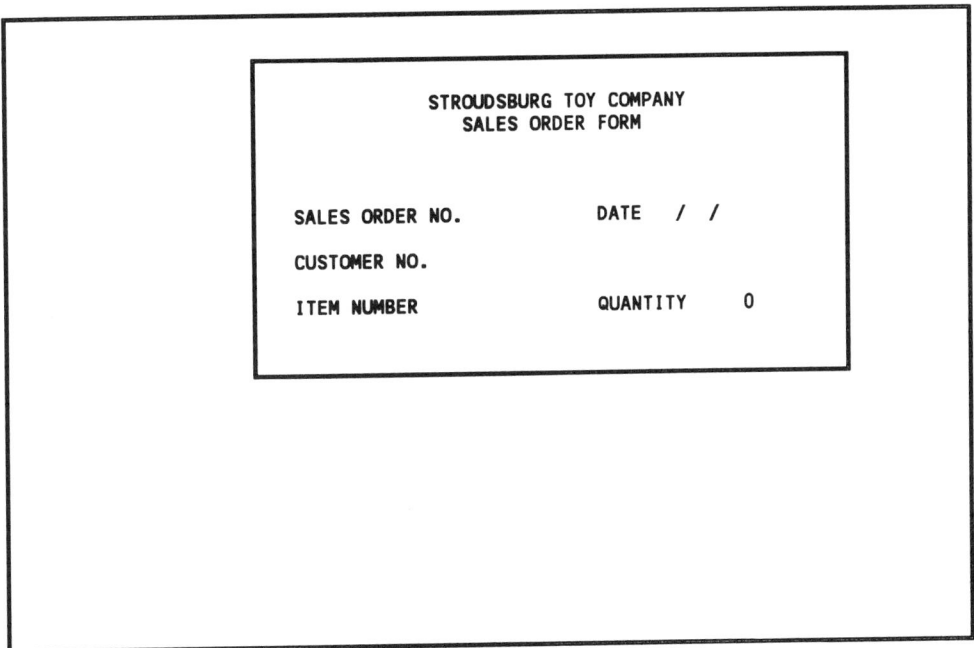

Figure 7-7 Sample Data Entry Form for the Sales_or Data File

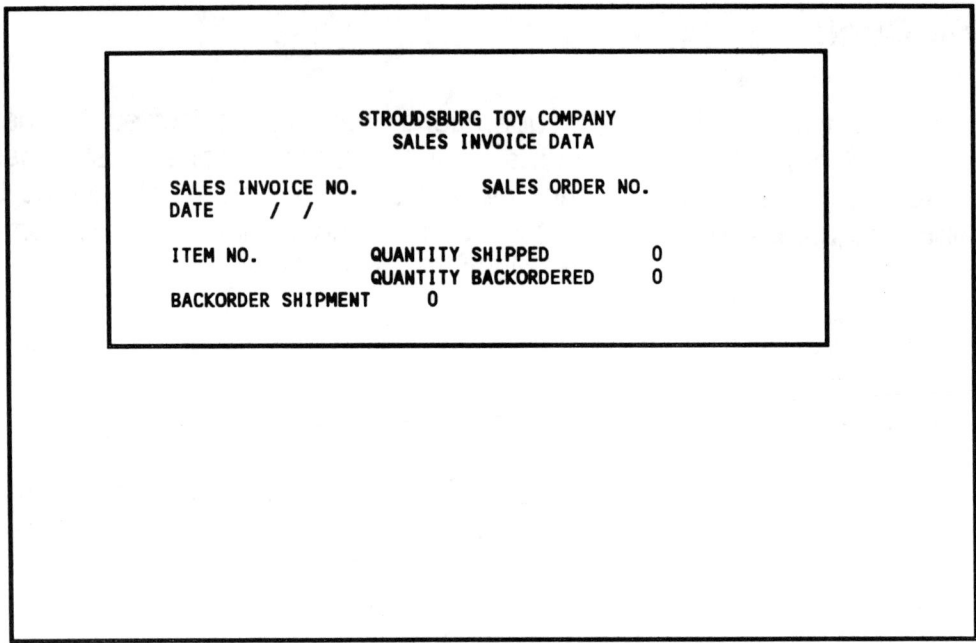

Figure 7-8 Sample Data Entry Form for the Sales_in Data File

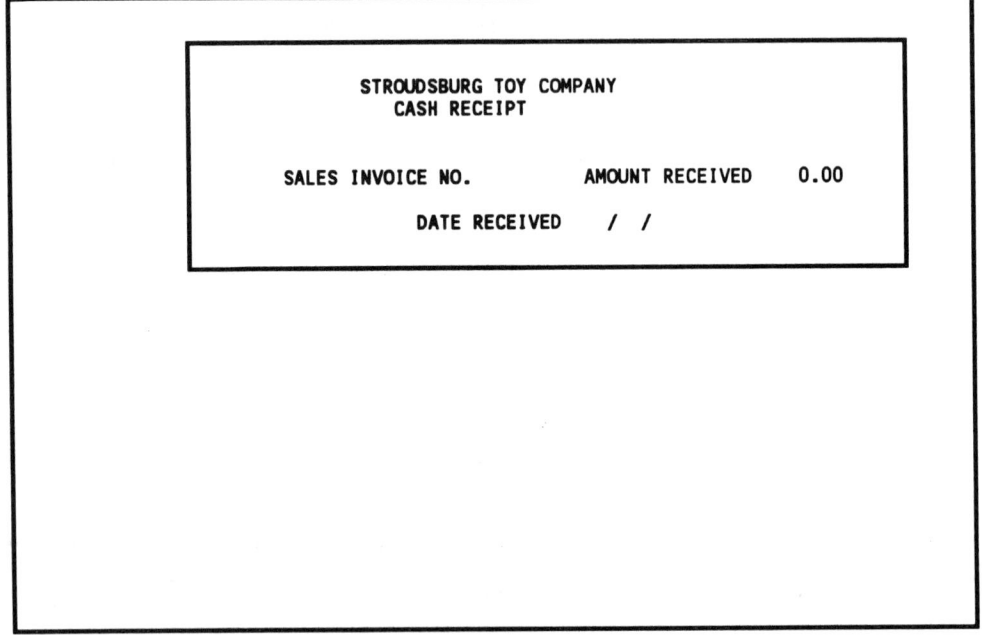

Figure 7-9 Sample Data Entry Form for the Cash_rec Data File

When you are finished creating these data entry forms, there is one other data entry form related to the revenue cycle. However, you do not need to design this form, the files corresponding to it are already included on the diskette that accompanied the book. You should copy these two files to your diskette:

- CUSTOMER.FMO
- CUSTOMER.SCR

After copying these files to your diskette, be sure to add the CUSTOMER.SCR file to your AIS_FILE catalog under the Forms panel. See Chapter 6 for information on how to add files to a catalog.

Expenditure Cycle

There are various data entry operations that are performed as part of the expenditure cycle. In order to institute some control over this process, Stroudsburg has asked you to design data entry screens as part of the expenditure cycle. Name the forms you are about to create the same as their corresponding data file. The names of the appropriate data files are shown below:

- PURCH_OR.DBF
- VOUCHER.DBF
- CASH_PAY.DBF

Figures 7-10 through 7-12 give you an idea as to how such data entry screens could appear. Feel free to design them as you want, but they should contain the same information as shown on the screen. The most important point that needs to be made is that you should not put any fields on the screen that do not appear on the Figures below. Also, remember to put some controls over the data entry process, using the techniques discussed in the tutorial. In the last chapter we will use these screens to record some expenditure transactions for Stroudsburg Toy Company.

When you are finished creating these data entry forms, there is one other data entry form related to the expenditure cycle. However, you do not need to design this form, the files corresponding to it are already included on the diskette that accompanied the book. You should copy these two files to your diskette:

- VOUCHER.FMO
- VOUCHER.SCR

Add the VOUCHER.SCR file to your AIS_FILE catalog, as described in Chapter 6.

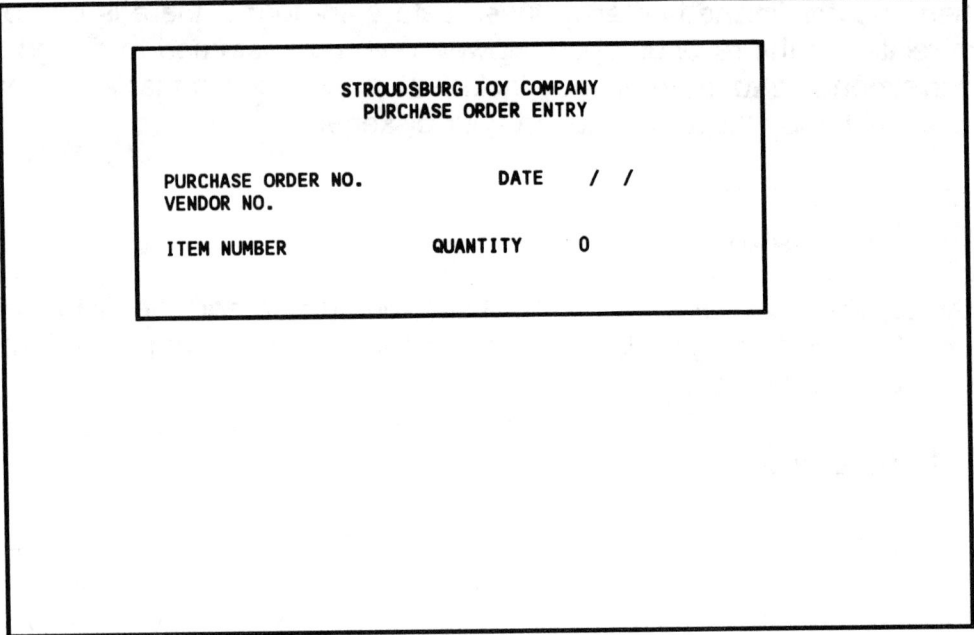

Figure 7-10 Sample Data Entry Form for the Purch_or Data File

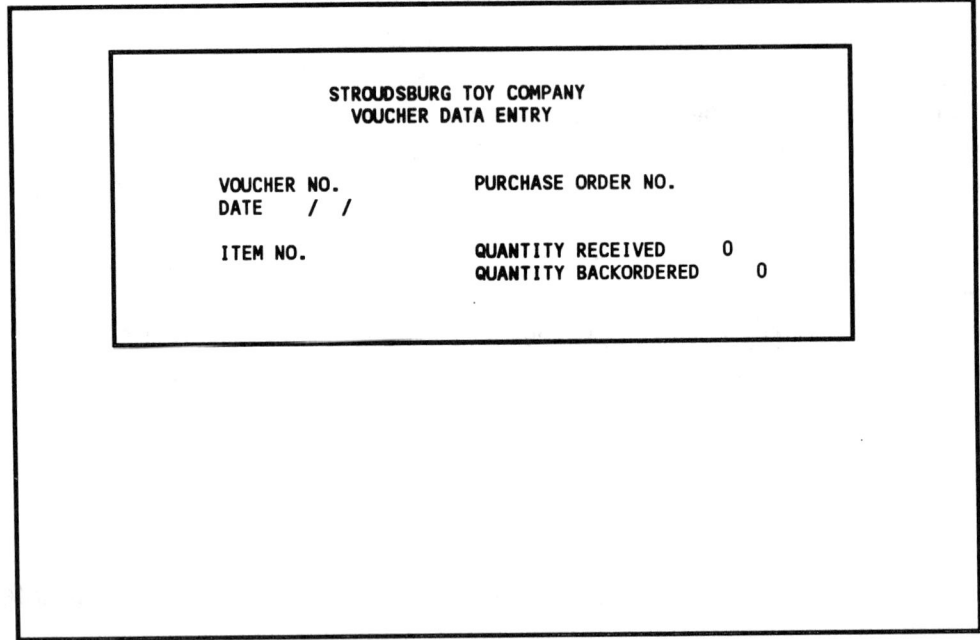

Figure 7-11 Sample Data Entry Form for the Voucher Data File

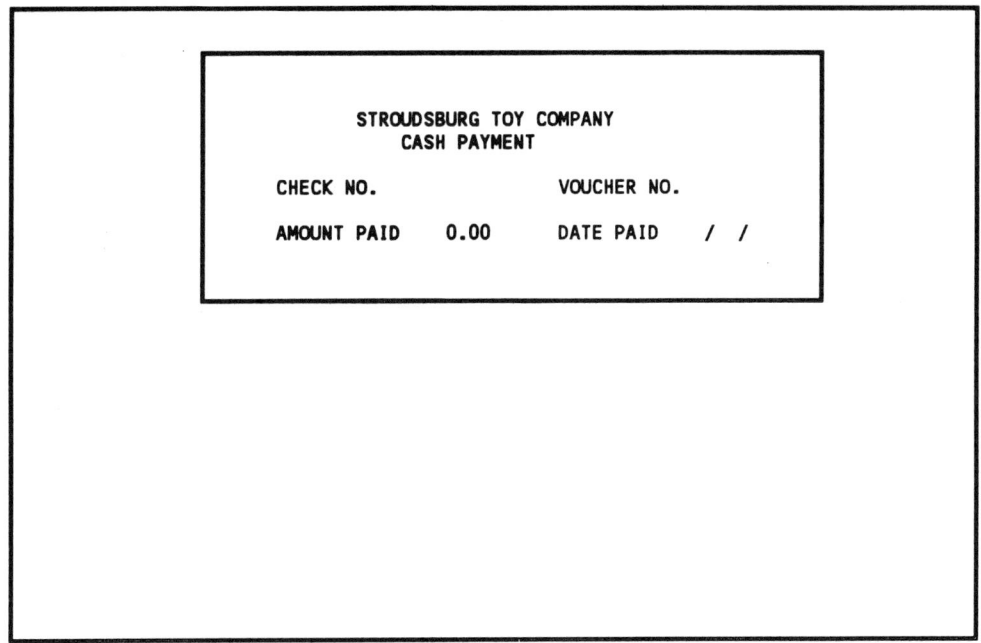

```
                    STROUDSBURG TOY COMPANY
                         CASH PAYMENT

       CHECK NO.                    VOUCHER NO.

       AMOUNT PAID     0.00         DATE PAID    /  /
```

Figure 7-12 Sample Data Entry Form for the Cash_pay Data File

Payroll Cycle

In order to add convenience as well as control to the process of recording critical payroll data, Stroudsburg Toy has asked you to design suitable input screens to aid in this task. Name the forms you create the same as their corresponding data file names. You will need to create five data entry screens. Figures 7-13 through 7-17 provide sample input screens to help you get started. When you are finished creating the screens, use them to enter payroll data into the system. Tables 7-2 through 7-6 provide the necessary data for these files. Do not worry about the *PDATE* field in the Payroll Master file or the *POSTED* field in the Time Card file. You may leave them blank for now; in the next chapter you will create a file that will automatically update these fields.

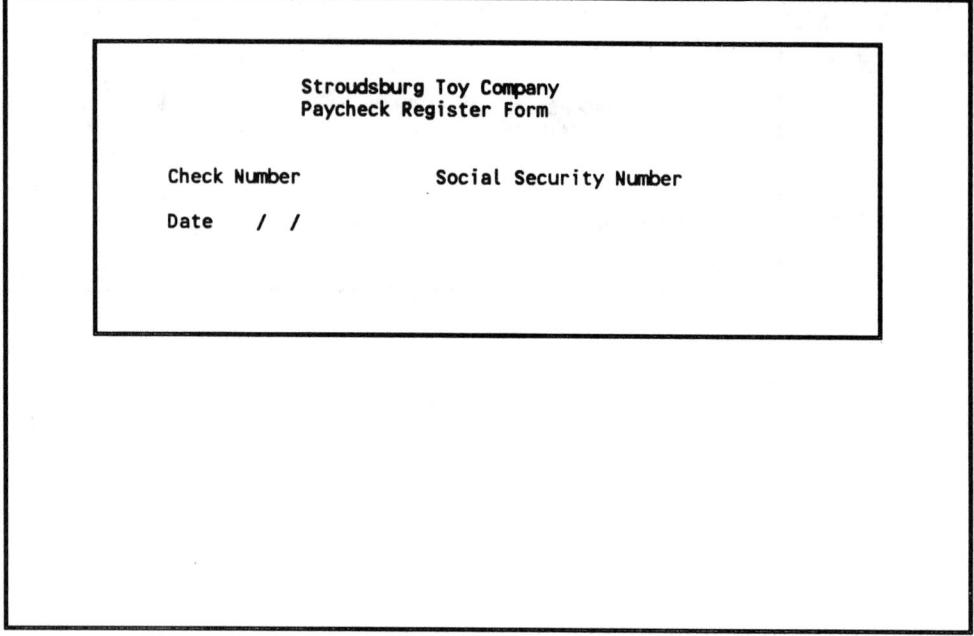

Figure 7-13 Sample Data Entry Form for the Paycheck Data File

PAYCHK_NO	SSN	DATE
2341	1111111111	08/31/91
2342	2222222222	08/31/91
2343	3333333333	08/31/91
2344	4444444444	08/31/91
2345	5555555555	08/31/91

Table 7-2 Data Entry for Paycheck Data File

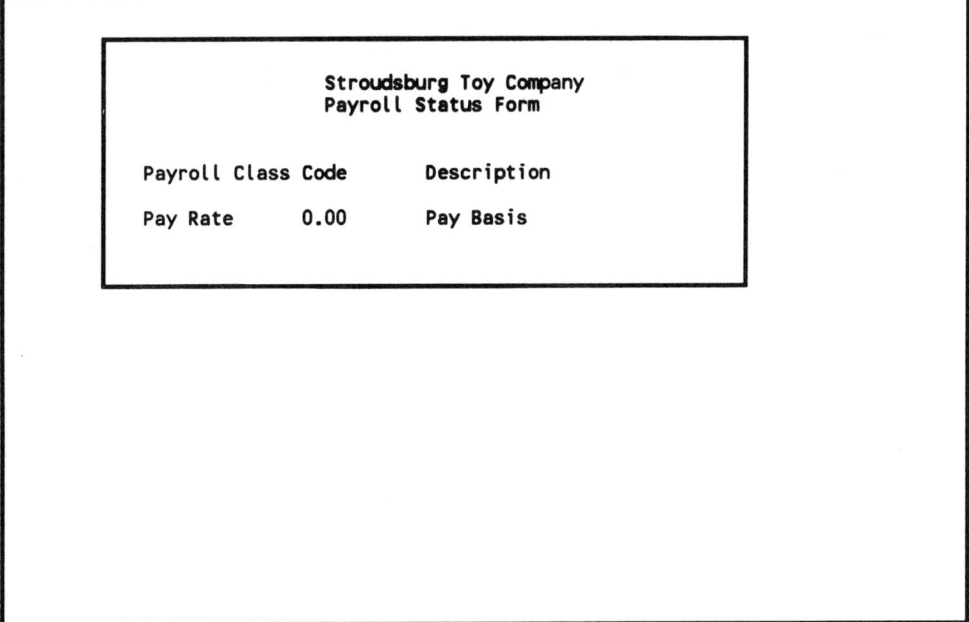

Figure 7-14 Sample Data Entry Form for the Pay_clas Data File

PAY_CLAS	CLAS_DESC	PAY_RATE	BASIS
A	President	5000.00	MONTHLY
B	Vice. Pres	3000.00	MONTHLY
C	Office Mgr	12.00	HOURLY
D	Store Mgr.	10.00	HOURLY
E	Part Timer	6.00	HOURLY

Table 7-3 Data Entry for Pay Classification Data File

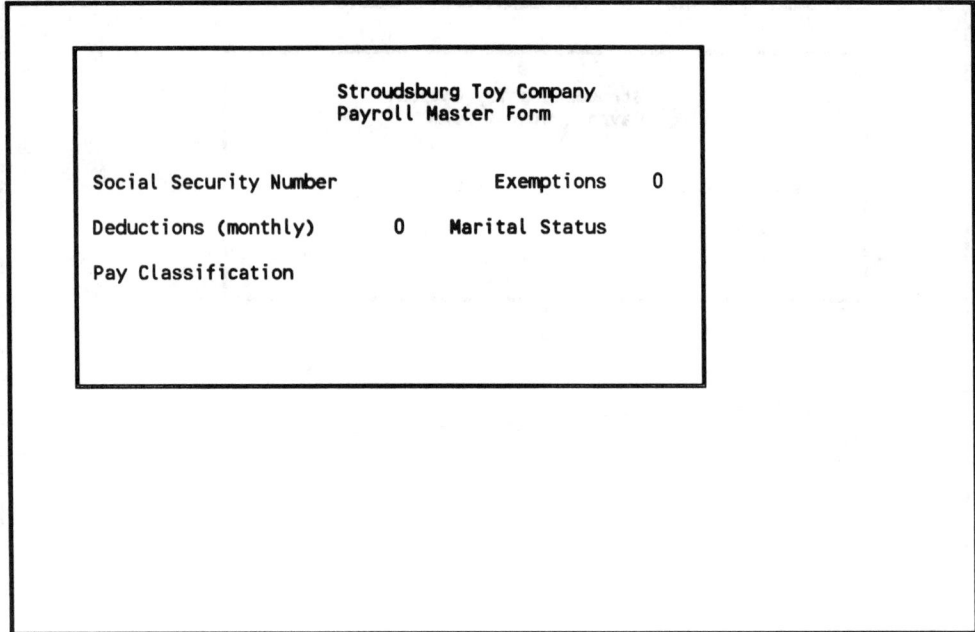

Figure 7-15 Sample Data Entry Form for the Pay_mast Data File

SSN	EXEMPTIONS	MARITAL_ST	PAY_CLAS	DEDUCTIONS	YTD_GRPAY	YTD_DEDUCT
111111111	2	M	A	1500.00	40000.00	12000.00
222222222	3	M	B	800.00	24000.00	6400.00
333333333	1	M	C	500.00	17000.00	4000.00
444444444	1	S	D	450.00	14000.00	3600.00
555555555	0	S	E	50.00	1950.00	400.00

Table 7-4 Data Entry for Payroll Master Data File

```
                        Stroudsburg Toy Company
                        Personnel Reference Form

        First Name                  Last Name
        Address
        City
        State          Zip Code

        Phone Number      -             Social Security Number
```

Figure 7-16 Sample Data Entry Form for the Personel Data File

SSN	LAST_NAME	FRST_NAME	ADDRESS	CITY	STATE	ZIP	HOME_PHONE
111111111	Jackson	Thomas	123 Lombard Street	Williamsburg	VA	23185	5261010
222222222	Jackson	William	456 South Street	Williamsburg	VA	23185	5262020
333333333	Mustafson	Lloyd	789 Chestnut Street	Williamsburg	VA	23185	5263030
444444444	Dalton	Susan	135 Ithan Avenue	Williamsburg	VA	23185	5264040
555555555	Fiveyard	Jimmy	2468 Appreciate Lane	Williamsburg	VA	23185	5265050

Table 7-5 Data Entry for Personel Data File

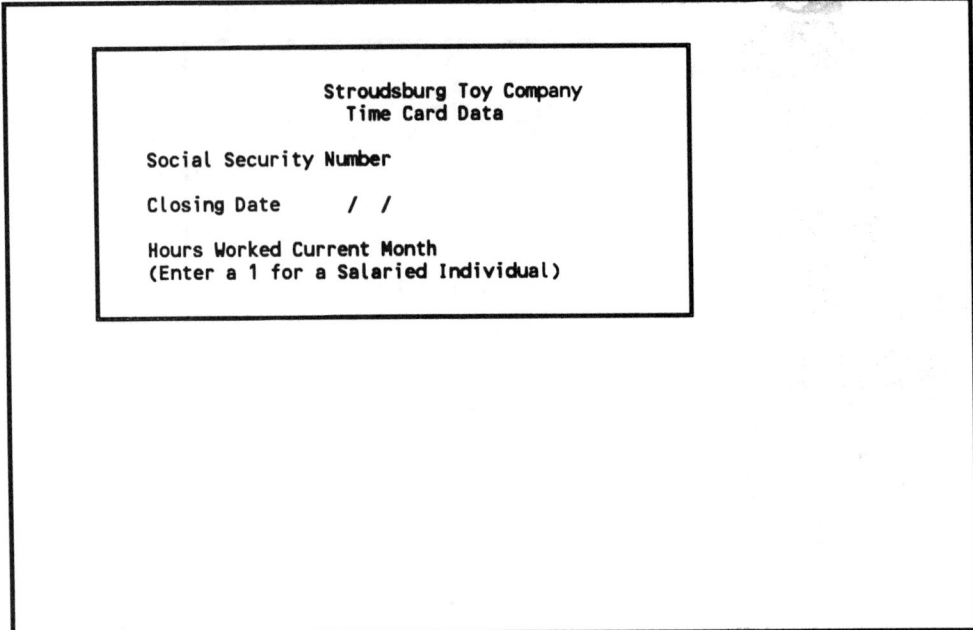

```
                    Stroudsburg Toy Company
                       Time Card Data

Social Security Number

Closing Date        /  /

Hours Worked Current Month
(Enter a 1 for a Salaried Individual)
```

Figure 7-17 Sample Data Entry Form for the Time_car Data File

SSN	HOURS	DATE
111111111	1	08/31/91
222222222	1	08/31/91
333333333	175	08/31/91
444444444	175	08/31/91
555555555	40	08/31/91

Table 7-6 Data Entry for Time Card Data File

Review questions

1. What must you do first before you can begin to create a form?
2. How do you add and edit text and labels on a form?
3. How do you add a field to a form?
4. What keys must be pressed to actually place a field on the form after you have selected the desired options?
5. What is meant by a template for a field?
6. How can you force all character data to be entered in upper-case letters?
7. How can you implement a limit check in dBASE?
8. How can you have a message displayed to help the user during data entry?
9. How can you implement a relationship check in dBASE?
10. How can you have a field displayed in financial format?
11. How do you save a Form?
12. How do you use a form for data entry?
13. How can you modify an existing Form?
14. How can you modify an existing field?
15. What is the difference between a Picture option and an Edit option?
16. How can you remove a field from the screen?
17. What are the filename extensions related to Forms?
18. Which filename extension is the one displayed in the Control Center?
19. What is the default data entry form?
20. How do you place a border around a Form?

CASE SOLUTION: PARADOX 3.5

PARADOX allows users to develop what are referred to as *Forms*. These forms can be used to display data already contained in tables or they may be used for data entry. The latter feature is what we will concentrate on in this chapter. Before you actually sit down to work with PARADOX, you would first design on paper what you want your data entry screen to look like. The form we will create in this tutorial is designed for adding new inventory items to our inventory master file. After looking at the data fields used in the inventory master file, let's assume that we have decided to create a form that looks like Figure 7-18.

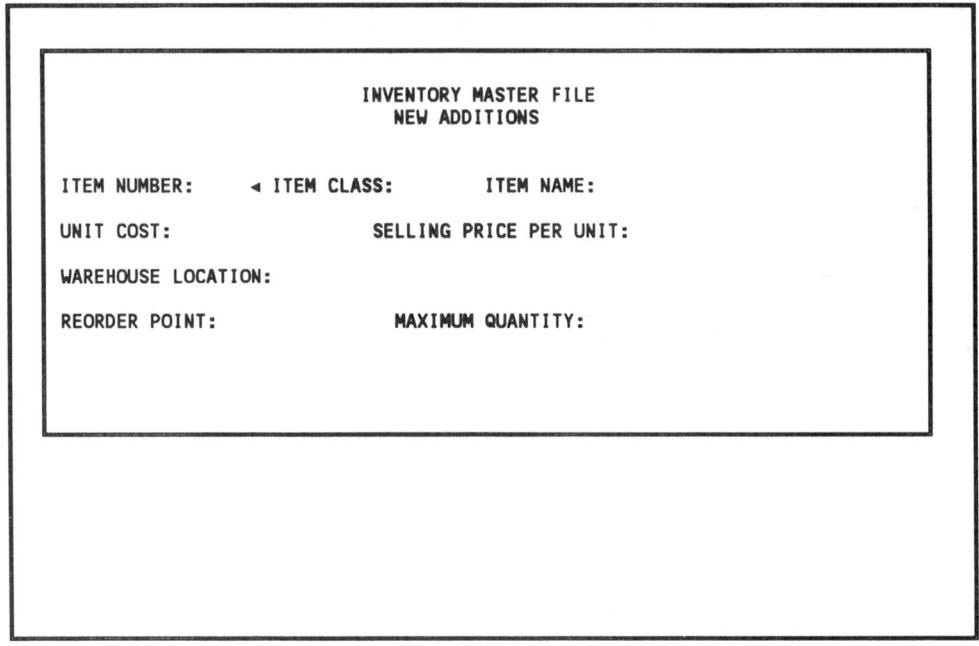

```
                          INVENTORY MASTER FILE
                             NEW ADDITIONS


ITEM NUMBER:        ◄ ITEM CLASS:        ITEM NAME:

UNIT COST:                     SELLING PRICE PER UNIT:

WAREHOUSE LOCATION:

REORDER POINT:              MAXIMUM QUANTITY:
```

Figure 7-18 Sample Data Entry Form for the Inv_mast Data Table

Designing a Data Entry Form

You are now ready to start working with PARADOX to create a form similar to Figure 7-18. After starting PARADOX, the first task is to switch to the appropriate drive and directory. The procedures for doing this are described in Chapter 6. Once you have done this, you should be back at the main menu, and the bottom right corner of your screen should indicate the current directory. This message will disappear from the screen once you press any key.

To begin creating your form, select **Forms** from the main menu followed by **Design**. Press **ENTER** to display the list of available data tables and then select Inv_mast. You are then asked which form number you wish to assign to this form. If you select Standard, then the form you are about to design would become the default form screen. This standard form would then be the one displayed when you utilize the

Form toggle switch (F7) discussed in Chapter 6. We will leave the standard form alone, and create your new form as custom form 1. Thus, move your cursor over to 1 and press **ENTER**. You are then asked to type in a form description of the form. It is useful from a control standpoint to provide some brief explanation of what this form is to be used for. You can just type in a phrase such as **Form for adding new inventory items**.

After doing this, your screen should look like Figure 7-19. *Note: if you need to exit from this tutorial before you have completed it, go to the section* Saving a Form. *When you are ready to work on the form again, read the section* Modifying a Form.

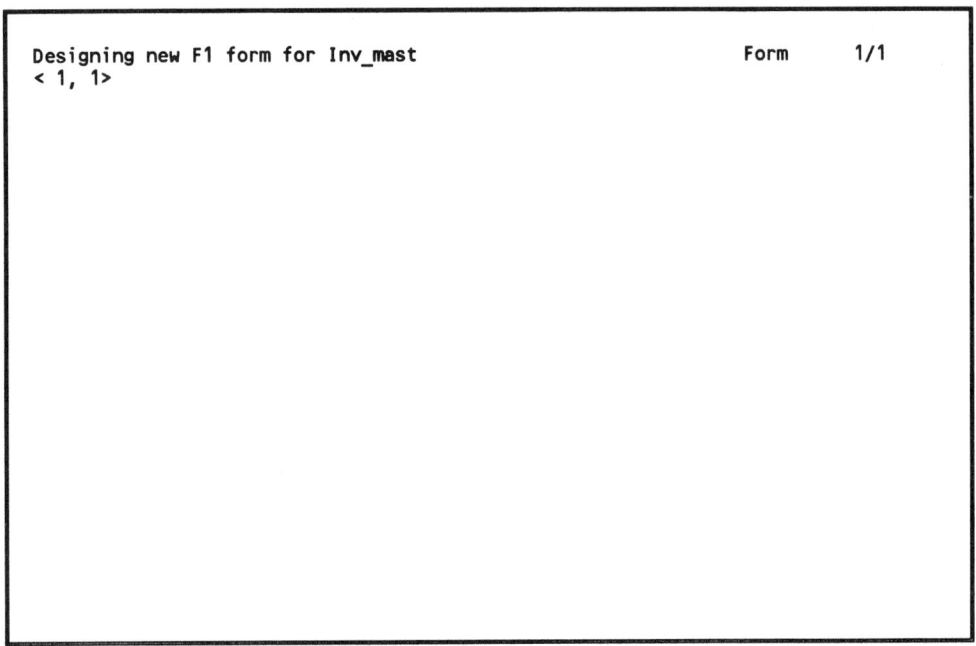

```
Designing new F1 form for Inv_mast                         Form      1/1
< 1, 1>
```

Figure 7-19 Blank Form Design Screen for Inv_mast Data Table

The first task you can work on is to put the heading on the top of the form. Be sure to leave room at the top of the screen for a border. You can use Figure 7-18 as a guide for putting the heading on the screen as well as the rest of the form. After typing in the heading, move the cursor down a couple of lines and type in the label **Item Number:** Labels serve as a prompt for the user to know what information is expected of them in the data entry process. To edit a label you may use the Backspace or Del keys to erase all or part of the text. After typing in this label, your screen should look like Figure 7-20.

The next objective is to add the item number field itself to the form, right next to its appropriate label. To do this, press **F10** to bring up the Forms menu and select **Field**, followed by **Place**, and finally select **Regular**. The top of your screen should now display all of the fields in the Inv_mast table. The field we want is ITEM_NO, so press **ENTER** when that field name is highlighted. PARADOX then instructs you to place the cursor at the desired location and press Enter. Your cursor is probably in the proper position, if not, move it one or two spaces to the right of the Item Number: label. Press **ENTER**, and the default width of the field is displayed, with each character space designated by a dash. If you need to resize the field for display purposes, you may do so with the **arrow keys**. The right arrow key makes the field wider, the left arrow key shortens the field width. The sizing of a field on a form does not affect the underlying width as designated when creating the table structure (Chapter 6). It merely affects how the data will be displayed on the form. For the Item Number field, there is no need to change the default width, so we can press **ENTER**, and the field is placed on the screen. At this point your screen should look like Figure 7-21.

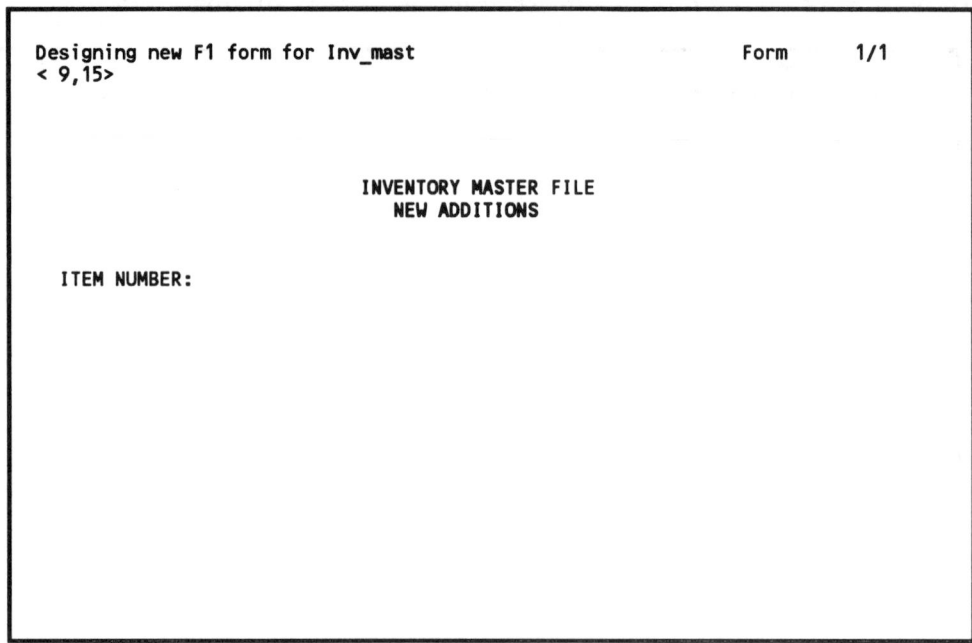

```
Designing new F1 form for Inv_mast                          Form      1/1
< 9,15>




                             INVENTORY MASTER FILE
                                NEW ADDITIONS


        ITEM NUMBER:
```

Figure 7-20 Data Entry Form after Typing in Heading and ITEM
NUMBER Label

The next field to add to the form is the Item Class field. First, type in its label, using Figure 7-18 as a guide and then repeat the steps above to place the ITEMCLASS field on the screen. Note that when you are given a list of field names to select form, ITEM_NO does not appear. This is a useful control PARADOX has implemented. Once a field is placed on a screen, it cannot be selected again. Continue to add the labels and fields to the display. The four dollar/numeric fields (UNIT_COST, UNIT_PRICE, REORD_PNT, and MAX_PNT) should be resized so that they are all eight characters wide. The default width for numbers of 17 is not necessary for this particular file. Be sure to type in the message at the bottom of the form **MAKE SURE ALL FIELDS ARE COMPLETE BEFORE CONTINUING**.

When you are finished, your screen should look like Figure 7-22. To see if you have all the right fields beside the correct labels, you can place your cursor anywhere on a field (i.e., on one of the dashed lines), and the top right corner of your screen indicates what the particular field is at that position.

```
Designing new F1 form for Inv_mast                    Form     1/1
< 9,20>




                          INVENTORY MASTER FILE
                             NEW ADDITIONS


       ITEM NUMBER:  ____
```

Figure 7-21 Data Entry Form after Adding the ITEM_NO Field to the Form

```
Designing new F1 form for Inv_mast                    Form     1/1
<16, 1>




                          INVENTORY MASTER FILE
                             NEW ADDITIONS


     ITEM NUMBER:  ____    ITEM CLASS:  ____    ITEM NAME:  _____

     UNIT COST:  _____        SELLING PRICE PER UNIT:  _____

     WAREHOUSE LOCATION:  _____

     REORDER POINT:  _____    MAXIMUM QUANTITY:  _____
```

Figure 7-22 Data Entry Form for Inv_mast Data Table after Adding all
Labels and Fields

Editing/Enhancing the Form Design

If you have made any mistakes in placing the fields at the appropriate places, you can move them to the correct places using options available through the Forms menu. To remove a field from a form, place your cursor on that field and press F10. From the menu, select Field and then Erase. You are asked to place the cursor on the appropriate field; if you have not done so, move the cursor to the field you wish to remove. Once your cursor is on the field, press ENTER, and the field is erased. You can then follow the procedures noted above on how to place a field at its proper place. Note that if there is a field already at the position where you wish to place a field, PARADOX will not allow you to do this. You must first move the existing field, either by erasing it or moving it.

You can move a field, its corresponding label if you desire, or an entire section of a form, by pressing F10, selecting Area, then Move, and then moving your cursor to the left upper corner of the area you wish to move. After doing this, press ENTER and then you are prompted to move the cursor to the lower right corner of the area you wish to move. Note that while you are doing this, the area that you wish to move is being highlighted. When you get to the end of the desired area, press ENTER once more. You can now use your arrow keys to position the highlighted area anywhere on the screen. When you have placed the area in the desired position, press ENTER to complete the move.

Once you are satisfied with the layout of your form and have the fields in the proper position, the last task is to add a border to the form to make it look more appealing. To do this, press **F10**, select **Border**, followed by **Place**, and then **Double-Line**. You are then asked to place the cursor at one of the corner positions for the border. Move your cursor to the upper left part of your screen, where you would like the upper left corner of your border to start. Be sure that the starting point is both above and to the left of any labels or fields on the screen. When you have found a proper position, press **ENTER**. This will lock in that corner for your border. Next, PARADOX instructs you to use the arrow keys to move to the diagonal corner for the border. Thus, move the cursor to the lower right corner of your screen. You will note that the border is expanded while you are moving the cursor. When you have found a position that does not have the border interfering with any field or label display, press **ENTER**. This will complete the border for your form. You are now ready to save the form. Your screen should now look like Figure 7-23.

Saving a form

To save your form, you need to issue the DO-IT! command. As you may have guessed by now, there are two ways to invoke this command; you can either press **F10** and select the **DO-IT!** option, or just press **F2**. After doing this, you are returned to the main menu. PARADOX has saved the form under the name INV_MAST.F1, with the .F1 extension indicating that this is the Form 1 associated with the INV_MAST table.

```
Designing new F1 form for Inv_mast                    Form  Ins 1/1
<20,80>


    ┌─────────────────────────────────────────────────────────────┐
    │                     INVENTORY MASTER FILE                     │
    │                        NEW ADDITIONS                          │
    │                                                               │
    │  ITEM NUMBER: ____   ITEM CLASS: ____   ITEM NAME: _____  │
    │                                                               │
    │  UNIT COST: _____      SELLING PRICE PER UNIT: _____      │
    │                                                               │
    │  WAREHOUSE LOCATION: _____                                   │
    │                                                               │
    │  REORDER POINT: _____      MAXIMUM QUANTITY: _____        │
    │                                                               │
    │                                                               │
    └─────────────────────────────────────────────────────────────┘
```

Figure 7-23 Completed Data Entry Form after Adding Border

Displaying a form

To use a particular form, you would need to be in a mode where it is appropriate for such a form to be displayed. Two such possibilities are when you are editing the records of a table, or when you are adding new records to a table. For now, we will just see what the form looks like when in the Edit mode.

From the main menu, select **Modify**, **Edit**, and then press **ENTER** to see a list of tables. Select the Inv_mast table and the table will be displayed in table view, i.e., rows and columns. To have the data displayed using the form you have just created, select **F10** to invoke the Edit menu. Select **Image**, **Pickform** and then **1** (which indicates the first custom designed form). The first record of the Inv_mast should now be displayed, similar to Figure 7-24. You can use the arrow keys to move from field to field and the PgUp and PgDn keys to move from record to record. Since there should be no need to edit the records at this time, you can exit from this screen by pressing **F10**, selecting **Cancel**, and then answering **Yes**.

After exiting from the Edit mode, you are returned to the View mode, which only allows a user to look at the data, but not change the data. To clear the screen, press **F8**. If you saw any problems while you were looking at the data using your form, you can modify the design of the form.

Modifying an existing form

To modify an existing form, you would select Forms, Change, press ENTER to display the tables, and then select Inv_mast table. You would then select 1 as the form, and the form that you created earlier will appear. At this point you may use the same procedures discussed above in the *Editing/Enhancing a Form* section to change any text or field information. When you are finished, you would save your changes by invoking DO-IT!. After doing so, you will be back at the main menu.

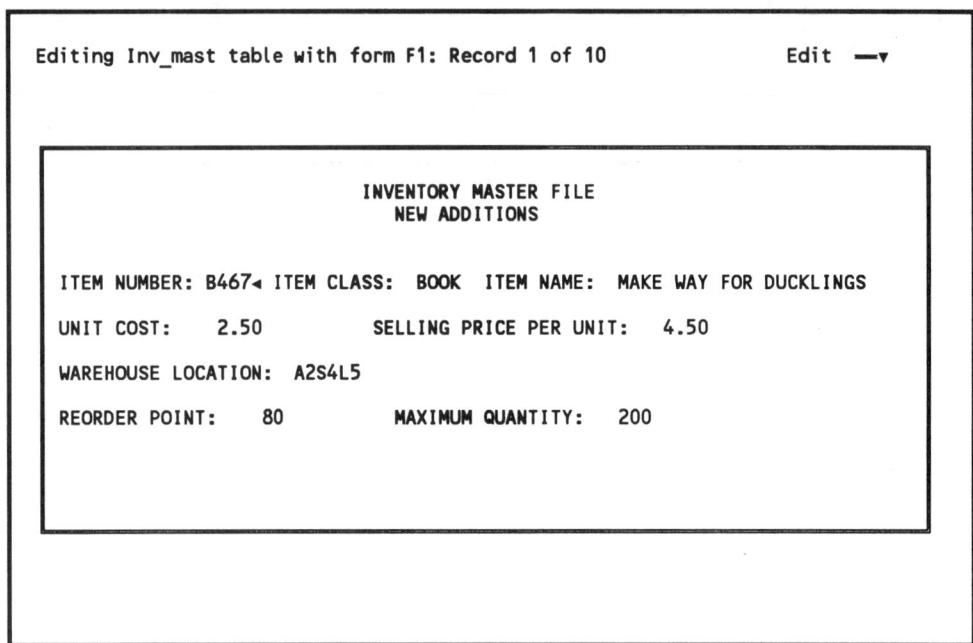

```
 Editing Inv_mast table with form F1: Record 1 of 10            Edit  ──▾


                          INVENTORY MASTER FILE
                              NEW ADDITIONS


   ITEM NUMBER: B467◂ ITEM CLASS:  BOOK  ITEM NAME:  MAKE WAY FOR DUCKLINGS

   UNIT COST:    2.50       SELLING PRICE PER UNIT:   4.50

   WAREHOUSE LOCATION:  A2S4L5

   REORDER POINT:    80      MAXIMUM QUANTITY:   200
```

Figure 7-24 Displaying the First Record in the Inv_mast Data Table Using Custom Form

Controlling data input

A firm relies on its database for a wide variety of applications, thus it is important that the data contained in the database be accurate, up to date, and consistent. In order to further this objective, it is extremely useful to have controls over the point in the accounting system where the data first enters the database. We can refer to this point as the *data entry process*. PARADOX offers a wide variety of controls designed to improve this process.

To gain some experience with these controls, we will use the Inv_mast table and implement controls over various parts of the table. In addition, the section on Database Integrity discusses another useful control. To start this process, select **Modify, Edit**, press **ENTER**, and select Inv_mast table. Press **F10** to display the Edit menu. The controls we wish to install are found under the ValCheck (for validity check) option. After you select **ValCheck**, you want to choose the **Define** option since we want to create some validity checks. PARADOX then asks you to move to the field we wish to place validity checks for the inventory master table. We will be putting some type of control over every field, so let's start with ITEM_NO.

First, move your cursor over to the Item_no column and press **ENTER**. For the Item_no field the type of control we will implement is a *Picture* option. Picture options allow the developer to control for the type of data that is entered for a particular field. In the case of the **Item_no field,** we want the first position to be a capital B, G, or T and the last three positions to be numeric characters.

The special characters needed to do this can be found through the on-line context sensitive Help system available in PARADOX. To access the Help system, press **F1**, and a help message is displayed concerning validity checks. To see specific information on the Picture option, move the cursor (it should be at the top of the screen on the menu line) to Pictures and press **ENTER**. The screen should then display the various special characters and how they control the type of data that may be entered in a field. We will be using several of these special Picture functions.

To return to our Inv_mast table, press **ENTER** to leave the help system. You will be returned to where you were before you accessed the Help system. Select the Picture option by moving your cursor to that option and pressing **ENTER**. For the Item_no field the type of Picture display we need is as follows: **&###** . This will force the first character to be a letter, and will convert the letter to capital if necessary. The last three characters indicate that those positions must be filled with numbers. You should note that this is not changing the underlying structure of this field; but how the data is displayed and entered. See Figure 7-25 as an example. After typing in these characters and pressing **ENTER**, you are returned to the table edit screen.

```
Picture:  &###                                              Edit
Enter a PAL picture format (e.g. ###-##-####).
INV_MAST┬ITEM_NO┬ITEMCLASS┬──────ITEM_NAME──────┬──UNIT_COST──┬──U
      1 │ B467 │ BOOK    │ MAKE WAY FOR DUCKLINGS │    2.50   │ ***
      2 │ G324 │ GAME    │ MONOPOLY               │    4.25   │ ***
      3 │ T219 │ TOY     │ TURTLE VAN             │   12.60   │ ***
      4 │ T418 │ TOY     │ ECTO MOBILE            │   11.40   │ ***
      5 │ G121 │ GAME    │ CANDYLAND              │    2.60   │ ***
      6 │ B119 │ BOOK    │ CASEY AT THE BAT       │    2.10   │ ***
      7 │ B187 │ BOOK    │ MIKE MULLIGAN          │    2.70   │ ***
      8 │ G043 │ GAME    │ KERPLUNK               │    6.80   │ ***
      9 │ B029 │ BOOK    │ GOODNIGHT MOON         │    3.60   │ ***
     10 │ T108 │ TOY     │ LEGO BLOCKS            │   12.70   │ ***
```

Figure 7-25 Adding a Picture Format to the ITEM_NO Field

At this point, you are ready to install controls over the remaining fields. These controls are shown below. The purpose of these controls will be discussed briefly. The brackets ({}) around BOOK,GAME,TOY for Item_class is designed to limit the entry in that field to one of the choices contained inside the brackets. For the user to select one of these choices, all that is needed is to press the first letter of the appropriate choice. The * in the ITEM_NAME picture means to repeat whatever type of character comes after the asterisk as many times as needed. Since the name of a particular inventory item varies, we do not want to restrict the entry to be of a certain length. The ! symbol permits any type of character, but if an alphabetic character is entered, PARADOX will convert it to uppercase. The low value of 0 for the numeric and dollar fields is designed to prevent entering negative numbers accidentally. This last control is often referred to as a *sign check* or *limit check*.

```
ITEM_CLASS -  Picture: {BOOK,GAME,TOY}
ITEM_NAME -   Picture: *!
UNIT_COST:    LowValue: 0
UNIT_PRICE:   LowValue: 0
WAREH_LOC:    Picture: &#&#&#
REORD_PNT:    LowValue: 0
MAX_PNT:      LowValue: 0
```

After you have installed these controls, save the validity checks by pressing **F2** for DO-IT!. You are returned to the View mode of the Inv_mast table. You can clear this from the screen by pressing **F8**.

Using a form

The last part of your tutorial is to add two new records to your Inv_mast table using the custom form you have created in this chapter. To do this from the main menu, choose **Modify, DataEntry**, press **ENTER** and select the Inv_mast table. When the data entry screen first appears, it is in its default table view mode. To use the custom form, press **F10**, select **Image, Pickform** and then choose form **1**. Your screen should look like Figure 7-26. The two records to add are shown in Table 7-7. Remember, just press B, G, or T to select the appropriate Item class. Purposely make mistakes as you input the data, such as trying to enter letters where numbers should be and vice versa. Also, try to input a negative number into one of the numeric fields. You should get an error message indicating that the number entered is not acceptable.

When you are finished, you can add the two new records to the existing table by pressing **F2**. This will add these records to the end of the Inv_mast table. Press **F8** to clear the screen.

```
DataEntry for Inv_mast table with form F1: Record 1 of 1          DataEntry


        ┌──────────────────────────────────────────────────────────────┐
        │                    INVENTORY MASTER FILE                      │
        │                      NEW ADDITIONS                            │
        │                                                               │
        │   ITEM NUMBER:     ◄ ITEM CLASS:        ITEM NAME:            │
        │                                                               │
        │   UNIT COST:                 SELLING PRICE PER UNIT:          │
        │                                                               │
        │   WAREHOUSE LOCATION:                                         │
        │                                                               │
        │   REORDER POINT:             MAXIMUM QUANTITY:                │
        │                                                               │
        │                                                               │
        └──────────────────────────────────────────────────────────────┘
```

Figure 7-26 Custom Data Entry Form for Inv_mast Data Table

Database integrity

The DBA, as well as everyone in the firm, should be concerned with making sure the database is accurate, consistent, and up-to-date. This is known as *database integrity*. At this point, your database is not consistent, since the inventory master data files contain two item numbers (G286 and T220) that are not in the other two inventory data files. You need to open up the other two inventory data files (INV_HIST and INV_TRAN) and add the two new item numbers to the files.

The first task is to build some integrity into these two tables so that only existing item numbers (from the inventory master table) can be used. To do this from the main menu, choose **Modify, DataEntry**, press **ENTER** and then select the Inv_tran table. After selecting this table, you are at the default data entry screen. The control you want to implement is referred to as a Table Lookup in PARADOX. Conceptually this is known as a *validity check*, since it checks for the validity, or existence of a particular data item.

To implement this feature, press **F10**, select **ValCheck, Define**, and then make sure your cursor is on the Item_no field. Press **ENTER** after you have selected the Item_no field and then select **TableLookup**. This feature will limit a user's choice for this field to the data in a corresponding table for the same field. Thus for this field the table we want to use is the Inv_mast table, so after pressing **ENTER**, select the Inv_mast from the list of tables. At this point your screen should look like Figure 7-27.

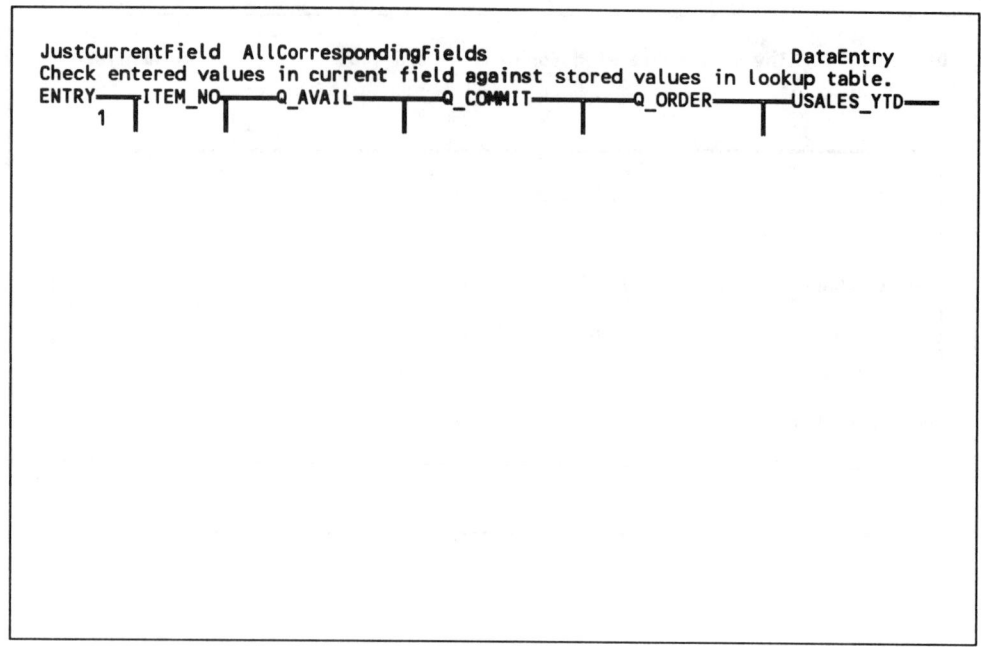

Figure 7-27 Selecting the Appropriate Lookup Option for the Inv_tran Data Table

Since we want to match just the Item_no field in the INV_TRAN table with the corresponding field in the INV_MAST table, you would select **JustCurrentField**. The last menu that appears asks whether you want the lookup table to be displayed, in this case the inventory master table, while you are inputting data. Since this control is designed to help users choose only existing item numbers, we would want the corresponding table displayed if necessary. To do this select the **HelpAndFill** option. After doing this, your screen should look like Figure 7-28. Note in the bottom right corner PARADOX indicates that the Table Lookup has been recorded.

To see how this feature works, let's add the two new inventory items to the Inv_tran table. As noted at the top of your screen, you can press **F1** for help with fill-in, which will display the Inv_mast table. After pressing F1, your screen should look like Figure 7-29. You can then go down to item number G286, and following the directions at the top of your screen, press F2 to select that record. You are then returned to the Data Entry screen for the inventory transaction table, and you will see that item number G286 has been added to your table. Be sure to add a "0" (zero) for the rest of the data fields. Repeat this process once more for item number T220. When you are finished, press **F2** to add these records to the end of the Inv_tran table. Press **F8** to clear the screen.

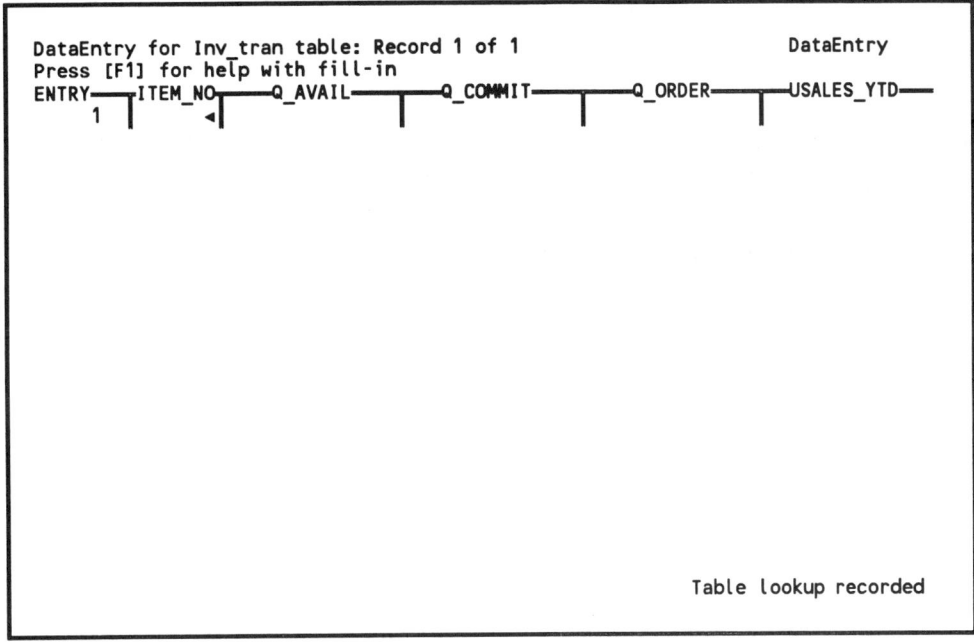

```
DataEntry for Inv_tran table: Record 1 of 1                    DataEntry
Press [F1] for help with fill-in
ENTRY──┬ITEM_NO┬──Q_AVAIL──┬──┬Q_COMMIT──┬──┬Q_ORDER──┬──┬USALES_YTD──┐
   1   │       │  ◄        │  │          │  │         │  │            │






                                            Table lookup recorded
```

Figure 7-28 Data Entry Screen for Inv_tran Data Table after Recording Table Lookup Option

```
Move to the record you want to select
Press [F2] to select the record; [Esc] to cancel; [F1] for help
INV_MAST┬ITEM_NO┬ITEMCLASS┬──────────ITEM_NAME──────────┬────UNIT_COST────┬────U
      1 │ B467  │ BOOK    │ MAKE WAY FOR DUCKLINGS        │         2.50    │ ***
      2 │ G324  │ GAME    │ MONOPOLY                      │         4.25    │ ***
      3 │ T219  │ TOY     │ TURTLE VAN                    │        12.60    │ ***
      4 │ T418  │ TOY     │ ECTO MOBILE                   │        11.40    │ ***
      5 │ G121  │ GAME    │ CANDYLAND                     │         2.60    │ ***
      6 │ B119  │ BOOK    │ CASEY AT THE BAT              │         2.10    │ ***
      7 │ B187  │ BOOK    │ MIKE MULLIGAN                 │         2.70    │ ***
      8 │ G043  │ GAME    │ KERPLUNK                      │         6.80    │ ***
      9 │ B029  │ BOOK    │ GOODNIGHT MOON                │         3.60    │ ***
     10 │ T108  │ TOY     │ LEGO BLOCKS                   │        12.70    │ ***
     11 │ G286  │ GAME    │ RISK                          │         5.25    │ ***
     12 │ T220  │ TOY     │ PIZZA THROWER                 │        11.60    │ ***
```

Figure 7-29 Using the Inv_mast Data File to Lookup an ITEM_NO for the Inv_tran Data Table

Conclusion

This completes the tutorial on using the Forms module of PARADOX. Ensuring the accuracy and reliability of the data that enters a firm's database is critical to the firm's success. With the proper use of editing controls, a DBMS can prevent a good number of errors from corrupting a database. These controls were discussed in the sections *Controlling Data Input* and *Database Integrity*.

FOLLOW-UP EXERCISES

Inventory Cycle

There are no additional forms that need to be created specific to the inventory cycle. However, what needs to be completed is the addition of the two new inventory records (item numbers G286 and T220) to the Inv_hist table. These two items should have already been added to the Inv_mast table and the Inv_tran table. Use the steps outlined above for creating a table lookup option in the Inv_hist table and use the lookup feature to add these two items to the Inv_hist table. As a reminder, however, be sure that you have added the two new inventory items discussed in this chapter to all three of your inventory data files.

Revenue Cycle

There are various data entry operations performed as part of the revenue cycle. In order to institute some control over the process, Stroudsburg has asked you to design data entry forms, with appropriate controls. The three tables we will design forms for are as follows:

- SALES_OR.DB
- SALES_IN.DB
- CASH_REC.DB

Figures 7-30 through 7-32 give you an idea as to how such data entry screens could appear. Feel free to design them as you want, but they should contain the same information as shown on the screen. When you are finished with the forms, you need to go back and install controls over the data entry process. For any POSTED, POSTEDIT, or PAID field define a ValCheck that has an F (for FALSE) as the default.

When you are finished creating these data entry forms and their corresponding controls, there is one other data entry form related to the revenue cycle. However, you do not need to design this form, the file corresponding to it is already included on the diskette that accompanied the book. You should copy this file to your diskette:

- CUSTOMER.F1

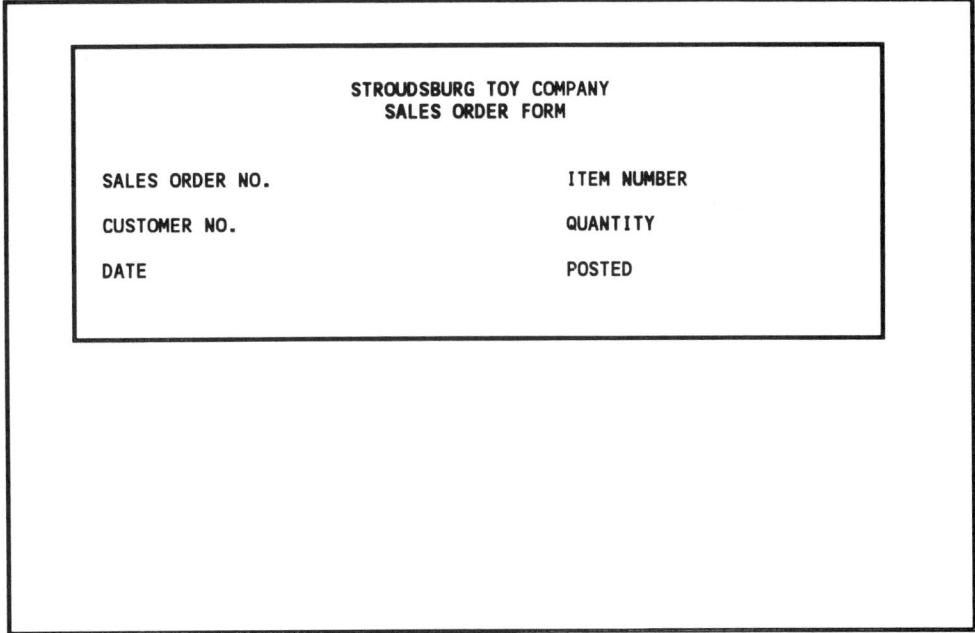

Figure 7-30 Sample Data Entry Form for the Sales_or Data Table

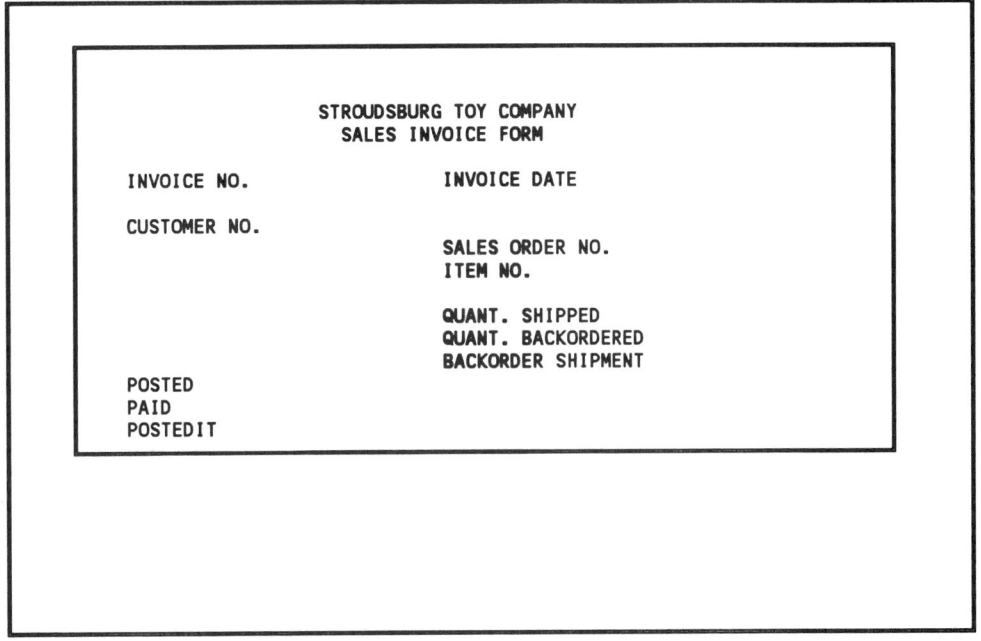

Figure 7-31 Sample Data Entry Form for the Sales_in Data Table

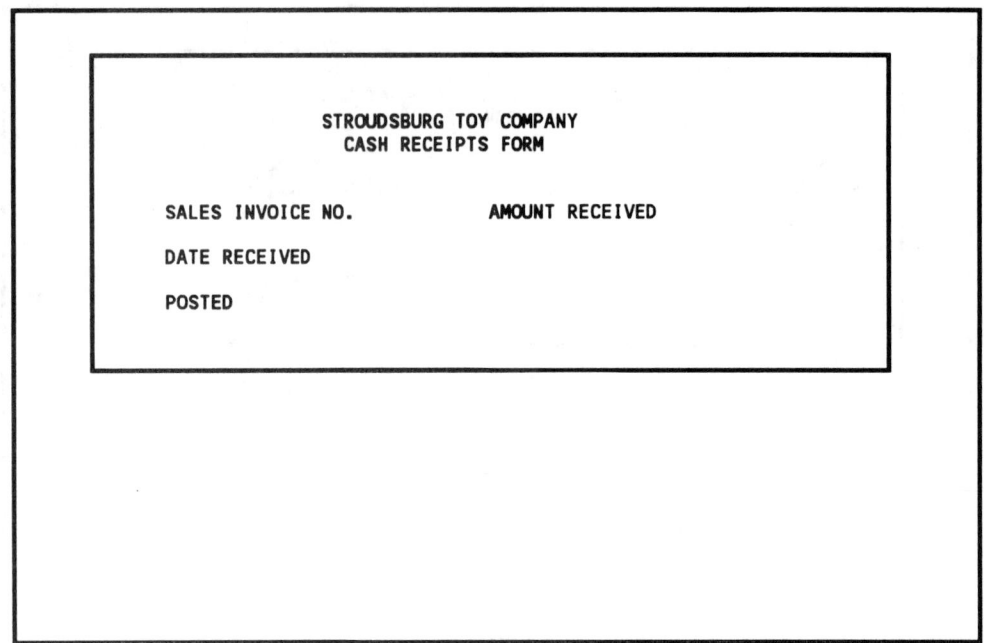

Figure 7-32 Sample Data Entry Form for the Cash_rec Data Table

Expenditure Cycle

There are various data entry operations performed as part of the expenditure cycle. In order to institute some control over the process, Stroudsburg has asked you to design data entry forms, with appropriate controls. The three tables we will design forms for are as follows:

- •PURCH_OR.DB
- •VOUCHER.DB
- •CASH_PAY.DB

Figures 7-33 through 7-35 give you a good idea as to how to design the forms. Feel free to design them as you want, but they should contain the same information as shown on the screen. When you are finished with the forms, you need to go back and install controls over the data entry process. For any POSTED, POSTEDIT, or PAID field define a ValCheck that has an F (for FALSE) as the default.

When you are finished creating these data entry forms and their corresponding controls, there is one other data entry form related to the revenue cycle. However, you do not need to design this form, the file corresponding to it is already included on the diskette that accompanied the book. You should copy this file to your diskette:

- • VENDOR.F1

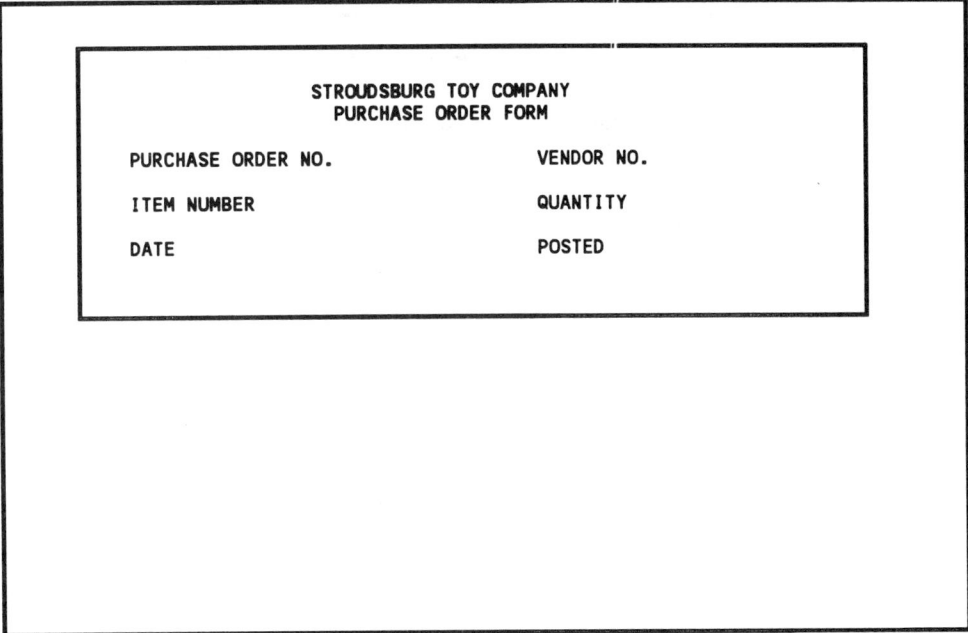

Figure 7-33 Sample Data Entry Form for the Purch_or Data Table

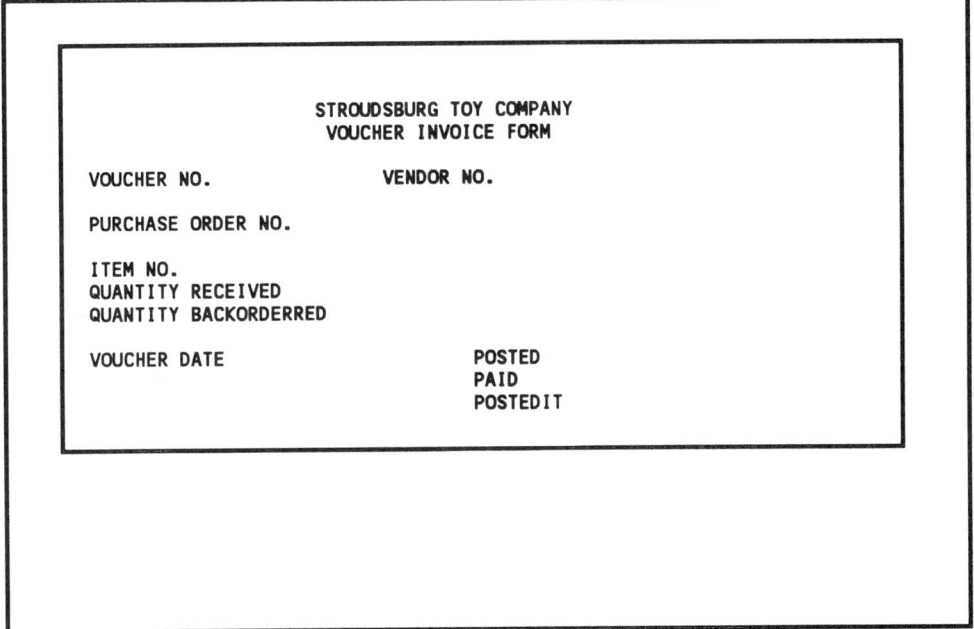

Figure 7-34 Sample Data Entry Form for the Voucher Data Table

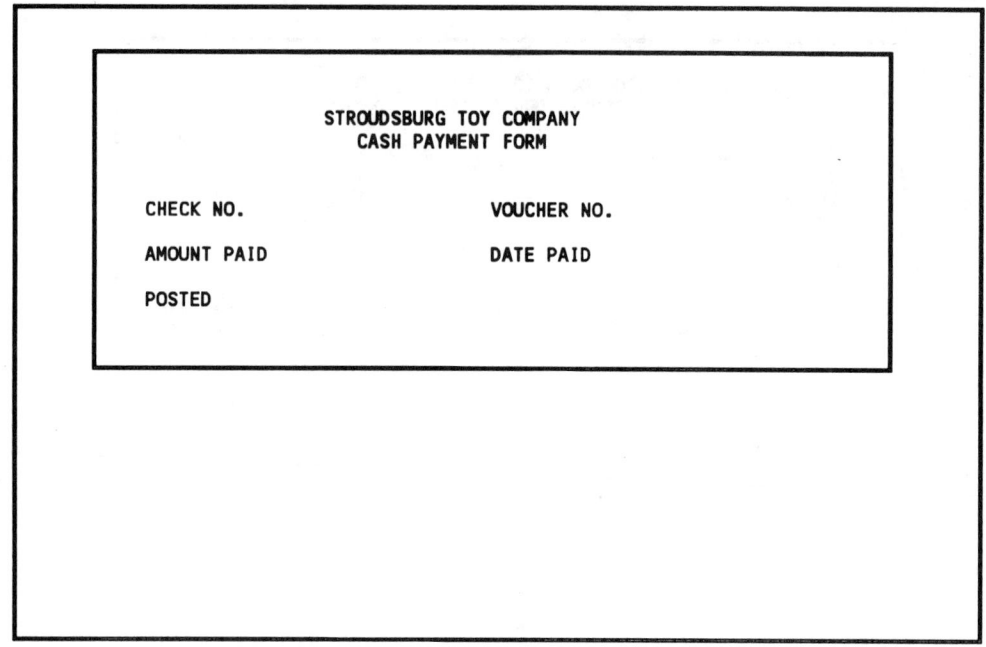

Figure 7-35 Sample Data Entry Form for the Cash_pay Data Table

Payroll Cycle

In order to add convenience as well as control to the process of recording critical payroll data, Stroudsburg Toy has asked you to design suitable input screens to aid in this task. You will need to create five data entry screens. Figures 7-36 through 7-40 provide sample input screens to help you get started. When you are finished creating the screens, you need to go back and install controls over the data entry process. When you are finished with that, use the forms to enter payroll data into the system. Tables 7-8 through 7-12 provide the necessary data for these files. Do not worry about the *DATE* field in the Payroll Master table. You may leave it blank for now; in the next chapter you will create a file that will automatically update that field. For the *POSTED* field in the Time Card table, place the field on the form and add a validity check that will place an "F" as the default value. Thus, when you enter the data, you may just skip over this field, and an F will be placed there automatically.

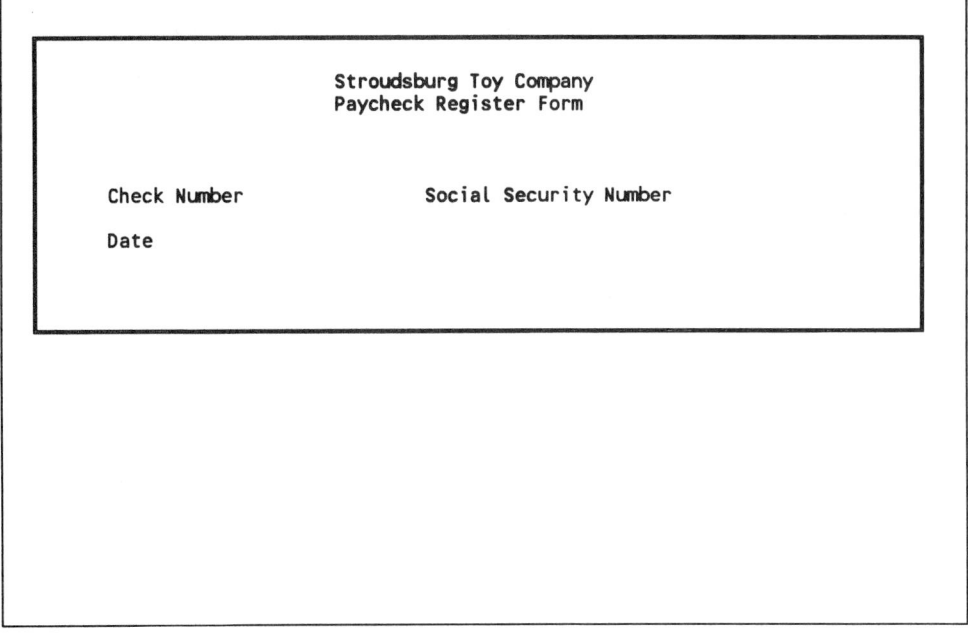

```
                        Stroudsburg Toy Company
                        Paycheck Register Form


        Check Number                Social Security Number

        Date
```

Figure 7-36 Sample Data Entry Form for the Paycheck Data Table

PAYCHK_NO	SSN	DATE
2341	1111111111	08/31/91
2342	2222222222	08/31/91
2343	3333333333	08/31/91
2344	4444444444	08/31/91
2345	5555555555	08/31/91

Table 7-8 Data Entry for Paycheck Data File

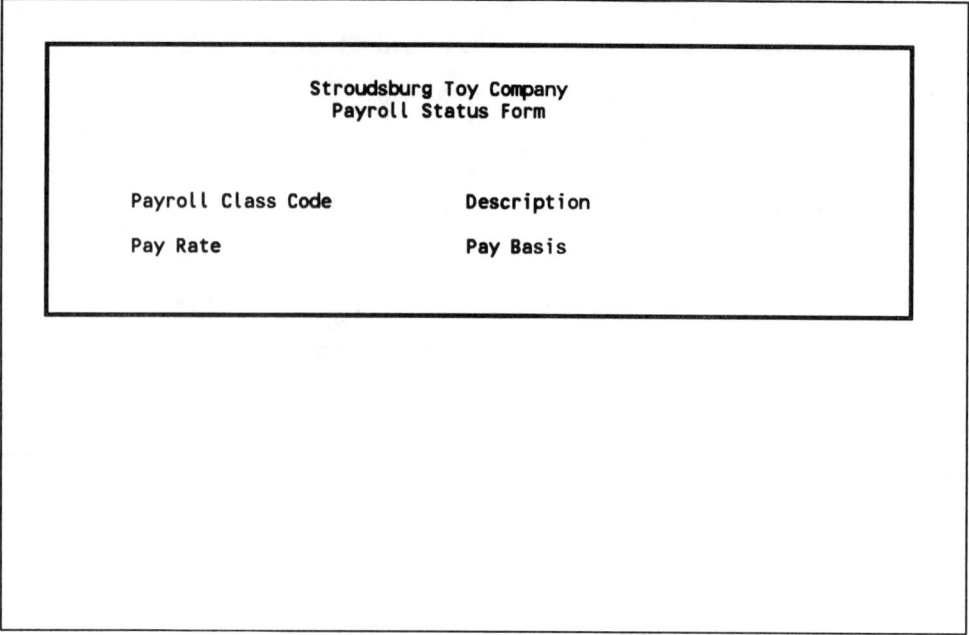

Figure 7-37 Sample Data Entry Form for the Pay_clas Data Table

PAY_CLAS	CLAS_DESC	PAY_RATE	BASIS
A	President	5000.00	MONTHLY
B	Vice. Pres	3000.00	MONTHLY
C	Office Mgr	12.00	HOURLY
D	Store Mgr.	10.00	HOURLY
E	Part Timer	6.00	HOURLY

Table 7-9 Data Entry for Pay Classification Data File

```
                        Stroudsburg Toy Company
                        Payroll Master Form


        Social Security Number              Exemptions

        Marital Status         Pay Classification

        Monthly Deductions
```

Figure 7-38 Sample Data Entry Form for the Pay_mast Data Table

SSN	EXEMPTIONS	MARITAL_ST	PAY_CLAS	DEDUCTIONS	YTD_GRPAY	YTD_DEDUCT
111111111	2	M	A	1500.00	40000.00	12000.00
222222222	3	M	B	800.00	24000.00	6400.00
333333333	1	M	C	500.00	17000.00	4000.00
444444444	1	S	D	450.00	14000.00	3600.00
555555555	0	S	E	50.00	1950.00	400.00

Table 7-10 Data Entry for Payroll Master Data File

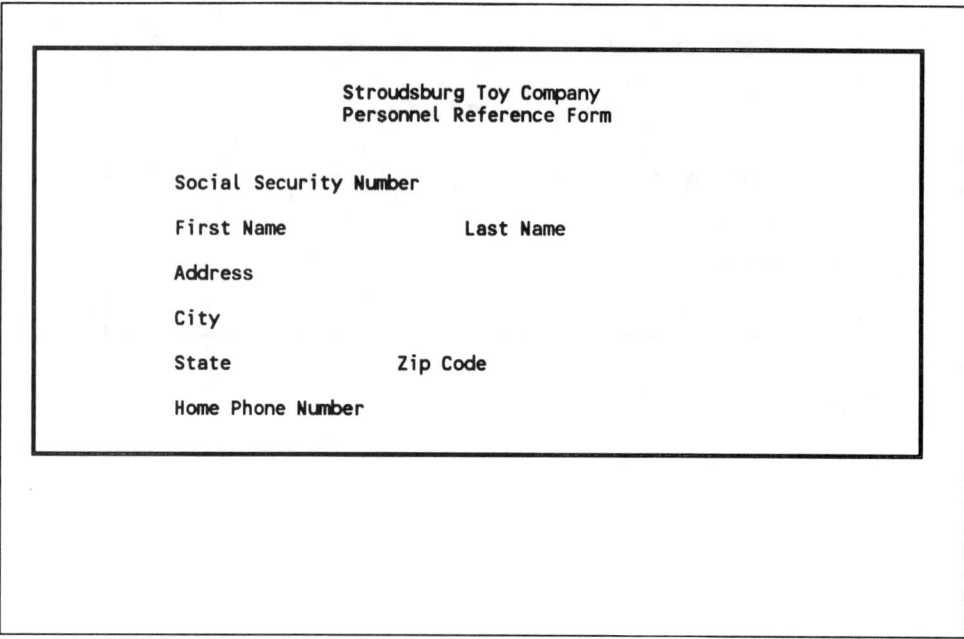

Figure 7-39 Sample Data Entry Form for the Personel Data Table

SSN	LAST_NAME	FRST_NAME	ADDRESS	CITY	STATE	ZIP	HOME_PHONE
111111111	Jackson	Thomas	123 Lombard Street	Williamsburg	VA	23185	5261010
222222222	Jackson	William	456 South Street	Williamsburg	VA	23185	5262020
333333333	Mustafson	Lloyd	789 Chestnut Street	Williamsburg	VA	23185	5263030
444444444	Dalton	Susan	135 Ithan Avenue	Williamsburg	VA	23185	5264040
555555555	Fiveyard	Jimmy	2468 Appreciate Lane	Williamsburg	VA	23185	5265050

Table 7-11 Data Entry for Personnel Data File

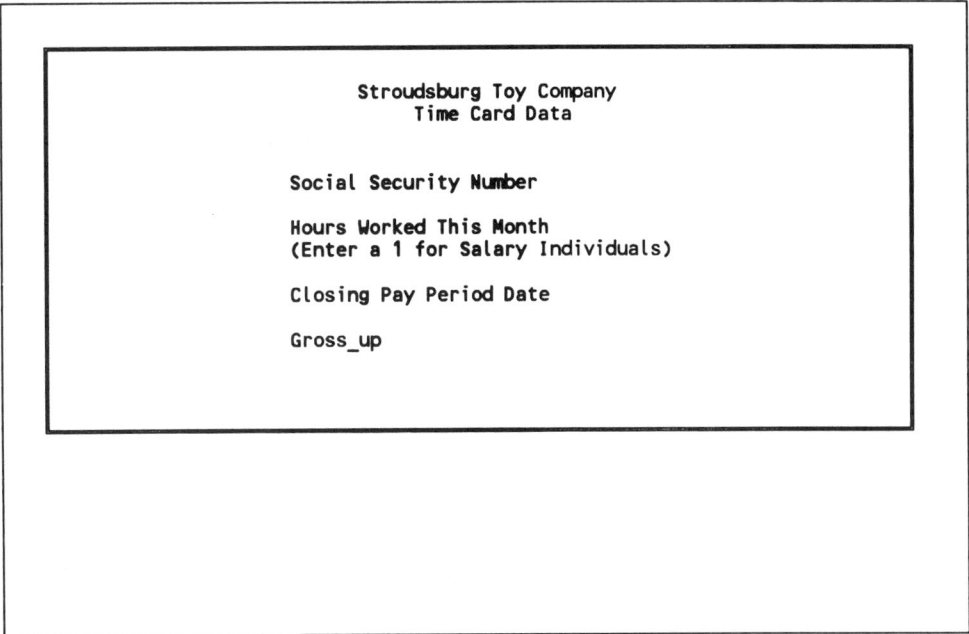

```
                    Stroudsburg Toy Company
                        Time Card Data


        Social Security Number

        Hours Worked This Month
        (Enter a 1 for Salary Individuals)

        Closing Pay Period Date

        Gross_up
```

Figure 7-40 Sample Data Entry Form for the Time_car Data Table

SSN	HOURS	DATE
111111111	1	08/31/91
222222222	1	08/31/91
333333333	175	08/31/91
444444444	175	08/31/91
555555555	40	08/31/91

Table 7-12 Data Entry for Time Card Data File

Review Questions

1. What must you do first before you can begin to create a form?
2. How do you add and edit text and labels on a form?
3. How do you insert a blank line on a form?
4. How do you add a field to a form?
5. What is meant by a template for a field?
6. How can you force all character data to be entered in upper-case letters?
7. How can you implement a limit check in PARADOX?
8. How can you implement a lookup (validity) check in PARADOX?
9. How do you save a Form?
10. How do you use a form for data entry?
11. How can you modify an existing Form?
12. How can you delete an existing field from a form?
13. What is the filename extension related to Forms?
14. What is the default data entry form?
15. How do you place a border around a Form?

CHAPTER 8
DESIGNING QUERIES TO VIEW AND UPDATE MULTIPLE FILES USING A DATABASE MANAGEMENT SYSTEM

INTRODUCTION

This chapter will teach you how to design queries, or views of the various data files. You will learn the three basic operations of the relational data model: *Project, Select,* and *Join.* You will learn how to use these queries to view files for relevant information as well as how to create update files that can be used to process transactions, in a batch mode. In the next chapter you will also see that queries can be used to help develop reports for management use. The query module is one of the more powerful features of a relational DBMS.

CASE: STROUDSBURG TOY COMPANY

Bill Jackson feels that the input side of the inventory database is now adequate due to the addition of user friendly prompts as well as the use of controls throughout the data entry process (Chapter 7). He believes the next step is to actually start using the data base for management purposes, such as checking the status of inventory items as well as to process some inventory-related transactions.

He would like you to develop a procedure which would allow someone to check the status of the inventory files to answer questions such as "Is it time to reorder any items?", or "What is the current value (cost) of my inventory?" He would also like to use the computer to update the inventory files when certain transactions occur, such as sales orders, shipments, purchases, and receipt of goods that affect the inventory database.

CASE SOLUTION: dBASE IV

The questions Bill would like to have answered, as well as the ability to process transactions, can both be accomplished through the proper design and use of *Queries.* A query allows the user to look at the data in various files in a multi-dimensional fashion. The user can design a query that will display only certain fields (a *Project* operation), a query that only displays records that meet a certain condition (a *Select* operation), and queries that combine data from several files (a *Join* operation). In addition, queries can be designed to update data in certain files using batch processing techniques.

Before you design a query, the systems designer should sit down with the users and find out what information they need in order to make appropriate decisions. Once this task has been completed, you are ready to use the computer to design the necessary query.

The first query you will design is one that will display the total value of inventory on hand at any given time. Since most users are more comfortable using the descriptions of inventory items rather than inventory item numbers, you have been asked to provide a listing of all inventory items showing their name, quantity on hand, unit cost, and total value. Management would like the data grouped according to the item class, such as books, toys, or games as well. If you recall the structure of the inventory files, the item name, unit cost and item class are maintained in the inventory master file, but the current quantity on hand is stored in the inventory transaction file. What is required is a way to join these two files together, and then display only certain information about each inventory item.

Creating View Queries

To begin creating your first query, make sure you are using the proper drive, directory and catalog. Once you are at the Control Center, move the cursor to the Query panel, and press **ENTER** on < create >. Your screen should look like Figure 8-1. This is the *Query design surface*, and the first menu option, Layout, is already displayed. The first task is to add the files necessary for our query to the design surface. As you may recall, we need two files, INV_MAST and INV_TRAN, in order to help Stroudsburg determine the value of their current inventory. To add these files to the design surface, select **Add file to query** and the names of the data files appear in a window on the right. Select INV_MAST and you will note that the field names for that file now appear at the top of your screen. This is known as a *File Skeleton*. Repeat this procedure to add the INV_TRAN file to your design. To access the Layout menu, press **Alt-L**, and then follow the steps above on how to add the file to your design surface.

Note: If you need to exit from this tutorial before you have completed it, go to the section Saving a view query. *When you are ready to work on the query again, read the section* Modifying a view query.

The next operation we will perform is to join the two files together. This is done by linking the two file skeletons together through a common field, or column. In this case, the common field is the ITEM_NO. To link two files together, you would move your cursor to the appropriate field in each file and type in the same word underneath each field name. The word we will use here is LINK1. You can move your cursor from field to field by using the Tab key, and you can move from file to file using F3 and F4. After you have typed **LINK1** under the ITEM_NO field for both files, the two files are effectively joined together.

You could have also joined the files together by placing your cursor in one of the common fields, pressing ALT-L and selecting the Create link by pointing option. This would have automatically placed the words LINK1 under the ITEM_NO field and then asked you to move your cursor to the corresponding common field in another table. You would then use F4 to move to the other table, position your cursor under the ITEM_NO, and press ENTER. The two tables would now be linked together.

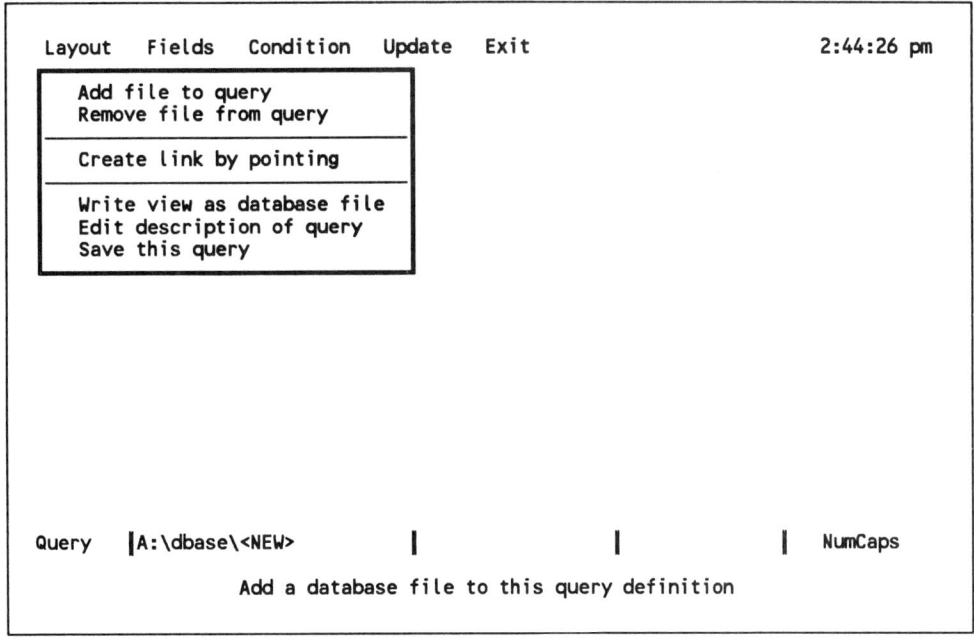

Figure 8-1 Layout Menu for Query Design Form

Your next task is to arrange the joined file in order of ITEM_NO. Place the cursor on the ITEM_NO field in the INV_MAST file. Bring up the Fields menu by pressing **ALT-F**, and select **Sort on this field**. Another window pops up allowing you to choose in which order you wish to sort. At this point your screen should look like Figure 8-2. Select Ascending ASCII by pressing **ENTER**. The linked file is now sorted by ITEM_NO.

The last field we need to add to our file skeleton is a *Calculated Field* which will show the total value of each inventory item. This value is equal to the unit cost times the quantity available. To add a calculated field, press **ALT-F** for the Fields menu and select **Create calculated field**. A new line is added to the file skeleton, and you can then build your calculated field. You must use fields that are currently on your query design surface. Type in the expression **(UNIT_COST*Q_AVAIL)**, and then press **ENTER**.

You now have all the necessary information to build the particular *View* that is needed. To select only certain fields to display in your query (a *project* operation), place your cursor on the fields that you want in the view and press **F5**. For this particular view, the fields we want to be included are as follows: ITEM_NO (you only need to select it from the INV_MAST file, not both), ITEM_CLASS, ITEM_NAME, Q_AVAIL, UNIT_COST, and the calculated field. When you go to add the Calculated field to the view, you are prompted for a field name. Call this field **TOT_COST**. After typing this in and pressing **ENTER**, the field is placed in the view.

After adding these fields, you will note two things have happened. First, the bottom of your screen now contains the fields you have just selected, and second, certain fields at the top of the screen have an ↓ beside their field names. This arrow indicates that a particular field is included in the view. If you have accidentally placed an incorrect field in a view, you can delete it by placing your cursor on the incorrect field and pressing F5 to delete it. We are now finished creating this view. The next section describes how to save the query.

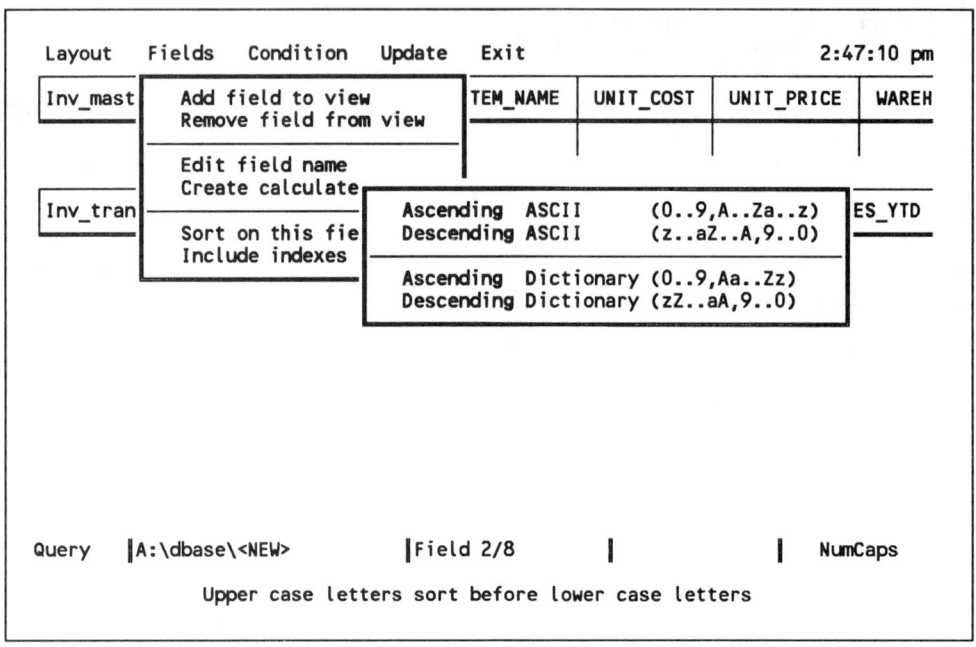

Figure 8-2 Sorting the Two Linked Data Files

Saving a View Query

The first step in saving the query is to give the view file a name. Press **ALT-L**, and move down to the Save this query option. After you press **ENTER**, you are asked for a file name. Name this file **INV_VAL**. When you have finished typing this in and pressing **ENTER**, the file is saved under that name. You should be aware that dBASE creates two different files. The file that contains your query screen design and the code that generates the query has a .QBE extension. When the query is actually used, a compiled program is generated, which has the extension .QBO. Your screen should now look like Figure 8-3.

You can now exit from the query design screen by pressing **ALT-E** and selecting **Save changes and exit**. While you have already saved the file, it is always a good idea, from a control standpoint, to issue a save command as your last command when completing a task. This ensures that if you have changed anything, and then forgotten to save those changes using the Layout options, that the changes will be saved upon exiting.

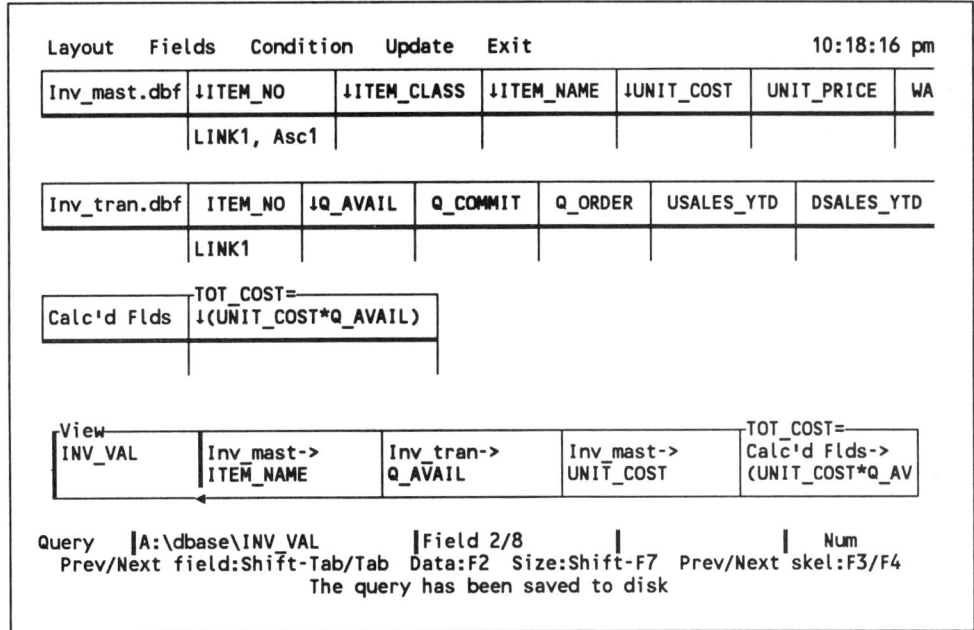

Layout	Fields	Condition	Update	Exit			10:18:16 pm

Inv_mast.dbf	↓ITEM_NO	↓ITEM_CLASS	↓ITEM_NAME	↓UNIT_COST	UNIT_PRICE	WA
	LINK1, Asc1					

Inv_tran.dbf	ITEM_NO	↓Q_AVAIL	Q_COMMIT	Q_ORDER	USALES_YTD	DSALES_YTD
	LINK1					

Calc'd Flds	┌TOT_COST─── ↓(UNIT_COST*Q_AVAIL)

┌View
| INV_VAL | Inv_mast-> ITEM_NAME | Inv_tran-> Q_AVAIL | Inv_mast-> UNIT_COST | ┌TOT_COST─── Calc'd Flds-> (UNIT_COST*Q_AV |

```
Query    |A:\dbase\INV_VAL        |Field 2/8        |            |  Num
   Prev/Next field:Shift-Tab/Tab Data:F2 Size:Shift-F7 Prev/Next skel:F3/F4
                     The query has been saved to disk
```

Figure 8-3 Completed INV_VAL View Query Screen

Using a View Query

To see what your file looks like, move your cursor to the INV_VAL file under the Query panel. You should note that when you highlight INV_VAL, the full name of the file (under the Panel area of the screen) is INV_VAL.QBE. Press **F2** and the screen that appears should match Figure 8-4. If it does not resemble this Figure, see the section on *Modifying a View Query*.

As you can see, information from both the INV_MAST and INV_TRAN have been combined, and only certain fields have been projected into the view. The entire view does not fit on the screen, just press **ENTER** or the arrow keys to move to different fields not on the screen. In addition, note that the inventory items have been grouped together by their class (books, games, or toys). You will also note that the bottom of the screen indicates that this is a *Read only* file. This means that no changes can be made directly to this file. If a user wants to change some of the data that appears in this file, they will have to access the *Source* files (INV_MAST and INV_TRAN) directly. This is a useful control device, since often we want people to be able to look at certain data, but do not want them to be able to make changes to those files.

```
   Records   Organize   Fields   Go To   Exit

  ITEM_NO ITEM_CLASS ITEM_NAME              Q_AVAIL UNIT_COST TOT_COST

  B029    BOOK       GOODNIGHT MOON             150      3.60          5
  B119    BOOK       CASEY AT THE BAT           130      2.10          2
  B187    BOOK       MIKE MULLIGAN              130      2.70          3
  B467    BOOK       MAKE WAY FOR DUCKLINGS     145      2.50          3
  G043    GAME       KERPLUNK                   155      6.80         10
  G121    GAME       CANDYLAND                   65      2.60          1
  G286    GAME       RISK                         0      5.25
  G324    GAME       MONOPOLY                    75      4.25          3
  T108    TOY        LEGO BLOCKS                 20     12.70          2
  T219    TOY        TURTLE VAN                 150     12.60         18
  T220    TOY        PIZZA THROWER                0     11.60
  T418    TOY        ECTO MOBILE                 45     11.40          5




  Browse   |A:\dbase\INV_VAL          |Rec 9/12        |View |ReadOnly|    Num
```

Figure 8-4 INV_VAL Query File, Sorted by Item Number

For example, a general ledger clerk may be interested in the total value of the inventory items, but that clerk should not be allowed to go in and adjust the inventory numbers directly; that should be done by an inventory control clerk. We would then have the inventory source files, e.g. INV_MAST, protected through a password scheme that only the inventory control clerk can access and modify. The general ledger clerk could then view the underlying data without altering the data.

You should also note that the view we have just created is a *Logical View* of the data, the underlying data files have not been physically changed at all. To verify this, first exit from the view by pressing **ALT-E**, and choosing **Exit**. When you are returned to the Control Center, you will note that the INV_VAL file is above the line in the Query panel. This indicates that this is an open file; to close the file press **ENTER** and select **Close view**. Next, move your cursor over to the data panel and highlight INV_MAST. Press **F2**, and the data in the file appears. Note that the file is still in the original order that you entered the data in Chapter 6, with the two new additions from Chapter 7 appearing at the end of the file. This represents the order in which the data is *physically* stored.

Modifying a view query

If your query did not look like Figure 8-4 and you feel it was a problem with the way you have designed the query, then dBASE allows you to modify the query design. You can recall the query design screen for a view file by highlighting the view file within the Query panel and pressing SHIFT-F2. You could also access the query design screen by pressing ENTER when the filename is highlighted within the Query panel and selecting Modify query.

You can also use the modify query feature if you had to save the query before it was in final form and you wish to pick up where you left off. Once you have decided to modify a query, your screen should display the query layout as you last saved it. To modify the query, there are several options available. To add a file to the query design, you would select the Add file to query option under the Layout menu. To remove a file from the design surface, you should select the Remove file from query option found under the Layout menu.

The F3 and F4 keys are used to move from one file skeleton to either the next file skeleton or the previous file skeleton. You can use the F5 key to either add or remove a field from the view file (the file that appears at the bottom of the screen). To rearrange the order of fields in the file view you can place your cursor on the field that you want to move and press F7. Following the instructions on the bottom of the screen, you would use the Tab key to move the field to its proper position and then press ENTER.

When you have completed all necessary changes to the query layout, save the query using the procedures described earlier, and then exit from the query design screen. To see if your query is now correct, display the view by pressing F2 while the filename is highlighted by the cursor in the Query Panel at the Control Center.

This completes our look at how to design a view query. We will use this particular view in the next chapter to help develop a report that can be printed.

Creating Update Queries

Stroudsburg Toy Company has decided to increase the selling price of all their books by 10 percent. Since Stroudsburg sells hundreds of different books, they want to make sure that all books are increased 10 percent. They believe that going into the INV_MAST file and going through each line item, finding a book and increasing its price 10 percent, would result in many clerical errors. A clerk may accidentally increase the price of a toy or game, they may miss a book or two, or they could make a numerical mistake recording the new price. They have asked you for help in updating the prices for their books.

This updating of selected records can be accomplished through the Query module of dBASE. The process is basically a two-stage one. In the first stage you will create a *filtering* condition that will select only those records that meet a certain criteria. This is referred to as a *Select* operator. The second step is to then define what the specific nature of the update is. While we will be creating an update query that involves only one file, we could use the data in one file as a basis for updating data in another file. An example of this type of operation is updating the quantity available in the inventory transaction file based on either units sold or units purchased. These types of transactions (sales and purchasing) would be kept in separate files, and would then be used to update the inventory transaction file. This is no more complex than the type of update query we will design below, and would use the methods described earlier to join the two files together. However, we will focus on a simple update query so that it is easier to see what has been accomplished through the update query.

To accomplish this update query, first find out what the current prices are for the 4 books contained in the INV_MAST file. You can either highlight the INV_MAST file from the Data panel and press F2 to display the file and look at the prices for the four books, or you could go to Chapter 6 and look up the prices from Table 6-1. Once you get the prices, write them down on a piece of paper so you can verify that the update has been performed correctly. As further proof, pick one inventory item that is not a book and write its price down also, to make sure that it does not change.

We can now begin the process of increasing the prices of all books by 10 percent. Move your cursor to the Query panel and press **ENTER** while you are on < create >. Following the procedures described previously, add the INV_MAST file to the design surface.

Note: If you need to exit from this tutorial before you have completed it, go to the section Saving an update query. *When you are ready to work on the query again, read the section* Modifying an update query.

The next task is to indicate that the only records to change are those that have been classified as books. This is known as a filtering condition, or in relational database terminology, as a Select operation. Using the **Tab** key, move your cursor to the ITEM_CLASS field. dBASE allows you to specify a variety of filter conditions, e.g., and, or, equal to, greater than, and less than. In this case, we want a filter condition that will only allow those records to be selected that have "BOOK" as their ITEM_CLASS.

There are a variety of ways to do this. One is to use the Conditions menu and build a filter condition in a separate box on the screen. This is generally used for more complex filtering conditions. Alternatively, we could go directly to the necessary field and type in the condition we want. We will use the second method, and will serve as an introduction to the importance of syntax in dBASE.

Move you cursor to the ITEM_CLASS field. Since ITEM_CLASS is a character type field, we will need to place quotes around the name of the item class we are filtering. If we were dealing with a date field, we would place the date inside curly braces {}. If it were a logical field, you would just put in .T. (for true conditions) or .F. (for false conditions). Numeric fields do not require any special coding considerations. The second issue concerning syntax is that dBASE is case sensitive. This means that "BOOK" is different from "Book" which is also different from "book". In other words, if all your data was in capital letters, and you asked dBASE to look for a record using small letters in your filtering condition, it would not find any matches.

Thus, you need to be careful that the text you use in the query is in the same case as the text in the data file. For this particular condition, we would type the following while in the ITEM_CLASS field: ="**BOOK**". (If the query does not work, check your INV_MAST data file to verify that you have used all capital letters for all the entries in ITEM_CLASS. We will discuss how to do this later). After you are finished typing ="**BOOK**", press **ENTER**. To see the results of your filter operation, we need to first put some fields in the view skeleton. Choose ITEM_NO, ITEM_CLASS, ITEM_NAME, and UNIT_PRICE by pressing **F5** when the cursor is on each of these fields. When you are finished, press **F2** and your screen should look like Figure 8-5. The screen should display only the four items that are books. By first checking your filter condition, you are placing a control over the potential risk of changing the wrong records. To return to the query design screen and continue with this update query, press **ALT-E**, and choose **Transfer to query design**.

```
 Records   Organize   Fields   Go To   Exit
┌────────┬──────────┬────────────────────────┬──────────────────────────┐
│ITEM_NO │ITEM_CLASS│ITEM_NAME               │UNIT_PRICE                │
├────────┼──────────┼────────────────────────┼──────────────────────────┤
│B467    │BOOK      │MAKE WAY FOR DUCKLINGS   │                      4.50│
│B119    │BOOK      │CASEY AT THE BAT         │                      4.30│
│B187    │BOOK      │MIKE MULLIGAN            │                      5.00│
│B029    │BOOK      │GOODNIGHT MOON           │                      7.00│
│        │          │                         │                          │
│        │          │                         │                          │
│        │          │                         │                          │
└────────┴──────────┴────────────────────────┴──────────────────────────┘
 Browse  |A:\dbase\<NEW>         |Rec 1/12      |View |      |   NumCaps
```

Figure 8-5 Results of Setting Filter Condition to BOOK for the Inv_mast Data File

If the query did not work properly, first check your filter condition, making sure that you have placed quotes around the word "BOOK". If it still does not work, save the query using the techniques described in the *Saving an update query* section below. Next, go to your INV_MAST data file, and press F2 to display the data. Make sure that all the ITEM_CLASS entries are capitalized; if not, make the necessary corrections. When you are finished doing this, return to your query using the techniques described in the *Modifying an update query* section.

The second stage of creating an update query is to specify exactly what you want done to the filtered records. To design your update, press **ALT-U**, and choose Specify update operation, by pressing **ENTER** on that option. Your screen should now look like Figure 8-6.

The menu choice that we are interested in is the first one, Replace values in Inv_mast.dbf. Since this option is already highlighted, press **ENTER** to select it. A message appears that indicates that if you want to proceed with the update option, then you must get rid of the view skeleton which appears at the bottom of the screen. Select **Proceed** and you will note that the view skeleton disappears, and at the top of your screen the word Replace now appears under the INV_MAST file name on your file skeleton.

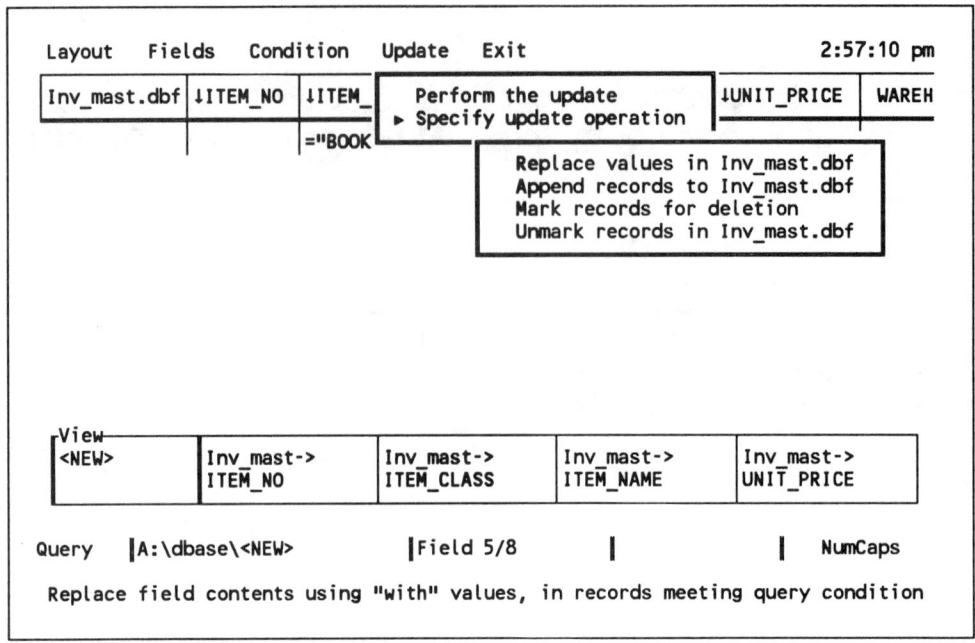

Figure 8-6 Selecting the Update Operation to be Performed on the
Inv_mast Data File

Every Replace command must be combined with a "with" condition in one of the fields. In this case, the field we want to replace (modify) is the UNIT_PRICE field. Move the cursor to that field and type in **WITH (UNIT_PRICE*1.10)**. This will complete the update query, so the last step is to save it.

Saving an update query

The first step in saving the update query is to give it a filename. Press **ALT-L** and select Save this query. After pressing **ENTER**, you are prompted for a filename; type in **PRICE_UP** and hit **ENTER**. You should note that dBASE saves update queries with two different extensions. The file you have just created has a .UPD extension. When the program is actually run, a new file is created with a .DBO extension. At this point your screen should look like Figure 8-7. You can now exit from the query module by pressing **ALT-E**, and selecting the **Save changes and exit** option.

You should now be back at the Control Center. If you look at the file names in your Query panel you will see the two files you have just created, INV_VAL and PRICE_UP. Note that the PRICE_UP file has an asterisk beside it. This indicates that it is an update file, and not just a view file.

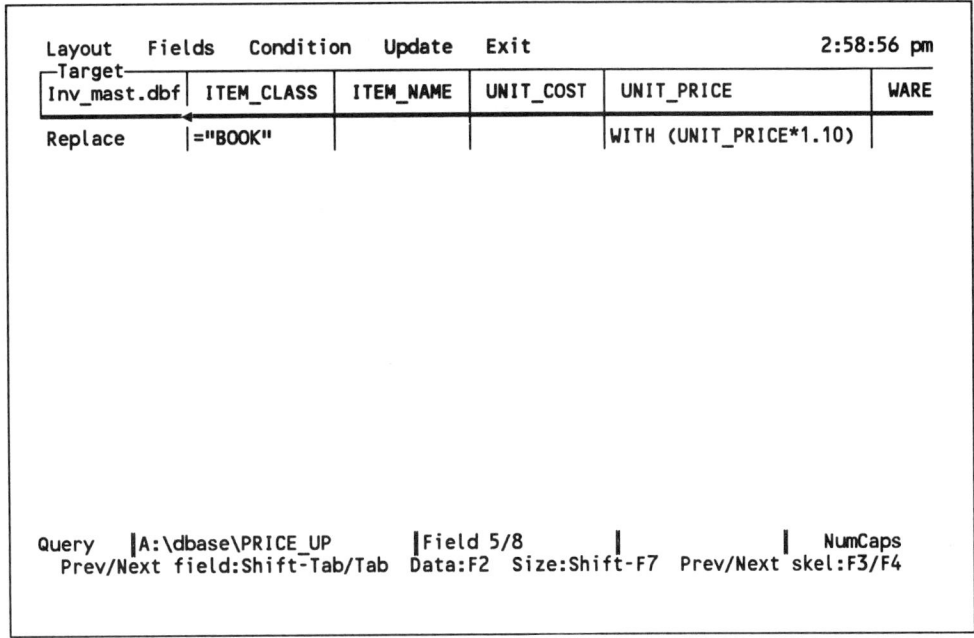

Figure 8-7 Completed Update Query Screen for Inv_mast Data File

Running an update query

To run the update query, highlight the PRICE_UP file, which is found in the Query panel. Notice that the full filename is displayed below the panel and has the .UPD extension. Press **ENTER** and then select the **Run update** option. As a control against accidental updating, you are asked if you are sure you want to perform the update. Respond **Yes**, and the update will be performed.

After completing the update, you will soon see that there is one major difference between a view query and an update query. A view query displays the data from the underlying data files, but does not change any of the data nor the order of the records in those files. On the other hand, the update query does physically change the affected file according to the update operation you designed.

To view the affected file, move your cursor over to the Data panel, highlight the INV_MAST file, and press **F2**. Hit **PgUp** and your screen should look like Figure 8-8. Find the four books and look at their prices, and compare them to the old prices. They all should reflect the 10 percent increase. In addition, look at the price of the non-book inventory item you had checked earlier and verify that it has remained constant.

If the update does not seem to have worked, you can modify the update query file. This process is described in the next section. However, to see if it works when you try it again, you must make sure the price data in the INV_MAST data file reflects the original price for all inventory items. This must be done before the update is run. This is most easily accomplished by displaying the affected file (INV_MAST) and editing the records using the techniques described in Chapter 6. The original prices are in Table 6-1. To return to the Control Center, press **Alt-E**, and choose **Exit**.

```
  Records    Organize    Fields    Go To    Exit

  ┌────────┬──────────┬────────────────────┬──────────┬───────────┬──────────┬───┐
  │ITEM_NO │ITEM_CLASS│ITEM_NAME           │UNIT_COST │UNIT_PRICE │WAREH_LOC │RE │
  ├────────┼──────────┼────────────────────┼──────────┼───────────┼──────────┼───┤
  │B467    │BOOK      │MAKE WAY FOR DUCKLINGS│    2.50 │      4.95 │A2S4L5    │ 8 │
  │G324    │GAME      │MONOPOLY            │     4.25 │      9.60 │A4S3L2    │ 6 │
  │T219    │TOY       │TURTLE VAN          │    12.60 │     22.50 │A3S2L4    │ 3 │
  │T418    │TOY       │ECTO MOBILE         │    11.40 │     21.90 │A3S3L6    │ 3 │
  │G121    │GAME      │CANDYLAND           │     2.60 │      4.80 │A4S3L1    │ 4 │
  │B119    │BOOK      │CASEY AT THE BAT    │     2.10 │      4.73 │A2S3L2    │ 7 │
  │B187    │BOOK      │MIKE MULLIGAN       │     2.70 │      5.50 │A2S3L5    │ 8 │
  │G043    │GAME      │KERPLUNK            │     6.80 │     14.90 │A4S2L4    │ 9 │
  │B029    │BOOK      │GOODNIGHT MOON      │     3.60 │      7.70 │A2S1L2    │ 4 │
  │T108    │TOY       │LEGO BLOCKS         │    12.70 │     18.40 │A3S1L4    │ 2 │
  │G286    │GAME      │RISK                │     5.25 │     11.60 │A4S3L7    │ 5 │
  │T220    │TOY       │PIZZA THROWER       │    11.60 │     21.50 │A3S2L5    │ 3 │
  └────────┴──────────┴────────────────────┴──────────┴───────────┴──────────┴───┘

  Browse  │A:\dbase\INV_MAST         │Rec 1/12        │File │         │    Num
```

Figure 8-8 Displaying the Results of the Price Update Query on the Inv_mast Data File

Modifying an update query

If your INV_MAST did not reflect the changes you had hoped for, or you had to save the query before it was in final form, you can modify the existing query design. To recall a query design screen for an update file, highlight that file within the Query panel and press SHIFT-F2. You can also access the query design screen by pressing ENTER when the filename is highlighted within the Query panel and selecting Modify query.

The techniques used to modify an update query are similar to those used when modifying a view query. Two important considerations are the syntax of your filtering conditions, and making sure that any updating formulas you have created are correct. When you have completed all necessary changes to the query layout, save the query using the procedures described above. To see if your update query is now correct, run the update following the instruction in the previous section. When it has finished running, look at the INV_MAST file to see if the prices of the books, and only the books, have increased 10 percent. If not, you may need to modify the query once more.

Conclusion

This completes the section on creating and using view and update queries. Queries are a powerful tool, and you can combine many functions such as filtering, joining, and updating on one query design surface. As noted earlier, we will use the INV_VAL query in the next chapter as the basis for a report.

FOLLOW-UP EXERCISES

Inventory Cycle

There is one other query that could be developed by Stroudsburg relating to its inventory function. This query will show when it is time to reorder a particular inventory item. The files needed to do this are the INV_MAST file and the INV_TRAN file. The steps that are necessary to carry this out are as follows:

1. After choosing the <create> option in the query panel, add the two files noted earlier to the design surface. Then join the two files together, using the ITEM_NO field as the common field.

2. Create a calculated field that will show the net units available. This is equal to the quantity available, plus the quantity on order from a vendor, but not yet received, minus the quantity committed to, but not yet shipped by us, to our customers. The field should be created as follows:

Q_AVAIL+Q_ORDER-Q_COMMIT

When you go to add this field to the view layout (Step 3), save it under the name REORD_CALC

3. Add the following fields to the view file:

ITEM_NO, ITEM_CLASS, ITEM_NAME, Q_AVAIL, Q_ORDER, Q_COMMIT, REORD_PNT, REORD_CALC

4. The final step is to put a filter condition on this query. The filter will be designed to display only those items which are at or below the reorder point. This can be accomplished by moving your cursor to the calculated field and adding a filter condition equal to the following: <=REORD_PNT. When you have finished adding the filter condition, save the query under the name REORDER, and then exit from the query design.

Revenue Cycle

NOTE: Before completing the exercise below, make sure that you have done the follow-up exercise related to the Inventory cycle. You should have created a view query named REORDER.
Stroudsburg Toy Company would like to be able to prepare a sales invoice that it could send to its customers. You realize that a great deal of the data that is appropriate for a sales invoice is contained in a variety of files. Your first task is to create a query that will combine several files relevant to the preparation of a sales invoice. The files and the steps you will need to do this are as follows (the files should all be found in the Data panel):

- SALES_INV
- SALES_OR
- INV_MAST
- CUSTOMER

1. With the cursor on the Query panel, press enter on <create>. Then add the four files above to the screen layout. Next, join the files together as follows:

SALES_IN and SALES_OR - You need a combination of fields to join these together. To do this, first join them together using SORDER_NO as link one. Next, use the ITEM_NO field as the second link.
SALES_IN and INV_MAST - the common field is ITEM_NO
CUSTOMER and SALES_OR - the common field is CUST_NO

2. Create a calculated field to represent the revenue for each line item on a sales invoice. Note that the sales invoice is used to record both regular shipments and backorder

shipments. Thus, we need to capture both of these in our calculation. The field should be created as follows:

UNIT_PRICE*(QUANT_SHIP+BACK_SHIP)

When you go to add this field to your view (next step), you will be prompted for a name. Use the name TOT_REV.

3. Since we only want to have invoices prepared for those invoices that have not yet been paid, we need to add a filter condition so that only unpaid invoices are selected. Under the PAID_SI field, add the filter condition .F.

4. Add fields to the view. The appropriate fields for the sales invoice are as follows:

SINV_NO   SORDER_NO ITEM_NO   ITEM_NAME QUANT_SHIP   QUANT_BACK
BACK_SHIP   UNIT_PRICE TOT_REV(the calculated field)   CUST_NO   CUST_NAME
  CUST_ADDR CUST_CITY CUST_STATE CUST_ZIP

When you are finished adding the fields to the view, save the query using the Save this query option under the Layout menu (ALT-L). Name this query SALES_IN. When you are finished, press ALT-E to exit, and select Save changes and exit. This will return you to the Command Center.

The second task Mr. Jackson would like you to accomplish is to design a query to update the accounts receivable master file (AR_MAST) based on sales invoice activity. This is the point in the revenue cycle at which Stroudsburg would recognize the revenue from a sale and then increase the customer's account balance. The files and the steps needed are the following:

- AR_MAST
- SALES_INV
- SALES_OR
- INV_MAST

1: After you have added the four files to the design surface, you can join them together using the following links:

SALES_IN and SALES_OR - You need a combination of fields to join these together. To do this, first join them together using SORDER_NO as link one. Next, use the ITEM_NO field as the second link.
SALES_OR and INV_MAST - the common field is ITEM_NO
SALES_OR and AR_MAST - the common field is CUST_NO

2: After the files have been joined, you can specify the update operation to be performed on the AR_MAST file. In this case, the update operation necessary is to replace the

CUR_BAL and the YTD_SALES values in the AR_MAST file to recognize the revenue from each customer.

3: Once this has been accomplished, save the file using the procedures discussed earlier. The name of this file should be AR_SALES. When finished recording the name, you can exit from the query design screen. When you are returned to the control center, you should see this file name in your query panel, with an asterisk next to it, indicating that this is an update file.

We will use these query files in Chapters 9 and 10, as well as several other query files that have been included on your dBASE IV diskette.

Expenditure Cycle

NOTE: Before completing the exercise below, make sure that you have done the follow-up exercise related to the Inventory cycle. You should have created a view query named REORDER.
Stroudsburg Toy Company would like to be able to prepare a voucher form that could be used as an authorization for payment to the vendor. You realize that the data necessary to design a voucher is contained in a variety of files. Your first task is to create a query that will combine several files relevant to the preparation of a voucher. The files and the steps you will need to do this are as follows (the files should all be found in the Data panel):

- VOUCHER
- PURCH_OR
- INV_MAST
- VENDOR

1. With the cursor on the Query panel, press enter on <create>. Then add the four files above to the screen layout. Next, join the files together as follows:

VOUCHER and PURCH_OR - You need a combination of fields to join these together. To do this, first join them together using PO_NO as link one. Next, use the ITEM_NO field as the second link.
VOUCHER and INV_MAST - the common field is ITEM_NO
VENDOR and PURCH_OR - the common field is VEND_NO

2. Create a calculated field to represent the total cost for each line item on the voucher. The field should be created as follows:

UNIT_COST*QUANT_REC
When you go to add this fieLd to your view (next step), you will be prompted for a name. Use the name TOT_COST.

3. Since we only need to prepare a voucher for those not yet paid, we need to add a filter condition to handle this, so that only the unpaid vouchers are selected. To do this, add the condition **.F.** under the PAID_VO field.

4. Add fields to the view. The appropriate fields for the voucher are as follows:

VOUCH_NO   PO_NO   INV_DATE   ITEM_NO   ITEM_NAME   QUANT_REC
QUANT_BACK   UNIT_COST   VEND_NO   TOT_COST(the calculated field)
VEND_NAME   VEND_ADDR   VEND_CITY   VEND_STATE   VEND_ZIP

When you are finished adding the fields to the view, save the query using the Save this query option under the Layout menu (ALT-L). Use the name VOUCHER. When you are finished, press ALT-E to exit, and select Save changes and exit.

The second task Mr. Jackson would like you to accomplish is to design a query to update the accounts payable master file (AP_MAST) based on voucher activity. This is the point in the expenditure cycle at which Stroudsburg recognizes the liability of their purchase and increases the balance owed to the vendor. Follow the steps above concerning how to begin creating a query. The files and the steps needed are the following:

- AP_MAST
- VOUCHER
- PURCH_OR
- INV_MAST

1: After you have added the four files to the design surface, you can join them together using the following links:

VOUCHER and PURCH_OR - You need a combination of fields to join these together. To do this, first join them together using PO_NO as link one. Next, use the ITEM_NO field as the second link.
PURCH_OR and INV_MAST - the common field is ITEM_NO
PURCH_OR and AP_MAST - the common field is VEND_NO

2: After the files have been joined, you can specify the update operation to be performed on the AP_MAST file. In this case, the update operation necessary is to replace the values in the CUR_BAL and the YTD_PURCH fields values in the AP_MAST file to recognize the liability associated with a purchase from each vendor.

3: Once this has been accomplished, save the file using the procedures discussed earlier. The name of this file should be AP_PURCH. When finished recording the name, you can exit from the query design screen. When you are returned to the control center, you should see this file name in your query panel, with an asterisk next to it, indicating that this is an update file.

We will use these query files in Chapters 9 and 10, as well as several other query files that have been included on your dBASE IV diskette.

Payroll Cycle

1. Create 2 view queries that will enable the user to create a monthly and year to date summary of payroll information. For the monthly summary, you will need to calculate a person's gross pay and their net pay, and limit the view to only the current month's payroll information. You will need data from all the files except the PAYCHECK file. For the year to date summary you will only need the PAY_MAST, PAY_CLAS, and PERSONEL data files. You can also calculate a person's year to date net pay. Since these two queries will be used as a basis for the reports in Chapter 9, it may be helpful to look at Figures 9-13 and 9-14 to get an idea of what fields will be necessary for those reports. These reports have been grouped by pay class.

2. Create two update queries. The first will update a person's year to date information based on the current month's payroll information and change the date in the PAY_MAST data file to reflect the most recent payroll period. The second query will change the POSTED field in the Time Card file to a true condition. This field is used to control the updating process so that only the most recent payroll transactions are used to update the Payroll Master file. Run these two queries when you are finished.

Review Questions

1. What is the difference between a view query and an update query?
2. What is the difference between a file skeleton and a view skeleton?
3. How do you join two or more data files together?
4. What is meant by a filter condition?
5. How can you add a calculated field to a query?
6. How do you add a data file to the query surface?
7. How can you perform a select operation in dBASE?
8. How can you perform a project operation in dBASE?
9. How do you save a query?
10. How do you run an update query?
11. Does a view query change any of the underlying data in the data files?
12. Does an update query change any of the underlying data in the data files?
13. What are the filename extensions for queries?
14. How do you add fields to the view skeleton?
15. How can you modify an existing query file?
16. What is meant by a read-only view?
17. Why are read-only files useful from a control perspective?

CASE SOLUTION: PARADOX 3.5

The questions Bill would like to have answered, as well as the ability to process transactions, can both be accomplished through the proper design and use of *Queries*. A query allows the user to look at the data in various files in a multi-dimensional fashion. The user can design a query that will display only certain fields (a *Project* operation), a query that only displays records that meet a certain condition (a *Select* operation), and queries that combine data from several files (a *Join* operation). In addition, queries can be designed to update data in certain files using batch processing techniques.

Before you design a query, the systems designer should sit down with the users and find out what information they need in order to make appropriate decisions. Once this task has been completed, you are ready to use the computer to design the necessary query.

The first query you will design is one that will display the total value of inventory on hand at any given time. Since most users are more comfortable using the descriptions of inventory items rather than inventory item numbers, you have been asked to provide a listing of all inventory items showing their name, quantity on hand, unit cost, and total value. Management would like the data grouped according to the item class, such as books, toys, or games as well. If you recall the structure of the inventory database, the item name, unit cost and item class are maintained in the inventory master table, but the current quantity on hand is stored in the inventory transaction table. What is required is a way to join these two tables together, and then display only certain information about each inventory item.

Indexing a table

In order to join two or more tables together, we need to make sure that they are arranged in the same manner, at least from a logical viewpoint. Arranging a table according to its *Primary key*, or uniquely identifying field, can either be done through Sorting or Indexing. Sorting will actually physically rearrange the records in a table based on the sorting field. Indexing creates another table containing just the indexing field and the physical record location of the corresponding record. Indexing is generally much more efficient.

The three tables you have created at this point can all be indexed on the same value, the item number. To create an index from the Main Menu, choose **Modify/Restructure** and then press **ENTER** to see a list of the tables you have created so far. Move the cursor over to the Inv_mast table, and press **ENTER**. The structure of the table should now be on your screen. To make a field be a key (indexing) field, you would place an asterisk after the description of the field type. Move your cursor over to the field type column for Item_no, and place an asterisk (*) after A4. After doing this, your screen should look like Figure 8-9. To save this new structure, press **F2**.

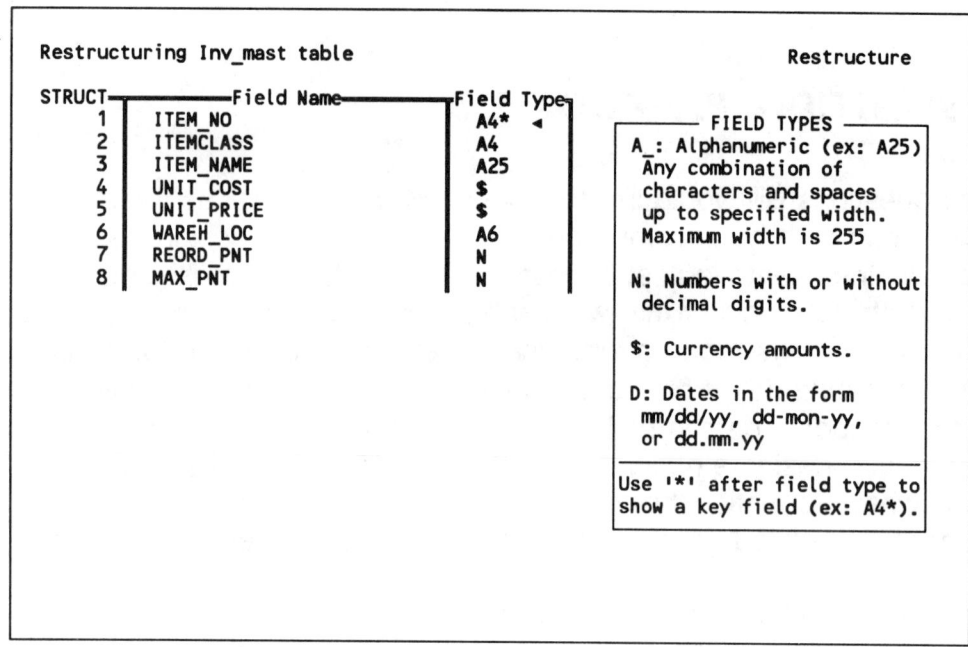

Figure 8-9 Adding an Index to the Inv_mast Data Table

Your screen will now display the contents of the Inv_mast table. Note that the order of the items is arranged according to the item number. Once you have marked a field as a key field, the table will always be displayed in order of the key field (unless you subsequently change the key field). To clear the screen, press **F8**.

One important detail that should be mentioned is that PARADOX requires that the key field always be the first field in a table; if it is not, you will get an error message indicating that the order of the fields is incorrect. Also, if several fields are required to uniquely identify a record, the fields must be in order of greatest importance, and must precede all non-key fields.

When you are finished indexing the Inv_mast table, repeat the same procedure for the Inv_tran and Inv_hist tables. Remember, if you want to clear the screen while viewing a table, press F8. You are now ready to design your first query, but first, a discussion on creating *Scripts*.

Recording and Using Scripts

In any transaction processing system, there are usually a series of procedures that are done repeatedly. Rather than having to design programs from scratch each time you wanted to perform a task, it would be much easier if you could somehow save the steps that you go through in completing a task, and then just run the saved steps. That is the essence of using *Scripts* in PARADOX.

A script is nothing more than a program or macro that will automatically perform a set of steps for you once you invoke the script. For our purposes, we will use the automatic keystroke capture ability of PARADOX to create our scripts. It is quite easy to use such scripts, as you will see. The basic concept behind this feature of PARADOX is as follows: first, you tell PARADOX to begin recording your keystrokes, second, you go through menu choices to carry out your objective, and third, when finished, you tell PARADOX to stop recording your keystrokes.

To start your first script, select **Script/BeginRecord**. You are asked to name the script; name this query **Inv_val**. After typing in the name and pressing **ENTER**, you are returned to the main menu. All keystrokes entered after this point are being saved by PARADOX in a macro that can later be played (used) whenever necessary.

Designing the Query

To start designing your query, select **Ask** from the main menu, press **ENTER** to display a list of tables, and select the Inv_mast table. After doing this, your screen should look like Figure 8-10. This is known as the query form. At the top of the screen it indicates the two function keys that are used frequently in queries, the F5 and F6 keys. The F5 key is used to indicate that a particular field is to be used as an example; this is shown by displaying the example in reverse video. The F6 key indicates that the field is to be part of the final query by placing a check mark in the field.

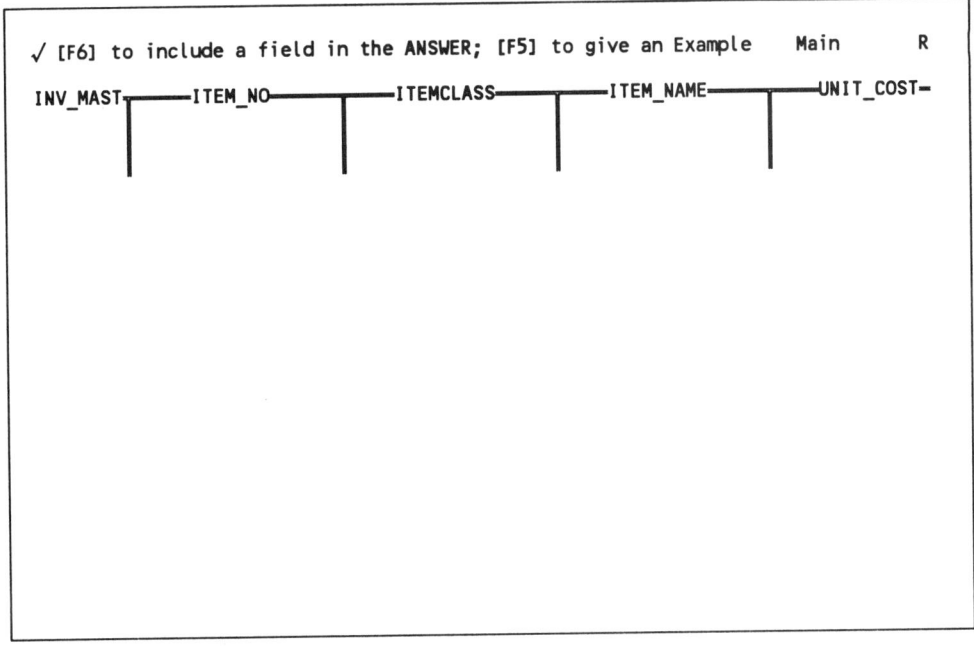

Figure 8-10 Query Form for Inv_mast Data Table

As noted earlier, the Inv_mast table does not have all the data that we want for this query, specifically, it does not have information on the quantity available, which is in the Inv_tran table. Thus, we need to add the Inv_tran table to our query as well, and link, or join the two tables together. To do this, first press **F10** to display the main menu at the top of the screen. Next, select **Ask**, press **ENTER**, and choose the Inv_tran table. Your screen should now have the structure of each table displayed on the screen. To move back and forth between the tables, press **F3** to move up and press **F4** to move down. We are now ready to join the two tables together through the use of common fields. For these two tables, the common field is the item number.

To tell PARADOX which two fields are the common fields, we place an example word in each common field. In this case, let's move our cursor to the Inv_mast table and move to the Item_no field. Press **F5** and type in the word **LINK1**. Note that the word is displayed in reverse video. After typing LINK1, press **ENTER**. When you are finished, press **F4** to move to the Inv_tran table, move to the Item_no field, press **F5** , and type in the word **LINK1**. After doing this, press **ENTER**, and the two tables are now joined together.

We are now ready to choose the fields we want to have displayed in our view. Press **F3** to return to the Inv_mast table and place your cursor in the Item_no field. Press **F6** to choose that field and you will see that a checkmark has been placed in that field. Your screen should look like Figure 8-11. The checkmark indicates that the field will be displayed when you view your query.

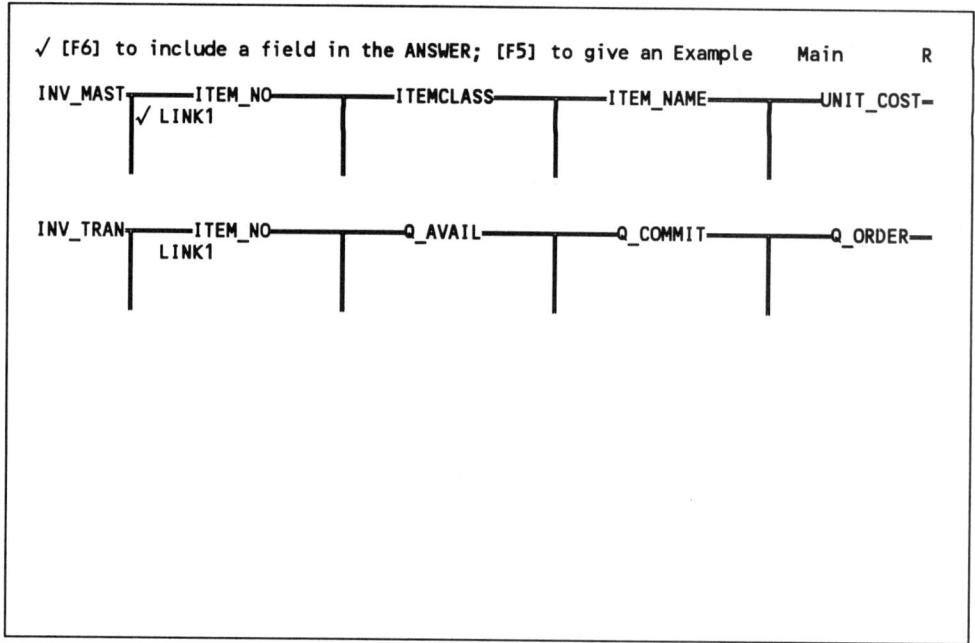

*Figure 8-11 Joining the Tables Together and Projecting the ITEM_NO
Field to be Displayed*

While you are using the Inv_mast table, place checkmarks under the item name, item class, and unit cost columns as well. While your cursor is in the unit cost field, press **F5**, type the acronym **UC**, and then press **ENTER**. UC should be displayed in reverse video. The purpose of doing this will be seen shortly, when we build a formula to calculate total cost of each inventory item.

Your next task is to move to the Inv_tran table, place your cursor under the Q_avail column and press **F6** to have this field displayed. Next, press **F5** so that this field can be used as an example, type in the letters **QA** and then press **ENTER**. Finally, we want to show for each inventory item the total dollar amount. This requires a calculation of the unit cost times the quantity available. To do this in PARADOX, you need to build the necessary formula. We will do this in the Q_avail column. Move your cursor to the Q_avail column. Place a comma after **QA** followed by a blank space and type **CALC**, which tells PARADOX to calculate whatever expression follows. The expression we need is **QA*UC**, but when we use these fields, we need to remember that QA and UC are examples of a particular field. Thus, after typing the word **CALC**, press **Spacebar** for a blank space, press F5 and type **QA***, and then press **F5** once more and type **UC**. After pressing ENTER, your screen should look like Figure 8-12. At this point, your formula is complete; be sure that **QA** and **UC** are both displayed in reverse video in your calculation.

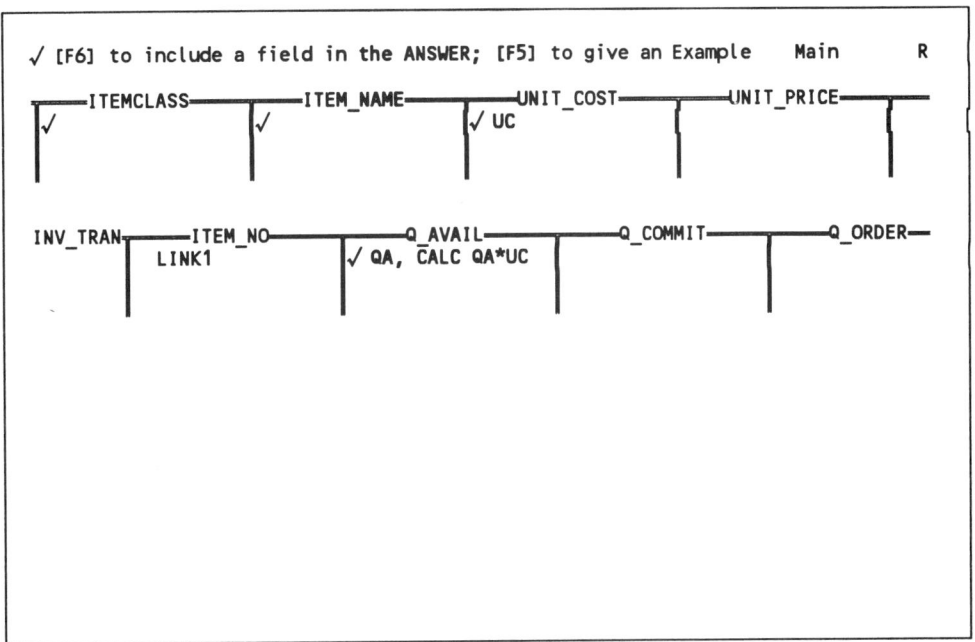

Figure 8-12 Query Form to Project Certain Fields and Calculate Total Cost

One last step is needed for formatting purposes. If we were to press DO-IT! right now, the calculated field would be displayed with the column heading QA*UC. It is useful to have more descriptive headings, which PARADOX allows us to create. Place your cursor in the Q_avail field. After UC press spacebar to put in a blank space and type the phrase **AS TOTAL COST** which will then display TOTAL COST as the column heading.

We are now ready to process the query. Press **F2** and a new table is displayed, known as an *Answer* table. See Figure 8-13. This table is the result of the above query. Note that the current answer table is too wide to fit on just one screen. To see the rest of the table, use the arrow keys to move either left or right. However, we can format the answer table so that all the necessary information is displayed on just one screen.

To get the answer table into a more useful format, press **F10** to bring up the main menu. Select **Image**, and then **ColumnSize**, which allows us to increase or decrease the width of any column. The top of your screen instructs you to move the cursor to the field

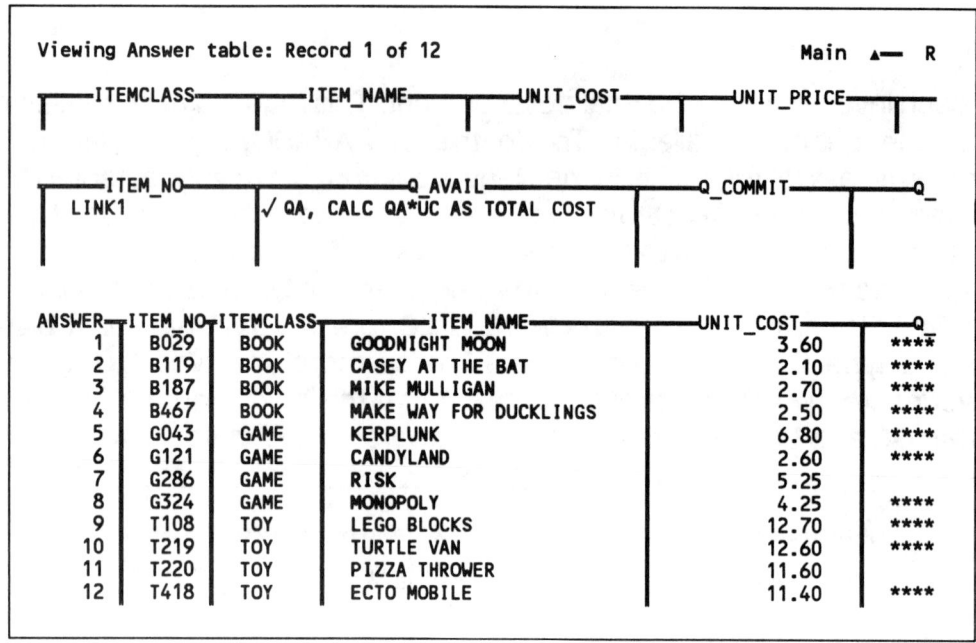

Figure 8-13 Results of the Query to Calculate and Display Total Costs

that you wish to resize. Move the cursor to the Item_name field and press **ENTER**. Use your left arrow key to shrink the size of the field, but not enough to erase part of the name of an item. When you are satisfied, press **ENTER**.

Repeat these steps with the unit cost field, the quantity available field, and the total cost field. When working with the numeric columns, you can tell if you have decreased its width too much because a series of asterisks will appear. If this happens, increase the size by at least two spaces by using your right arrow key. When you are finished with the last field and have pressed **ENTER**, move your cursor over to the far left. You should now be able to see the entire view on just one screen. See Figure 8-14 as an example.

The last part of this exercise is to clear the screen of everything but the answer table. Be careful not to erase your answer table when doing this. First, move the cursor off of the answer table by pressing the **F3** key, which will move the cursor up to the Inv_tran query form. While the Inv_tran query form is highlighted, press **F8** to clear it from the screen. Note that the Answer table is once more the table that is highlighted. Move your cursor to the Inv_mast query form by pressing **F3** once more, and then pressing F8 to erase the Inv_mast query form from the screen. The only display that should be left on your screen at this point is the Answer table.

These steps complete the design of this query. Remember, however, that we are recording this as a script. To end the script, press **F10**, select **Script**, and then **EndRecord**. The steps you have just gone through are now recorded under the name Inv_val, and can be played back at any time.

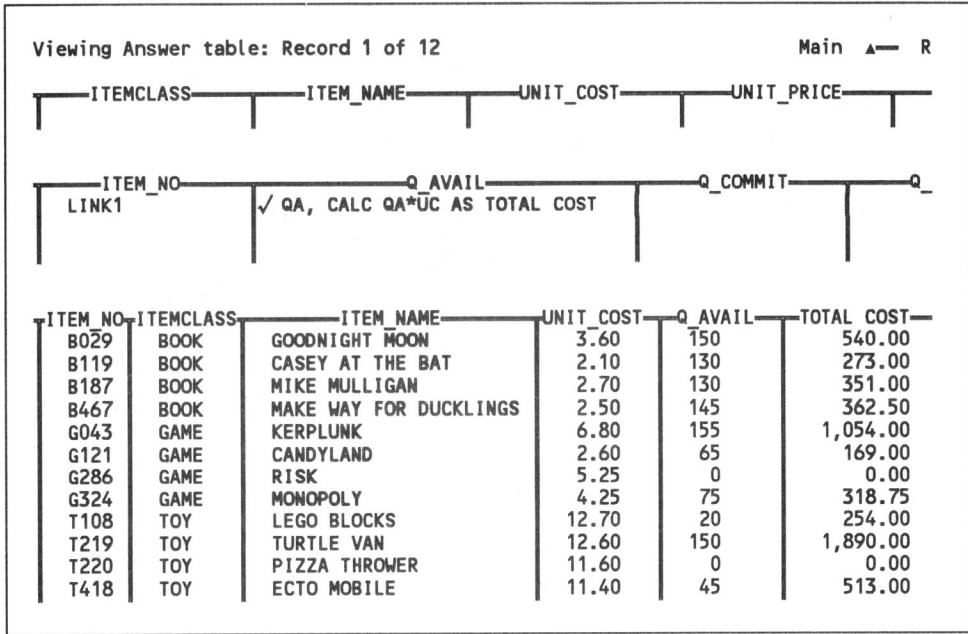

Figure 8-14 Revised Answer Table after Resizing Certain Fields

Playing a script

To play back this script, first clear your screen by pressing **F8**. Then select **Script**, **Play** and press **ENTER** to display a list of scripts. Select Inv_val and PARADOX will run through the steps you have used to create that query, and after a short time, the screen should display the Answer table as you have designed it. If it does not, the best advice at this point is to re-create the script from scratch, following the steps above, starting with Recording scripts. We are now ready to create the other major type of query operation that will be useful to Stroudsburg, known as *update* queries. Clear the screen by pressing **F8**.

Creating an Update Query

Stroudsburg Toy Company has just decided to increase the selling price of all their books by 10 percent. Since Stroudsburg sells hundreds of different books, they want to make sure that all books are increased 10 percent. They believe that going into the INV_MAST file and going through each line item, finding a book and increasing its price 10 percent, would result in many clerical errors. A clerk may accidentally increase the price of a toy or game, miss a book or two, make a numerical mistake recording the new price. They have asked you for help in updating the prices for their books.

The query option in PARADOX can also be used to update records in a table that meet certain "filtering" conditions. While we will only create an update query that involves one table, we could use the data in one file as a basis for updating data in another file. An example of this type of operation is updating the quantity available in the inventory transaction table based on either units sold or units purchased. These types of transactions (sales and purchasing) would be kept in separate tables, and would then be used to update the inventory transaction table. This is no more complex than the type of update query we will design below, and would use the methods described earlier to join the two files together. However, we will focus on a simple update query so that it is easier to see what has been accomplished through the update query.

Before we start, first select **View** from the main menu, press **ENTER** and choose the Inv_mast table. Move your cursor over to the unit price field, and write down on a sheet of paper what the current prices are for the four books. Select one non-book item and write down its price as well. When you are finished, press **F8** to remove the table from the screen. We can use this information to see if our query works properly.

Select **Ask** from the main menu, press **ENTER** and choose Inv_mast. Move your cursor over to the Itemclass column and type in the word **BOOK**. This acts as a filter condition to limit any processing of this table to just books. It is critical that you type in the word exactly as it is typed in the underlying data table. If you were to type in **book** (lowercase), PARADOX would not find any books in the Inv_mast table (assuming that you have used capital letters to type the Item_class field information). Next, move your cursor over to the unit price field, press **F5** and type in **UP**. This should now be displayed in reverse video. Next, place a comma after **UP** followed by a blank space and type **CHANGETO UP*1.10**. BE sure to press F5 before you type in the UP part of the formula. After doing this, your screen should look like Figure 8-15.

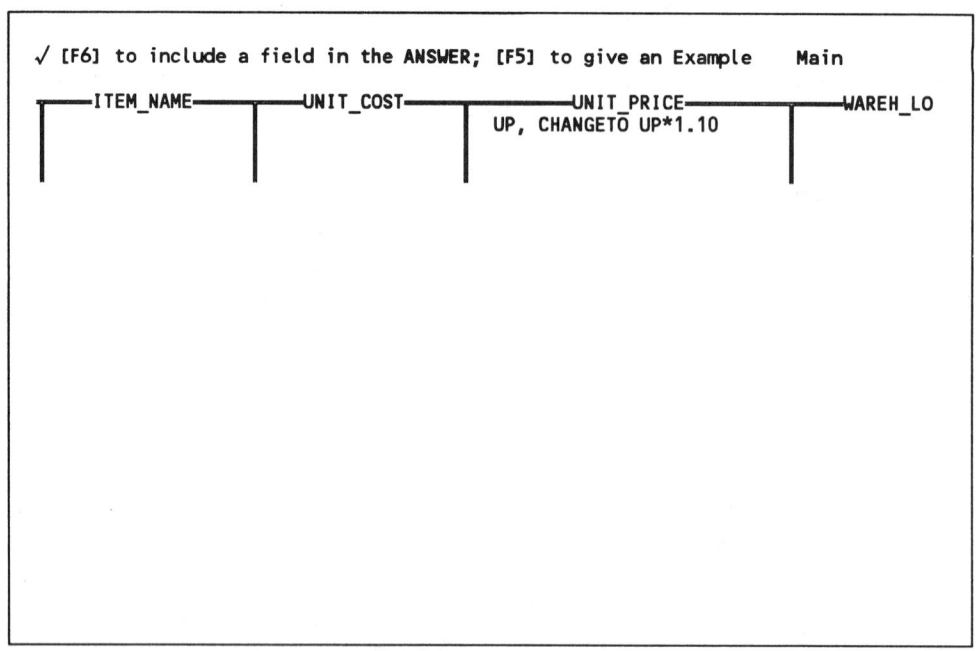

Figure 8-15 Update Query for the Inv_mast Data Table

You are now ready to run the update. Press **F2**, and your screen will soon look like Figure 8-16. The table that is displayed represents the set of records that were changed as a result of this update. Thus, only those inventory items that are classified as books should be displayed. Move over to the price field, and you will note that it

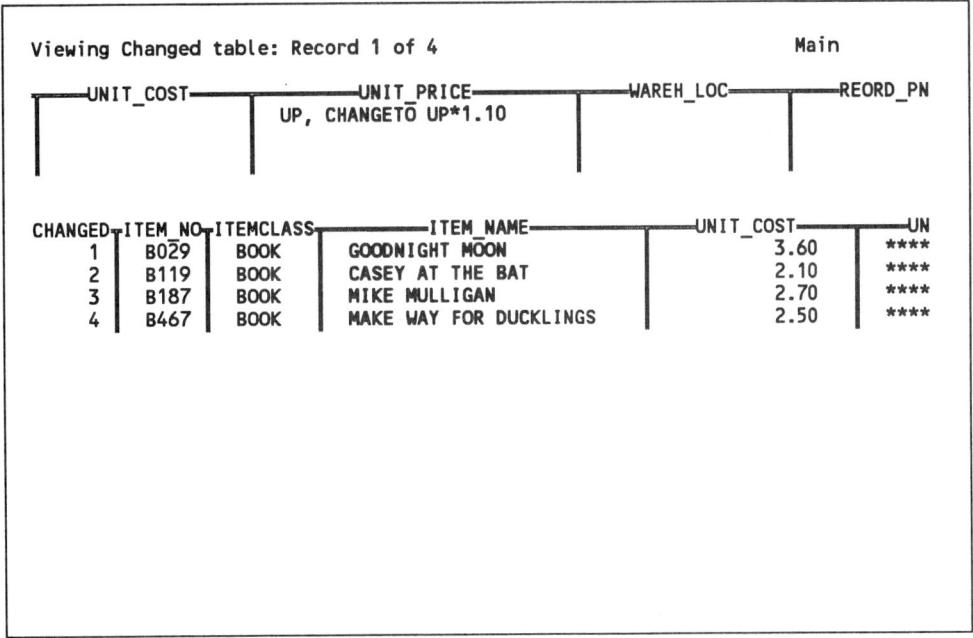

```
Viewing Changed table: Record 1 of 4                              Main
┌─────UNIT_COST─────┬────────UNIT_PRICE────────┬──────WAREH_LOC──────┬──────REORD_PN
│                   │   UP, CHANGETO UP*1.10    │                     │
│                   │                           │                     │
│                   │                           │                     │
│                   │                           │                     │

CHANGED┬ITEM_NO┬ITEMCLASS┬────────ITEM_NAME────────┬─────UNIT_COST─────┬──────UN
   1   │ B029  │  BOOK   │ GOODNIGHT MOON           │          3.60     │   ****
   2   │ B119  │  BOOK   │ CASEY AT THE BAT         │          2.10     │   ****
   3   │ B187  │  BOOK   │ MIKE MULLIGAN            │          2.70     │   ****
   4   │ B467  │  BOOK   │ MAKE WAY FOR DUCKLINGS   │          2.50     │   ****
```

Figure 8-16 Answer Table Displaying the Affected Records for the Price Update Query

shows the old prices. This is because this is only a view of the records from the old table that were changed, not what the actual changes were. To see what the new table looks like, press **F8** twice to clear the screen. Select **View**, press **ENTER**, and choose **Inv_mast**. The entire inventory master table should now be displayed. Move your cursor over to the unit price field, and compare the prices of the books with what you had written on a piece of paper before the update. The prices should reflect a 10 percent increase. See Figure 8-17 for comparison. Not only should the books have increased 10 percent, but the prices of the other items should not have increased. Be sure to check this as well.

If you have made a mistake, the best plan of attack to is to first edit the Inv_mast table to get the prices back to their original values. You can edit a table using the steps discussed in Chapter 6. Use Table 6-4 to get the original prices. If one of the records has an asterisk beside it, it means that the value exceeds the width of the field. To edit this type of field, first press **ALT-F5** to display the entire field, and then proceed with your normal editing procedures. After editing the table, press F2 to save the changes, and then try to design and run the update query once more.

```
Viewing Inv_mast table: Record 1 of 12                          Main
┌ITEMCLASS┬─────ITEM_NAME─────┬──UNIT_COST──┬──UNIT_PRICE──┬WA
│ BOOK    │ GOODNIGHT MOON    │      3.60   │      7.70    │
│ BOOK    │ CASEY AT THE BAT  │      2.10   │      4.73    │
│ BOOK    │ MIKE MULLIGAN     │      2.70   │      5.50    │
│ BOOK    │ MAKE WAY FOR DUCKLINGS │ 2.50   │      4.95    │
│ GAME    │ KERPLUNK          │      6.80   │     14.90    │
│ GAME    │ CANDYLAND         │      2.60   │      4.80    │
│ GAME    │ RISK              │      5.25   │     11.60    │
│ GAME    │ MONOPOLY          │      4.25   │      9.60    │
│ TOY     │ LEGO BLOCKS       │     12.70   │     18.40    │
│ TOY     │ TURTLE VAN        │     12.60   │     22.50    │
│ TOY     │ PIZZA THROWER     │     11.60   │     21.50    │
│ TOY     │ ECTO MOBILE       │     11.40   │     21.90    │
```

Figure 8-17 Viewing the Updated Inv_mast Data Table

Conclusion

This completes the section on creating view and update queries, as well as the fundamentals of creating and playing scripts. Queries and scripts are powerful tools, and you can combine many functions such as filtering, joining, and updating into one query and then play it as a script. We will the INV_VAL query in the next chapter as the basis for a report.

FOLLOW-UP EXERCISES

Inventory Cycle

There is one other query that could be developed by Stroudsburg relating to its inventory function. This query would show when it is time to reorder a particular inventory item. The files needed to do this are the Inv_mast table and the Inv_tran table. The steps that are necessary to carry this out are as follows:

1. From the main menu, select **Ask**, press **ENTER**, and choose Inv_mast.

2. Place a checkmark under item number, and then press **F5** to type in **LINK1** as an example.

3. Place a checkmark under the item class, item name, and reorder point fields.

4. Bring up the main menu (**F10**), select **Ask**, press **ENTER**, and choose Inv_tran.

5. Under the item number field, press **F5** and type **LINK1**. The two tables are now joined together.

6. Place a checkmark under quantity available, press **F5**, and type in **QA**.

7. Place a checkmark under quantity committed, press **F5**, and type in **QC**.

8. Place a checkmark under quantity ordered, press **F5** and type in **QO**. Follow this with a comma, then a blank space and then type **CALC QA+QO-QC as Balance** making sure to press **F5** each time for QA, QO, and QC. These should all be displayed in reverse video.

9. Press **F3** to return to the Inv_mast query form, place the cursor under the reorder point field, press **F5** and type in **RP**. Follow this with a comma, then a blank space, and then type >QA+QO-QC. Make sure that you press **F5** each time for QA, QO, and QC, so that each one is displayed in reverse video.

10. Press **F10**, select **Script**, and then **QuerySave**. Name the query **REORDER**. To run this script in the future, select Script, then Play, press ENTER and choose REORDER. To view the results of the query you would then press F2.

Revenue cycle

NOTE: Before completing the exercise below, make sure that you have done the follow-up exercise related to the Inventory cycle. You should have created a view query named REORDER.
Stroudsburg Toy Company would like to be able to prepare a sales invoice that it could send to its customers, but it only wants to send the invoice to those customers who have not paid. This first query will limit the selection of invoices to those invoices that have not been paid. We will then use the results of this query to mail out the appropriate invoices.
The steps needed to develop this query are as follows.

1. From the main menu, select **Ask**, press **ENTER**, and choose Sales_in. Place a checkmark in the far left column, under the name of the table. This has the effect of placing check marks in each field.

2. Move the cursor over to the Paid_si field and type in **F**. This will allow only those invoices which have not yet been paid to be selected as part of the query.

3. Press **F10** and select **Scrip**t and **QuerySave**. Name this query **Unpaidsi** and then press **ENTER**.

4. Whenever you want to process this query, select Script/Play and choose Unpaidsi. The query form you created will appear and you can run the query by pressing F2.

The second task Mr. Jackson would like you to accomplish is to develop an update query to reflect sales invoicing activity. This update will update a customer's account in terms of increasing both the current balance and the year to date sales of a customer. To accomplish this procedure in PARADOX requires multiple queries. The following steps guide you through the necessary queries. Since this does involve many steps, it is best to save them in a script.

1. Select **Script, BeginRecord** from the main menu and name the script **Ar_sales**. After doing this, you are returned to the main menu.

2. Use the **Ask** command and press **ENTER** to bring up a list of tables. Choose Sales_in table and then place a checkmark in the table name column (far left). This should automatically place a checkmark in each field. For the Item_no field, place an example called **LINK1**. For the quantity shipped field, place an example called **QS** and for the backshipped field, place an example called **BS**. Next, move the cursor to the POSTED field and type **F** . This will limit the updating process to only those transactions that have not yet been posted to the AR master file.

3. Press **F10** and select **Ask** again. Press **ENTER**; the table to use this time is the Inv_mast table. Place the example **LINK1** in the Item_no field, and the example **UP** in the unit price field. After placing UP in the unit price field, follow this with a comma and a

blank space and then type: **CALC (QS+BS)*UP AS TOTREV**. This is the formula to determine total revenue for each sale. Be sure to press **F5** before typing in the field name abbreviations. Press **F2** to process the query, then press **ALT-F8** to clear the screen.

4. From the main menu, select **Ask**, press **ENTER** and select the table called Answer. Place a checkmark in the customer number field and under the TOTREV field type **CALC SUM**. These two steps tell PARADOX to sum the total dollar value of all invoices, by customer. Press **F2** to process the query and then press **ALT-F8** to clear the screen.

5. From the main menu, select **Ask**, press **ENTER** and choose the Answer table again. Note that this is different table than the answer table in step 3. In the customer number field place an example called **LINK1**, and in the Sum of TOTREV field place the example **TR**. Press **F10** to bring up the menu and select **Ask**. Press **ENTER** and choose the Ar_mast table and place the example **LINK1** in the customer number field. In the current balance column, place the example: **CB, CHANGETO CB+TR**. In the Year to date sales column, place the example **YTDS, CHANGETO YTDS+TR**. Press **F2** to process the query and **ALT-F8** to clear the screen. This completes the update process.

6. From the main menu select **Scripts** and then **EndRecord**. This script will be used in Chapter 10.

Expenditure Cycle

   NOTE: Before completing the exercise below, make sure that you have done the follow-up exercise related to the Inventory cycle. You should have created a view query named REORDER.
   Stroudsburg Toy Company would like to be able to prepare a voucher form that could be used as an authorization for payment to the vendor. However, there is no need to have one prepared for a voucher that has already been paid.
   The steps needed to develop this query are as follows.

1. From the main menu, select **Ask**, press **ENTER**, and choose Voucher. Place a check mark in the far left column, under the name of the table. This has the effect of placing check marks in each field.

2. Move the cursor over to the Paid_vo field and type in **F** to select only those invoices which have not been paid. This will limit the selection of vouchers to only those vouchers that have not yet been paid.

3. Press **F10** and select **Script, QuerySave**. Name this query **Unpaidvo** and press **ENTER**.

4. Whenever you want to process this query, select Script/Play and choose Unpaidvo. The query form you created will appear and you can run the query by pressing F2.

   The second task Mr. Jackson would like you to accomplish is to develop an update query to reflect voucher activity. This update will update a vendor's account in terms of increasing both the current balance and the year to date purchases from a vendor. To accomplish this procedure in PARADOX requires multiple queries. The following steps guide you through the necessary queries. Since this does involve many steps, it is best to save them in a script.

1. Select **Script, BeginRecord** from the main menu and name the script **Ap_purch**. After doing this, you are returned to the main menu.

2. Use the **Ask** command, press **ENTER** and choose the Voucher table. Place a checkmark in the table name column. This should place a checkmark in each field. For the Item number field, place an example called **LINK1** in the field. For the quantity received, place an example called **QR**. Next, move the cursor to the POSTED field and type **F** . This will limit the updating process to only those transactions that have not yet been posted to the AP master file.

3. Press **F10** and select **Ask** again. Press **ENTER** and the table to use this time is the Inv_mast table. Place the example **LINK1** in the Item_no field, and the example **UC** in the unit cost field. After placing UC in the unit cost field, follow this with a comma and a blankspace and then type: **CALC QR*UC AS TOTCOST**. This is the formula to determine

total cost of each purchase. Be sure to press **F5** before typing in the field name abbreviations. Press **F2** to process the query, then press **ALT-F8** to clear the screen.

4. From the main menu, select **Ask**, press **ENTER** and choose the table called Answer. Place a checkmark in the vendor number field and under the TOTCOST field type **CALC SUM**. These two steps tells PARADOX to sum the total dollar value of all vouchers, by vendor. Press **F2** to process the query and then press **ALT-F8** to clear the screen.

5. From the main menu, select **Ask**, press **ENTER** and choose the Answer table again. Note that this is a different table than the answer table in step 3. In the vendor number field place an example called **LINK1** and in the Sum of TOTCOST field place the example **TC**. Press **F10** to bring up the menu, select **Ask** and then press **ENTER**. Choose the Ap_mast table and place the example **LINK1** in the vendor number field. In the current balance column, place the example: **CB, CHANGETO CB+TC**. In the Year to date purchases column, place the example: **YTDP, CHANGETO YTDP+TC**. Press **F2** to process the query and **ALT-F8** to clear the screen. This completes the update process.

6. From the main menu select **Scripts** and then **EndRecord**. This script will be used in Chapter 10.

Payroll Cycle

1. Create a view query that will limit the selection of payroll records to only the most current period. You will want to join the PAY_MAST and TIME_CAR data tables together to do this. Also, check off all the fields in the PAY_MAST data table. This will be useful in the next chapter. Save the query using the SaveQuery option under the scripts menu.

2. Create two update queries. The first will update a person's year to date information based on the current month's payroll information and change the date in the PAY_MAST data table to reflect the most recent payroll period. The second query will change the POSTED field in the Time Card table to a true condition. This field is used to control the updating process so that only the most recent payroll transactions are used to update the Payroll Master table. Run these two queries when you are finished.

Review Questions

1. What is the difference between a view query and an update query?
2. How do you select a field for display in a query?
3. What is meant by a common field?
4. How do you join two or more data tables together?
5. What is meant by a filter condition?
6. How can you add a calculated field to a query?
7. How do you add a data file to the query surface?
8. How can you create an index for a data file?
9. What is the difference between indexing and sorting?
10. How can you perform a select operation in PARADOX?
11. How can you perform a project operation in PARADOX?
12. What is meant by a script?
13. How can you begin recording keystrokes for use in a script?
14. How do you play a script?
15. Does a view query change any of the underlying data in the data files?
16. Does an update query change any of the underlying data in the data files?
17. What is meant by an Answer table?
18. What is meant by saying a view is read-only?
19. Why are read-only files useful from a control perspective?

CHAPTER 9
DESIGNING AND PRINTING REPORTS USING A DATABASE MANAGEMENT SYSTEM

INTRODUCTION

This chapter will teach you how to design reports, or outputs, using your DBMS. In doing this task, you will learn how to group similar data together for reporting purposes as well as how to control the printer. Since the outputs of any DBMS are generally the most critical part of an accounting system, the reports are generally designed first. This helps the systems designer to know what the user wants from the system, then he or she can backtrack and determine the necessary data files to help create these reports. The design of the reports is saved until the end in this casebook since you need the data files on hand in order to create the reports. Thus, we can assume that the conceptual design of the reports to be developed in this chapter was the first step in the systems design process, but that the actual physical design from a software standpoint was last.

CASE: STROUDSBURG TOY COMPANY

Tom Jackson believes that the design of the inventory database is right on schedule. Looking back at what has been accomplished, Mr. Jackson notes that the inventory data files have been created and data entry screens and controls have been designed. The most recent task completed was the creation of queries to view or update the information contained in one or more files. He believes that the last necessary component is the creation of outputs, or reports, which can be used for either internal or external purposes. He has asked you to help in the design of these reports.

CASE SOLUTION: dBASE IV

To create a report in dBASE IV, you first need to tell dBASE which data file or query file your report will be using as a source of data. For this tutorial, we will be using the INV_VAL query file. To select this file, move your cursor to the Query Panel, highlight the INV_VAL file, and press **ENTER**. Next, select **Use view**, and you will note after a short wait that this file now appears above the line in the Query panel, indicating that it is now the active file.

Having selected the INV_VAL file, we are now ready to start creating a report that can present the data in this file in a useful manner. Move your cursor over to the Reports panel, and press **ENTER** on <create>. After doing this, your screen should look like Figure 9-1. This is the *Report Design* screen, with the Layout menu options already displayed.

Note: If you need to exit from this tutorial before you have completed it, go to the section Saving a report. *When you are ready to work on the report again, read the section* Modifying a report.

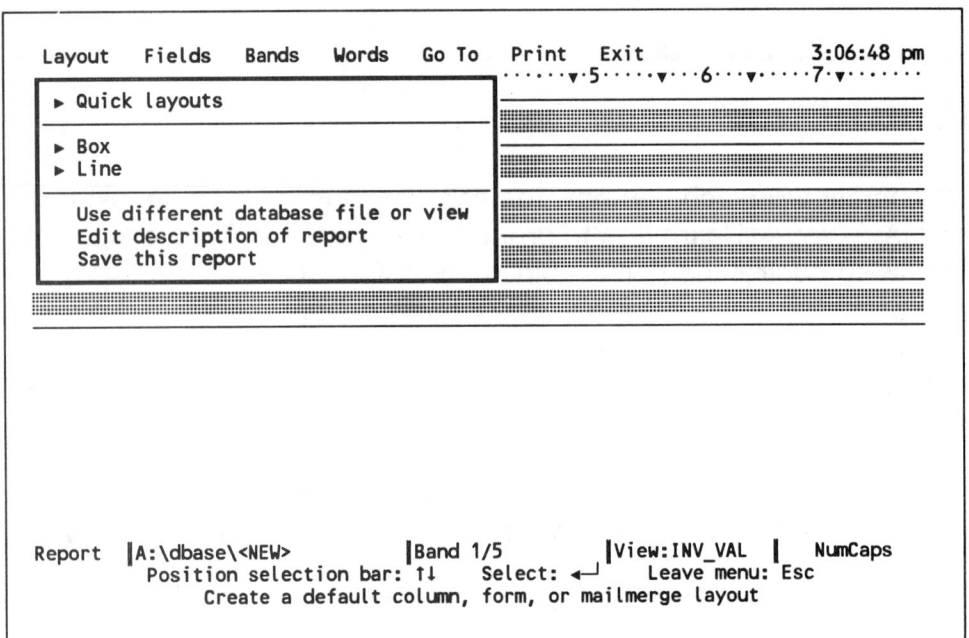

Figure 9-1 Layout Menu for A New Report Design Screen

Creating a Report

dBASE offers a "*default*" report design, which often provides a useful starting point for creating your own report. This option is found under Quick layouts. However, we will learn how to build the report from scratch, which will be more useful from a pedagogical standpoint. If you press **ESC** at this point, you are given a blank design screen. Your screen should look like Figure 9-2.

As you can see, the report screen contains 5 separate areas or *Bands*. The function of each of these is described briefly below.

• Page Header Band: This section of the report is used to indicate what would appear at the top of each page of the report. dBASE has as a default to display the current date and the page number.

• Report Intro band: This part of the report is used to give a brief description of the report that will be generated. It appears just once in the report, after the Page Header Band has been printed for the first page.

• Detail Band: This part of the report displays the actual contents of the file for the fields and records you select.

• Report Summary band: This section is used to summarize the entire report. A common use of the Report Summary Band is to total numeric fields for the report. As with the Report Intro Band, this appears just once for the entire report, on the last page.
• Page Footer Band: This last section is used to indicate what would appear at the bottom of each page of the report.

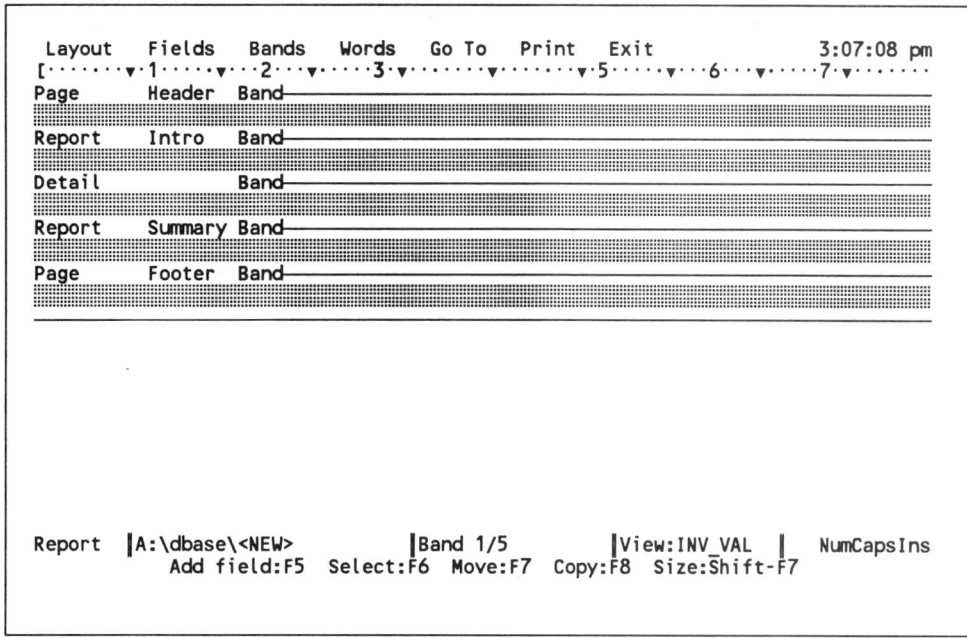

Figure 9-2 Blank Report Design Screen for INV_VAL Query File

In addition to these five sections, there are also Group Intro and Group Summary bands that can be added to the report design. We will see how to do this later, and discuss the purpose of those two sections at that time.

The first task you can do is to add the column labels that are to appear in the Page Header band. This is similar to the idea of adding labels in forms. The column labels are used to make it easier for someone reading the report to understand what the various columns of data represent. Use Figure 9-3 as a guide to creating appropriate column labels. Be sure to leave a blank line below the column labels. To put a blank line on the screen, make sure that the INS key has been activated. You can tell if it is active by looking at the bottom right part of your screen. If the Ins key has been activated, you should see the word **Ins**. If it is not there, press the **INS** key, and you will see that word in the lower right corner of the screen. To insert a blank line, all you need to do is press **ENTER** while the **INS** key is activated.

Once you are finished placing the column headings on the screen, the next task to accomplish is to delete a line. Move your cursor to the blank line below the Report Intro Band. Since we will not be putting a report introduction with this report, there is no need to have this blank line. To delete the line, press **CTRL-Y**.

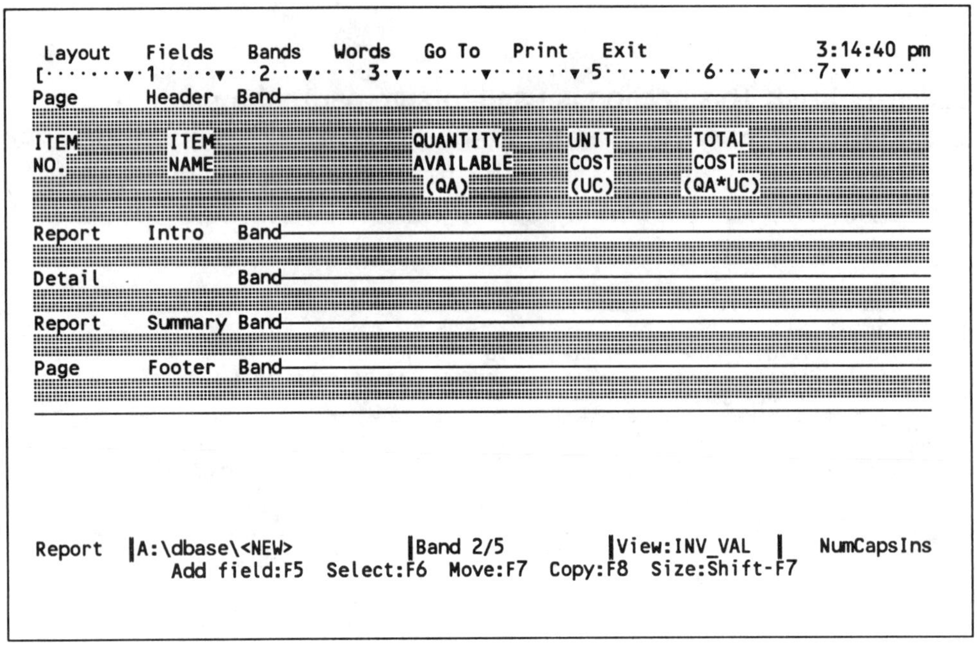

```
    Layout   Fields   Bands   Words    Go To    Print    Exit            3:14:40 pm
    [········▼·1····▼···2··▼····3·▼··········▼····▼···6··▼······7·▼·····
    Page       Header  Band──────────────────────────────────────────────────

    ITEM        ITEM                    QUANTITY      UNIT       TOTAL
    NO.         NAME                    AVAILABLE     COST       COST
                                        (QA)          (UC)       (QA*UC)


    Report     Intro   Band────────────────────────────────────────────────

    Detail             Band────────────────────────────────────────────────
    Report     Summary Band────────────────────────────────────────────────
    Page       Footer  Band────────────────────────────────────────────────




    Report    |A:\dbase\<NEW>        |Band 2/5        |View:INV_VAL  |  NumCaps Ins
               Add field:F5  Select:F6 Move:F7  Copy:F8 Size:Shift-F7
```

Figure 9-3 Report Design Screen with Column Headings Added to
the Surface

The next part of the report to work on is the Detail Band. First, move your cursor down to the blank line below the Detail Band line. Place your cursor so that it as at the far left, lined up under the ITEM NO. column heading (in the Page Header band). The Detail band is where the actual contents of the underlying data or query file are displayed. To do this, press **ALT-F** for Fields, and select **Add Field**. The names of all the fields associated with the current data file or query view are displayed on your screen. See Figure 9-4. Select **ITEM_NO**, and a window pops up allowing you to design how you want this field displayed. Since the default format is acceptable, you only need to press **CTRL-END** to place the field on the report design surface.

Follow these same steps to add the other fields (ITEM_NAME, Q_AVAIL, UNIT_COST and TOT_COST) to your report, being careful to have your cursor in the right place before you begin to add the field. If a field does end up in the wrong position, i.e., under the wrong column heading, place your cursor on the field display and press **DEL** to erase it. You can then place the field in its proper position.

The default display for all of the fields is acceptable, except for the TOT_COST field. After selecting this field to add, and the window pops up displaying the field characteristics, press **ENTER** while the cursor is on the Template option. Change the template to have only five characters displayed before the decimal point. Press **ENTER** after making this adjustment, and then press **CTRL-END** to save your changes. When you are finished adding all of the data fields, your screen should look like Figure 9-5.

The last major task to complete for this report is to add a *Group Band*. When you add a Group band, two new sections appear on the design layout, the Group Intro Band and the Group Summary Band. The Group Intro band is used to display what heading will appear each time a new group is started (e.g. books). This would then be followed by the detail (e.g., the item number, the item name) of that group. The Group Summary band is used to present summary information (e.g. total value) for the group (e.g. books) after displaying the detail data for that group.

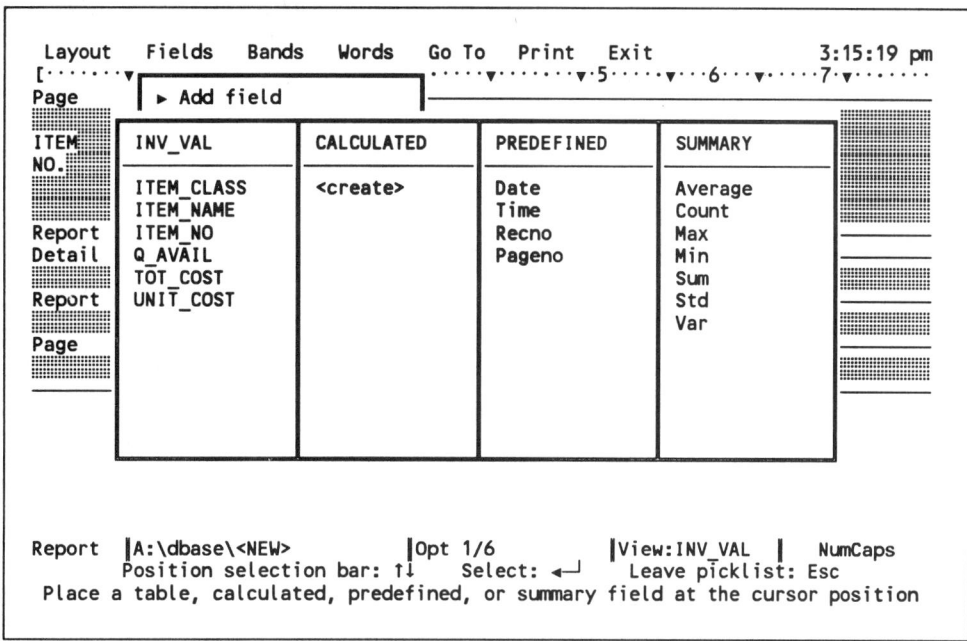

```
   Layout   Fields   Bands   Words   Go To   Print   Exit            3:15:19 pm
   [······▼·······················▼·····▼·5····▼···6··▼····7·▼······
   Page       ▶ Add field
   ░░░░░┌─────────────┬─────────────┬─────────────┬─────────────┐░░░░░░░
   ITEM░│ INV_VAL     │ CALCULATED  │ PREDEFINED  │ SUMMARY     │░░░░░░░
   NO.░░│             │             │             │             │░░░░░░░
   ░░░░░│ ITEM_CLASS  │ <create>    │ Date        │ Average     │░░░░░░░
   ░░░░░│ ITEM_NAME   │             │ Time        │ Count       │░░░░░░░
   Report│ ITEM_NO     │             │ Recno       │ Max         │
   Detail│ Q_AVAIL     │             │ Pageno      │ Min         │
   ░░░░░│ TOT_COST    │             │             │ Sum         │░░░░░░░
   Report│ UNIT_COST   │             │             │ Std         │
   Page  │             │             │             │ Var         │░░░░░░░
   ░░░░░│             │             │             │             │░░░░░░░
   ░░░░░│             │             │             │             │
         └─────────────┴─────────────┴─────────────┴─────────────┘


   Report  │A:\dbase\<NEW>        │Opt 1/6      │View:INV_VAL │  NumCaps
           Position selection bar: ↑↓   Select: ◄┘   Leave picklist: Esc
      Place a table, calculated, predefined, or summary field at the cursor position
```

Figure 9-4 Adding a Field to the Report Design Screen

```
   Layout   Fields   Bands   Words   Go To   Print   Exit            3:17:27 pm
   [······▼·1····▼····2···▼·····3·▼·········▼········▼·5····▼···6··▼····7·▼······
   Page       Header  Band
   ░░░░░░░░░░░░░░░░░░░░░░░░░░░░░░░░░░░░░░░░░░░░░░░░░░░░░░░░░░░░░░░░░░░░░░░░
   ITEM░░░░░░ ITEM░░░░░░░░░░░░QUANTITY░░░░UNIT░░░░TOTAL░░░░░░░░░░░░░░░░░░░
   NO.░░░░░░░ NAME░░░░░░░░░░░░AVAILABLE░░░COST░░░░COST░░░░░░░░░░░░░░░░░░░░
   ░░░░░░░░░░░░░░░░░░░░░░░░░░░░(QA)░░░░░░░(UC)░░░░(QA*UC)░░░░░░░░░░░░░░░░░░
   Report   Intro  Band
   Detail          Band
   XXXX░░XXXXXXXXXXXXXXXXXXXXXXXXXXXX░░999░░░░░░999.99░░░99999.99░░░░░░░░
   Report   Summary Band
   Page     Footer  Band


   Report  │A:\dbase\<NEW>        │Line:0 Col:66  │View:INV_VAL │  NumCapsIns
           Add field:F5  Select:F6  Move:F7  Copy:F8  Size:Shift-F7
```

Figure 9-5 Report Design Screen after Adding all Fields to the Detail Band

We want our report to show the information on inventory value separately for each Item Class (BOOK, GAME, or TOY). To add a Group band, first move your cursor to the Report Intro band and press **ALT-B**. The Band menu should now be displayed. Select **Add a group band**, and another box will appear. From this box, we will specify how we want to group our report. With the cursor on Field value, press **ENTER**, and a menu box is displayed showing all the field names for the current data file or query view. Move your cursor to ITEM_CLASS and press **ENTER**. When you are finished doing this, you are returned to the report design screen, which should look like Figure 9-6. Note that at the bottom of the screen there is a message indicating that the report is grouped by ITEM_CLASS.

```
   Layout   Fields   Bands   Words   Go To   Print   Exit           3:18:32 pm
   [······▼·1·····▼··2··▼····3·▼··········▼·5·····▼···6··▼···7·▼·········
   Page        Header   Band─────────────────────────────────────────────────

   ITEM        ITEM                QUANTITY      UNIT       TOTAL
   NO.         NAME                AVAILABLE     COST       COST
                                   (QA)          (UC)       (QA*UC)


   Report   Intro   Band──────────────────────────────────────────────────────
   Group  1 Intro   Band──────────────────────────────────────────────────────

   Detail           Band──────────────────────────────────────────────────────
   XXXX  XXXXXXXXXXXXXXXXXXXXXXXXXX   999      999.99     99999.99
   Group  1 Summary Band─────────────────────────────────────────────────────

   Report   Summary Band──────────────────────────────────────────────────────

   Page     Footer  Band──────────────────────────────────────────────────────



   Report  |A:\dbase\<NEW>         |Band 3/7        |View:INV_VAL |   NumCapsIns
              Add field:F5   Select:F6   Move:F7   Copy:F8   Size:Shift-F7
                                Group by ITEM_CLASS
```

Figure 9-6 Adding a Group Band to the Report Design

The first section we will work on is the Group Intro band. Move your cursor to the blank line below the Group Intro band and type the words **ITEM CATEGORY:** at the far left margin. Next, move your cursor to the right one or two spaces and add the ITEM_CLASS field to the display. This can be done by pressing **ALT-F**, and selecting **Add field**. Choose **ITEM_CLASS**, and when the default format is displayed, press **CTRL-END** to accept it. Next, move your cursor a couple of spaces to the right and type **Inventory values as of** and then press **ALT-F**. From the fields menu, select the **Date** type field found under the Predefined column and press **ENTER**. The effect of these steps is to display the name of the inventory category that is about to be displayed in detail. The detail band will list the desired data for the individual records that fall within that group.

The next section to modify is the Group Summary Band. We want the report to show the total dollar value of each inventory classification. To do this, first move your cursor to the blank line under the Group Summary Band, and move the cursor so that it is under the Total Cost column label. Press **ALT-F** and select **Add field**. The type of field we wish to display here is a *Summary* field, so move your cursor over to the last column displayed, which has the heading SUMMARY. The type of operation needed is to sum the individual records for the total cost field. Move the cursor down to Sum, and press **ENTER**.

A box appears requesting certain information. The only necessary information is to note which Field to summarize on. However, from a control standpoint it is useful to give these summary calculations a name as well. Thus, with the cursor on the Name option, press **ENTER**, and type in the name **GRP_DOL**. The GRP part of the name will help us to remember that this field is summarizing a field within a group, and not for the entire report. Press **ENTER** when you are finished typing in the name. Next, move your cursor down to Field to summarize on and press **ENTER**. The list of field names appears; select **TOT_COST**. Modify the size of the template as necessary. To save this field, press **CTRL_END**. You should now see the field displayed on your screen. The next task is designed to make the report easier to understand by placing a label next to this field. Move your cursor to the far left margin while in the Group Summary band, and type the label **Subtotal for category**. At this point, your screen should look like Figure 9-7.

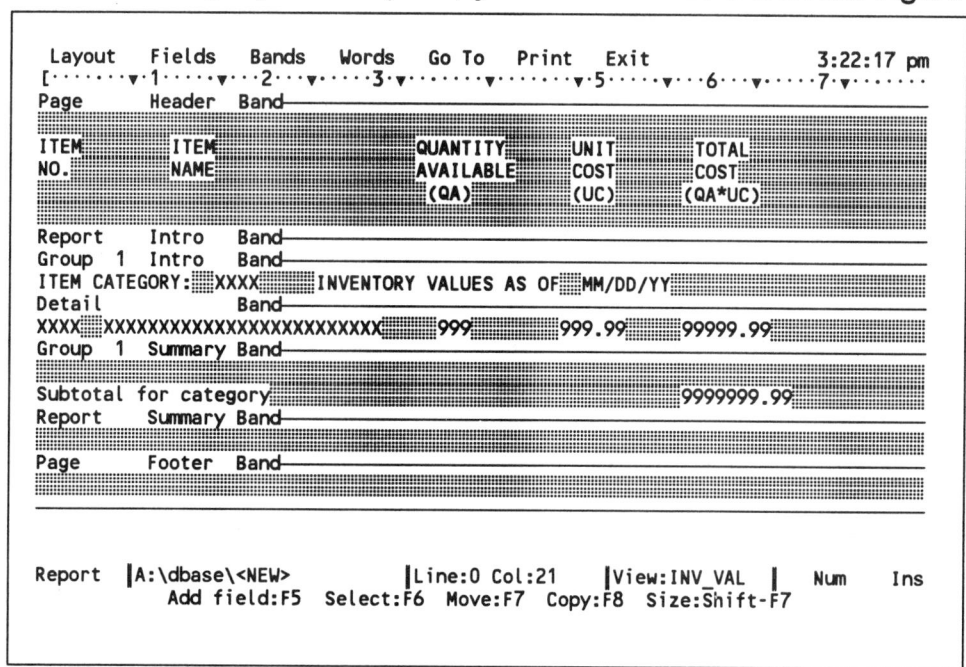

Figure 9-7 Adding Labels and Fields to the Group Intro and Group Summary Bands

The last part of the report we need to modify is the Report Summary Band, so move your cursor to this section. The field we will add in this section will summarize the entire report, for all inventory classifications. Thus, we only need to add a field under the total cost column.

Move the cursor under the TOTAL COST column and follow the procedures above on how to add a Summary field. For the Name, use **RPT_DOL**, to indicate this is a summary field for the entire report, as opposed to just summarizing for a particular group.

For the Field to summarize on, select **TOT_COST**. Modify the template size as necessary. Save this by pressing **CTRL_END**. You should be back at the report layout screen. Type in a label for descriptive purposes at the far left margin titled `Total Inventory Value for all Categories`. After completing this, your screen should look like Figure 9-8.

The last issue related to designing this report concerns formatting. The report will appear much clearer if each Group Band is printed on a separate page. This is helpful since it may be confusing to see a group band start in the middle of one page, and continued on the next. A user would have to refer to the previous page to see which item category is currently being displayed. To control for this, there is an option under the Band menu to have each band start on a separate page.

```
  Layout    Fields   Bands   Words   Go To   Print   Exit              3:24:00 pm
  [······▼·1····▼···2····▼····3·▼······▼·······▼·5····▼··6···▼··7·▼·····
  Page       Header  Band────────────────────────────────────────────────

  ITEM         ITEM                    QUANTITY     UNIT      TOTAL
  NO.          NAME                    AVAILABLE    COST      COST
                                       (QA)         (UC)      (QA*UC)

  Report    Intro   Band─────────────────────────────────────────────────
  Group  1  Intro   Band─────────────────────────────────────────────────
  ITEM CATEGORY: XXXX      INVENTORY VALUES AS OF MM/DD/YY
  Detail            Band─────────────────────────────────────────────────
  XXXX XXXXXXXXXXXXXXXXXXXXXXXXXXX     999       999.99     99999.99
  Group  1  Summary Band─────────────────────────────────────────────────

  Subtotal for category                                     9999999.99
  Report    Summary Band─────────────────────────────────────────────────

  Total inventory value for all categories                  9999999.99
  Page       Footer  Band────────────────────────────────────────────────


  Report   |A:\dbase\<NEW>        |Line:1 Col:0    |View:INV_VAL |  Num   Ins
            Add field:F5  Select:F6  Move:F7  Copy:F8  Size:Shift-F7
```

Figure 9-8 Completed Report Design for Inventory Value Report

To implement this option, move the cursor to the Group Intro Band line and press **ALT-B**. Move your cursor down to Begin band on new page and press **ENTER** to toggle the choice between Yes and No. When you have set the choice to **Yes**, press **ESC** to exit from the Band menu.

This completes the basic set-up of the report. Before we actually save the report, the next section will briefly discuss some of the printing options available within dBASE.

Controlling the report print-out

dBASE IV supports a wide variety of printers. When dBASE was originally installed on your computer, the person who installed the program was asked to select a default printer. However, this is not crucial to having your reports print out correctly, dBASE can still print a report on a printer that is not the same as the original default printer set-up during installation.

You can control a wide variety of printing options through the Print menu options. For example, you can set the width of your margins, the number of lines to print on a page, whether to eject a page after or before you begin printing (or both), and the number of copies to print. In general there is often not a need to change the default settings already stored by dBASE. If you run into problems in printing a report, you may need to ask your lab consultant for help, since it could be one of many potential problems, most likely not related to dBASE itself.

Saving a report

You are now ready to save this report. To do this, press **ALT-L**, and move the cursor down to Save this report. After pressing **ENTER**, you are prompted for a file name. For this report, use the name **INV_VAL** and press **ENTER** when you are finished typing the name. dBASE will now generate the program code related to the design of this report. dBASE creates three files related to each individual report that is designed. The design of the report itself has the extension .FRM. The program code that will generate the report has a .FRG extension, while the compiled code has a .FRO extension. When dBASE has finished generating the program code and saved the report, you may exit by pressing **ALT-E** and selecting **Save changes and exit**. After doing this, you are back at the Control Center. The report file name INV_VAL is now displayed in the Report panel.

Printing a report

After saving the report, you can now see what the output looks like by printing the report. Before printing the report, make sure that your printer is on and that the top of the page is set correctly. Next, place your cursor on the **INV_VAL** file in the Report panel (note the complete filename displayed below the panel area has a .FRM extension), and press **ENTER**. You are then given a set of printing options which can be used to refine the nature of your output. We will ignore any special options available. Select **Print report**, and after a brief wait another menu box appears. Select **Begin printing now**, and in a short time dBASE will start to print your report. When the report is completed, you are returned to the control center.

dBASE also allows the user to see what the report will look like without actually printing it. This can be done by selecting View report on screen from the Print menu. This is useful for testing the report before it is actually printed.

Figure 9-9 displays the first page of the printout. If your report does not look like this, or some of the numbers are different, you may need to go back and modify the report format; the next section discusses how to do this.

Modifying a report

If your report did not look like Figure 9-9 and you feel it was a problem with the way you have designed the report, or you had to save the report before it was in final form, dBASE allows you to modify the report format. You can recall the report design screen for a specific report file by highlighting that report within the report panel and pressing Shift-F2. You could also access the report design screen by pressing Enter when the filename is highlighted within the report panel and selecting Modify report.

After doing this, your screen should have the report layout as you last saved it. To modify the report, you can use the features described earlier such as CTRL-Y to delete an entire line, and the DEL or BACKSPACE keys to erase text or fields. To modify a field, highlight the field, press ALT-F and select Modify field. Remember to press CTRL-END when you are finished modifying a field so that any changes made are properly saved.

```
ITEM        ITEM                 QUANTITY      UNIT      TOTAL
NO.         NAME                 AVAILABLE     COST      COST
                                 (QA)          (UC)      (QA*UC)

ITEM CATEGORY:   BOOK        INVENTORY VALUES AS OF  08/01/91

B029   GOODNIGHT MOON              150         3.60      540.00
B119   CASEY AT THE BAT            130         2.10      273.00
B187   MIKE MULLIGAN               130         2.70      351.00
B467   MAKE WAY FOR DUCKLINGS      145         2.50      362.50

Subtotal for category                                  1526.50
```

Figure 9-9 Printout of First Page of INV_VAL Report

After completing all necessary changes to the report layout, save the report using the procedures described above. To see if your report is now correct, try to print the report, following the instructions in the previous section.

Conclusion

This completes the section on creating and printing reports in dBASE IV. To get more practice at it, attempt the follow-up case(s) at the end of the Chapter. Reporting is an important feature of any DBMS, so it is vital that you gain an understanding of how to design useful reports.

FOLLOW-UP EXERCISES

Inventory Cycle

Using the view file you created in the last chapter (REORDER), design a report that will show a listing of those items that need to be reordered. In addition, have the report grouped by Item classification. Figure 9-10 provides a general layout for such a report. Save the report using the name REORDER.

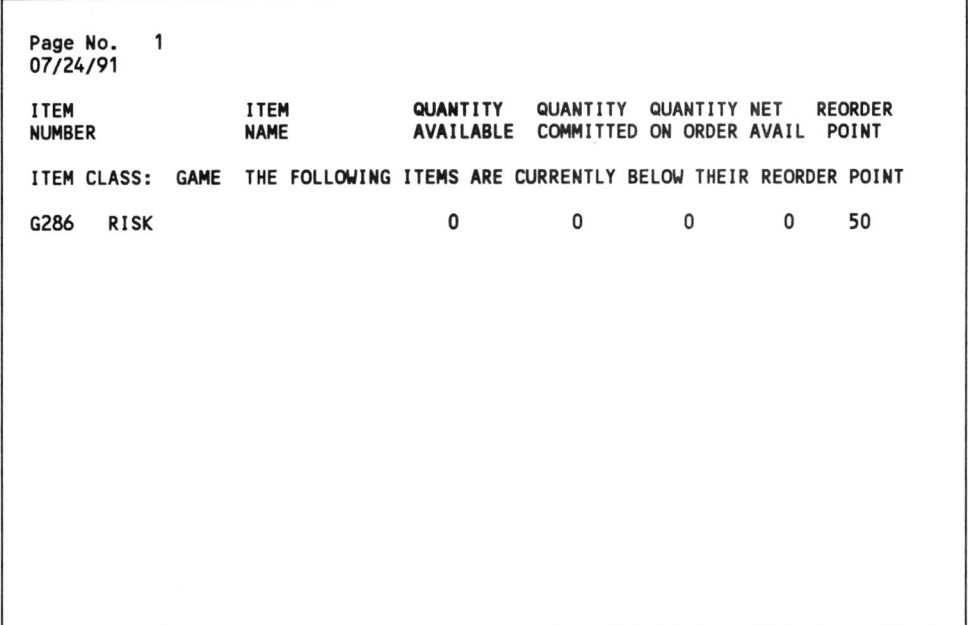

```
Page No.    1
07/24/91

ITEM                  ITEM           QUANTITY   QUANTITY  QUANTITY NET    REORDER
NUMBER                NAME           AVAILABLE  COMMITTED ON ORDER AVAIL  POINT

ITEM CLASS:   GAME   THE FOLLOWING ITEMS ARE CURRENTLY BELOW THEIR REORDER POINT

G286   RISK                            0          0         0        0     50
```

Figure 9-10 Sample Report Layout for Reorder Report

Revenue Cycle

NOTE: Before completing the exercise below, make sure that you have done the follow-up exercise related to the Inventory cycle. You should have created a report named REORDER.
Using the query view file you created in the previous chapter (SALES_IN), design a report that can serve as the invoice that will be mailed to the customer. This report should be grouped by sales invoice number. Figure 9-11 shows a sample invoice that can be created using the SALES_IN view file. Save the report using the name SALES_IN.

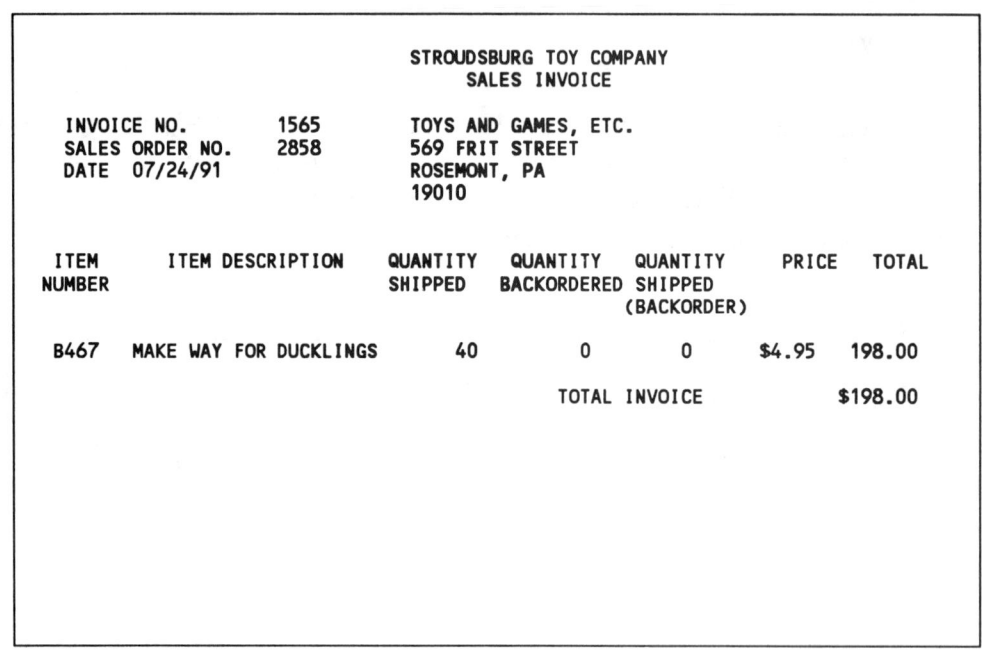

Figure 9-11 Sample Report Layout for Sales Invoice Report

Expenditure Cycle

NOTE: Before completing the exercise below, make sure that you have done the follow-up exercise related to the Inventory cycle. You should have created a report named REORDER.

Using the view file you created in the previous chapter (VOUCHER), design a report that can serve as the voucher for internal recordkeeping. This report should be grouped by voucher number. Figure 9-12 shows a sample voucher that can be created using the VOUCHER view file. Save the report using the name VOUCHER.

```
                              STROUDSBURG TOY COMPANY
                                  VOUCHER INVOICE

        VOUCHER NO.        2162    TONKER, INC.
        PURCHASE ORDER NO. 1251    4796 TYLER STREET
        DATE   07/24/91            CINCINATTI, OH
                                   43875


        ITEM       ITEM DESCRIPTION      QUANTITY   QUANTITY    COST    TOTAL
        NUMBER                           RECEIVED   BACKORDERED

         B029 GOODNIGHT MOON                90          0       $3.60   $324.00

                                                  TOTAL INVOICE         $324.00
```

Figure 9-12 Sample Report Layout for Voucher Report

Payroll Cycle

Create two reports using the view queries you designed Chapter 8. One report will summarize the monthly payroll, the second report will summarize year to date payroll. Use Figures 9-13 and 9-14 as guides. Note that the reports are grouped on the basis of payment, either monthly or hourly.

```
                      Stroudsburg Toy Company

Payroll Summary for the Month Ending 08/30/91

SSN                 Name                    Gross Pay  Deductions  Net Pay

Monthly Payroll for MONTHLY wage earners

111111111 Thomas Jackson                      5000.00    1500.00   3500.00
222222222 William Jackson                     3000.00     800.00   2200.00

Total monthly payroll for MONTHLY wage earners 8000.00   2300.00   5700.00
```

Figure 9-13 Sample Report Layout for Monthly Payroll Report

```
                      Stroudsburg Toy Company

Year to date payroll summary
as of 08/31/91


SSN                 Name                    Gross Pay   Deductions  Net Pay

Year to date Payroll for MONTHLY wage earners

111111111    Thomas Jackson                 40000.00    12000.00   28000.00
222222222    William Jackson                24000.00     6400.00   17600.00

Total of year to date payroll for          64000.00    18400.00   45600.00
MONTHLY wage earners
```

Figure 9-14 Sample Report Layout for Year to Date Payroll Report

Review Questions

1. What is the first step that must be done before you can begin designing a report?
2. What is the difference between using a view or database for creating a report?
3. What are the purposes of the five basic parts of a report?
4. What is meant by a Group Band?
5. How do you add a Group Band to a report?
6. What must you do to the data before you can add a Group Band?
7. How do you add a summary field to a report?
8. How do you save a report?
9. How can you modify a report?
10. How can you move a field or label around the report surface?
11. What are the filename extensions dBASE uses with reports?
12. What is meant by Quick Layout?
13. How can you look at a report without printing it?
13. How do you print a report once it has been created?
14. How can you get just one group band to print per page?
15. What controls are necessary over reports?
16. Does dBASE allow multiple data files to be used in a single report?
17. How do you delete a field from the report design surface?
18. How can you insert a blank line into a report?
19. Is a summary field stored as part of a company's database?
20. What is the difference between a Report Summary and a Group Summary?

CASE SOLUTION: PARADOX 3.5

To begin designing a report in PARADOX, select **Report** from the main menu. Choose **Design** from the submenu, press **ENTER** for a list of tables to use, and select the Inv_mast table. You are then asked which report you wish to design; we will designate this report as report 1, so select **1.** After doing so, you are asked for a report description. It is useful for documentation purposes to provide a brief explanation of the report. Let's call this report **Inventory value summary report**. After typing this in and pressing **ENTER**, your final submenu asks whether you want Tabular or Free form layout. Since we will be designing the report from scratch, select **Free form.** After doing this, your screen should look like Figure 9-15.

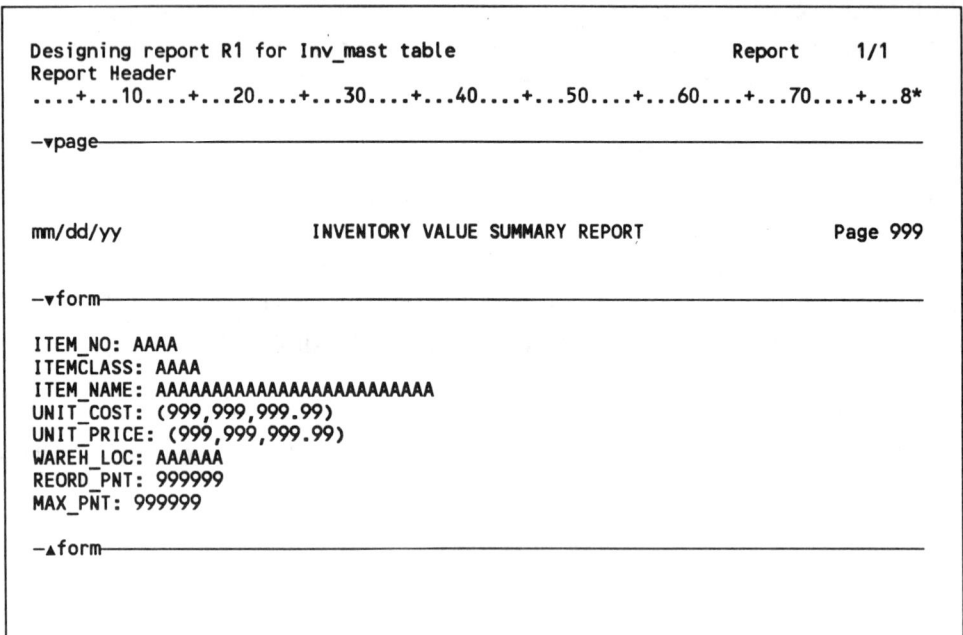

```
Designing report R1 for Inv_mast table                    Report    1/1
Report Header
....+...10....+...20....+...30....+...40....+...50....+...60....+...70....+...8*

—▼page—————————————————————————————————————————————————


mm/dd/yy                  INVENTORY VALUE SUMMARY REPORT         Page 999


—▼form—————————————————————————————————————————————————

ITEM_NO: AAAA
ITEMCLASS: AAAA
ITEM_NAME: AAAAAAAAAAAAAAAAAAAAAAAAAAAA
UNIT_COST: (999,999,999.99)
UNIT_PRICE: (999,999,999.99)
WAREH_LOC: AAAAAA
REORD_PNT: 999999
MAX_PNT: 999999

—▲form—————————————————————————————————————————————————
```

Figure 9-15 Default Report Layout for Free Form Design for the Inv_mast Data Table

This screen is the report design screen. There are five sections currently on your screen, and it will be useful to explain the purpose of each one before we begin creating the report. If you use your up and down arrow keys you can move through the various parts of the report design. Notice the top left of your screen and you will see the name of the section change depending where your cursor is at that point in time. The following is a brief description of each section.

• Report Header: This part of the report is used to give a brief description of the report that will be generated. It appears just once in the report.
• Page Header: This section of the report is used to indicate what will appear at the top of each page of the report. PARADOX has as a default to display the current date and the page number.

• Form Band: This part of the report displays the actual contents of the file for the fields and records you select.

• Page Footer: This section is used to indicate what will appear at the bottom of each page of the report.

• Report Footer: This section is used to summarize the entire report. A common use of the Report Footer is to total numeric fields for the report. As with the Report Header, this appears just once for the entire report, on the last page.

In addition to these five sections, you can also add Group Header and Group Footer sections that can be added to the report design. We will see how to do this later, and discuss the purpose of these two sections at that time.

The first job is to delete the information in the Form Band so that we can start with an empty report design. Before doing this, press the Ins key to turn it on. The top right of your screen should display Ins after doing this. Move your cursor down to the Form band and place your cursor at the far left of the Item_no line. To delete a line, press **CTRL-Y**. Repeat this procedure until all of the lines in the Form band are eliminated. It will be helpful to delete some of the extra lines in the other sections at this time as well. While you are in the Page header section, be careful not to erase the page number/date line. After erasing the form band lines and the extra blank lines, your screen should look like Figure 9-16.

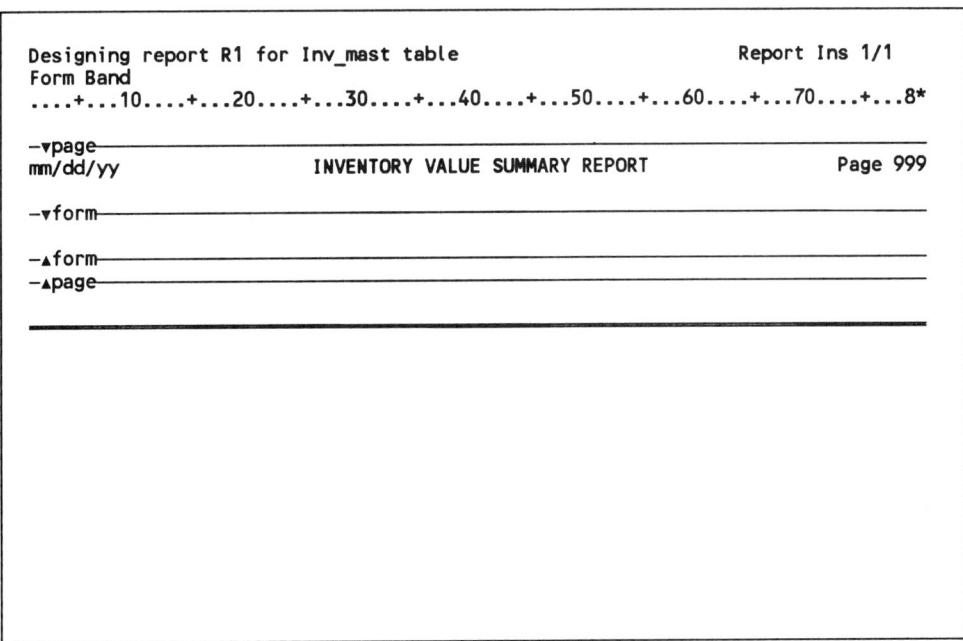

```
Designing report R1 for Inv_mast table                    Report Ins 1/1
Form Band
....+...10....+...20....+...30....+...40....+...50....+...60....+...70....+...8*

─▼page─────────────────────────────────────────────────────────────────
mm/dd/yy                   INVENTORY VALUE SUMMARY REPORT            Page 999

─▼form─────────────────────────────────────────────────────────────────

─▲form─────────────────────────────────────────────────────────────────
─▲page─────────────────────────────────────────────────────────────────
```

Figure 9-16 Report Layout after Deleting Unnecessary Lines

The next task is to add what PARADOX refers to as *Group Bands*. A group band will add a Group header section and a Group footer section to your report. The Group header is used to display what heading will appear each time a new group is started (e.g. books). This would then be followed by the detail (e.g., the item number, the item name) of that group, as designated in the Form section. The Group footer section is used to present summary information (e.g. total value) for the group (e.g. books) after displaying the detail data for that group.

To add a Group section, place your cursor on a line between the page header section and the form band section. For example, place your cursor on the line below where PARADOX has displayed the date and page number in the Page Header section. When you have positioned your cursor correctly, press **F10** to bring up the report menu. Select **Group, Insert, Field** and choose **Item_class**. You are then asked where you want to place the group band. Since your cursor is already in the proper place, press **ENTER**. Your screen should now look like Figure 9-17.

```
Designing report R1 for Inv_mast table                        Report Ins 1/1
Page Header
....+...10....+...20....+...30....+...40....+...50....+...60....+...70....+...8*

─▼page─────────────────────────────────────────────────────────────────────
mm/dd/yy                     INVENTORY VALUE SUMMARY REPORT            Page 999

─────▼group ITEMCLASS───────────────────────────────────────────────────────

─▼form──────────────────────────────────────────────────────────────────────

─▲form──────────────────────────────────────────────────────────────────────

─────▲group ITEMCLASS───────────────────────────────────────────────────────
─▲page──────────────────────────────────────────────────────────────────────

═══════════════════════════════════════════════════════════════════════════
```

Figure 9-17 Adding a Group Band to the Report Layout

Next, we will add a report title and the column headings that will appear at the top of each page, along with the date and page number. Move your cursor to the Page Header section and on the line below the date/page number add the heading as shown in Figure 9-18. Next, put in the headings for the 5 columns (Item number, item name, unit cost, quantity available and total cost). Use Figure 9-18 as a guide. You can press **ENTER** when you need to add a new line to the report design surface. If the ENTER key does not add a new line to the report, make sure that the INS key has been pressed. When you are finished adding the column headings, press **ENTER** once more to add a blank line. After doing this, use your arrow keys to move down to the blank line in the Group Header section. The top left of your screen indicates which section of the report you are currently in.

In this section, we will put in a heading that indicates what particular category (class) is currently being shown on the report. Thus, with your cursor in the group header section, type in the label **Item Category:**. Move your cursor over one or two spaces with the right arrow key. We are now ready to add the Itemclass field to the report

```
Designing report R1 for Inv_mast table                Report Ins 1/1
Page Header
....+...10....+...20....+...30....+...40....+...50....+...60....+...70....+...8*

—▼page—————————————————————————————————————————————————————————————————
mm/dd/yy                    INVENTORY VALUE SUMMARY REPORT              Page 999
                              STROUDSBURG TOY COMPANY

ITEM            ITEM                        UNIT        QUANTITY       TOTAL
NO.             NAME                        COST        AVAILABLE      COST
————▼group ITEMCLASS——————————————————————————————————————————————————————

—▼form————————————————————————————————————————————————————————————————————

—▲form————————————————————————————————————————————————————————————————————

————▲group ITEMCLASS——————————————————————————————————————————————————————
—▲page————————————————————————————————————————————————————————————————————

_____
```

Figure 9-18 Adding a Page Heading and Column Headings to the Report Layout

design. To add a field, press **F10** to bring up the menu. Select **Field, Place, Regular** and choose the **Itemclass** field. You are then asked to position the cursor to where you want to place this field. Since your cursor should be in the correct place (right beside the Item Category label, you can press **ENTER**. If your cursor is not beside the label Item Category: that you have typed, move it there now and press ENTER. You are then asked if you want to change the display width. Since we will not change the default display, press **ENTER**, and the field will be placed on the report surface. Your screen should look like Figure 9-19.

We are now ready to start adding the actual detail we want in our report. Move your cursor down to the Form band. It is within the Form band that we will add the fields to match the column headings we designed in the Page Header section.

To add each field to the display, follow the procedure used earlier when you added the item class field to the report. This is done by pressing **F10**, selecting **Field, Place, Regular,** and choosing, while under the first column heading, the Item_no field. You want this field to be at the far left of your Form band, so if you are not there, be sure to move your cursor to that position when you are prompted as to where to place the field. When you are in the right position, press **ENTER**. You are then asked if you want to change the width; we will use the default, so press **ENTER** again. At this point your screen should look like Figure 9-20.

```
Designing report R1 for Inv_mast table                    Report Ins 1/1
Group Header for ITEMCLASS                                       ITEMCLASS
....+...10....+...20....+...30....+...40....+...50....+...60....+...70....+...8*

—vpage—————————————————————————————————————————————————————————————
mm/dd/yy                   INVENTORY VALUE SUMMARY REPORT         Page 999
                              STROUDSBURG TOY COMPANY

ITEM           ITEM                    UNIT        QUANTITY      TOTAL
NO.            NAME                     COST        AVAILABLE     COST

————vgroup ITEMCLASS——————————————————————————————————————————————
ITEM CATEGORY:  AAAA
—vform—————————————————————————————————————————————————————————————

—▲form—————————————————————————————————————————————————————————————

————▲group ITEMCLASS——————————————————————————————————————————————
—▲page—————————————————————————————————————————————————————————————


```

Figure 9-19 Adding the ITEM CATEGORY Label and ITEMCLASS Field to the Report Layout

```
Designing report R1 for Inv_mast table                    Report Ins 1/1
Form Band
....+...10....+...20....+...30....+...40....+...50....+...60....+...70....+...8*

—vpage—————————————————————————————————————————————————————————————
mm/dd/yy                   INVENTORY VALUE SUMMARY REPORT         Page 999
                              STROUDSBURG TOY COMPANY

ITEM           ITEM                    UNIT        QUANTITY      TOTAL
NO.            NAME                     COST        AVAILABLE     COST

————vgroup ITEMCLASS——————————————————————————————————————————————
ITEM CATEGORY:  AAAA
—vform—————————————————————————————————————————————————————————————
AAAA
—▲form—————————————————————————————————————————————————————————————

————▲group ITEMCLASS——————————————————————————————————————————————
—▲page—————————————————————————————————————————————————————————————


```

Figure 9-20 Adding the ITEM_NO Field to the Report Layout

Follow the same procedure to add the item name field to the report design. The next step is to add the Unit Cost field. Follow the same procedures as above for adding a field. The only special consideration is that you should change the display width to three characters (before the decimal point) and accept the default of two decimal places.

When you get to the next field to add, the quantity available, there is a special procedure that is needed to place this field on the report surface, since it is not found in the Inv_mast table, which is the table we are using as the basis for our report, but is stored in the Inv_tran table. The PARADOX reporting module allows the user to link, or join, two or more tables together and then use any of the fields from this combination of tables. All that is needed in order to join two tables together is a common field. If you recall from the previous chapter, the common field for these two tables is the Item_no.

To link these two tables together, press **F10** followed by **Field, Lookup, Link**. You are now asked which table you want to link; press **ENTER** to display the list of tables and select Inv_tran. You are then to link the Item_no field from the Inv_tran table to a field in the Inv_mast table. The list of fields for the Inv_mast table are displayed. The field we want is the Item_no field, so move your cursor to that field (if necessary) and press **ENTER**. The two tables are now linked together.

We are now ready to add the quantity available field to the report. Follow the same steps as before for adding a field to the report, i.e., press **F10** followed by **Field, Place, Regular**. At this point, the fields for the Inv_mast table are displayed. However, if you hit the left arrow key once, or the right arrow key several times, one of the displayed menu items in the list is [Inv_tran->]. This represents the Inv_tran table, so press **ENTER** when your cursor highlights this choice and a listing of the fields for the Inv_tran table is displayed. Select **Q_avail**, making sure you are placing the field in the appropriate column position, and then press **ENTER**. For this field we will adjust the default width of the field. Make the field 4 positions wide by using your arrow keys to shorten the width, and then press ENTER. Next you are asked how many decimal places are needed; press **ENTER** to accept the default of **0**. After doing this, your screen should look like Figure 9-21. Note at the top left of your screen the phrase [Inv_tran->q_avail]. This is the full notation for describing a field in PARADOX. The first part of the phrase indicates the table, and followed by a dash (the minus sign) and a greater than symbol, followed by the name of the appropriate field in that table. Knowing this syntax will be useful later on in helping us to build *Calculated fields* .

The last field to be added to your report is the Total Cost field, which is different than the other fields since this is a calculated field, and not found in any specific table. To add a calculated field to the report, you need to build the formula used in the calculation. The following steps describe how to do this. Press **F10** and select **Field, Place, Calculated**. You are now asked to type in the expression. PARADOX requires that you place [ ] around any field you use in the expression. The calculation needed to measure total cost is quantity available times unit cost. To express this in PARADOX syntax you would type in: **[unit_cost]*[inv_tran->q_avail]** as the formula. See Figure 9-22 for guidance. Note that the quantity available field is identified by first typing in the name of the table that the field is stored in (since it is not in the Inv_mast table) followed by the name of the field. Press **ENTER** when you are finished creating the formula; you are then

```
Designing report R1 for Inv_mast table                      Report Ins 1/1
Form Band                                                [Inv_tran->Q_AVAIL]
....+...10....+...20....+...30....+...40....+...50....+...60....+...70....+...8*

—▼page─────────────────────────────────────────────────────────────────────
mm/dd/yy                    INVENTORY VALUE SUMMARY REPORT          Page 999
                               STROUDSBURG TOY COMPANY

ITEM            ITEM                    UNIT          QUANTITY      TOTAL
NO.             NAME                    COST          AVAILABLE     COST
────▼group ITEMCLASS────────────────────────────────────────────────────────
ITEM CATEGORY:  AAAA
—▼form──────────────────────────────────────────────────────────────────────
AAAA    AAAAAAAAAAAAAAAAAAAAAAAAAAAAAA     (999.99)    9999
—▲form──────────────────────────────────────────────────────────────────────

────▲group ITEMCLASS────────────────────────────────────────────────────────
—▲page──────────────────────────────────────────────────────────────────────


━━━━━━━━━━━━━━━━━━━━━━━━━━━━━━━━━━━━━━━━━━━━━━━━━━━━━━━━━━━━━━━━━━━━━━━━━━━━━━
```

*Figure 9-21 Adding the Q_AVAIL Field from the Inv_tran Table to the
        Report Layout*

```
Expression:  [UNIT_COST]*[INV_TRAN->Q_AVAIL]                 Report Ins 1/1
Calculation from fields in a record -- e.g. [Quan] * [Unit-Price].
....+...10....+...20....+...30....+...40....+...50....+...60....+...70....+...8*

—▼page─────────────────────────────────────────────────────────────────────
mm/dd/yy                    INVENTORY VALUE SUMMARY REPORT          Page 999
                               STROUDSBURG TOY COMPANY

ITEM            ITEM                    UNIT          QUANTITY      TOTAL
NO.             NAME                    COST          AVAILABLE     COST
────▼group ITEMCLASS────────────────────────────────────────────────────────
ITEM CATEGORY:  AAAA
—▼form──────────────────────────────────────────────────────────────────────
AAAA    AAAAAAAAAAAAAAAAAAAAAAAAAAAAAA     (999.99)    9999
—▲form──────────────────────────────────────────────────────────────────────

────▲group ITEMCLASS────────────────────────────────────────────────────────
—▲page──────────────────────────────────────────────────────────────────────


━━━━━━━━━━━━━━━━━━━━━━━━━━━━━━━━━━━━━━━━━━━━━━━━━━━━━━━━━━━━━━━━━━━━━━━━━━━━━━
```

Figure 9-22 Formula for Calculating Total Cost of Each Inventory Item

asked to move it to the appropriate place on the screen. When you have positioned the field correctly, (under the Total cost column heading) press **ENTER**. Next, you need to adjust the size of the field display. Narrow the width to five positions before the decimal place, press **ENTER** and press **ENTER** once more to select the default decimal place width of two. After doing this your screen should look like Figure 9-23.

```
Designing report R1 for Inv_mast table                        Report Ins 1/1
Form Band                                      [UNIT_COST]*[INV_TRAN->Q_AVAIL]
....+...10....+...20....+...30....+...40....+...50....+...60....+...70....+...8*

─▼page──────────────────────────────────────────────────────────────────────
mm/dd/yy                      INVENTORY VALUE SUMMARY REPORT         Page 999
                                 STROUDSBURG TOY COMPANY

ITEM            ITEM                        UNIT        QUANTITY      TOTAL
NO.             NAME                        COST        AVAILABLE     COST

────▼group ITEMCLASS─────────────────────────────────────────────────────────
ITEM CATEGORY:  AAAA
─▼form───────────────────────────────────────────────────────────────────────
AAAA    AAAAAAAAAAAAAAAAAAAAAAAAAAAA       (999.99)    9999        (99,999.99)
─▲form───────────────────────────────────────────────────────────────────────

────▲group ITEMCLASS─────────────────────────────────────────────────────────
─▲page───────────────────────────────────────────────────────────────────────

═══════════════════════════════════════════════════════════════════════════
```

Figure 9-23 Adding the Calculated Field to the Report Layout

This completes the Form band section of the report. The next section to work on is the Group Footer section. Move your cursor down to this section, and the first step is to press **ENTER** so that a new blank line is added. On the second blank line, type the words **Subtotal for Category**. Next, move your cursor one or two positions to the right and then add the Itemclass field to the screen. Press **F10, Field, Place, Regular** and select **Itemclass**.

After doing this, move your cursor to the right so that it lines up under the Total Cost field shown in the form band. We are going to add a field here that will summarize the total value of all inventory items for the particular category displayed in the form band. To do this, press **F10, Field, Place, Summary, Calculated**. When you are asked to type the expression, type in the same formula noted above for the Total Cost field in the form band: **[unit_cost]*[inv_tran->q_avail]**. When you are finished typing in this expression, press **ENTER**, and you are asked what sort of Summary this is, select **Sum**. You are then asked whether you are summing for just a group (PerGroup) or for the entire report (Overall). Since we are in the Group Footer section, select **PerGroup**. For the next couple of prompts, just follow the guidelines discussed earlier. Adjust the display width to seven characters, and keep the number of decimal places at 2. After completing this, your screen should look like Figure 9-24.

Since we would like to have each item category printed on separate pages, we need to tell PARADOX to start a new page after each group is finished. To do this, move down one line using the down arrow key and press **ENTER**. In the far left margin of this blank line type **PAGEBREAK**, making sure to use capital letters. This command will have the affect of starting each group on a new page. Your screen should look like Figure 9-25.

```
Designing report R1 for Inv_mast table                        Report Ins 1/1
Group Footer for ITEMCLASS  Total for [UNIT_COST]*[INV_TRAN->Q_AVAIL], per group
....+...10....+...20....+...30....+...40....+...50....+...60....+...70....+...8*
─────────────────────────────────────────────────────────────────────────────
─▼page───────────────────────────────────────────────────────────────────────
mm/dd/yy                    INVENTORY VALUE SUMMARY REPORT              Page 999
                             STROUDSBURG TOY COMPANY

ITEM            ITEM                    UNIT        QUANTITY       TOTAL
NO.             NAME                    COST        AVAILABLE      COST

────▼group ITEMCLASS──────────────────────────────────────────────────────────
ITEM CATEGORY:  AAAA
─▼form────────────────────────────────────────────────────────────────────────
AAAA    AAAAAAAAAAAAAAAAAAAAAAAAAAAA    (999.99)    9999           (99,999.99)
─▲form────────────────────────────────────────────────────────────────────────

SUBTOTAL FOR CATEGORY  AAAA                                        (999,999.99)
────▲group ITEMCLASS──────────────────────────────────────────────────────────
─▲page────────────────────────────────────────────────────────────────────────


━━━━━━━━━━━━━━━━━━━━━━━━━━━━━━━━━━━━━━━━━━━━━━━━━━━━━━━━━━━━━━━━━━━━━━━━━━━━━━━━
```

Figure 9-24 Adding a Label and Summary Field to the Group Footer Band

```
Designing report R1 for Inv_mast table                        Report Ins 1/1
Group Footer for ITEMCLASS
....+...10....+...20....+...30....+...40....+...50....+...60....+...70....+...8*
─────────────────────────────────────────────────────────────────────────────
─▼page───────────────────────────────────────────────────────────────────────
mm/dd/yy                    INVENTORY VALUE SUMMARY REPORT              Page 999
                             STROUDSBURG TOY COMPANY

ITEM            ITEM                    UNIT        QUANTITY       TOTAL
NO.             NAME                    COST        AVAILABLE      COST

────▼group ITEMCLASS──────────────────────────────────────────────────────────
ITEM CATEGORY:  AAAA
─▼form────────────────────────────────────────────────────────────────────────
AAAA    AAAAAAAAAAAAAAAAAAAAAAAAAAAA    (999.99)    9999           (99,999.99)
─▲form────────────────────────────────────────────────────────────────────────

SUBTOTAL FOR CATEGORY  AAAA                                        (999,999.99)
PAGEBREAK
────▲group ITEMCLASS──────────────────────────────────────────────────────────
─▲page────────────────────────────────────────────────────────────────────────


━━━━━━━━━━━━━━━━━━━━━━━━━━━━━━━━━━━━━━━━━━━━━━━━━━━━━━━━━━━━━━━━━━━━━━━━━━━━━━━━
```

Figure 9-25 Adding a PAGEBREAK for Each New Group

The last part of the report to work on is the Report Footer section. Move your cursor to this section, which follows the Page Footer section. You may need to press ENTER while on the Page line and then use your down arrow key to move into the Report Footer section. The first task we will take care of is to use a new page to display the Report Footer information. To do this, type **PAGEBREAK** on the first line in the report footer, and then press **ENTER**. Be sure to use capital letters. On the next line, type the words **TOTAL INVENTORY VALUE FOR ALL CATEGORIES** and then move the cursor underneath the Total cost column and repeat the procedures above on how to add a summary, calculated field to the report. The only difference is that when you are asked whether the Sum should be calculated PerGroup or Overall, select **Overall** this time. Adjust the width of the field accordingly, and when you are finished, your screen should look like Figure 9-26. You can preview, on screen, what the report will look like by pressing **F10** and selecting **Output, Screen**.

```
Designing report R1 for Inv_mast table                    Report Ins 1/1
Report Footer                        Total for [UNIT_COST]*[INV_TRAN->Q_AVAIL]
....+...10....+...20....+...30....+...40....+...50....+...60....+...70....+...8*

─▼page───────────────────────────────────────────────────────────────────
mm/dd/yy                    INVENTORY VALUE SUMMARY REPORT            Page 999
                            STROUDSBURG TOY COMPANY

ITEM           ITEM                      UNIT        QUANTITY      TOTAL
NO.            NAME                      COST        AVAILABLE     COST

────▼group ITEMCLASS──────────────────────────────────────────────────────
ITEM CATEGORY:  AAAA
─▼form────────────────────────────────────────────────────────────────────
AAAA    AAAAAAAAAAAAAAAAAAAAAAAAAAAAAA   (999.99)    9999          (99,999.99)
─▲form────────────────────────────────────────────────────────────────────

SUBTOTAL FOR CATEGORY  AAAA                                        (999,999.99)
PAGEBREAK
────▲group ITEMCLASS──────────────────────────────────────────────────────
─▲page────────────────────────────────────────────────────────────────────
PAGEBREAK
TOTAL INVENTORY VALUE FOR ALL CATEGORIES                          (999,999.99)
───────────────────────────────────────────────────────────────────────────
```

Figure 9-26 Completed Report Layout for Inventory Value Report

Saving/modifying the report form

To save the report, press **F2**. PARADOX will save the report with the extension .R1, indicating that this is report number 1 associated with the Inv_mast table. If you need to modify the report at a later date, select, from the main menu, **Report, Change**, press **ENTER** and select Inv_mast as the table and report **1** as the appropriate report.

To erase a field from the report, place your cursor on the field and press F10 followed by selecting Field, Erase, and then pressing ENTER. To erase a label, you can use the DEL key or the BACKSPACE key. To put a blank line in your report, press ENTER. Remember, this will only insert a blank line if the INS key has been pressed. If you want to delete an entire line, press CTRL-Y when your cursor is at the far left margin. These operations represent the majority of changes that may be necessary to your report. Once you are satisfied with the report layout, you can view the report on the screen by pressing F10 and selecting Output followed by Screen. If the report appears correct at this point press F2 to save the changes.

Printing the report

Since we will just use the default settings for printing that PARADOX has been installed with, we will not discuss printer settings. It should be pointed out however that there are several printing options available within PARADOX to allow the user to customize the format of the printed report.

At this point, we will create a script that can print this report out by just selecting the appropriate script and playing it. From the main menu, select **Script, BeginRecord** and name the script **Prt_inv**. After pressing **ENTER** you are returned to the main menu. At this point, all keystrokes will be recorded as a program that can later be run whenever necessary. From the main menu, select **Report, Output** and press **ENTER** to get a list of tables. Select **Inv_mast**, and then Report **1**. You are then asked where you would like the output to be sent, select **Printer**. In a short time, PARADOX will begin to print your report. When it is finished, you are returned to the main menu. Select **Script, EndRecord** and you are finished recording your printing program. Figure 9-27 shows the first page of the printout. To run this in the future from the main menu, select Script, Play, press ENTER and choose Prt_inv as the script to play.

Conclusion

This completes the section on creating and printing reports using PARADOX. To get more practice at it, attempt the follow-up case(s) at the end of the Chapter. Reporting is an important feature of any DBMS, so it is vital that you gain an understanding of how to design useful reports.

```
   7/31/91                 INVENTORY VALUE SUMMARY REPORT              Page   1
                              STROUDSBURG TOY COMPANY

   ITEM        ITEM                     UNIT      QUANTITY      TOTAL
   NO.         NAME                     COST      AVAILABLE     COST

   ITEM CATEGORY:  BOOK
   B029    GOODNIGHT MOON               3.60        150          540.00
   B119    CASEY AT THE BAT             2.10        130          273.00
   B187    MIKE MULLIGAN                2.70        130          351.00
   B467    MAKE WAY FOR DUCKLINGS       2.50        145          362.50

   SUBTOTAL FOR CATEGORY  BOOK                                  1,526.50
```

Figure 9-27 Printout of First Page of Inventory Value Report

FOLLOW-UP EXERCISES

Inventory cycle

Based on the query you created last chapter known as REORDER, prepare a report that will print the results of that query. To do this, first start by beginning to record a script, naming it PRT_REOR. Next, select Script, Play, press ENTER and choose REORDER. (If this script is not displayed, you may have to go back to the previous chapter and create the script). Press F2 to process the query. When PARADOX is finished processing this query, the results are shown in an answer table. Press ALT-F8 to clear the screen. Select Report, Design, press ENTER, and choose the Answer table. Select 1, give it a brief description and then choose Free form. Design the report so that it looks like Figure 9-28. The report should be grouped by Itemclass. When you are finished, press F2 to save the report. Finally, from the main menu, select Report, Output and then press ENTER to see a list of tables. Select Answer and then select Printer as the output device. When it is finished printing, select Script, EndRecord. You can now play this script at any time by selecting the PRT_REOR script from the menu.

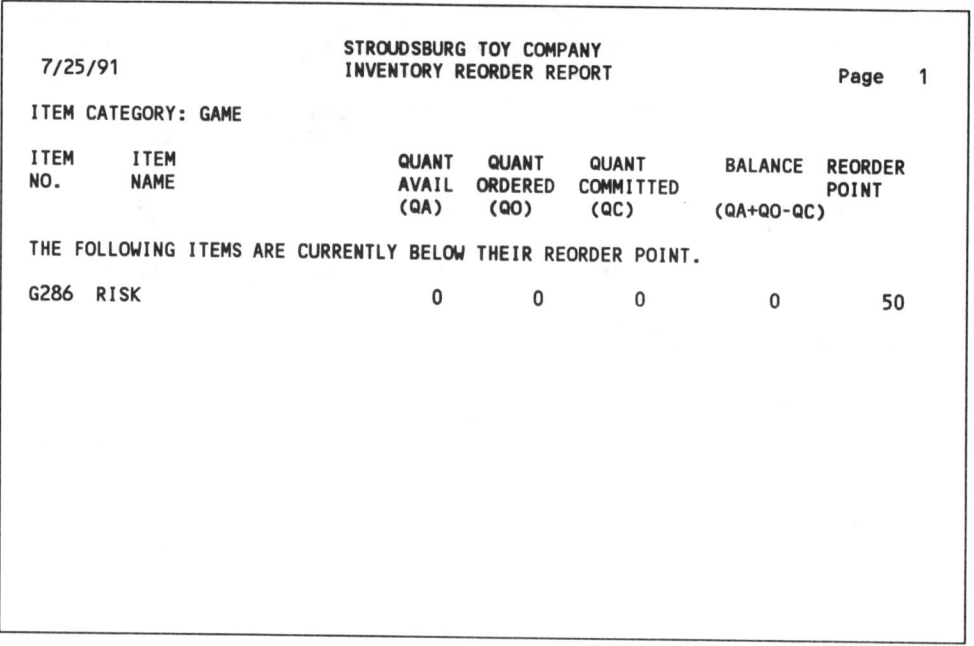

Figure 9-28 Sample Report Layout for Reorder Report

Revenue Cycle

NOTE: Before completing the exercise below, make sure that you have done the follow-up exercise related to the Inventory cycle. You should have created a report named REORDER.

Create a report for the sales invoice file that looks like Figure 9-29. To do this, you will need to start the report with the Sales_in table and then link the Sales_or table, the Inv_mast table and the Customer table to the Sales_in table. When linking, use the matching field from the Sales_in table. Be sure to group the report by sales invoice number.

The second part of this exercise is to create a script that will print out only those sales invoices for those that are unpaid. In the last chapter you created a query that would display such a listing. What is needed is a way to combine that query with the report you have just created. To start, go through the steps necessary to begin recording a script. Name the script PRT_SI. After pressing ENTER and returning to the main menu, select Script, Play, press ENTER and select Unpaidsi. Press F2 to process the query. When this query is finished, the answer table is displayed on the screen.

We are now ready to combine this answer with the report form. To do this, first press ALT-F8 to clear the screen. Next, select Tools, Copy, JustFamily and press ENTER. PARADOX is ready to copy all the files associated with one table, such as form files and report files, to another table. You are first asked for the *source* table, which in this case is the Sales_in table, so select that table. For the *target* table, select Answer, then select Replace. Press Alt-F8 to clear the screen.

```
                                                        Page    1
  INVOICE NO.        1565          TOYS AND GAMES, ETC.
  SALES ORDER NO.    2858          569 FRIT STREET
  INVOICE DATE       8/17/91       ROSEMONT              , PA   19010

  ITEM         ITEM               QUANT    QUANT    BACK    UNIT      TOTAL
  NO.          NAME               SHIP     BACK.    SHIP    PRICE

  B467    MAKE WAY FOR DUCKLINGS    40       0        0      4.95     198.00

                                  TOTAL INVOICE                       198.00
```

Figure 9-29 Sample Report Layout for Sales Invoice Report

The last step is to now print the report. Select Report, Output and press ENTER. Select the Answer table, report 1 and select Printer as the output device. When the report is finished printing, select Script, EndRecord. To play this in the future, just select the PRT_SI script.

Expenditure cycle

NOTE: Before completing the exercise below, make sure that you have done the follow-up exercise related to the Inventory cycle, creating a report named REORDER.

First, create a report for the Voucher table that looks like Figure 9-30. To do this, you will need to start with the voucher table and then link the Purch_or table, the Inv_mast table and the Vendor table to the Voucher table. When linking, just use the matching field from the Voucher table. Be sure to group the report by voucher number.

The second part of this exercise is to create a script that will print out only those vouchers for those that are unpaid. In the last chapter you created a query that would display such a listing. What is needed is a way to combine that query with the report you have just created. To start, go through the steps necessary to begin recording a script. Name the script PRT_VO. After pressing ENTER and returning to the main menu, select Script, Play, press Enter and select Unpaidvo. Press F2 to process the query. When this query is finished, the answer table is displayed on the screen.

We are now ready to combine this answer with the report form. To do this, first press ALT-F8 to clear the screen. Next, select Tools, Copy, JustFamily, and press ENTER. PARADOX is ready to copy all the files associated with one table, such as form files and report files, to another table. You are first asked for the *source* table, which in this case is the Voucher table, so select that table. For the *target* table, select Answer, then select Replace. Press Alt-F8 to clear the screen.

```
                                                      Page    1


        VOUCHER NO.        2161        MISMILLAN BOOK CO.
        PURCAHSE ORDER NO. 1250        567435 OLDE STREET
        VOUCHER DATE       8/27/91     NEW YORK                ,NY   43985

        ITEM        ITEM              QUANT.  QUANT.  UNIT     TOTAL
        NO.         NAME              REC.    BACK.   COST     COST

        B119                           80       0      2.10     168.00

                      TOTAL AMOUNT OF VOUCHER NO.  2161          168.00
```

Figure 9-30 Sample Report Layout for Voucher Report

The last step is to now print the report. Select Report, Output and press ENTER. Select the Answer table, and report 1 and select Printer as the output device. When the report is finished printing, select Script, EndRecord. To play this in the future, just select the PRT_VO script.

Payroll Cycle

Create two reports for Stroudsburg. One report will summarize the monthly payroll, the second report will summarize year to date payroll. Use Figures 9-31 and 9-32 as guides. Note that these reports are grouped by pay basis, either monthly or hourly. In addition, for the monthly payroll summary, you will need to use the view query you developed in the last chapter so that the report only prints the current month's payroll data. It is advisable that after creating the reports, you create a script for printing the reports.

```
                         Stroudsburg Toy Company
               Payroll Summary for the Month Ending  8/31/91

    Soc. Sec. No.       Name          Gross Pay      Deductions     Net Pay

    Basis for payment HOURLY

    333333333  Lloyd    Gustafson      2,100.00        500.00      1,600.00
    444444444  Susan    Dalton         1,750.00        450.00      1,300.00
    555555555  Jimmy    Fiveyard         240.00         50.00        190.00

    Total for HOURLY  wage earners      4,090.00      1,000.00      3,090.00
```

Figure 9-31 Sample Report Layout for Monthly Payroll Report

```
                         Stroudsburg Toy Company

    Year to Date Payroll Summary
    as of  8/31/91

    Soc. Sec.         Name            Gross Pay      Deductions     Net Pay
    No.

    Year to date payroll for HOURLY  wage earners

    333333333  Lloyd    Gustafson     17,000.00       4,000.00     13,000.00
    444444444  Susan    Dalton        14,000.00       3,600.00     10,400.00
    555555555  Jimmy    Fiveyard       1,950.00         400.00      1,550.00

    Total year to date payroll for
    HOURLY   wage earners             32,950.00       8,000.00     24,950.00
```

Figure 9-32 Sample Report Layout for Year to Date Payroll Report

Review Questions

1. What is the first step that must be done before you can begin designing a report?
2. What are the purposes of the five basic parts of a report?
3. What is meant by a Group Band?
4. How do you add a Group Band to a report?
5. How do you add a summary field to a report?
6. How do you save a report format?
7. How can you modify a report?
8. What is the filename extension PARADOX uses with reports?
9. How can you look at a report without printing it?
10. How do you print a report once it has been created?
11. How can you get just one group band to print per page?
12. What controls are necessary over reports?
13. Does PARADOX allow multiple data tables to be used in a single report?
14. How do you delete a field from the report design surface?
15. How can you insert a blank line into a report?
16. Is a summary field stored as part of a company's database?
17. What is the difference between a Report Summary and a Group Summary?

CHAPTER 10
TRANSACTION PROCESSING AND CONTROLS USING A DATABASE MANAGEMENT SYSTEM

INTRODUCTION

The purpose of this chapter is to integrate the previous 4 chapters to see how a Database management system can support the transaction processing and information requirements of the accounting cycle. This chapter will provide you with some sample data and lead you through either the Revenue or Expenditure cycle, depending on which one you have been doing throughout these database exercises. Due to the limitations inherent in using only the menu structures of the database software, and not the powerful programming languages which accompany them, some of the steps are done for one small, but necessary operation. Keep in mind that some of the steps we will go through would normally be combined in a true transaction processing system. However, the level of detail that the steps take you through are useful from a learning perspective, since they help you understand all that is needed in the successful design of such a system.

CASE STUDY: STROUDSBURG TOY COMPANY

Mr. Jackson feels that it is time to test the database system you have designed for his toy company. He would like you to utilize all the features you have built for the system. This includes the use of data entry forms, searching (querying) the database for information, updating the accounting files based on transactions, and providing reports for management use.

Mr. Jackson would like you to go through one entire accounting cycle, and test the effectiveness of the system. He has asked you to work on either the revenue cycle or the expenditure cycle, and trace a transaction from its beginning to its final disposition. He has provided you with the transactions relevant to each of these cycles for the month of September. Mr. Jackson is continuing to use a manual accounting and information system. However, if the results of the DBMS agree with what he has done manually, it will convince him to make the switch to a computerized system.

CASE SOLUTION: dBASE IV

Included on the dBASE IV disk that came with this text are several files that you will be using to test the system you have developed in the past four chapters. The files correspond for the most part to either the revenue cycle or the expenditure cycle. Some of the files, such as the inventory files you have been working on for the tutorials, are needed for both cycles. The next part of this chapter is divided into two sections, one for the revenue cycle, the other for the expenditure cycle.

One item to note is that you will be entering data as part of this exercise. Entering the data as a set and then processing that entire set of data is known as *batch processing*. You could have an *online processing* system in dBASE if you wanted, but that would entail the development of customized programs through the dBASE programming language.

Revenue Cycle

The first item we will discuss is the files you will be using and the purpose of each one as it relates to the revenue cycle. We will go through the files in the order we have covered them in this book: Data files, Form (input) files, Query files, and Report files. Note that some of these files have already been used in earlier chapters; this section provides a useful summary of those files you did not create in an earlier chapter.

Data files

• AR_MAST.DBF - This file contains data relating to each customer's current outstanding balance, as well as a summary of all sales Stroudsburg has made to each customer for the current year.
• CASH_REC.DBF - This file contains data relating to customer payments to Stroudsburg.
• CUSTOMER.DBF - This file contains basic data on each customer, such as name and address, as well as credit information.
• SALES_IN.DBF - This file is used to store data concerning a sales transaction after the goods have been shipped to the customer, and Stroudsburg is ready to bill for those goods.
• SALES_OR.DBF - This file contains basic data concerning a sales transaction, such as who the customer is, and what items were ordered.
• You also need the three inventory files created in Chapter 6 (INV_HIST.DBF, INV_MAST.DBF, and INV_TRAN.DBF)

Forms files

• CUSTOMER.FMO/.SCR - This form is used to add new customers or make changes to the basic data of existing customers.
• You will also need the forms files created in Chapter Two (SALES_IN.FMO/.SCR, SALES_OR.FMO/.SCR, and CASH_REC.FMO/.SCR)

Query and update files

• BACKORD.QBE - This is a view query that will show a list of all sales invoices which have existing backorders, including the item that has been backordered.
• AR_CASH.UPD - This is an update file that is used to update the AR_MAST.DBF file to reflect customer payments.

- BACKSHIP.UPD - This update file is used to update the SALES_INV file based on the shipment of previously backordered inventory items.
- CR_POST.UPD - This file will update the CASH_REC.DBF file to indicate that the transaction has been posted.
- INV_HIST.UPD - This update file will add the current month's sale to this sales history file at the end of the month, as well as move each month's sales back one more month.
- ITRAN_SO.UPD and ITRAN_SI.UPD - These two files are used to update the inventory transaction file (INV_TRAN). The ITRAN_SO will update the quantity committed to, while the ITRAN_SI update will affect the quantity available, the quantity committed to, as well as the dollar amounts (revenue and cost) of each invoiced sale.
- NU_MONTH.UPD - This file is used to clear out the data concerning the current month's sales activity at the end of the month. This data has already been sent to the history file noted above.
- POST_PDS.UPD- This file will update the SALES_IN.DBF file to indicate whether an invoice has been paid. The assumption with this file is that each invoice is paid in full.
- SI_POST.UPD, SO_POST.UPD and SIPOSTAR.UPD - These three files are used to indicate that the sales invoice and sales order transactions have been posted to the necessary files.
- You will also need the query and update files created in Chapter Three (INV_VAL.QBE, REORDER.QBE, SALES_IN.QBE, and AR_SALES.UPD)

Report Files

- There are no additional reports contained on the disk. All the report files you need for this exercise are ones you have created in earlier chapters.

Your first task is to copy the necessary files from the diskette that came with this casebook. After doing this, make sure that you add all of these files to your AIS_FILE.CAT catalog file. Your screen, after switching into the AIS_FILE.CAT catalog, should look like Figure 10-1. Move through each panel to check if the above files exist. If they do not, you will have to go back to the chapter where they were created and complete those exercises. Once you have all of these files, you are ready to process the sample data.

Transaction processing

This section will lead you step by step through the revenue cycle. As noted earlier, the system you have created does not mimic one in the real world, since it is designed to teach you about the revenue cycle as well as dBASE IV. We have only scratched the surface of dBASE' capabilities, since we limited ourselves to operating from the Control Center. dBASE IV contains a powerful programming language that can be used to customize a database system for any organization.

```
Catalog  Tools  Exit                                          12:27:50 am
                            dBASE IV CONTROL CENTER

                         CATALOG: A:\DBASE\AIS_FILE.CAT

      Data         Queries        Forms        Reports      Labels    Applications
   ┌─────────────┬─────────────┬─────────────┬─────────────┬─────────────┬─────────────┐
   │ <create>    │ <create>    │ <create>    │ <create>    │ <create>    │ <create>    │
   ├─────────────┼─────────────┼─────────────┼─────────────┼─────────────┼─────────────┤
   │ AR_MAST     │ BACKORD     │ CASH_REC    │ INV_VAL     │             │             │
   │ CASH_REC    │ INV_VAL     │ CUSTOMER    │ REORDER     │             │             │
   │ CUSTOMER    │ REORDER     │ INV_MAST    │ SALES_IN    │             │             │
   │ INV_HIST    │ SALES_IN    │ SALES_IN    │             │             │             │
   │ INV_MAST    │ *AR_CASH    │ SALES_OR    │             │             │             │
   │ INV_TRAN    │ *AR_SALES   │             │             │             │             │
   │ SALES_IN    │ *BACKSHIP   │             │             │             │             │
   │ SALES_OR    │ *CR_POST    │             │             │             │             │
   └─────────────┴─────────────┴─────────────┴─────────────┴─────────────┴─────────────┘

   File:          New file
   Description: Press ENTER on <create> to create a new file


    Help:F1  Use:◄┘  Data:F2  Design:Shift-F2  Quick Report:Shift-F9  Menus:F10
```

*Figure 10-1 Control Center for Revenue Cycle after Adding Necessary
Files to Catalog*

When you are finished going through the following steps, you should have a better understanding of what the various parts of the revenue cycle are from a systems perspective. You should pay special attention to the controls that are needed at each stage of the process. You should also have a better understanding of dBASE IV when you are finished and a strong sense of accomplishment at having designed a fairly useful sales transaction processing system from scratch.

The revenue cycle: step by step

Note: After several of the following steps you are returned to the Control Center and there may be some open files, i.e., above the horizontal line. Be sure to close these files by moving over to the Data or Query panel and closing the file by highlighting the file above the horizontal line, pressing ENTER and selecting the Close file option.

STEP ONE: The starting point of the revenue cycle for Stroudsburg is the sales order. To record sales orders, use the **SALES_OR** file found in the FORMS panel. Press **F2** to display the data, and then press **ALT-R** for the `Records` menu, and select the **Add new records** option. At this point you can begin to record the sales orders. The data needed for the sales orders is shown in Table 10-1. Note that there is another field in this file, the POSTED field. However, this field is not input by the user, rather, it is part of the updating process we will go through later.

When you have finished inputting the data, you may exit from the data entry screen by pressing **ALT-E** and selecting **Exit**.

SORDER_NO	ORD_DATE	CUST_NO	ITEM_NO	QUANT_ORD
2866	09/05/91	C104	B467	40
2866	09/05/91	C104	G121	25
2867	09/08/91	C102	T418	20
2868	09/12/91	C110	B187	30
2868	09/12/91	C110	T108	15
2868	09/12/91	C110	G324	10
2869	09/18/91	C101	B119	60
2869	09/18/91	C101	B467	70

Table 10-1 Data Entry for Sales Order Data File

STEP TWO: In this step we will update the inventory transaction file to reflect the sales order data. The appropriate file to use here is the **ITRAN_SO** file in the Query panel. The sales order data will be used to update the quantity committed field. Since the sale is not yet formalized, we do not reduce the quantity available field at this time. To run an update query press **ENTER** when the file is highlighted, select **Run update**, and answer **Yes** to the question concerning if you are sure you want to run the update.

STEP THREE: This step is used to update the SALES_OR data file to indicate that it has been posted to the INV_TRAN file. The file to be run here is called **SO_POST**, and can be found under the Query panel.

STEP FOUR: This step is used to record the actual shipment of an order. Use the **SALES_IN** data entry file found in the Form panel. To add the new data, the sequence of keystrokes is **F2**, followed by **ALT-R**, followed by **Add new records**. Note once more that the POSTED field is not part of the data entry process at this stage. To exit when you are finished, press **ALT-E** and select **Exit**. The data needed for the sales invoice file is shown in Table 10-2.

SINV_NO	SORDER_NO	INV DATE	ITEM_NO	QUANT_SHIP	QUANT_BACK	BACK_SHIP
1569	2859	09/04/91	T108	0	0	5
1569	2859	09/04/91	G043	0	0	30
1570	2861	09/07/91	T219	30	0	0
1570	2861	09/07/91	T108	15	15	0
1570	2861	09/07/91	B029	40	0	0
1570	2861	09/07/91	G121	25	0	0
1571	2863	09/10/91	G121	40	50	0
1572	2864	09/12/91	B467	20	0	0
1572	2864	09/12/91	G121	0	60	0
1573	2865	09/13/91	T418	20	0	0
1573	2865	09/13/91	T108	0	30	0
1573	2865	09/13/91	G043	25	0	0
1574	2866	09/15/91	B467	40	0	0
1574	2866	09/15/91	G121	0	25	0

Table 10-2 Data Entry for Sales Invoice Data File

STEP FIVE: We are now ready to update the inventory transaction file to reflect the actual shipment of goods. The update file to run here is **ITRAN_SI**, which is found within the Query panel. This will reduce the quantity available, reduce the quantity committed to, and record the revenue and cost of each item sold. Follow the procedures noted in Step Two for running an update query.

STEP SIX: This step is used to update the SALES_IN data file to indicate that it has been posted to the INV_TRAN file. The file to be run here is called **SI_POST**, and can be found under the Query panel.

STEP SEVEN: In this step, we will update each customer's account to reflect any sales activity, as evidenced by a sales invoice. This file is named **AR_SALES** and is found under the Query panel.

STEP EIGHT: After updating the accounts receivable subsidiary accounts, Stroudsburg needs to mark these sales invoices as being posted, so that they are not posted twice to the subsidiary ledger. In this step, you will run the **SIPOSTAR** file found under the Query panel. This is similar in nature to Step Three, and is a control feature.

STEP NINE: Stroudsburg is now ready to send out sales invoices to its customers for unpaid invoices. This step will produce reports for each customer in regards to their accounts. The name of the file to be used is **SALES_IN**, found under the Reports panel. After selecting this report, you would then select Print report, and then print it to the printer or to the screen. Note that these invoices reflect the updated selling prices for the books from Chapter 3. If the goods were shipped to the customer prior to this price increase, the customer would pay the old price. The invoice to those customers would have to be manually corrected.

STEP TEN: In this step we will specifically account for the items shipped on backorders, so that we can clear the old backorders from our records. This is accomplished by running the update file **BACKSHIP**, found in the Query panel. The reason for doing this is tied in with the next step, where we take a look at all items that are currently on backorder. If we did not perform this step, then even the old backorders which have since been satisfied would appear in that query.

STEP ELEVEN: As noted in Step Seven, Stroudsburg would like to look at the status of all backordered items. This is simply a view of selected data from a set of files. The file to be used here is named **BACKORD**, which is found in the Query panel. Note that this filename does not have an asterisk beside it, since it is not an update file. Press ALT-E to exit, and be sure to close the open file when you are returned to the Control Center.

STEP TWELVE: At this stage of the revenue cycle, Stroudsburg will record the receipt of cash from customers who have received invoices (Step 11). We will assume here that each invoice is paid in full; i.e., whatever goods Stroudsburg has shipped are paid for in full when the customer makes payment. The file to be used is found under the Forms panel and is named **CASH_REC**. Table 10-3 represents cash receipts for the current period. Follow the procedures found in Step One concerning how to add data to a file.

SINV_NO	REC_AMT	DATE_REC
1565	180.00	09/02/91
1566	1533.50	09/06/91
1568	736.00	09/10/91
1569	539.00	09/14/91
1570	1379.00	09/17/91
1572	99.00	09/22/91

Table 10-3 Data Entry for Cash Receipt Data File

STEP THIRTEEN: This step is used to update the customers' accounts to reflect cash receipts from paid sales invoices (Step Twelve). The update file to be used in this step is found under the Query panel and is named **AR_CASH**.

STEP FOURTEEN: The step performed here is similar to those performed in Steps Three, Six, and Eight, in that it is a control device to prevent a cash receipt from being posted more than once to a customer's account. This program, named **CR_POST**, is found under the Query panel and marks off each cash receipt as being posted after Step Thirteen has been run.

STEP FIFTEEN: This step will update the sales invoice data file to indicate whether a particular invoice has been paid. Again, this is a control feature designed to prevent sending out invoices if the account has already been paid. It also allows Stroudsburg to get a listing of all unpaid invoices after this update has been performed. The name of the update file used in this step is **POST_PDS**, and can be found under the Query panel.

STEP SIXTEEN: In this step we will update the INV_HIST data file to summarize the past month's sales activity by item number. In addition, this update program will move each month's sales activity back one month to create an historical file of sales activity for the past twelve months. The file to be run is **INV_HIST**, found in the Query panel.

STEP SEVENTEEN: This is a simple but necessary update program to set the balance of current month's sales to 0, so that a new month's sales activity can begin to be recorded. The name of this update file is **NU_MONTH**, found under the Query panel.

STEP EIGHTEEN: This is the last step, and is designed to produce a report summarizing which inventory items need to be reordered since their balance has fallen below the reorder point. The name of this report is **REORDER**, and can be found under the Reports panel.

It should be noted that there are a variety of other reports that can be prepared form the files you have available. However, the two reports that you have printed are fundamental to the revenue cycle. Your instructor could ask you to design some other reports that management may find useful.

Expenditure Cycle

The first item we will discuss is the files you will be using and the purpose of each one as it relates to the expenditure cycle. We will go through the files in the order we have covered them in this book: data files, form (input) files, query files, and report files. Note that some of these files have already been used in earlier chapters; this section provides a useful summary of those files you did not specifically create in an earlier chapter.

Data files

• AP_MAST.DBF - This file contains data relating to each vendor's current outstanding balance, as well as a summary of all purchases Stroudsburg has made from each vendor for the current year.
• CASH_PAY.DBF - This file contains data relating to vendor payments made by Stroudsburg.
• VENDOR.DBF - This file contains basic data on each vendor, such as name and address, as well as discount information.
• VOUCHER.DBF - This file is used to store data concerning a purchase transaction after the goods have been received by Stroudsburg, and Stroudsburg is ready to pay for those goods.
• PURCH_OR.DBF - This file contains basic data concerning a purchase transaction, such as who the vendor is, and what items are being purchased.
• You also need the three inventory files created in Chapter One (INV_HIST.DBF, INV_MAST.DBF, and INV_TRAN.DBF)

Forms files

• VENDOR.FMO/.SCR - This form is used to add new vendors or make changes to the basic data of existing vendors.
• You will also need the forms files created in Chapter Two (VOUCHER.FMO/.SCR, PURCH_OR.FMO/.SCR, and CASH_PAY.FMO/.SCR)

Query and update files

• AP_CASH.UPD - This is an update file that is used to update the AP_MAST.DBF file to reflect payments to vendors.
• CP_POST.UPD - This file will update the CASH_PAY.DBF file to indicate that the transaction has been posted.
• ITRAN_PO.UPD and ITRAN_VO.UPD - These files are used to indicate that the purchase order and voucher transactions have been posted to the inventory transaction file. The ITRAN_PO file will update the quantity ordered field and the ITRAN_VO file will update the quantity available and quantity ordered fields.
• POST_PDV.UPD- This file will update the VOUCHER.DBF file to indicate whether a voucher has been paid. The assumption with this file is that each voucher is paid in full.

• PO_POST.UPD, VO_POST.UPD, and VOPOSTAP.UPD- These three files are used to indicate that the voucher or purchase order have been posted to the necessary files.
• You will also need the query and update files created in Chapter Three (INV_VAL.QBE, REORDER.QBE, VOUCHER.QBE, and AP_PURCH.UPD)

<u>Report Files</u>

There are no additional reports contained on the disk. All the report files you need for this exercise are ones you have created in earlier chapters.

Your first task is to copy the necessary files from the diskette that came with this casebook. After doing this, make sure that you add all of these files in your AIS_FILE.CAT catalog file. Your screen, after switching into the AIS_FILE.CAT catalog, should look like Figure 10-2. Move through each panel to check if the above files exist. If they do not, you will have to go back to the chapter where they were created and complete those exercises. Once you have all of these files, you are ready to process the sample data.

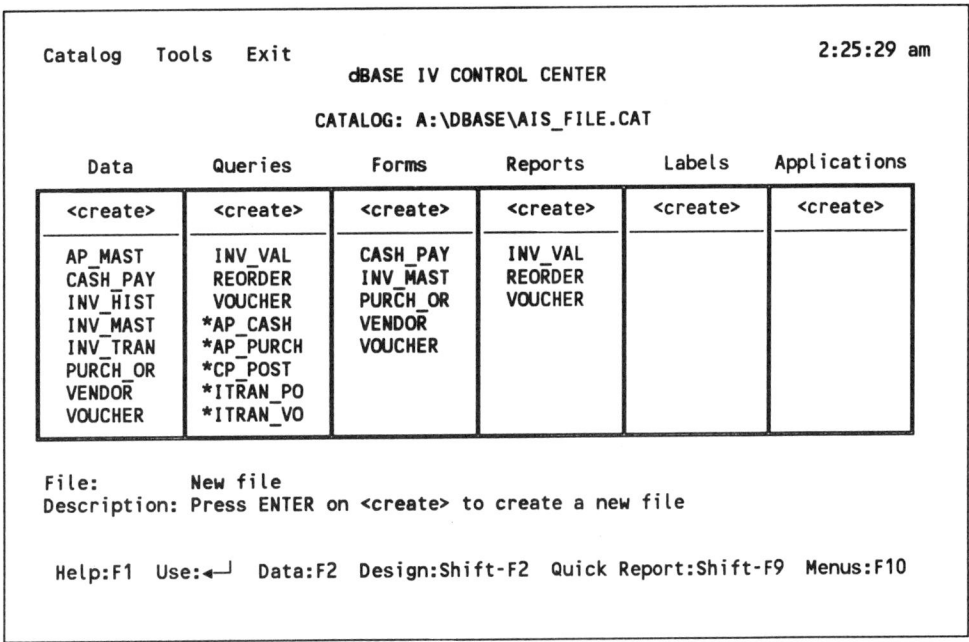

Figure 10-2 Control Center for Expenditure Cycle after Adding Necessary Files to Catalog

Transaction processing

This section will lead you step by step through the expenditure cycle. As noted earlier, this system you have created likely does not mimic one in the real world, since it is designed to teach you about the expenditure cycle as well as dBASE IV. We have only scratched the surface of dBASE' capabilities, since we limited ourselves to operating from the Control Center. dBASE IV contains a powerful programming language that can be used to customize a database system for any organization.

When you are finished going through the following steps, you should have a better understanding as to what the various parts of the expenditure cycle are from a systems perspective. You should pay special note to the controls that are needed at each stage of the process. You should also have a better understanding of dBASE IV when you are finished and a strong sense of accomplishment at having designed a fairly useful purchase transaction processing system from scratch.

The expenditure cycle: step by step

Note: After several of the following steps you are returned to the Control Center and there may be some open files, i.e., above the horizontal line. Be sure to close these files by moving over to the Data or Query panel and closing the file by highlighting the file above the horizontal line, pressing ENTER and selecting the Close file option.

STEP ONE: The starting point of the expenditure cycle for Stroudsburg is the purchase order. To record purchase orders, use the **PURCH_OR** file found in the FORMS panel. Press **F2** to display the data, and then press **ALT-R** for the **Records** menu, and select the **Add new records** option. At this point you can begin to record the purchase orders. The data needed for the purchase orders is shown in Table 10-4. Note that there is another field in this file, the POSTED field. However, this field is not input by the user, rather, it is part of the updating process we will go through later.

When you have finished inputting the data, press **ALT-E** and select **Exit**.

PO_NO	PUR_DATE	ITEM_NO	QUANT_PUR	VEND_NO
1256	09/02/91	G286	160	V103
1257	09/08/91	T220	100	V105
1258	09/19/91	B467	120	V101
1259	09/25/91	G286	30	V102
1260	09/26/91	T418	60	V104
1260	09/26/91	T219	50	V104
1261	09/28/91	G043	80	V103
1261	09/28/91	G324	70	V103

Table 10-4 Data Entry for Purchase Order Data File

STEP TWO: In this step we will update the inventory transaction file to reflect the purchase order data. The appropriate file to use here is the **ITRAN_PO** file in the Query panel. The purchase order data will be used to update the quantity ordered field. Since the purchase is not yet formalized, we do not increase the quantity available field at this time. To run an update query press **ENTER** when the file is highlighted, select **Run update**, and answer **Yes** to the question concerning if you are sure you want to run the update.

STEP THREE: This step is used to update the PURCH_OR data file to indicate that it has been posted to the INV_TRAN file. The file to be run here is called **PO_POST**, and can be found under the Query panel.

STEP FOUR: This step is used to record the actual receipt of an order. Use the **VOUCHER** data entry file found in the Form panel. To add the new data, the sequence of keystrokes is **F2**, followed by **ALT-R**, followed by **Add new records**. Note once more that the POSTED field is not part of the data entry process at this stage. To exit from the data entry process, press **ALT-E** and select **Exit**. The data needed for the voucher file is shown in Table 10-5.

VOUCH_NO	PO_NO	INV DATE	ITEM_NO	QUANT_REC	QUANT_BACK
2163	1252	09/03/91	T108	90	0
2164	1253	09/05/91	G121	130	0
2165	1254	09/07/91	G121	60	0
2166	1255	09/09/91	T418	80	0
2167	1256	09/10/91	G286	160	0
2168	1257	09/14/91	T220	100	0
2169	1258	09/27/91	B467	120	0
2170	1260	09/30/91	T418	60	0
2170	1260	09/30/91	T219	50	0

Table 10-5 Data Entry for Voucher Data File

STEP FIVE: We are now ready to update the inventory transaction file to reflect the actual receipt of goods. The update file to run is **ITRAN_VO**, which is found within the Query panel. This will increase the quantity available and reduce the quantity ordered fields. Follow the procedures noted in Step Two for running an update query.

STEP SIX: This step is used to update the VOUCHER data file to indicate that it has been posted to the INV_TRAN file. The file to be run here is called **VO_POST**, and can be found under the Query panel.

STEP SEVEN: In this step, we will update each vendor's account to reflect any receipt of goods, as evidenced by a voucher. This file is named **AP_PURCH** and is found under the Query panel.

STEP EIGHT: After updating the accounts payable subsidiary accounts, Stroudsburg needs to mark these vouchers as being posted, so that they are not posted twice to the subsidiary ledger. In this step, you will run the **VOPOSTAP** file found under the Query panel. This is similar in nature to Step Three, and is a control feature.

STEP NINE: Stroudsburg is now ready to prepare a formal voucher which will be used to control cash payments. This document would be kept with a copy of the purchase order, receiving report and vendor's invoice as authorization to make payment. The name of the file to be used is **VOUCHER**, found under the Reports panel. After highlighting this file and pressing ENTER, select the Print report option and you may then print the report to the Printer or the Screen.

STEP TEN: At this stage of the expenditure cycle, Stroudsburg will record the payment of cash to vendors who have been authorized to be paid based on a completed voucher. We will assume here that each vendor invoice is paid in full; i.e., whatever goods Stroudsburg has received are paid for in full, regardless of backorders. The file to be used is found under the Forms panel and is named **CASH_PAY**. Follow the procedures found in Step One concerning how to add data shown in Table 10-6 to a file.

CHECK_NO	VOUCH_NO	AMOUNT_PD	DATE_PD
3092	2162	324.00	09/06/91
3093	2161	168.00	09/07/91
3094	2163	1143.00	09/13/91
3095	2164	338.00	09/15/91
3096	2165	156.00	09/17/91
3097	2166	912.00	09/19/91
3098	2167	840.00	09/20/91
3099	2168	1160.00	09/24/91

Table 10-6 Data Entry for Cash Payments Data File

STEP ELEVEN: This step is used to update the vendors' accounts to reflect cash payments from authorized vouchers. The update file to be used in this step is found under the Query panel and is named **AP_CASH**.

STEP TWELVE: The step performed here is similar to those performed in Steps Three, Six, and Eight in that it is a control device to prevent a cash payment from being posted more than once to a vendor's account. This program, named **CP_POST**, is found under the Query panel and marks off each cash payment as being posted after Step Eleven has been run.

STEP THIRTEEN: This step will update the voucher data file to indicate whether a particular voucher has been paid. Again, this is a control feature designed to prevent the preparation of a voucher if the account has already been paid. It also allows Stroudsburg to get a listing of all unpaid vouchers after this update has been performed. The name of the update file used in this step is **POST_PDV**, and can be found under the Query panel.

STEP FOURTEEN: This is the last step, and is designed to produce a report summarizing which inventory items need to be reordered since their balance has fallen below the reorder point. Note that since we have only dealt with the purchase of items, there will be no inventory items that need to be ordered. Thus, there will be no reports generated. However, this report is mentioned since it basically is a bridge between the revenue and expenditure cycle. The name of this report you would normally run is **REORDER**, and can be found under the Reports panel.

It should be noted that there are a variety of other reports that can be prepared form the files you have available. However, the report that you have printed is fundamental to the expenditure cycle. Your instructor could ask you to design some other reports that management may find useful.

Payroll Cycle

Process the following set of payroll data (Tables 10-7 through 10-9) for the month of September. When you are finished entering the data, the following order of events may be helpful:

1. Run the query that updates the payroll master file to reflect revised year to date totals and changes the date to the most recent payroll period.

2. Print the monthly summary report.

3. Print the year to date summary report.

4. Run the query that will change the POSTED field to a true condition.

SSN	HOURS	DATE
111111111	1	09/30/91
222222222	1	09/30/91
333333333	150	09/30/91
444444444	160	09/30/91
555555555	60	09/30/91

Table 10-7 Data Entry for Time Card Data File

PAY_CLAS	CLAS_DESC	PAY_RATE	BASIS
A	President	6000.00	MONTHLY
B	Vice. Pres	4000.00	MONTHLY
C	Office Mgr	14.00	HOURLY
D	Store Mgr.	12.00	HOURLY
E	Part Timer	7.50	HOURLY

Table 10-8 Data Entry for Recording Pay Rate Change (Hint: Use PAY_CLAS Form)

PAYCHK_NO	SSN	DATE
2346	1111111111	09/30/91
2347	2222222222	09/30/91
2348	3333333333	09/30/91
2349	4444444444	09/30/91
2350	5555555555	09/30/91

Table 10-9 Data Entry for Paycheck Data File

Conclusion

This chapter completes your review of the accounting cycle as well as your introduction to dBASE IV. To see if your programs have worked correctly, ask your instructor for a copy of the various data files to see if your files contain the same data. If you want to continue your study of dBASE, there are many fine books available that can help with this task. At this point, you are probably ready to move into some of the more advanced topics such as programming, so be sure the book you select offers such topics.

There are no formal review question related to this chapter. If you want to review this chapter, the easiest way to do it is to make up additional data and see how dBASE processes it.

CASE SOLUTION: PARADOX 3.5

Included on your PARADOX disk that came with this text are several files that you will be using to test the system you have developed in the past four chapters. The files relate for the most part to either the revenue cycle or the expenditure cycle. Some of the files, such as the inventory files you have been working on for the tutorials, are needed for both cycles. The next part of this chapter is divided into two sections, one for the revenue cycle, the other for the expenditure cycle.

One item to note is that you will be entering data as part of this exercise. Enter all the data at the same time. Entering the data as a set and then processing that entire set of data is known as *batch processing*. You could have an *online processing* system in PARADOX if you wanted, but that would entail the development of customized programs through the PARADOX programming language.

Revenue Cycle

The first item we will discuss is the files you will be using and the purpose of each one as it relates to the revenue cycle. We will go through the files in the order we have covered them in this book: data files, form (input) files, query files, and report files. Note that some of these files have already been used in earlier chapters; this section provides a useful summary of those files you did not specifically create in an earlier chapter.

Data files and Index files

• AR_MAST.DB - This file contains data relating to each customer's current outstanding balance, as well as a summary of all sales Stroudsburg has made to each customer for the current year.
• CASH_REC.DB - This file contains data relating to customer payments to Stroudsburg.
• CUSTOMER.DB - This file contains basic data on each customer, such as name and address, as well as credit information.
• SALES_IN.DB - This file is used to store data concerning a sales transaction after the goods have been shipped to the customer, and Stroudsburg is ready to bill for those goods.
• SALES_OR.DB - This file contains basic data concerning a sales transaction, such as who the customer is, and what items they want.
• Associated with each of these data files there are index files. These have the same name, except for the extension. The extension for the index files is .PX. Thus, the sales order file has an index file name SALES_OR.PX. You copied these files to your disk in Chapter 6. There are also files with a .VAL extension (e.g., SALES_OR.VAL). These represent the validity checks associated with each table. There should be .VAL files for the SALES_OR, SALES_IN, and CASH_REC files from when you designed the input forms and the corresponding controls for these tables in Chapter 7.
• You also need the three inventory files created in Chapter One (INV_HIST.DB, INV_MAST.DB, and INV_TRAN.DB), as well as the index and validity check files associated with each of these files.

Forms files

- CUSTOMER.F1 - This form is used to add new customers or make changes to the basic data of existing customers.
- You will also need the forms files created in Chapter Two (SALES_IN.F1, SALES_OR.F1, and CASH_REC.F1)

Query, Update and Other Scripts

- BACKORD.SC - This is a view query that will show a list of all sales invoices which have existing backorders, including the item that has been backordered.
- AR_CASH.SC - This is an update file that is used to update the AR_MAST.DB file to reflect customer payments.
- BACKSHIP.SC - This update file is used to update the SALES_INV file based on the shipment of previously backordered inventory items.
- CR_POST.SC - This file will update the CASH_REC.DB file to indicate that the transaction has been posted.
- INV_HIST.SC and INVHIST.SC - These files will add the current month's sale to this sales history file at the end of the month, as well as move each month's sales back one more month.
- ITRAN_SO.SC and ITRAN_SI.SC - These two files are used to update the inventory transaction file (INV_TRAN). The ITRAN_SO will update the quantity committed to, while the ITRAN_SI update will affect the quantity available, the quantity committed to, as well as the dollar amounts (revenue and cost) of each invoiced sale.
- NU_MONTH.SC - This file is used to clear out the data concerning the current month's sales activity at the end of the month. This data has already been sent to the history file noted above.
- POST_PDS.SC- This file will update the SALES_IN.DB file to indicate whether an invoice has been paid. The assumption with this file is that each invoice is paid in full.
- SI_POST.SC, SO_POST.SC and SIPOSTAR.SC - These three files are used to indicate that the sales invoice and sales order has been posted to the necessary files.
- SALORD.SC, SALINV.SC, and CASHREC.SC - These scripts are used in conjunction with the forms created earlier and are designed to automate data entry.
- PRT_SI.SC and PRT_REOR.SC - These scripts are designed to automate the printing process for their respective reports. These scripts were created in Chapter 9.
- You will also need the query and update scripts created in Chapter Three (INV_VAL.SC, REORDER.SC, SALES_IN.SC, and AR_SALES.SC)

Report Files

There are no additional reports contained on the disk. All the report files you need for this exercise are ones you have created in earlier chapters.

Transaction processing

This section will lead you step by step through the revenue cycle. As noted earlier, this system you have created does not mimic one in the real world, since it is designed to teach you about the revenue cycle as well as PARADOX. We have only scratched the surface of PARADOX' capabilities, since we limited ourselves to operating from the Menu system. PARADOX contains a powerful programming language that can be used to customize a database system for any organization.

When you are finished going through the following steps, you should have a better understanding as to what the various parts of the revenue cycle are from a systems perspective. You should pay special note to the controls that are needed at each stage of the process. You should also have a better understanding of PARADOX when you are finished and a strong sense of accomplishment at having designed a fairly useful sales transaction processing system from scratch.

The revenue cycle: step by step

STEP ONE: The starting point of the revenue cycle for Stroudsburg is the sales order. To record sales orders, play the **SALORD** `script`. The data needed for the sales orders is shown in Table 10-10. Note that there is another field in this file, the POSTED field. Just press ENTER when you come to this field. PARADOX will automatically enter a "F" for this field. Later, we will change this field through an update query. When you have finished inputting the data, press **F2**. Press **F8** to clear the screen.

SORDER_NO	ITEM_NO	CUST_NO	QUANT_ORD	ORD_DATE
2866	B467	C104	40	09/05/91
2866	G121	C104	25	09/05/91
2867	T418	C102	20	09/08/91
2868	B187	C110	30	09/12/91
2868	T108	C110	15	09/12/91
2868	G324	C110	10	09/12/91
2869	B119	C101	60	09/18/91
2869	B467	C101	70	09/18/91

Table 10-10 Data Entry for Sales Order Data Table

STEP TWO: In this step we will update the inventory transaction table to reflect the sales order data. The appropriate file to use here is the **ITRAN_SO** script, so play this script. The sales order data will be used to update the quantity committed field. Since the sale is not yet formalized, we do not reduce the quantity available field at this time.

STEP THREE: This step is used to update the SALES_OR data table to indicate that it has been posted to the INV_TRAN table. The script to play here is called **SO_POST**, and can be found under the Script/Play menu.

STEP FOUR: This step is used to record the actual shipment of an order. Use the **SALINV** script to add the new data. Note once more that the POSTED, PAID, and

POSTEDIT fields can be ignored, and PARADOX will automatically enter "F" for these fields. When you are finished, press F2. The data needed for the sales invoice file is shown in Table 10-11. Press **F8** to clear the screen.

SINV_NO	INV_DATE	CUST_NO	SORDER_NO	ITEM_NO	QUANT_SHIP	QUANT_BACK	BACK_SHIP
1569	09/04/91	C107	2859	T108	0	0	5
1569	09/04/91	C107	2859	G043	0	0	30
1570	09/07/91	C101	2861	T219	30	0	0
1570	09/07/91	C101	2861	T108	15	15	0
1570	09/07/91	C101	2861	B029	40	0	0
1570	09/07/91	C101	2861	G121	25	0	0
1571	09/10/91	C104	2863	G121	40	50	0
1572	09/12/91	C110	2864	B467	20	0	0
1572	09/12/91	C110	2864	G121	0	60	0
1573	09/13/91	C107	2865	T418	20	0	0
1573	09/13/91	C107	2865	T108	0	30	0
1573	09/13/91	C107	2865	G043	25	0	0
1574	09/15/91	C104	2866	B467	40	0	0
1574	09/15/91	C104	2866	G121	0	25	0

Table 10-11 Data Entry for Sales Invoice Data Table

STEP FIVE: We are now ready to update the inventory transaction table to reflect the actual shipment of goods. The update file to run here is **ITRAN_SI**, which is found within the Script/Play menu. This script will reduce the quantity available, reduce the quantity committed to, and record the revenue and cost of each item sold.

STEP SIX: This step is used to update the SALES_IN data table to indicate that it has been posted to the INV_TRAN table. The script to play here is called **SI_POST**, and can be found under the Script/Play menu.

STEP SEVEN: In this step, we will update each customer's account to reflect any sales activity, as evidenced by a sales invoice. This script is named **AR_SALES**.

STEP EIGHT: After updating the accounts receivable subsidiary accounts, Stroudsburg needs to mark these sales invoices as being posted, so that they are not posted twice to the subsidiary ledger. In this step, you will play the **SIPOSTAR** script. This is similar in nature to Step Three, and is a control feature.

STEP NINE: Stroudsburg is now ready to send out sales invoices to its customers for unpaid invoices. That is the purpose of this step, to produce reports for each customer in regards to their accounts. The name of the script to be used is **PRT_SI**, which you created in the last chapter.

STEP TEN: In this step we will specifically account for the items shipped on backorders, so that we can clear those from our records. This is accomplished by running the script **BACKSHIP**. The reason for doing this is tied in with the next step, where we take a look at all items that are currently on backorder. If we did not perform this step, then even the old backorders which have since been satisfied would appear in that query.

STEP ELEVEN: As noted in Step Seven, Stroudsburg would like to look at the status of all backordered items. This is simply a view of selected data from a set of files. The script to be used here is named **BACKORD**. When you are finished viewing the file, press **F8** to clear the screen.

STEP TWELVE: At this stage of the revenue cycle, Stroudsburg will record the receipt of cash from customers who have received invoices (Step 11). We will assume here that each invoice is paid in full; i.e., whatever goods Stroudsburg has shipped are paid for in full when the customer makes payment. The script to be used is named **CASHREC**. Table 10-12 represents cash receipts for the current period. Follow the procedures found in Step One concerning how to add this data to a table. When you are finished, press **F2** to add the data to the Cash_rec file and then press **F8** to clear the screen.

SINV_NO	REC_AMT	DATE_REC
1565	180.00	09/02/91
1566	1533.50	09/06/91
1568	736.00	09/10/91
1569	539.00	09/14/91
1570	1379.00	09/17/91
1572	99.00	09/22/91

Table 10-12 Data Entry for Cash Receipts Data Table

STEP THIRTEEN: This step is used to update the customers' accounts to reflect cash receipts from paid sales invoices (Step 12). The script to be used in this step is called **AR_CASH**.

STEP FOURTEEN: The step performed here is similar to those performed in Steps Three, Six, and Ten in that it is a control device to prevent a cash receipt from being posted more than once to a customer's account. This script is named **CR_POST** and marks off each cash receipt as being posted after Step Twelve has been run.

STEP FIFTEEN: This step will update the sales invoice data file to indicate whether a particular invoice has been paid. Again, this is a control feature designed to prevent sending out invoices if the account has already been paid. It also allows Stroudsburg to get a listing of all unpaid invoices after this update has been performed. The name of the script used in this step is **POST_PDS**.

STEP SIXTEEN: In this step we will update the INV_HIST data table to summarize the past month's sales activity by item number. In addition, this update program will move each month's sales activity back one month to create an historical file of sales activity for the past twelve months. The name of the script is **INV_HIST**.

STEP SEVENTEEN: This is a simple but necessary update program to set the balance of current month's sales to 0, so that a new month's sales activity can begin to be recorded. The name of this update script is **NU_MONTH**.

STEP EIGHTEEN: This is the last step, and is designed to produce a report summarizing which inventory items need to be reordered since their balance has fallen below the reorder point. The name of this script is **PRT_REOR**, and which you created in Chapter 4.

It should be noted that there are a variety of other reports that can be prepared from the tables you have available. However, the two reports that you have printed are fundamental to the revenue cycle. Your instructor could ask you to design some other reports that management may find useful.

Expenditure Cycle

The first item we will discuss is the files you will be using and the purpose of each one as it relates to the expenditure cycle. We will go through the in the order we have covered them in this book: data tables, form (input) files, query files, and report files. Note that some of these files have already been used in earlier chapters; this section provides a useful summary of those files you did not specifically create in an earlier chapter.

Data files

• AP_MAST.DB - This file contains data relating to each vendor's current outstanding balance, as well as a summary of all purchases Stroudsburg has made from each vendor for the current year.
• CASH_PAY.DB - This file has data relating to vendor payments made by Stroudsburg.
• VENDOR.DB - This file contains basic data on each vendor, such as name and address, as well as discount information.
• VOUCHER.DB - This file is used to store data concerning a purchase transaction after the goods have been received by Stroudsburg, and Stroudsburg is ready to pay for those goods.
• PURCH_OR.DB - This file contains basic data concerning a purchase transaction, such as who the vendor is, and what items are being purchased.
• Associated with each of these data files there are index files. These have the same name, except for the extension. The extension for the index files is .PX. Thus, the purchase order file has an index file name PURCH_OR.PX. You copied these to your disk in Chapter 6. There are also files with a .VAL extension (e.g., PURCH_OR.VAL). These represent the validity checks associated with each table. There should be .VAL files for the PURCH_OR, VOUCHER, and CASH_PAY files from when you designed the input forms and the corresponding controls for these tables in Chapter 7.
• You also need the three inventory files created in Chapter One (INV_HIST.DB, INV_MAST.DB, and INV_TRAN.DB), as well as the index and validity check files associated with each of these files.

Forms files

• VENDOR.F1 - This form is used to add new vendors or make changes to the basic data of existing vendors.
• You will also need the forms files created in Chapter Two (VOUCHER.F1, PURCH_OR.F1, and CASH_PAY.F1)

Query, Update, and Other Scripts

• AP_CASH.SC - This is an update file that is used to update the AP_MAST.DB file to reflect payments to vendors.
• CP_POST.SC - This file will update the CASH_PAY.DB file to indicate that the transaction has been posted.

• ITRAN_PO.SC and ITRAN_VO.SC - These two files are used to update the inventory transaction TABLE (INV_TRAN). The ITRAN_PO will update the quantity ordered, while the ITRAN_VO update will affect the quantity available, and the quantity ordered.

• POST_PDV.SC- This file will update the VOUCHER.DB file to indicate whether a voucher has been paid. The assumption with this file is that each voucher is paid in full.

• PO_POST.SC, VO_POST.SC and VOPOSTAP.SC - These three files are used to indicate that the purchase order and voucher transactions have been posted to the necessary files.

• PURORD.SC, VOUCH.SC, and CASHPAY.SC - These scripts are used in conjunction with the forms created earlier and are designed to automate data entry.

• PRT_VO.SC and PRT_REOR.SC - These scripts are designed to automate the printing process for their respective reports. These scripts were created in Chapter 9.

• You will also need the query and update script files created in Chapter Three (INV_VAL.SC, REORDER.SC, VOUCHER.SC, and AP_PURCH.SC)

Report Files

There are no additional reports contained on the disk. All the report files you need for this exercise are ones you have created in earlier chapters.

Transaction processing

This section will lead you step by step through the expenditure cycle. As noted earlier, this system you have created likely does not mimic one in the real world, since it is designed to teach you about the expenditure cycle as well as PARADOX. We have only scratched the surface of PARADOX' capabilities, since we limited ourselves to operating from the Menu system. PARADOX contains a powerful programming language that can be used to customize a database system for any organization.

When you are finished going through the following steps, you should have a better understanding as to what the various parts of the expenditure cycle are from a systems perspective. You should pay special note to the controls that are needed at each stage of the process. You should also have a better understanding of PARADOX when you are finished and a strong sense of accomplishment at having designed a fairly useful purchase transaction processing system from scratch.

The expenditure cycle: step by step

STEP ONE: The starting point for the expenditure cycle is the purchase order. To record purchase orders, use the **PURORD** script. The data needed for the purchase orders is shown in Table 10-13. Note that there is another field in this file, the POSTED field. Just press ENTER when you get to this field and PARADOX will automatically place an "F" in this field. Later, we will change this field using an update query. Be sure to press **F2** when you are finished recording all the data. Press **F8** to clear the screen.

PO_NO	VEND_NO	ITEM_NO	QUANT_PUR	PUR_DATE
1256	V103	G286	160	09/02/91
1257	V105	T220	100	09/08/91
1258	V101	B467	120	09/19/91
1259	V102	G286	30	09/25/91
1260	V104	T418	60	09/26/91
1260	V104	T219	50	09/26/91
1261	V103	G043	80	09/28/91
1261	V103	G324	70	09/28/91

Table 10-13 Data Entry for Purchase Order Data Table

STEP TWO: In this step we will update the inventory transaction table to reflect the purchase order data. The appropriate file to use here is the **ITRAN_PO** script. The purchase order data will be used to update the quantity ordered field. Since the purchase is not yet formalized, we do not increase the quantity available field at this time.

STEP THREE: This step is used to update the PURCH_OR data table to indicate that it has been posted to the INV_TRAN table. The script to be run here is called **PO_POST**.

STEP FOUR: This step is used to record the actual receipt of an order. Use the **VOUCH** script to add the new data. Note once more that the POSTED, PAID, and POSTEDIT fields are not part of the data entry process, just press ENTER and PARADOX will automatically assign an "F" to these fields. The data needed for the voucher file is shown in Table 10-14. When you are finished, press **F2**. Press **F8** to clear the screen.

VOUCH_NO	VEND_NO	PO_NO	ITEM_NO	QUANT_REC	QUANT_BACK	INV_DATE
2163	V104	1252	T108	90	0	09/03/91
2164	V101	1253	G121	130	0	09/05/91
2165	V101	1254	G121	60	0	09/07/91
2166	V106	1255	T418	80	0	09/09/91
2167	V103	1256	G286	160	0	09/10/91
2168	V105	1257	T220	100	0	09/14/91
2169	V101	1258	B467	120	0	09/27/91
2170	V104	1260	T418	60	0	09/30/91
2170	V104	1260	T219	50	0	09/30/91

Table 10-14 Data Entry for Voucher Data Table

STEP FIVE: We are now ready to update the inventory transaction table to reflect the actual receipt of goods. The script to run is **ITRAN_VO**. This will increase the quantity available and reduce the quantity ordered fields.

STEP SIX: This step is used to update the VOUCHER data table to indicate that it has been posted to the INV_TRAN table. The script to play here is called **VO_POST**, and can be found under the Script/Play menu.

STEP SEVEN: In this step, we will update each vendor's account to reflect any receipt of goods, as evidenced by a voucher. This script is named **AP_PURCH**.

STEP EIGHT: After updating the accounts payable subsidiary accounts, Stroudsburg needs to mark these vouchers as being posted, so that they are not posted twice to the subsidiary ledger. In this step, you will play the **VOPOSTAP** script. This is similar in nature to Step Three, and is a control feature.

STEP NINE: Stroudsburg is now ready to prepare a formal voucher which will be used to control cash payments. This document would be kept with a copy of the purchase order, receiving report and vendor's invoice as authorization to make payment. The name of the script to be used is **PRT_VO**, which you created in the last chapter.

STEP TEN: At this stage of the expenditure cycle, Stroudsburg will record the payment of cash to vendors who have been authorized to be paid based on a completed voucher. We will assume here that each vendor invoice is paid in full; i.e., whatever goods Stroudsburg has received are paid for in full, regardless of backorders. The script to be used is named **CASHPAY**. Follow the procedures found in Step One concerning how to add the data shown in Table 10-15 to a file. When you are finished, press **F2** to add the data to the Cash_pay file, and then **F8** to clear the screen.

VOUCH_NO	CHECK_NO	AMOUNT_PD	DATE_PD
2162	3092	324.00	09/06/91
2161	3093	168.00	09/07/91
2163	3094	1143.00	09/13/91
2164	3095	338.00	09/15/91
2165	3096	156.00	09/17/91
2166	3097	912.00	09/19/91
2167	3098	840.00	09/20/91
2168	3099	1160.00	09/24/91

Table 10-15 Data Entry for Cash Payments Data Table

STEP ELEVEN: This step is used to update the vendors' accounts to reflect cash payments from authorized vouchers. The script to be used in this step is named **AP_CASH**.

STEP TWELVE: The step performed here is similar to those performed in Steps Three and Seven, in that it is a control device to prevent a cash payment from being posted more than once to a vendor's account. This script, named **CP_POST**, marks off each cash payment as being posted after Step Eleven has been run.

STEP THIRTEEN: This step will update the voucher data table to indicate whether a particular voucher has been paid. Again, this is a control feature designed to prevent the preparation of a voucher if the account has already been paid. It also allows Stroudsburg to get a listing of all unpaid vouchers after this update has been performed. The name of the script used in this step is **POST_PDV**.

STEP FOURTEEN: This is the last step, and is designed to produce a report summarizing which inventory items need to be reordered since their balance has fallen below the reorder point. Note that since we have only dealt with the purchase of items, there will be no inventory items that need to be ordered. Thus, there will be no reports generated. However, this report is mentioned since it basically is a bridge between the revenue and expenditure cycle. The name of the script you would normally run is **PRT_REOR**.

It should be noted that there are a variety of other reports that can be prepared from the files you have available. However, the report that you have printed is fundamental to the expenditure cycle. Your instructor could ask you to design some other reports that management may find useful.

Payroll Cycle

Process the following set of payroll data contained in Tables 10-16 through 10-18 for the month of September. When you are finished entering the data, the following order of events may be helpful:

1. Run the query that updates the payroll master file to reflect revised year to date totals and changes the date to the most recent payroll period.

2. Print the monthly summary report.

3. Print the year to date summary report.

4. Run the query that will change the POSTED field to a true condition.

SSN	HOURS	DATE
111111111	1	09/30/91
222222222	1	09/30/91
333333333	150	09/30/91
444444444	160	09/30/91
555555555	60	09/30/91

Table 10-16 Data Entry for Time Card Data File

PAY_CLAS	CLAS_DESC	PAY_RATE	BASIS
A	President	6000.00	MONTHLY
B	Vice. Pres	4000.00	MONTHLY
C	Office Mgr	14.00	HOURLY
D	Store Mgr.	12.00	HOURLY
E	Part Timer	7.50	HOURLY

Table 10-17 Data Entry for Recording Pay Rate Change

PAYCHK_NO	SSN	DATE
2346	1111111111	09/30/91
2347	2222222222	09/30/91
2348	3333333333	09/30/91
2349	4444444444	09/30/91
2350	5555555555	09/30/91

Table 10-18 Data Entry for Paycheck Data File

Conclusion

This chapter completes your review of the accounting cycle as well as your introduction to PARADOX. To see if your programs have worked correctly, ask your instructor for a copy of the various data files to see if your files contain the same data. If you want to continue your study of PARADOX, there are many fine books available that can help with this task. At this point, you are probably ready to move into some of the more advanced topics such as programming, so be sure the book you select offers such topics.

There are no formal review question related to this chapter. If you want to review this chapter, the easiest way to do it is to make up additional data and see how PARADOX processes it.

NOTES

NOTES

NOTES

NOTES

NOTES

NOTES

NOTES

NOTES

NOTES

NOTES

NOTES